Yvonne Nolan

with Colette Burgess, Colin Shaw,
Debby Railton & Nicki Pritchatt

HEALTH & SOCIAL CARE
(Adults) 3rd edition

www.pearsonschoolsandfe.co.uk

✓ Free online support
✓ Useful weblinks
✓ 24 hour online ordering

0845 630 44 44

362 NOL

Heinemann

Part of Pearson

Heinemann is an imprint of Pearson Education Limited, Edinburgh Gate, Harlow, Essex, CM20 2JE.

www.pearsonschoolsandfecolleges.co.uk

Heinemann is a registered trademark of Pearson Education Limited

Copyright © Yvonne Nolan 2011 for Units SHC 31, SHC 32, SHC 33, SHC 34, HSC 024, HSC 025, HSC 036, HSC 037, HSC 038, HSC 3003, HSC 3013, HSC 3020
Copyright © Nicki Pritchatt 2011 for Units HSC 3004, HSC 3029, DEM 301
Copyright © Colette Burgess and Colin Shaw 2011 for Unit HSC 2028
Copyright © Debby Railton 2011 for Unit HSC 3047
Copyright © Julia Barrand, Royal National Institute of Blind People (RNIB) 2011 for Unit SS MU 3.1
Typeset by Saxon Graphics Ltd, Derby
Original illustrations © Pearson Education Ltd 2011
Illustrated by Andrew Cameron/Karate Grafika
Cover design by Wooden Ark
Picture research by Emma Whyte
Cover photo/illustration © plainpicture/Stockwerk

The rights of the authors to be identified as authors of this work have been asserted by them in accordance with the Copyright, Designs and Patents Act 1988.

First published 2011

14 13 12 11
10 9 8 7 6 5 4 3 2

British Library Cataloguing in Publication Data
A catalogue record for this book is available from the British Library.

ISBN 978 0 435 03197 8

Printed in Spain by Grafos S.A, Barcelona.

Every effort has been made to contact copyright holders of material reproduced in this book. Any omissions will be rectified in subsequent printings if notice is given to the publishers.

Websites
Pearson Education Limited is not responsible for the content of any external Internet sites. It is essential for tutors to preview each website before using it in class so as to ensure that the URL is still accurate, relevant and appropriate. We suggest that tutors bookmark useful websites and consider enabling students to access them through the school/college intranet.

Contents

Three further units are included on the CD-ROM:

Acknowledgements

The publisher would like to thank Jane Kellas for providing the further reading features for each unit.

The publisher would like to thank the following for their kind permission to reproduce their photographs:

(Key: b-bottom; c-centre; l-left; r-right; t-top)

Alamy Images: Ace Stock Ltd 78, Alex Segre 302, JR Bale 349, Greg Balfour Evans 258, Big Cheese Photo LLC 267, Peter Cavanagh 197, Chris Fredriksson 104, Cultura 365, Cultura RM 92, DavidHills.net 384cr, DBurke 79, Paul Doyle 177, Enigma 264, Fancy CD/13, Ian Shaw 85, Ilene MacDonald 265, Imagebroker 280, 351, Imagebroker 280, 351, Itani Images 78br, Juice Images 69, Lisa F young cd/17, mediablitzimages (uk) Limited 307, Nikreates 221, Oleksiy Maksymenko 20, P-59 Photos 209, Paul Doyles 310, Paula Solloway 20t, Peter Titmuss cd/15, Photofusion Picture library 26, 78tr, Photofusion Picture Library 26, 78tr, Picture Contact 360, Picture Press 3, Red Green Blue New Media Ltd Gonta 217, Science Photo Library 384, Shout 158, Steve Skjold 14, Steve Skjold 14, Anna Stowe 246, Tim Gander 91; **Bellman & Symfon:** 19; **Corbis:** Steve Prezant 23; **Digital Vision:** Rob van Petten 29; **Fotolia.com:** Glenda Powers 239; **Getty Images:** 114, Altrendo 243, 253, Altrendo 243, 253, Chris Baker 207, Barry Austin photography 99, Comstock CD/9, Design Pics / Kristy-Anne Glubish 252, John Kelly 152, Ryan McVay 46, Ryan McWay CD/10, Yellow dog productions 117; **iStockphoto:** Ben Blankenburg 238, Christine Glade 303, franz pfluegl 340t, Martin Novak 385, S.P. Rayner 120, Willie B. Thomas 132, Catherine Yeulet 144; **Pearson Education Ltd:** David Sanderson 218, Gareth Boden 8, Jules Selmes 98, 210, 210/2, 210/3, 210/4, 210/5, 210/6, 60, 214 Lord and Leverett 5, 25, 25b, 171, 171b, Richard Smith 211, 211/1, 211/2, 211/4, 211/5, 306, MindStudio 50, 63, Rob Judges 45, Tudor Photography 170; **Photolibrary.com:** asia images 78tc, Britain on View 34; **Plainpicture Ltd:** Briljans 47; **Science Photo Library Ltd:** Life In View 388, victor habbick visions 187; **Shutterstock.com:** 1, Adam Borkowski 78bc, Andresr 51, 161, Charles Taylor 261, clearviewstock CD/2, cozyta 337, Edhar 68c, Elena Rostunova 298, Fedorov Oleksiy 113, Iv Mirin 226, Maksim Shmeljov CD/1 (a), Mark William Richardson 175, mihalec 367, Monkey Business Images 64, Mushakesa 75, nikkytok 157, Orange Line Media 386, Photoroller 234, Radhoose 313, robcocquyt 108, ssguy 141, Stocklite 350, Viacheslav A. Zotov 291, Viktor1 181, Vladitto 103, Yuri Arcurs 145, 183, Yuriy Boyko 229

Every effort has been made to trace the copyright holders and we apologise in advance for any unintentional omissions. We would be pleased to insert the appropriate acknowledgement in any subsequent edition of this publication.

Introduction

This book is designed to cover the knowledge you will need for the new Level 3 Health and Social Care Diploma. If you have previously worked on S/NVQ qualifications, the style of the Diploma is very different.

The knowledge and skills will be assessed differently and the way you learn and the type of evidence you may need to provide will be different, but overall, the knowledge and skills that you need in order to do your job remain the same.

Apart from the updates to cover the transformation in social care and the personalisation agenda, people who work in social care still need the same skills and the same understanding of how and why things are done.

The major changes in the way that social care is planned for and delivered have brought about very significant improvements by putting people in control of their lives and giving them real choice about which services they need and how they want them delivered.

Putting people at the heart of what we do means that services fit into their lives, not the other way around. It is a very exciting time to be working in social care as the new approaches are implemented across the UK and people are able to control budgets and organise their own care and support.

You have a wonderful opportunity to be part of the changes and to contribute to supporting people to participate fully in society and to be in control of their own lives and make their own choices. I hope that this book will help you to achieve your Diploma and support your professional development in this most challenging but rewarding career.

I wish you every success in your studies and in your future in social care.

Yvonne Nolan

How to use this book

Look out for the following special features as you work through the book.

Case study
Real-life scenarios that explore key issues and broaden your understanding

Activity
A pencil and paper icon marks opportunities for you to consolidate and/or extend learning, allowing you to apply the theoretical knowledge that you have learned to health and social care situations

Doing it well
Information around the skills needed to perform practical aspects of the job. These are often in the form of checklists that you can tick off point by point to confirm that you are doing things correctly

Reflect
Reflect features have thought bubbles, to remind you that they are opportunities for you to reflect on your practice

Key term
Look out for the keyhole symbol that highlights these key terms – clear definitions of words and phrases you need to know

Functional skills
The building blocks icon indicates where you can demonstrate your English, mathematics or ICT skills while carrying out an activity or answering a case study

Getting ready for assessment
Information to help you prepare for assessment, linked to the learning outcomes for the unit

Legislation
Summarises all the laws referred to in a unit

Further reading and research
Useful for continuing professional development, including references to websites, books and agencies

Unit SHC 31

Promote communication in health, social care or children's and young people's settings

Communication is about the way people reach out to one another. It is an essential part of all relationships, and the ability to communicate well with people who use services and people with whom you work is a basic requirement for doing your job.

Communication is not just speech, or using language – we use touch, facial expressions and body movements when we are communicating with people individually or in groups, and there are many means of written and electronic communication that are widely used today.

It is important that you learn to communicate well even where there are differences in people's abilities and methods of communication; people communicate in many different ways and at different levels.

Recording information is important and serves many valuable purposes. You need to understand the significance of what you record and how it is recorded, and the requirements relating to record keeping and to confidentiality.

This unit will help you to understand how all of the different aspects of communication can be used in order to build and develop relationships, and to improve your practice as a social care professional.

In this unit you will learn about:

- **why effective communication is important in the work setting**
- **how to meet the communication and language needs, wishes and preferences of individuals**
- **how to overcome barriers to communication**
- **how to apply principles and practices relating to confidentiality.**

1. Understand why effective communication is important in the work setting

1.1 Different reasons why people communicate

Communication is much more than talking — it is about how people respond to each other in many different ways, such as touch, facial expression, body movements and dress. There is also written communication, the telephone and electronic messages.

> ### Reflect
>
> *You* are the most important tool you have for doing your job. As a social care worker, your own ability to relate to others and to understand them is vital. Whether you work with one person as a personal assistant or with a wider group of people in their own homes or in residential or hospital care, your work is all about good communication.
>
> How does this make you feel? Do you find it a bit daunting? Or is it an exciting challenge?

Developing relationships

Communication is the basis of all relationships, regardless of whether the relationships are personal or professional, and regardless of the nature of the communication. As people communicate, a relationship is formed. This is usually a two-way process as each person involved gets to know the other through a process of communicating and sharing information.

When you support someone, you will get to know and talk to them, and a relationship will grow. Professional relationships are built on respect, trust and good communication. Professional requirements and the **Code of Practice** relevant to the country you work in bind you to deliver a certain standard of service and behaviour. These are set in the UK by the following organisations:

- Scottish Social Services Council
- Care Council for Wales
- General Social Care Council (England)
- Northern Ireland Social Care Council.

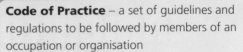

> ### Key term
>
>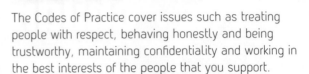
>
> **Code of Practice** – a set of guidelines and regulations to be followed by members of an occupation or organisation

The Codes of Practice cover issues such as treating people with respect, behaving honestly and being trustworthy, maintaining confidentiality and working in the best interests of the people that you support.

In your role, you will need to form relationships with a wide range of people including:

- people who use the services
- family and friends of the people you work for
- managers
- colleagues from your own organisation
- colleagues from other organisations.

1.2 How communication affects relationships in the work setting

Relationships are important

In relationships, the building of trust and understanding between people makes it easier to get things done. If you work as part of a team, you will need to work alongside colleagues and share a workload. If there are good relationships, then working becomes easier because people will co-operate and trust develops.

The key relationships are with the people you support. Your skills in building a relationship will be an important part of ensuring that the identified outcomes are met. People who have decided that they want some support in their lives need to be sure that they are working with someone who is honest and trustworthy, can keep confidences and is committed to working in their best interests. Once people feel reassured about all of these aspects, they are more likely to feel confident to move towards achieving the outcomes they have identified.

Why do you think good relationships are important?

Relationships with colleagues and other professionals are vital if people are to work together effectively. Respecting the expertise and value of the work of others is an essential building block of a good professional relationship. Take the time and trouble to find out what other people do; ask about their training and their skills, and think about what you can learn from them. Remember that all those who work with someone are important and everyone makes an essential contribution.

Doing it well

Effective working relationships

There are some key pointers to effective working relationships.

- Respect and value everyone's contribution.
- Keep to any agreements made with colleagues.
- Be on time for meetings.
- Take your fair share of the workload.
- Ask questions if you do not understand.
- Share your knowledge where it can help others.
- Follow agreed procedures to resolve any disputes or conflicts.
- Learn from the knowledge and skills of colleagues.
- Follow agreed procedures for decision making.

Stages of an interaction

A one-off episode of communication between people is called an 'interaction'. As you spend time in communication with someone, the nature of the interaction will go through changes.

- **Stage 1:** Introduction, insignificant information. This is the stage at which both parties decide whether they want to continue the discussion, and how comfortable they feel. Body language and non-verbal communication are very important at this stage.
- **Stage 2:** Main contact, significant information. The middle of any interaction is likely to contain the 'meat', and this is where you will need to use active listening skills (such as maintaining eye contact or leaning forwards when you are listening) to ensure that the interaction is beneficial and that it meets the needs of the person you are working with.
- **Stage 3:** Reflect, wind up, end positively. Ending in a positive way where all participants are left feeling that they have benefited from the interaction is very important. You may find that you have to end an interaction because of time restrictions, or you may feel that enough has been covered — the other person may need a rest, or you may need a break!

At the end of an interaction, you should always try to reflect on the areas you have covered, and offer a positive and encouraging ending, for example: 'I'm glad you've talked about how unhappy you've been feeling. Now we can try to work at making things better.'

Even if the content of an interaction has been fairly negative, you should encourage the person to see the fact that the interaction has taken place as being positive in itself.

If you are called away before you have had a chance to wind up an interaction properly with a person, make a point of returning to end things in a positive way. If you say, 'I'll be back in a minute', make sure that you do go back.

2. Be able to meet the communication and language needs, wishes and preferences of individuals

2.1 Communication and language needs, wishes and preferences of individuals

Any relationship comes about through communication. In order to provide effective support for people, you must learn to be a good communicator. You will have to know how to pick up the messages that are being communicated from others, and be able to communicate effectively with others without always having to use words.

When we meet and talk with people, we will usually be using two language systems. We will use a verbal or spoken language, and **non-verbal communication**

or **body language**. If you understand the importance of non-verbal communication, you will be able to use it to improve your own skills when you communicate with someone. About 93 per cent of what you communicate to others is understood without you speaking a word.

> ### Key terms
>
> **Non-verbal communication** – a way of communicating without words, through body language, gestures, facial expression and eye contact
>
> **Body language** – the ways in which people communicate without speaking, such as through posture and how they arrange their bodies

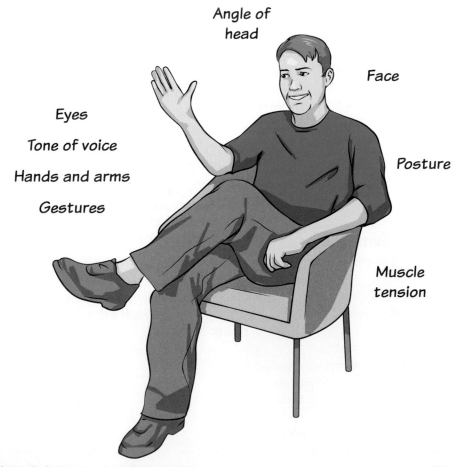

Think about what your body language is saying.

Body language is the way in which we pick up most of the messages people are trying to give us – and some that they are not! For example, sitting in a relaxed way, facing the person who is talking to you and leaning slightly forward says that someone is interested and ready to listen. Sitting slightly turned away from someone with arms and legs folded says that the person is not listening or not interested in hearing what is being said.

What does this body language tell you?

Activity 1

Emotions

Do this with a friend or colleague.

1. Write the names of several emotions (such as anger, joy, sadness, disappointment or fear) on pieces of paper.
2. One of you should pick up a piece of paper. Your task is to communicate the emotion written on the paper to your partner, without saying anything.
3. Your partner then has to decide what the emotion is and say why. Make sure that you list all the things that made you aware of the emotion being expressed. Then change places and repeat the exercise. Take it in turns, until all the pieces of paper have been used.
4. At the end, discuss with your partner what you have discovered about communication as a result of this exercise.

If you record this activity, it may provide some supporting material towards achieving the learning outcome.

When you carried out Activity 1, there will have been quite a few clues about what your partner was trying to communicate. It is not only the expressions on people's faces that tell you about how they feel, but also the way they use the rest of their bodies (non-verbal communication).

Effective communication requires the ability to understand your own and other people's non-verbal behaviour. Our body language sends messages to other people – often unintentionally. You will need to learn to be very aware of the messages that you are giving to people through your own body language.

2.2 Factors to consider when promoting effective communication

Research shows that people pay far more attention to facial expressions and tone of voice than they do to spoken words. For example, in one study, words contributed only seven per cent towards the impression of whether or not someone was liked; tone of voice contributed 38 per cent and facial expression 55 per cent. The study also found that if there was a contradiction between facial expression and words, people believed the facial expression.

The eyes

We can often pick up the feelings and thoughts of other people by looking at their eyes. Our pupils become dilated (bigger) when we are excited, or when we are attracted to or interested in someone. A fixed stare may send the message that the person is angry. Looking away is often interpreted as showing boredom in European cultures, or we may see it as a sign of someone not being truthful. Shy people may be reluctant to make eye contact at all.

The face

Faces can send very complex messages but we can read them easily – even in diagram form. For example,

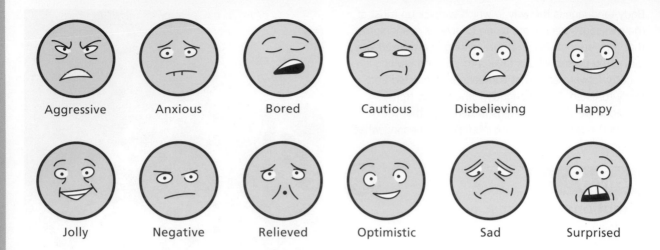

Aggressive · Anxious · Bored · Cautious · Disbelieving · Happy

Jolly · Negative · Relieved · Optimistic · Sad · Surprised

How little does it take for you to understand the emotion?

emoticons in electronic messaging are very simple cartoons, but they convey the intended message very clearly.

Our faces often indicate our emotional state. When a person is sad, they may look down, there may be tension in the face and the mouth will be closed. The muscles in the person's shoulders are likely to be relaxed, but their face and neck may show tension. Anger is shown through tense facial muscles, often with frowns and fixed lines around the mouth; sometimes people's faces are flushed when they are angry. A happy person will have wide-open eyes that make contact with you, and they will smile.

Voice tone

If we talk quickly in a loud voice with a fixed tone, people may see us as angry. A calm, slow voice with varying tone may send a message of being friendly. Tone of voice, along with facial expression, can show concern, interest, disbelief, boredom, irritation and a host of other emotions.

Body movement and posture

The ways we walk, move our heads, sit, cross our legs and so on send messages about whether we are tired, happy, sad or bored. Sitting with crossed arms can mean 'I'm not taking any notice' or 'I disagree with you'. Leaning back or to one side can send the message that you are relaxed or bored. Leaning forward can show interest, sympathy or concern. Standing or sitting face

to face can send a message of being formal or being angry. A slight angle can create a more relaxed and friendly feeling.

Muscle tension

The tension in our feet, hands and fingers can tell others how relaxed or how tense we are. If people are very tense, their shoulders might stiffen, their face muscles might tighten and they might sit or stand rigidly. The face might have a firmly closed mouth with lips and jaws clenched tight. A tense person may breathe quickly and become hot, because deep breathing is not possible when the body is tense.

Gestures

Gestures can help us to understand what a person is saying. Some gestures carry a generally agreed meaning of their own within a culture; for example, in some cultures it is considered very rude to show the soles of your feet, or to give a thumbs-up sign. When people are excited, they may move their arms or hands quickly to accompany what they are saying. Some people gesture when they speak far more than others. We do not necessarily learn gestures from watching others; they may be more deeply rooted in our speech development. Iverson and Goldin-Meadow carried out research in 1998 comparing the speech and gestures of people who had been blind from birth and those who had not. The results showed that the gestures were similar in both groups.

Touch

Touching another person can send messages such as care, affection, power over them or sexual interest. The social setting and other body language usually help people to understand what touch might mean. You should not make assumptions about touch; some people are not happy to be touched, so while for many people a hug or holding a hand may be a welcome demonstration of care and support, others may find it unacceptable. Always check first – 'Do you need a hug?' or 'Are you OK with this?' is a simple way to check if people are comfortable with being touched.

Personal space

The space between people usually indicates how friendly or intimate the conversation is. People in different cultures have different assumptions about how close people should be when they are talking. People in some cultures are much more inclined to touch each other than in others. For example, in Arab cultures, men will hug and kiss on meeting. This is not generally done in the UK, but it is slowly becoming more acceptable among younger people.

When talking to strangers, we may keep an arm's length apart. The ritual of shaking hands indicates that you have been introduced – you may come closer. When you are friendly with someone, you may accept

the person coming even closer to you. Close family and sexual partners are able to be closest. Research has shown that there are 'zones' within which we are comfortable; there is a:

- public zone – strangers tend to maintain a distance, usually more than about two metres – unless squashed together on a train or in a crowd!
- social zone – acquaintances can come slightly closer
- personal zone – friends are accepted into this zone
- intimate zone – usually reserved for close family and partners.

Respecting someone's personal space is very important when you are working. If you enter someone's personal space without asking or explaining, it is disrespectful and the person may feel very uncomfortable with it.

2.3 Communication methods and styles to meet individual needs

There are many different ways to communicate. You have already looked at the importance of non-verbal communication, but there are other methods and styles of communication that are useful when you are thinking about how to meet people's communication needs.

| Intimate zone (touching) | Personal zone (less than 1 metre) | Social zone (1–2 metres) | Public zone (2 metres +) |

Does this work for you?

Using the right level and type of language is important in ensuring that you are understood. People can speak with different degrees of formality or informality. For example, if you went to a hospital reception, you might expect the person on duty to greet you with a formal phrase, such as 'Good morning, how can I help you?'. You would not expect an informal greeting such as you may hear used between friends: 'Hello mate, what's up then?' or 'How's it going?'

The degree of formality or informality establishes a context. At a hospital reception you are unlikely to want to spend time making friends and chatting things over with the receptionist. You may be seeking urgent help; your expectations of the situation might be that you want to be taken seriously and be put in touch with professional services as soon as possible. You might see the situation as a very formal encounter. If you were treated informally, you might interpret this as not being taken seriously, or not respected.

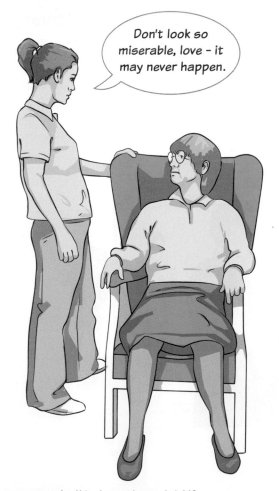

> Don't look so miserable, love – it may never happen.

Can you see why this does not sound right?

Methods of communication

Communicating may not always be about speaking, or even non-verbal communication. You can communicate in many other ways — for example, telephone, email, texting, writing, using interpreters for languages or signing or using pictures.

Some methods of communication are appropriate in specific contexts; for example, telephone conversations are useful for making arrangements or passing on information. The telephone may not necessarily be the most appropriate form of communication where someone is upset or if there is a difficult issue to be discussed, and it can also be a difficult means of communication for people who have a hearing impairment or understanding difficulties.

What do you think is being communicated here?

Texting can also be useful for short messages making arrangements or passing on information. Increasingly, people of all ages are texting, but this may be a problematic means of communication for people who have difficulties in using their hands or have a visual impairment.

Email and other types of electronic communication, such as voice-over Internet communication, can be a very valuable way of people keeping in touch and sending large amounts of information, or pictures. It has limitations, and issues such as confidentiality need to be considered, but it has provided many people with an effective means of maintaining contact with family and friends. Email is also used to communicate between professionals and can be a useful way of sharing large amounts of information. However, there are risks when email is not secure and great care must be taken to follow organisational policy when sharing information through email.

Communication with someone whose language you do not speak needs to be undertaken using an interpreter if necessary. Some limited communication about simple matters can often be achieved using visual signs, but for serious communication about complex or important issues, the services of a professional interpreter are essential. This includes British Sign Language (BSL), which is the first language for many people who are deaf or hearing-impaired. Signing is a professional skill

and requires considerable training in order to learn it, as does any language. There are other communication systems using signs and symbols, such as Makaton, that are less complex and can be learned to a useful standard in a shorter time period. These may be helpful in supporting communication with some people.

People who have a limited ability to speak because of accident or illness, such as a stroke, may be able to communicate using picture cards. These can communicate simple messages, but are not suitable for dealing with complex personal issues.

2.4 Reactions to communication

How do you work out what another person might be feeling? Look at a person's facial expression. Much of what emotions you identify will be in their eyes, but the eyebrows and mouth also tell you a lot about what someone is feeling.

Notice whether someone is looking directly at you or not. Lack of eye contact can be an indication that all is not well. It may be that the person is not feeling

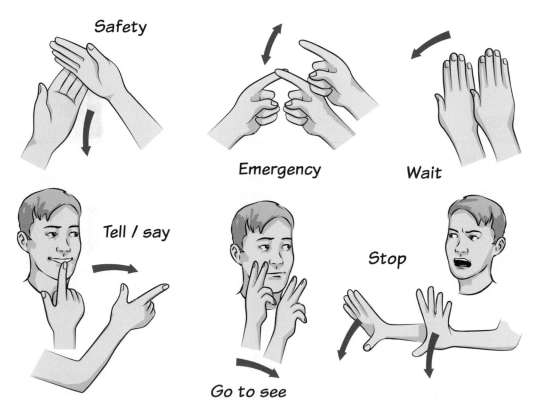

Safety

Emergency

Wait

Tell / say

Go to see

Stop

Can you learn these and try using them?

confident. They may be unhappy, or feel uneasy about talking to you. You will need to follow this up. Some clear, simple questions may help to clear up any problems:

- 'Are you OK to talk?'
- 'Is something bothering you?'
- 'Would you feel happier talking to someone else?'

All of these are non-threatening conversation openers that should help people to explain any issues.

Look at how a person sits. Are they relaxed and comfortable, sitting well back in the chair, or tense and perched on the edge of the seat? Are they slumped in the chair with their head down? People who are feeling well and cheerful tend to hold their heads up, and sit in a relaxed and comfortable way. A person who is tense and nervous, or who feels unsure and worried, is likely to reflect that in the way they sit or stand. Observe hands and gestures carefully. Someone twisting their hands, or fiddling with hair or clothes, is signalling tension and worry. Frequent little shrugs of the shoulders or spreading of the hands may indicate a feeling of helplessness or hopelessness.

Remember that you can often learn as much by observing as by what you hear. It is important to learn to 'listen with your eyes'.

People who are distressed

An important part of responding appropriately is recognising when people are distressed and knowing how to deal with it. There are definite and measurable physical effects caused by strong emotional responses. It is useful to be aware of the effects of emotions, as they can often be an early indicator of a potentially highly charged or dangerous situation. The physical effects of strong emotion can be:

- the pupils dilate, the eyelids open wider than usual and the eyes protrude
- the speed and strength of a person's heartbeat is increased
- blood pressure is increased and blood is forced towards the surface of the body; this is clearly noticeable in flushing of the face and neck
- the hair can stand up, causing goose pimples
- breathing patterns will change and a person may breathe more rapidly
- the lung function alters to allow up to 25 per cent more oxygen to be absorbed
- more sweat is produced — this can often be identified as a 'cold sweat'
- the salivary glands are inhibited — resulting in a dry mouth
- the digestive system is affected — the gastric fluids are reduced and blood is withdrawn from the digestive organs
- there is an increase in adrenaline — this reinforces all effects and increases blood clotting.

Case study

Recognising body language

Mr Morris has severe arthritis and his mobility is very poor. He has some incontinence of urine. The arthritis in his hands, elbows and shoulders means that he is not able to carry out basic domestic tasks, but he can wash and dress, although he is slow and sometimes cannot manage the buttons.

His wife had cared for him at home, with the help of a very supportive neighbour and volunteers from the local church, until a few weeks ago, when she suffered a massive stroke and died. Mr Morris has one son who lives 200 miles away. The son came at once when his mother died, and has stayed for a couple of weeks with his father. However, he now has to return to work and has helped his father to work out a support plan as a

matter of urgency. Mr Morris' support from his neighbour and the church will continue, but some personal support from an agency that the family have chosen will back this up. The first visit of the agency worker is today.

1. What would you expect the facial expression of Mr Morris to be when the visitor arrives?
2. Allowing for his physical difficulties, how do you think he would be sitting?
3. What do you think he would be doing with his hands?
4. What emotions and feelings is Mr Morris likely to be expressing through his body language?
5. How could his care worker support him to communicate?

These physical changes prepare the body for 'fight or flight' — in other words, to challenge a difficult situation or to run away.

There are other very noticeable effects in people in a highly emotional state. They will often have what appears to be increased energy. For example, they may not speak, but shout; they may not sit or stand still, but run or walk about; they may slam doors and even throw furniture or objects around.

Another apparent effect of strong emotional responses is a temporary lessening of the awareness of pain. This often occurs when people act regardless of severe injury, as on the battlefield or in an accident or other emergency. It is only when the immediate threat has passed that they become aware of their injuries.

Signs and signals of distress

When you have a close working knowledge of someone's behaviour over a period of time, it becomes easy to identify when they are becoming distressed. You will find that you have become tuned in to individual behaviour and can recognise the small signs that indicate a change in mood. However, you may not always know someone so well.

There are some general indications that a person is becoming distressed which you may find helpful to recognise. You are most likely to notice:

- changes in **voice** — it may be raised or at a higher pitch than usual
- changes in **facial expression** — this could be scowling, frowning, snarling
- changes in **eyes** — pupils could be dilated and eyes open wider
- **body language** demonstrating agitation and people may adopt an aggressive stance, leaning forwards with fists clenched
- the **face and neck** may be reddened
- there may be excessive **sweating**
- people's **breathing patterns** may change and they may breathe faster than normal.

You may notice a significant change in usual behaviour when someone is becoming distressed. For example, someone who is normally talkative may become quiet and someone who is normally quiet may start to shout or talk very quickly. Other examples are someone who is normally lively becoming still and rigid, or someone who is normally relaxed starting to walk around waving their arms.

You need to be aware of changes in normal behaviour, even if they are far less extreme than these examples. Sometimes a subtle change in behaviour can indicate someone is becoming distressed, and you are far more likely to notice subtle changes in people whom you know well and have worked with over a period of time.

Case study

Signs of distress

Liz is an older lady who has been in a residential home for the past three years. Like most of the residents, she has her own chair and she likes to sit in a corner of the main lounge. Liz is normally bright and chatty and talks happily with the staff and other residents.

As with many residential settings, there is a regular influx of new residents, who usually adapt to the setting extremely well. However, the previous week a new resident, Maria, was admitted who, like Liz, was very talkative and friendly, but she would continue to talk at great length and quite loudly for long periods of time. For the first couple of days Liz appeared to join in and respond to Maria's conversation, but staff noticed she gradually responded less and less, and appeared to be becoming more unhappy. One morning a staff member went into the lounge, where Maria was talking as usual, and noticed that Liz was sitting in her corner with her head down but bolt upright in her chair with her arms bent and fists clenched, and breathing faster than usual. When the staff member crouched down to talk to Liz, they noticed she had bright red cheeks.

1. What conclusions would you reach about Liz's state of mind from looking at the physical indications?
2. What would be the next step you would take?
3. What are the potential responses from Liz?
4. What would be a satisfactory outcome?

How people control strong emotions

In growing and developing, most of us learn to control our powerful emotions. The sight of a two-year-old lying on the floor in a supermarket kicking and screaming is not uncommon — it is one that is accepted as normal behaviour for a child of that age. On the other hand, it is not socially acceptable for an adult to do the same thing, however much we may want to on occasions! We do not behave this way in public because we have been socialised into behaviour that is accepted as the norm in society. However, some people do find it beneficial and therapeutic to have a tantrum in the privacy of their homes, to get relief from the rage they feel.

Have you ever felt like doing this?

Reflect

Consider how you deal with emotions. Think of the occasions when you have felt strong and powerful emotions but managed to keep them under control and not show your distress publicly, and other occasions when you have shown public distress. Try to identify the difference in circumstances and the factors that caused the two different responses.

1. Was the difference about the people who were present?
2. Was it the circumstances of the occasion?
3. Was it about your emotional state at the time?

Thinking about all the factors will help you to understand the ways in which you deal with strong emotions.

Causes of distress and potential triggers for behaviour

Most people behave within the accepted norms of society most of the time. However, on occasions the emotions may become too powerful or the normal control which people exercise over their emotions may relax, resulting in a display of emotion and distress. People can become highly emotional for all sorts of reasons, but being aware of potential **triggers** for emotional behaviour can be helpful when you are preparing to respond to a challenging situation. People commonly become distressed when:

- they receive bad or worrying news
- there are problems with a relationship that is important to them

- there is an overload of work or family pressures
- they have serious money, work or family issues
- they are reacting to the behaviour of others towards them
- they are in an environment that they find frustrating or restricting
- they are in an environment that they find intensely irritating
- they are deprived of information and are fearful
- they have full information about a situation and they remain fearful of it
- they are anxious about a forthcoming event
- they are unable to achieve the objectives they have set themselves.

Key term

Trigger – an event that causes other events

You will come across different reasons and triggers for emotional behaviour depending on the setting in which you work.

I just can't go on like this.

How many stress triggers can you see here?

Doing it well

Non-verbal communication

- Make sure that you maintain eye contact with the person you are talking to, although looking away occasionally is normal and you should avoid staring.
- Be aware of what you are doing and try to think why you are losing attention.
- Sit where you can be comfortably seen, not where someone has to turn in order to look at you.
- Sit a comfortable distance away from the person – not so far that any sense of closeness is lost, but not so close that you invade their space.
- Show by your gestures that you are listening and interested in what people are saying, such as nodding occasionally to show you are receptive.
- Avoid folded arms or crossed legs, as these can indicate that you are closed rather than open to what someone is expressing.
- Lean towards someone to show that you are interested in what they are saying. You can use leaning forwards quite effectively at times when you want to emphasise your interest or support. Then move backwards a little at times when the content is a little lighter.
- Using touch to communicate your caring and concern is often useful and appropriate. Many people find it comforting to have their hand held or stroked, or to have an arm around their shoulders.
- Be aware of a person's body language, which should tell you if they find touch acceptable.
- Always err on the side of caution if you are unsure about what is acceptable in another culture – for example, with regard to touching.
- Think about age and gender in relation to touch. An older woman may be happy to have her hand held by a female care worker, but may be uncomfortable with such a response from a man.
- Ensure that you are touching someone because you think it will comfort them, and not because you feel helpless and cannot think of anything to say.

Activity 2

Triggers

Identify six potential triggers for emotional behaviour that relate to your own work setting. Explain why they are particularly relevant to the person or people you work with, and what you would expect to see.

If you record this activity, it may contribute towards the achievement of learning outcome 1.

Functional skills

English: Speaking and listening

Take part in a discussion with a small group of colleagues about six potential triggers for emotional behaviour that relate to your work setting. Ensure all participants take an active role by asking questions and picking up on points made by others. Present your ideas concisely and use clear speech at all times.

Is this contact welcome?

Activity 3

Comfort zone

Do this with at least one other person – two or three is even better.

1. Think of an incident or situation which is quite important and significant to you. Stand still in the middle of a room and begin to tell your partner about your significant incident.

2. Your partner should start at the edge of the room and slowly move closer and closer to you. At the point where you feel comfortable talking to your partner, say 'Stop'. Mark this point and measure the distance from where you are standing.

3. They should then continue moving closer. At the point where you feel that your partner is too close, say 'Stop' again. Mark this point and measure the distance from where you are standing.

4. Change places and repeat the exercise.

You may find that you and your partner(s) have different distances at which you feel comfortable, but it is likely to be in the range of three to five feet (one to one and a half metres).

If you can video this activity and support that with a written account, or just write a reflective account including how you felt and an explanation of why, you may be able to use it to support the achievement of learning outcome 1.

Listening effectively

Communication is a two-way process. This may sound obvious, but a great deal of communication is wasted because only one of the parties is communicating. Think about setting up communication between two radios – when a link is established, the question is asked: 'Are you receiving me?' The answer comes back: 'Receiving you loud and clear.' Unfortunately, human beings do not do this exercise before they talk to each other!

If no one is listening and receiving the information a person is trying to communicate, it is just a waste of time. Learning how to listen is a key task for anyone working in care.

How can you tell when someone is really listening?

You may think that you know how to listen and that it is something you do constantly. After all, you are hearing all sorts of noises all day long – but simply hearing sounds is not the same thing as actively listening.

For most people, feeling that someone is really listening makes a huge difference to how confident they feel about talking. You will need to learn about ways in which you can show people you are listening to what they are saying.

Yes, I'm really interested, go on.

You can tell me anything. I'm very friendly and approachable.

No, it's fine. I've got plenty of time – don't feel you have to hurry.

Why would behaviour like this not encourage someone to keep talking?

Reflect

Think about a time you have talked to someone you felt was really interested in what you were saying and listening carefully to you. Try to note down all the little signals that made you so sure they were really listening. Did the fact you thought the person was really listening to you make it easier to talk? How can you make sure that you give out the same signals to the people who are talking to you?

Spending some time thinking about this will help you to improve your listening skills.

Using body language

The messages are made clear by such things as facial expression or maintaining eye contact, leaning forwards when you are listening, or having an open and relaxed posture.

Your body language will let people know that you really are listening to what they are saying. Practise your listening skills in just the same way you would practise any other skill — you can learn to listen well.

Doing it well

Listening
- Look at the person who is talking to you.
- Maintain eye contact, without staring.
- Nod your head to encourage the person to talk and to show that you understand.
- Use 'aha', 'mm' and similar expressions which indicate that you are still listening.
- Lean slightly towards the person who is speaking – this indicates interest and concern.
- Have an open and interested facial expression, which should reflect the tone of the conversation – happy, serious, and so on.

Using the right words

Body language is one key to effective listening, but what you say in reply is also important. You can back up the message that you are interested and listening by checking that you have understood what has been said to you. Using sentences beginning 'So...' to check that you have got it right can be helpful. 'So it's only since you had the fall that you are feeling worried about being here alone.' 'So you were happy with the service before the hours were changed.' You can also use expressions such as 'So what you mean is...' or 'So what you are saying is...'

Short, encouraging phrases used while people are talking can show concern, understanding or sympathy. Phrases such as 'I see', 'Oh dear', 'Yes' or 'Go on' all give the speaker a clear indication that you are listening and want them to continue.

Using questions

Sometimes questions can be helpful to prompt someone who is talking, or to try to move a conversation forward. There are two different kinds of questions. Questions that can be answered with just 'yes' or 'no' are **closed questions** — for example, 'Would you like to go out today?'

An **open question** needs more than 'yes' or 'no' to answer it. 'What is your favourite kind of outing?' is an open question. Open questions usually begin with:

- what
- how
- why
- when
- where.

Depending on the conversation and the circumstances, either type of question may be appropriate. For example, if you are encouraging someone to talk because they have always been quiet, but have suddenly begun to open up, you are more likely to use open questions to encourage them to carry on talking. On the other hand, if you need factual information or you just want to confirm that you have understood what has been said to you, then you may need to ask closed questions.

Key terms

Closed question – a question that requires only 'yes' or 'no' as an answer

Open question – a question that cannot be answered by just 'yes' or 'no'; it often begins with a 'how' or a 'why', for example. This sort of question encourages people to talk more

One of the main points to remember when listening is that whatever you say, there should not be too much of it! You are supposed to be listening, not speaking. There are some don'ts for good listening.

- Don't interrupt — always let people finish what they are saying, and wait for a gap in the conversation.
- Don't give advice — even if asked. You are not the person concerned, so you cannot respond to questions beginning, 'If you were me...' Your job is to encourage people to make their own decisions, not to tell them what to do. If you are pushed for an answer, you should respond with something like: 'Well, I'm not you, so what I would do isn't the point — now let's look at your options...'
- Don't tell people about your own experiences — you are there as a listener, not to make people listen while you talk about yourself.
- Don't ever dismiss fears, worries or concerns by saying, 'That's silly' or 'You shouldn't worry about that' — people's fears are real and should not be made to sound trivial.

Activity 4

Open and closed questions

What type of question is each of the following?

- 'Are you feeling worried?'
- 'What sort of things worry you?'
- 'Do you want to join in the games tonight?'
- 'Is your daughter coming to visit?'
- 'Why were you cross with Marge this morning?'
- 'Were you cross with Marge this morning?'
- 'What have you got planned for when your daughter comes to visit?'
- 'Do you live here alone?'
- 'How do you feel about living alone?'

Think of some more of your own and note how they could apply to people you support.

If you record the questions and explain the links to the people you support (without giving any information that could identify people), it may be able to contribute to your achievement of learning outcome 1.

3. Be able to overcome barriers to communication

This learning outcome looks at potential difficulties in establishing communication. Difficulties can be the result of barriers to communication and misunderstandings can often happen if barriers are not completely overcome.

3.1 How people from different backgrounds may use and/or interpret communication methods in different ways

Your first port of call to find out about communication issues is the person with whom you are communicating. However, you can discover a great deal about possible communication issues by simply observing someone. You can find out about how a person communicates and the differences between their way of communicating and your own.

Observation should be able to establish:

- which language is being used
- if a person experiences any hearing or visual impairment
- if they have any physical illness or disability
- if they have a learning disability.

Any of these factors could have a bearing on how well you will be able to communicate with someone, and what steps they may want you to take to make things easier. Observation will give you some very good clues to start with, but you should work with the person to establish exactly what is needed to assist communication. You may also consider supporting this by:

- asking colleagues who have worked with the person before and who are likely to have some background information and advice
- consulting other professionals who have worked with the person and may have knowledge of means of communication which have been effective for them
- reading previous case notes or case histories
- finding out as much as you can about a person's particular illness or disability – the most useful sources of information are likely to be the specialist agencies for the particular condition

- talking to the person's family or friends. They are likely to have a great deal of information that will have developed over a long period of time, and are likely to be a very useful source of advice and help.

3.2 Barriers to effective communication

There are many barriers that can be put in the way of someone who wants to communicate. You will need to understand how to recognise these and to learn how you can work with someone to overcome them.

Communication barriers can include:

- either of you having a sensory impairment
- a physical illness or disability, such as a stroke or confusion
- a learning disability
- people speaking different languages
- cultural differences
- different styles of speech
- distress, where somebody is so upset that they are unable to communicate.

3.3 Ways to overcome barriers to communication

Physical barriers

Communication can also be hindered by physical and environmental factors. Always provide a private situation if you have personal matters to discuss – it is rarely the case that the best that can be arranged is to pull the curtains around a bed. You need to think about the surroundings. People find it difficult to talk in noisy, crowded places. A communal lounge with a television on is not a good place for effective communication.

Remember the temperature – make sure it is comfortable. Think about lighting. Is it too dark or too bright? Is the sun in someone's eyes? Make sure that you do not sit with your face in shadow. It is very disconcerting not to be able to see someone's face when talking to them – remember what you have learned about non-verbal communication.

It is important when communicating with someone that they can see your face and hear what you are saying.

Doing it well

Key points for communicating

- Never take communication for granted.
- Not everyone communicates in the same way.
- It is your responsibility to support the person to communicate.
- As far as possible, plan ahead and think what you will need to take into account.
- It is important when communicating with someone that they can see your face and hear what you are saying.

Remember you need to understand what barriers can get in the way so that you can make sure they do not. If the person you are working with has decided that communication is a part of their life that needs support, then your role is to work with them to overcome as many of the obstacles to communication as possible.

Thinking about obstacles

Never assume that you or anyone can be heard, understood and responded to without first thinking about the person involved. Check first to ensure you are supporting someone to communicate as effectively as possible by working with them to overcome as many challenges and barriers as possible.

The first and most important step is to find out what support someone is looking for to achieve the outcomes they want. They may already be able to communicate quite well and just need some additional support in specific areas, or they may want you to offer extensive support and help them to develop a whole strategy for communicating.

For example, someone may be profoundly deaf but use British Sign Language; they may just need some support to ensure that an interpreter is available for key communications. They may also need the services of a note-taker in order to complete a qualification to get the job that will provide independence – the identified outcome.

Alternatively, someone may have become visually impaired through an age-related condition such as **macular degeneration** and may be quite confident in getting around indoors, but looking for support when going out. This will contribute towards achieving the outcome of feeling more confident and meeting more people that was the identified outcome for the support plan. Your role is always to work alongside people to achieve the outcomes in the support plan by building on what they can already do.

Key term

Macular degeneration – an eye disease that results in blurred vision and can cause blindness

Different people will respond to barriers and difficulties in different ways; some will be ready to have a go and be keen to meet any challenges head on, whereas others will be put off and find it hard to overcome barriers. You need to understand how each person is reacting and ensure that they are doing things in the way that they have chosen, not in the way that you think may be best for them.

Communication is affected by many different factors including:

- hearing loss
- physical disability
- visual impairment
- learning disabilities
- dementia/confusion
- language differences
- distress.

Hearing loss

If someone is profoundly deaf, you will need to find out from them what sort of support they have chosen. If someone uses British Sign Language (BSL), you will need to have a BSL interpreter available. If someone uses a hearing aid, check that it is operating efficiently if you seem to be having communication problems.

Consider the level of someone's hearing. Many people are hard of hearing, but this may not be a profound hearing loss. It can mean that they have difficulty hearing where there is background noise and other people talking.

A loss or reduction of ability to hear clearly can cause major differences in the ability to communicate. It is very difficult for somebody who does not hear sounds at all or hears them in a blurred and indistinct way to be able to respond and to join in unless others are making the effort to overcome the barriers. The result can be that people feel very isolated and excluded from others around them. This can lead to understandable frustration and anger.

Profound deafness is not as common as partial hearing loss. People are most likely to suffer from loss of hearing of certain sounds at certain volumes or at certain pitches, such as high sounds or low sounds. It is also very common for people to find it difficult to hear if there is background noise — many sounds may jumble together, making it very hard to pick out the voice of one person. There are electronic devices called 'personal listeners' that can support people to hear more clearly

in noisy environments. **Loop systems** can support people to hear sounds in a public place, such as music, a film or a lecture. Similar technology can be used to support people's ability to hear television or radio broadcasts in their own home.

> ### Key term
>
> **Loop system** – a system enabling partially deaf people to hear dialogue and sound in theatres, cinemas and so on

A personal listener.

Hearing loss can also have an effect on speech, particularly for those who are profoundly deaf and are unable to hear their own voices as they speak. This can make communication doubly difficult and frustrating if others are not sufficiently aware of the barriers that may be facing these people.

Some people may be able to lip read, while for many, BSL is their first language. BSL is estimated to be a first or preferred language for between 30,000 and 70,000 people in the UK. Some deaf people may use Makaton, a system for developing language that uses speech, signs and symbols to help people with hearing difficulties to communicate and to develop their language skills. It may involve speaking a word and performing a sign using hands and body language. There is a large range of symbols that may help people with a learning difficulty to recognise an idea or to communicate with others.

Would this be a valuable skill for you?

People who are deaf or hard of hearing can use telecommunication services, such as minicoms or the typetalk service. These allow a spoken conversation to be translated in written form using a form of word processor, and the responses are then translated into speech and relayed to a hearing person. These services have provided a major advance in enabling people who are hard of hearing or profoundly deaf to use telephone equipment. For people who are less severely affected by hearing impairment, there are facilities such as telephone receivers with adjustable volume that allow conversations to be heard more clearly.

Doing it well

Supporting communication for someone with a hearing impairment

- Use a BSL interpreter if necessary. BSL is a language and if you cannot communicate, you need an interpreter – as with any other language.
- Try to reduce any background noise as far as possible.
- Check with the person concerned that any means of hearing support, for example, a hearing aid, is working properly, is fitted correctly and that the batteries are working.
- Ensure that you are sitting in a good light, not too far away, and that you speak clearly and slowly – but do not shout or exaggerate words. Shouting simply distorts your face and makes it more difficult for a person with hearing loss to be able to read what you are saying.
- Remember the importance of non-verbal communication.
- Do not cover your mouth with your hand while you are speaking and try not to sit with your face in shadow.
- Do not shout or speak directly into a person's ear or hearing aid.
- Be prepared to write things down if someone prefers this.

Case study

Solving communication problems

Mr Talan lives alone. For many years he has been well known in the neighbourhood. He was never particularly chatty, but always said a polite 'Good morning' on his way to the shops, and had a smile and a kind word for the children. His wife died about 15 years ago. They had only one son, a soldier killed in action many years previously.

Recently, Mr Talan's health began to deteriorate. He had a bad winter with a chest infection and a nasty fall in the snow. This seemed to shake his confidence, and he chose to have a support worker twice a week. Neighbours began to notice that Mr Talan no longer spoke to them, and he failed to acknowledge the children. His outings to the shops became less frequent.

Jean, his support worker, was worried that he hardly responded to her cheerful chat as she worked. She realised that Mr Talan's hearing was deteriorating.

After medical investigations, Mr Talan chose to use a hearing aid. He began to be much more like his old self – he spoke to people again, smiled at the children and enjoyed his visits to the shops.

1. How do you think Mr Talan felt when he began to have problems hearing people?
2. Why do you think he reacted in the way he did?
3. What other factors might Jean have thought were causing Mr Talan's deterioration?
4. How are people likely to have reacted to Mr Talan?

Physical disability

If someone is physically disabled, you will need to consider whether you need to change how you respond to their communication and think about whether body language may be different from what you would expect.

How would you interpret this body language? You could be very wrong.

Depending on the disability, it can be evident in different ways. People who have suffered strokes, for example, may have reduced communication abilities because of conditions such as **dysphasia**. This condition is very distressing for the person and for family and friends who are trying to communicate. Often this is coupled with a loss of movement and a difficulty in using facial muscles to form words.

Key term

Dysphasia – a problem with finding the right words or interpreting the meanings of words spoken

Following a stroke or other brain injury, people have to work out ways of coping with dysphasia. Many people find that they prefer people to communicate with them using some simple rules.

- Use very simple, short sentences, speaking slowly, and be prepared to wait while the person processes what you have said and composes a reply.
- Use gestures – they can make it easier for people to understand what you are trying to get across.
- Use drawing, writing or flashcards to help understanding.
- Use simple, closed questions that only need a 'yes' or 'no' answer.
- Avoid long, complicated sentences with interrelated ideas. For example, do not say, 'It's almost dinner time I think, so how long is it since you ate something and have you thought about what you would like?' Instead, say, 'Are you hungry? Would you like fish? Would you like chicken?' and so on, until the person has told you what they want to eat.

Case study

Identifying Mr Pritchard's wishes

Jane is working with Mr Pritchard, who has very poor speech following a stroke. He is making noises and is clearly trying to indicate something to her. He is moving his hand and eyes in the direction of the window. Jane asks if he wants the window open – he gets more agitated and shakes his head. She then asks if he wants the curtains drawn – he shakes his head again.
She thinks about what they were talking about before he started to try to tell her something – it was about his family, and his children and grandchildren coming to

visit. She asks if it is the photo on the windowsill he wants – he nods and smiles.

Jane sits with him for a few more minutes and talks about the people in the photograph, making sure that any questions just need a nod or shake of the head.

1. How did Jane work out what he wanted?
2. How else could she have done this?
3. What could have happened if she had not been able to work out what he wanted?

In some cases, the communication difficulty is a symptom of a disability. Illnesses, such as motor neurone disease or cerebral palsy, can also lead to difficulties in making speech, although not in understanding it.

- The person will understand perfectly what you are saying, but the challenge lies in communicating with you.
- There is no need for you to speak slowly, although you should allow time for a response.
- You will have to become familiar with the sound of the person's voice; it can take a while to tune in to understanding the voice of someone who has an illness affecting the facial, throat or larynx muscles.

Other types of disability may have no effect at all upon voice production or the thought processes that produce spoken words, but the lack of other body movements may mean that non-verbal communication may be difficult or not what you would expect. It is easy to misunderstand or get the wrong impression about someone's attitudes and feelings if the non-verbal clues you expect to see are simply not there.

Visual impairment

Visual impairment can result in many communication difficulties. Not only is someone unable to pick up the visual signals that are being given out by the person speaking, but, because they are unaware of these signals, they may also fail to give appropriate signals in return. This lack of non-verbal communication and inability to receive and interpret non-verbal communication can lead to misunderstandings about a person's attitudes and behaviour. It means that communications can easily be misinterpreted, or it could be thought that they are behaving in an inappropriate way.

Do not rely on your facial expressions to communicate your interest and concern — use words and touch where appropriate. If you are asked to find out any information, remember to check the format it needs to be in. This may be large print, Braille or audio. If you need any further information, the Royal National Institute of Blind People (RNIB) will be able to advise you about local sources of supplies.

Hello. I'm Jeff and I'm going to be the person who is mainly responsible for looking after you while you are in here...

Good morning, Ralph. It's Solange. How are you?

You need to think carefully about the way you address people who have an impairment.

People should have their eyes tested regularly in order to check their prescription and health.

Communicating with people who have visual impairment

- Let them know you are there first. One way to do this is by touching, but check that the person is comfortable with this approach.
- Make sure that you introduce yourself when you come into a room. A simple 'Hello John, it's Sue' is all that is needed so that you do not 'arrive' unexpectedly.
- You may need to use touch more than you would in speaking to a sighted person, because your facial expressions and body movements will not be seen. So, if you are expressing concern or sympathy, it may be appropriate to touch someone's hand or arm at the same time that you are saying you are concerned and sympathetic.
- Ask the person what communication suits them best – do not impose your idea of appropriate styles of communication. Most people who have a visual impairment know very well what they can and cannot do, and if you ask they will tell you exactly what they need you to do in order to provide support.
- Do not decide that you know the best way to help. Never take the arm of someone who is visually impaired to help them to move around. Allow the person to take your arm or shoulder and direct you.

For people with limited vision, it may be important to use language to describe things that a sighted person may take for granted, such as non-verbal communication or the context of certain comments. Touch may be an important aspect of communication; some registered blind people can work out what you look like if they can touch your face.

One of the commonest ways that people decide to deal with a relatively minor visual impairment is to use glasses or contact lenses. It may be worth reminding people to check that these are clean and the correct prescription. You might also remind older people that it is advisable to have their eyes tested every year, in order to check for diseases such as glaucoma. You might advise younger people to have their eyes checked every two years.

Learning disabilities

The spectrum of learning disability is so wide, both in terms of specific disabilities and the effect on people's lives, that it is almost impossible to be prescriptive about how a learning disability affects communication. For some people there may be almost no noticeable effect on communication, while for others a learning disability may result in a significant loss of speech, hearing, vision and apparent level of understanding.

Broadly, the effect of learning disabilities is to limit the ability of a person to understand and process information. This means it is very much a case of finding out from the person what support they are looking for and how this fits into supporting the achievement of their identified outcomes.

Where the nature of the learning disability is such that communication is seriously limited, the support plan should clearly identify the level and type of support required, and also the family or friends who are able to discuss this.

It is also possible that a learning disability may mean that someone will have a short attention span, so this can result in communications having to be repeated several times or perhaps paraphrased in an appropriate form. You should have gathered sufficient information about the person to know the level of understanding that they have – how simply and how often you need to explain things, and the kinds of communication which are likely to be the most effective.

Many people with a learning disability respond well to physical contact and are able to relate and communicate on a physical level more easily than on a verbal level. This will vary between people and you should be prepared to use a great deal of physical contact and hugs when communicating, if you know that this is something to which the person responds.

Dementia/confusion

This condition is most prevalent in older people, although it can happen to younger people and can sometimes be caused through a brain injury following an accident. People with **dementia** can ultimately lose the ability to communicate, but in the early stages it involves short-term memory loss to the extent of being unable to remember the essential parts of a conversation or a recent exchange.

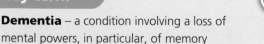

Key term

Dementia – a condition involving a loss of mental powers, in particular, of memory

People with memory disorders often substitute inappropriate words, although it is sometimes possible to see the connection. For example, 'tablecloth' may be substituted for 'carpet' or 'rope' for 'scarf'. However, it is not always possible to make sense of such conversations.

People may also have what appear to be delusions; a 90-year-old woman may say, 'My mother visited me yesterday.' On the surface, such a statement appears to be irrational. However, as part of a support plan, it is very important not to challenge the rationality

of what is being said. The most important thing is to make the older person feel valued and respected. Perhaps you know that the visitor was, in fact, a daughter, and she has simply used an incorrect word. There is no need to challenge or correct the communication; the important thing is that the person feels safe and respected.

Sometimes someone may be disorientated and make statements about needing to go to work or to go home to look after the children. Once again, it is important not to argue, but rather to try to divert the conversation in a way that interests and values the person. For example:

Mrs M:	I must go home and get the tea ready for my children.
Support worker:	All right, shall we walk to your room, then? You might want your coat.
Mrs M:	Yes, that's right, you're so kind.
Support worker [now in Mrs M's room]:	Is this photograph of your son and daughter?
Mrs M:	Yes, that's right.
Support worker:	They've both got married now – aren't they both grown-up?
Mrs M:	Yes, I'm very proud of them – they're coming to visit me tomorrow.
Support worker:	That's wonderful. Why don't we go downstairs and have a cup of tea?
Mrs M:	Yes, that would be very nice – you're so kind to me.

In the exchange above, the support worker has avoided arguing about logic, and instead has gently helped Mrs M to remember the age her children are now. Throughout the conversation, the support worker has shown respect for Mrs M.

How do you think this lady feels?

3.4 Strategies that can be used to clarify misunderstandings

Language differences

Where a person speaks a different language from the people providing support, it can be an isolating and frustrating experience. The person may become distressed and frightened, as it is very difficult to establish exactly what is happening and they are not in a position to ask or to have any questions answered. They may feel excluded from everything and will find making relationships with support workers extremely difficult. Misunderstandings may well occur.

How are misunderstandings being overcome here?

Make sure that you know what language someone is comfortable with — do not assume it is the same as yours without making certain! Find out if you need to provide any translation facilities, or written information in another language. If translation is needed, your team leader or manager should be able to help you to arrange it. Your local adult services department will have a list of interpreters, as will the police or the consulate or embassy of the country the person is from. Where you are in the position of supporting someone who speaks a different language, you will need the services of an interpreter for any serious discussions or communication.

You should always use professional interpreters wherever possible. It may be very tempting to use other members of the family — very often children have excellent language skills — but it is inappropriate in many support situations. This is because:

- their English and their ability to interpret may not be at the same standard as a professional interpreter's, and misunderstandings can easily occur
- the person may wish to discuss matters which are not appropriate to be discussed with children, or they may not want members of the family involved in very personal discussions about health or support issues.

It is unlikely that you would be able to have a full-time interpreter available throughout your period of supporting someone, so it is necessary to consider alternatives for encouraging everyday communication.

Be prepared to learn words in the person's language that will help communication. You could try to give the person some words in your language if they are willing and able to learn them.

There are other simple techniques such as flashcards or sign language that you may wish to try that can help basic levels of communication.

How would you feel about doing this?

The suggestions given are not exhaustive and you will come up with many that work for the person you are supporting. The most effective way of communicating with a person who speaks a different language is through non-verbal communication. A smile and a friendly face are understood in all languages, as are a concerned facial expression and a warm and welcoming body position.

However, be careful about the use of gestures – gestures that are acceptable in one culture may not be acceptable in all. For example, a thumb extended upwards in some cultures would mean 'great, that's fine, OK', but in many cultures it is an extremely offensive gesture. If you are unsure which gestures are acceptable in another culture, make sure that you check before using any which may be misinterpreted.

Distress

If people are upset as the result of an outside event, such as the death of a close friend or relative, or because they have received some other bad news, there is probably little you can do to prevent the distress. However, the way you communicate with them and the way you handle the situation can often reduce it.

You must be careful not to pressurise people to discuss more than they want to. You could also offer them a choice of talking to another member of staff or a relative or friend, if they appear to be unwilling to discuss their worries with you.

Your acknowledgement and recognition of their distress may be sufficient for some people, and they may be able to deal with their unhappiness or grief themselves if they know that they can obtain additional support from you if necessary.

Support workers need to give people the chance to decide whether they want to talk about the causes of distress.

The effects of your interactions

You need to be aware of the ways in which you are using your own communication skills to interact with someone who is distressed. While you are taking into account the person's body language and the clues of non-verbal communication, you will need to be conscious of the messages your own non-verbal communication is sending. You need to demonstrate openness with an open, welcoming position, but do not move in on somebody's personal space as this often heightens tension. Make eye contact in a way that demonstrates you are willing to listen.

It is important that with anyone who is clearly distressed or displaying anger or excitement, you approach them in a calm and non-threatening way. It is unlikely that there will be risks to you or to other people, but if at any point you feel your personal safety, or that of others, is at risk, you should immediately summon help.

Getting help

No one is able to deal with every situation with which they are faced, and you may feel that a particular situation is beyond your capability. This is nothing to be ashamed of. Knowing your own limitations is important and demonstrates a higher degree of maturity and self-awareness than taking risks. Contact other members of your team or other professional colleagues with the experience or skills to deal with the situation. Never hesitate to summon help when you feel unsure in dealing with a person in distress.

Someone who is very upset can become aggressive in some circumstances. If you notice that a person is becoming aggressive or changing from crying or expressing anger to shouting or throwing things, then you should immediately summon help.

Anger is not always directed at others; it can be turned inwards and be directed against the person. You may be faced with a distressed, hurt and angry person who makes it clear that they intend to self-harm. In this case you have a responsibility to take immediate action to protect them. You must also advise the person that you will have to take these steps to protect them and attempt to stop them from harming themselves. Remember, it is never acceptable to allow someone to do harm to themselves. There is more information on protecting people in Unit HSC 024.

How to offer support

When communicating with someone who is distressed, one of the first things to do is to find out what support they want. Sometimes all people need is having their hand held to enable them to go on coping with the distress themselves. Providing unwanted support can sometimes be as damaging and as unhelpful as too little or none. The risks of providing unwanted support are that people may:

- feel they are disempowered and are no longer able to help or support themselves — this is likely to damage their self-esteem or self-confidence
- feel you have interfered and they have been forced to reveal more about themselves and their personal life than they would have wished to
- become over-dependent on you for help and support, which may reduce their ability to manage their own lives.

On the other hand, offering too little or no help can mean that people may:

- feel they are isolated and there is nobody who cares for them or is interested in their problems
- feel they are unworthy and not liked
- get very angry and frustrated at the apparent lack of care or interest from the rest of the world.

The level of help and support you offer must always be the decision of the person concerned. Wherever possible, this should be done through a process of discussion. Questions should be open-ended and clear, and designed to establish the correct level of support, such as, 'I can see you're very upset — would it help to talk to me about it?' or 'I can see you're very upset — would you like me to find you someone to talk to?'

There may be circumstances in which it is not possible to discuss this with people, perhaps because they are extremely agitated or angry, or are in an exceedingly distressed state and unable to hold a calm conversation. It may even be that they are threatening to harm themselves or others. In these circumstances you will need to judge how best to intervene. You could try acting in the same way as you would when dealing with somebody who was calmer. For example, if you put your hand on the shoulder of someone who is sobbing and clearly very upset, the result could be that the person either shakes you off and walks away, or turns to you for a hug.

No! I don't want you to touch me. It won't help!

Attempts to comfort someone in distress may not always be welcome.

Broadly, the support you will be asked for will probably fall into one of three categories, as shown in Table 1.

Form of support	Description
Practical support	Giving information, offering a hug or hand-holding, making a telephone call, providing transport or other practical assistance, contacting someone on behalf of the distressed person or meeting an appropriate professional.
Emotional support	Using listening skills, using counselling skills.
Immediate emergency assistance	Summoning immediate help from a colleague, a senior member of staff, an appropriate professional or the emergency services.

Table 1: Forms of support.

3.5 How to access extra support or services to enable individuals to communicate effectively

You will need to ensure that you have access to sources of information and the appropriate resources that can be offered in particular circumstances. There are specialist organisations which will offer particular support for those who are bereaved, for those who are experiencing relationship difficulties or for those who are feeling depressed and may harm themselves. You should be sure that you can access all the relevant contact details.

Empathy

You should not attempt to offer counselling unless you have been adequately trained and had the opportunity for supervised practice. However, do not underestimate the support you will be able to provide by using good communication skills and a genuine empathy and care for the people you support — you can encourage them to express how they feel about what is causing them worry, anxiety or distress.

Empathy involves the skill of developing an accurate understanding of the feelings and thoughts of another person. It involves being able to understand the world of another person and the feelings that they may have. Empathising with another person is a skill that develops from good active listening, and it is a characteristic of a caring attitude, where a person can see beyond their own assumptions about the world and can imagine the thoughts and feelings of someone who is quite different. It means that you can 'walk a mile in someone else's shoes'.

Many situations can be resolved and the distress significantly reduced if the person can talk to someone who has good listening skills and can offer clear, practical advice and information. It can also simply be a matter of showing that someone cares enough to sit and hold their hand for half an hour, or to offer a big hug!

If you feel the situation calls for more support than you can offer, it is important that you recognise this and refer it to someone else as required.

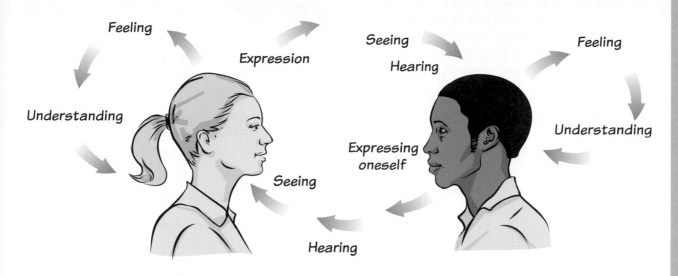

Feeling

Expression

Understanding

Seeing

Hearing

Seeing

Hearing

Feeling

Understanding

Expressing oneself

Developing a sense of empathy may involve a communication cycle of active listening.

Does this make you feel good? Why?

How distress can affect you

It can be very upsetting to deal with someone who is displaying powerful emotions. People's stories or experiences can be so moving and distressing that you may feel very grateful, or perhaps even guilty, for your own happier circumstances. On the other hand, if you are having difficulties yourself, you could find these echoed or brought to the surface by dealing with a person in distress. In this case it is important to talk to your supervisor or line manager as soon as possible and arrange for someone else to continue to offer support.

Feeling concerned, upset or even angry after a particularly emotional experience with a person is normal. Such a response is not in any way a reflection on the quality of your work or your ability as a support worker. After such an experience, most people are likely to continue to think about it for some time. One of the best ways to deal with this is to discuss it with your line manager or supervisor, or with a close friend or relative, always bearing in mind the principles of confidentiality. After a period of time you may come to terms with what happened. However, if you find it is interfering with your work, either with the particular person or with other people, there are plenty of sources of help available to you, both within and outside your workplace. Talk to your line manager or supervisor for advice on gaining access to any help you need.

The distress of others, whether in the form of anger, sadness or anxiety, will always be upsetting for the person who works with them. However, if you are able to develop your skills and knowledge so that you can identify distress, work towards reducing it and offer effective help and support to those who are experiencing it, then you are making a useful and meaningful contribution to the provision of quality care.

Reflect

Think about a situation at work when a person became distressed while you were communicating with them. If this has not happened to you at work, think about a situation with a friend or in your family.

1. What action did you take?
2. Do you think you handled the situation sensitively?
3. What effect did it have on you?

Check the information stored in your workplace about support for people in distress or at risk from self-harming.

4. Be able to apply principles and practices relating to confidentiality

4.1 The meaning of the term confidentiality

Confidentiality involves keeping information safe and only passing it on where there is a clear right to it and a clear need to do so. Confidentiality is an important right for everyone because:

- people may not trust a support worker who does not keep information confidential
- people may not feel valued or able to keep their self-esteem if their private details are shared with others
- people's safety may be put at risk if details of their property and habits are shared publicly.

A professional service which maintains respect for people must keep private information confidential. There are legal requirements under the **Data Protection Act 1998** to keep personal **records** confidential.

> ### Key terms
>
> **Data Protection Act 1998** – a law to ensure the safety of data held
>
> **Records** – information that is written and retained, either electronically as a computer record, or on paper as a hard copy. Records must be accessible, stored securely and be easily retrievable if necessary

Looking after information

Once something is written down or entered on to a computer, it becomes a permanent record. For this reason, you must be very careful what you do with any files, charts, notes or other written records. They must always be stored somewhere locked and safe. People should be very careful with files that leave the workplace. There are many stories about files being stolen from cars or left on buses!

Records kept on computers must also be kept safe and protected. If you work for an organisation, your workplace will have policies relating to records on computers, which will include access being restricted by a password, and the computer system being

protected against the possibility of people hacking into it (accessing it illegally).

If you work as a personal assistant, the person you work for may have records on a computer, or kept as written documents. You must check with your employer the steps they want you to take to keep information safe and secure. They may have a password-protected file, a firewall on their computer or use antivirus software. Someone who is directing their own services has the same rights to confidentiality and to have their personal information kept securely.

> ### Reflect
>
> 1. Do you always think about keeping information safe?
> 2. If you are working in someone's home, does keeping information secure seem less important than if you are working at a hospital or residential care home?
> 3. Do you sometimes leave files lying about?
> 4. Do you always make sure that neighbours or other visitors are not able to access personal information?
> 5. Think about your own practice in relation to confidentiality – does it really measure up?

Since the Access to Personal Files Act 1987, people can see their personal files. The Data Protection Act 1998 gives people a right to see the information recorded about them. This means that people can see their medical records, or social services files. Since January 2005, the Freedom of Information Act 2000 has provided people with a right to access general information held by public authorities, including local authorities and the National Health Service. Personal information about other people cannot be accessed and is protected by the Data Protection Act.

The information that you write in files should be clear and factual. Do not include irrelevant information, or opinions that are not backed up by facts, and write only about the person concerned. Sign and date the information. Anything you write should be true and able to be justified.

If you work as a personal assistant, you will keep only the records that your employer asks you to keep. Direct Payments may require certain information to be recorded, and it can be useful to keep some notes for reviews and providing feedback on how well a support plan is working out.

Doing it well

Recording information

The purpose of a file is to reflect an accurate and up-to-date picture of a person's situation, and to provide a record that can be referred to at some point in the future. Some of it may be required to be disclosed to other agencies, and the person it has been written about will have access to it. Always think about what you write. Make sure it is ACES:

- Accurate
- Clear
- Easy to read
- Shareable.

See Unit HSC 038 for more information regarding maintaining accurate and complete records for people.

All information, however it is stored, is subject to the rules laid down in the Data Protection Act 1998, which covers medical records, social service records, credit information, local authority information and so on. Anything relating to a person, whether fact or opinion, is personal data.

Anyone processing personal data must comply with the eight enforceable principles of good practice laid down in the Data Protection Act 1998. These say that data must be:

- fairly and lawfully processed
- processed for limited purposes
- adequate, relevant and not excessive
- accurate
- not kept for longer than necessary
- processed in accordance with the data subject's rights
- kept secure
- not transferred to countries without adequate protection.

All of the organisations responsible for inspecting quality in the delivery of social care in the UK (see Table 2) also have national minimum standards about how confidentiality must be maintained. The inspectors from each of these organisations will check the systems for recording and storing information, and make sure that they comply with regulations.

In addition to the requirements on organisations, all people who work in social care, regardless of whether it is for a large organisation or an individual employer, should be bound by the professional **Codes of Practice** of the regulatory bodies (see Table 2).

Key term

Code of Practice – guidelines for professional behaviour that set out clearly the expectations of those who are working in a professional area

Country	Inspecting organisation	Regulatory body
England	Care Quality Commission	General Social Care Council
Wales	Care and Social Services Inspectorate for Wales	Care Council for Wales
Scotland	Care Commission	Scottish Social Services Council
Northern Ireland	Regulation and Quality Improvement Authority	Northern Ireland Social Care Council

Table 2: Organisations responsible for inspecting and regulating the quality of social care.

Activity 5

Compliance

1. Take the last six actions you have performed with information. These could include:
   - writing records/notes
   - entering data on to a computer
   - sharing information with someone manually or electronically
   - receiving information in writing or electronically.

2. Check each of the six actions with the Data Protection Act principles listed earlier, the national minimum standards for the UK country you work in and the professional Code of Practice to see if they comply.

3. If they do – excellent! If not, think about what changes need to be made and how you can go about making them.

The purpose of keeping records

Records are kept for a variety of purposes. The method of recording is likely to depend on the purpose for which it is required. The information could be:

- needed for making decisions
- intended to provide background knowledge and understanding for another worker

Functional skills

English: Writing

You have been asked to keep written records on people you are working with to provide an accurate and up-to-date picture of somebody's situation. These are formal documents that may be used by others in your team or outside agencies. Ensure that your records are laid out clearly and concisely, and are organised in an appropriate format. You should check the records so that spelling, punctuation and grammar are accurate.

- about family and contacts of people who are important to a person
- passed to another professional who is also involved in providing a caring service
- passed from yourself to a colleague over a short space of time, to ensure that the care you provide offers an element of continuity
- used to help in planning and developing services.

If people's records are not managed safely, there can be a whole range of consequences. Poor information and record storage can result in much more than a few lost pieces of paper or the odd deleted email.

Case study

Gary's support plan

Gary is 27 years old and works as an administrator in a small factory. He is paraplegic following a motorbike accident nine years ago. Gary employs a team of personal assistants using Direct Payments.

Recently, a neighbour came to the door with a file he said he had found in the local pub. It was Gary's support plan and contained notes that the PAs made about any issues and what was done. There was not very much in there; his PAs were not very good about maintaining it and Gary had never thought it particularly important.

However, this incident made him very uncomfortable and he realised how much of his personal information was in there. As a result Gary was:

- embarrassed about how much the neighbour now knew about him
- worried about who else might have seen it
- angry with the PA who had left it in the pub
- angry with himself for not realising the importance and sensitivity of the information earlier
- determined to set procedures in place for information to be more secure in future.

1. Who was at fault here?
2. Why do you think the incident happened?
3. What needs to change, and how should this be done?

4.2 Ways to maintain confidentiality in day-to-day communication

The most common way in which workers breach confidentiality is by chatting about work with friends or family. It is very tempting to discuss the day's events with your family or friends over a drink or a meal. It is often therapeutic to discuss a stressful day, and helps get things into perspective. But you must make sure that you talk about issues at work in a way that keeps people's details confidential and anonymous.

For example, you can talk about how an encounter made you feel without giving any details of the other people involved. You can say, 'Today this person accused me of stealing all their money — at first I was so angry I didn't know what to say! What would you have done?' The issue can be discussed without making reference to gender, ethnicity, age, physical description, location or any other personal information that might even remotely identify the person concerned. The issue is how you felt and what you should do, and you are always free to discuss yourself.

It might be considered a breach of your professional code of conduct to discuss a person's details with people who do not have a need to know. The essential issue is trust; even if no one can identify the name of the person involved, others might perceive you as displaying a lack of respect if you talk about the personal characteristics of the people you work with in public places.

Imagine you were in a restaurant and you overheard staff from a local clinic saying: 'You wouldn't believe how ugly some of the patients are! The other day we had this 40-year-old, dark-haired woman — lives in Meadow Close — she had a face like the back of a bus. Well, the operation went wrong — but I mean, what's she got to live for anyway?' Now imagine that you were about to attend that clinic. Would you want those staff to look after you?

The principle of confidentiality is about trust and confidence in professional workers, not only about protecting the identity of people.

You also need to be sure that you do not discuss one person you support with another whom you also support. You may not think you would ever act in that way, but it is so easy to do, with the best of intentions.

Imagine the scene. Someone says, 'Ethel doesn't look too good today', and your well-meant response is, 'No, she doesn't. She's had a bit of an upset with her son. She'd probably be really glad of some company later, if you've got the time.' This is the type of response that can cause

Have you ever discussed work with friends?

great distress and, above all, distrust. If the woman you have spoken to later says to Ethel, 'Sue said you were a bit down because of the upset with your son,' Ethel is not going to know how much you have said. As far as she knows, you could have given her whole life history to the woman who enquired. The most damaging consequence of this breach of confidentiality is the loss of trust. This can have damaging effects on a person's self-esteem, confidence and general well-being.

In this case, the best way to respond to the woman's comment would have been, 'Don't you think so? Well, perhaps she might be glad of some company later if you've got the time.'

Reflect

Think of a time when you have told someone something in confidence and later discovered that they had told other people. Try to recall how you felt about it. You may have felt angry or betrayed. Perhaps you were embarrassed and did not want to face anyone. Note down a few of the ways you felt.

1. Have you ever betrayed someone's confidence – even accidentally?
2. Are you honestly always as careful as you should be about what you say and to whom you say it?

Policies of the organisation

Every organisation will have a policy on confidentiality and the disclosure of information. You must be sure that you know what both policies are in your workplace.

The basic rule is that all information a person gives, or that is given on their behalf, to an organisation is confidential and cannot be disclosed to anyone without the consent of the person. You will need to support people in contributing to and understanding records and reports concerning them, and ensure they understand how the rules of confidentiality affect them.

Passing on information with consent

In many cases, the passing on of information is routine and related to the care of the person concerned. For example, medical information may be passed to a hospital, residential home or private care agency. However, this is only with the agreement of the person concerned. Even if they have chosen to commission a particular service, you must still make it clear that information will have to be shared. Do not assume that the person will realise this, and do not assume that they will not object. Always ask; it just takes a simple 'So now that you've chosen the agency, you do realise that we'll have to pass on the information in your records? Are you OK about this?'

But it is essential that only information that is required for the purpose is passed on. For example, it is not necessary to tell the hearing aid clinic that Mr Sampson's son is currently serving a prison sentence. However, if Mr Sampson became seriously ill and the hospital wanted to contact his next of kin, you would need to pass that information on. The hearing aid clinic would, however, need to know that Mr Sampson's hearing had been getting worse for the past couple of months.

Case study

Security and confidentiality

Evergreens Care Home is a 14-bed residential unit for elderly people with moderate care needs. It does not have a computerised record system. All the records on the residents, including their drug regimes, are stored in folders kept in a filing cabinet behind the reception desk.

One day, one of the residents, Mr Tedesco, is in great distress. He says he found his record folder lying on the reception desk and took a quick look inside. He saw that the doctor had recommended he have some tests for prostate cancer. Mr Tedesco had told the staff about

his urinary problems, but had no idea there was a risk of cancer. He is very upset and also angry that 'the staff didn't tell me the truth'.

1. What are the security and confidentiality issues in this situation?
2. How can the staff respond to Mr Tedesco's immediate distress?
3. What actions could be taken to improve security and confidentiality at Evergreens?

Situation	Example
There is a significant risk of harm to someone	An older person tells you that she switches off the heating as soon as there is no one in the house, in order to save money. She asks you not to tell anyone because her daughter will make a fuss. She may be at risk of harm from the cold.
A person is in danger of being abused	A man explains that his son takes his money, but asks you not to tell anyone because his son will be angry and the man is frightened of him. He is experiencing financial abuse.
There is a significant risk of harm to others	A man lives in a terraced house piled high with newspapers and rubbish. Apart from the vermin, he has told you that he lights fires in the hearth with some of the old newspapers — he begs you not to tell anyone because he is terrified that 'they' will make him move out of his home. There is a serious risk of fire, not only in his house, but of it spreading to other houses.
There is a risk to the support worker's health or well-being	A man is very aggressive and becoming violent, placing you at risk. You know that he can be calm at times and usually responds well to you, but recently, he has been becoming more and more aggressive.

Table 3: Situations where confidentiality may need to be broken.

4.3 The potential tension between maintaining confidentiality and disclosing concerns

People have a right to confidentiality, but also a responsibility in relation to the rights of others. Confidentiality often has to be kept within boundaries, and the rights of others have to be balanced with the person's rights. For example, a support worker may have to tell their manager something learned in confidence, or may have to seek medical assistance for someone.

Some situations may mean that you have to pass on information, because keeping it to yourself could result in harm to the person you are supporting, to someone else or to you.

All of the situations in Table 3 involve only sharing information with a manager in order to decide what action to take. You must not share information any further without consultation with senior colleagues.

If you are directly employed as a personal assistant and are concerned about the well-being of your employer, you may have to pass on information to the relevant organisation: social services, doctor or police. These are not easy decisions to make and you will have to be very

clear why you think that someone is not able to take decisions that are in their own best interests. This may be because they are ill or confused, or because they are afraid of someone else.

You cannot decide to pass on confidential information simply because you think that your employer would be better off if they acted in a different way, or if they had this or that help or assistance. You must only do this when you have good reason to believe that there is a risk of serious harm.

Decisions about breaking confidentiality are about balancing the risks — you must ask yourself: 'Are the risks of the distress at my breaking confidentiality greater than the risks posed to a person's health and well-being by the circumstances?'

Taking a decision that you know will damage a relationship you have built up with someone over a period of time is always hard to do. If at all possible, you should discuss the circumstances with a manager or senior colleague before deciding on action.

The well-being of the person you are supporting is always the deciding factor.

Confidentiality and the need to know

Good practice involves asking people if you can let other people know things. It would be wrong to pass on even the date of a person's birthday without asking them first. Some people might not want others to celebrate their birthday — for example, Jehovah's Witnesses believe that it is wrong to do so. Whatever you know should be kept private unless you are told by the person concerned that it is acceptable to share the information. The exception to this rule is that information can be passed on when others have a need to know it. Some examples of people who have a 'need to know' are:

● managers — they may need to help make decisions which affect the person
● colleagues — they may be working with the same person
● other professionals — they may also be working with the person and need to be kept up to date.

However, information should always be shared with the knowledge and consent of the person concerned. You must always explain that you will be passing on information, and what the information is, so that people do not imagine that you will be telling others everything about them. When people have a need to know, they only need to know enough to do their job.

When information is passed to other professionals, it should be on the understanding that they keep it confidential. It is important to check that people asking for information are who they say they are. If you answer the telephone and the caller says they are a social worker or other professional, you should explain that you must call back before giving any information. Phoning back enables you to be sure that you are talking to someone at a particular number or within a particular organisation. If you meet a person you do not know, you should ask for proof of identity before passing on any information.

Relatives will often claim that they have a 'right to know'. The most famous example of this was Victoria Gillick, who went to court in order to try to gain access to her daughter's medical records. She claimed that she had the right to know whether her daughter had been given the contraceptive pill. Her GP had refused to tell her and she took the case all the way to the House of Lords, but the ruling was not changed and she was not given access to her daughter's records. The rules remain the same. Even for close relatives, the information is not available unless the person agrees.

It is difficult, however, if you are faced with angry or distressed relatives who believe that you have information they are entitled to. One situation you could encounter is where a son or daughter, for example, believes that they have the right to be told about medical information in respect of a parent. Another example is where someone is trying to find out a person's whereabouts. The best response is to be clear and assertive, but to demonstrate that you understand it is difficult for them. Do not try to 'pass the buck' and give people the idea that they can find out from someone else. There is nothing more frustrating than being passed from one person to another without anyone being prepared to tell you anything. It is important to be clear and say, for example, 'I'm sorry. I know you must be worried, but I can't discuss any information unless your mother agrees', or 'I'm sorry, I can't give out any information about where Jennifer is living now. But if you would like to leave me a name and contact details, I will pass on the message and she can contact you.'

Has the doctor said anything more about my mother's illness?

I expect your mother would like to talk to you directly – shall I show you to her room?

Sometimes it is possible to ask relatives to discuss issues directly with people.

Legislation

- Access to Personal Files Act 1987
- Data Protection Act 1998
- Freedom of Information Act 2000

Getting ready for assessment

Learning outcome 1 requires you to demonstrate your knowledge of why communication is important in your work setting. You may be asked to prepare assignments or projects about the reasons for communication and about the impacts of communication on how you work with others. Your projects or assignments should ideally include examples from your own work setting, or from some previous experience of communicating and relating to others in a work setting. Assessors will be looking to see that you can understand what lies behind communication, but also that you can see how it affects the way you work.

Learning outcome 2 requires you to demonstrate evidence of your communication skills in order to achieve it. You will need to be able to show, probably in a real work situation, that you are able to find out the best way to communicate with someone. You will need to show that you are able to do this through checking with the person concerned, communication with carers, family and friends if appropriate, and by reference to records and any other relevant supporting professionals. An assessor will be looking to see that you are able to take into account all the factors that affect communication. You will also have to demonstrate that you are sensitive to the effect of your communication on others and that you can adjust your responses to take account of a person's reactions.

This may be observed by an assessor during your normal day-to-day work while other skills are being assessed, or you may have to set up a specific observation where you can demonstrate your communication skills. If you are not confident that you are ready for assessment, work with a friend or colleague and ask them to feed back on how your communications made them feel.

Learning outcome 3 requires you to demonstrate the skills you have in overcoming barriers to communication as well as showing that you understand the ways in which people from different cultures and backgrounds communicate. This is likely to be assessed in a real work situation by an assessor observing you working. They will want to see you demonstrate that you can recognise any difficulties that people may experience, such as sensory impairment or speaking a different language, and find ways to deal with the problem. You may be able to demonstrate this by showing how you can use recorded material for giving information to people with a visual impairment, and by always announcing yourself when you walk into a room. You may be able to show how you can speak clearly, in order to enable a deaf person to read your lips.

You need to be able to show that you can maintain confidentiality, and that you understand why it is important and some of the dilemmas that it can create. Some of this may be in the form of assignments in which you will be able to explain the importance of secure storage and recording systems. The assignments may be written, or may be presentations or projects. The assessment requires you to explain – this means that you must include reasons and consequences, not just a description of secure systems. You need to answer the question 'why?'. Make sure that you use words and phrases like 'because', 'so that', 'in order to' and 'as a result of'.

Think about examples of systems you know or have used, and include them for your assessor to see that you know how to apply your knowledge in practice. You could comment on what you have found to work well and what has not worked so well – but do not forget to say why.

Further reading and research

In this unit you have covered aspects of communication to help you build and develop relationships, as well as ways to improve your practice as a professional care worker. Below are details of further opportunities to research this subject. The list is not exhaustive and some you may find more interesting and useful than others.

- www.direct.gov.uk (Data Protection Act 1998, Rights and Responsibilities)
- www.dh.gov.uk (Department of Health – Data Protection Act 1998, patient choice, sensory impairment)
- www.arcos.org.uk (ARCOS – Association for Rehabilitation of Communication and Oral Skills, tel: 01684 576795)
- www.scie.org.uk (Social Care Institute for Excellence)
- www.rnib.org.uk (Royal National Institute of Blind People)
- www.sense.org.uk (Sense)
- www.deafblind.org.uk, www.deafblindscotland.org.uk (Deafblind)

- www.rnid.org.uk (RNID – Royal National Institute for Deaf People)
- www.alzheimers.org.uk (Alzheimer's Society)
- www.askmencap.info (Mencap – fact sheets on communication and people with learning disabilities)
- Butler, S. (2004) *Hearing and Sight Loss,* Age Concern and RNIB
- Caldwell, P., Stevens, P. (2005) *Creative Conversations: Communicating with People with Learning Disabilities,* Pavilion Publishers
- Iverson J and Goldin-Meadow S. (1998) *Nature,* 196 228
- Malone, C., Forbat, L., Robb, M. and Seden, J. (2004) *Relating Experience: Stories from Health and Social Care: An Anthology about Communication and Relationships,* Routledge
- Moss, B. (2007) *Communication Skills for Health and Social Care,* Sage Publications Ltd
- Thomson, H. and Meggitt, C. (2007) *Human Growth and Development,* Hodder Headline

Unit SHC 32

Engage in personal development in health, social care or children's and young people's settings

The knowledge and skills addressed in this unit are key to working effectively in all aspects of your practice. It is essential to know how to evaluate your work and how you can improve on what you do, and to understand the factors that have influenced your attitudes and beliefs.

With the major changes, new policies and ongoing research in this sector, you need to make sure that you are up to date in work practices and knowledge, and aware of current thinking. This is not an option but a duty that you accept when you choose to become a professional worker in the social care sector. The people that you support have a right to expect that your practice is always of a high standard and up to date.

In this unit you will learn about:

- **what is required for competence in own work role**
- **how to reflect on practice**
- **how to evaluate own performance**
- **how to agree a personal development plan**
- **how to use learning opportunities and reflective practice to contribute to personal development.**

1. Understand what is required for competence in own work role

1.1 Duties and responsibilities of your work role

The specific duties and responsibilities of your job will vary depending on your role and the employer you work for. If you work for a large employer, whether in the public, private or voluntary sectors, you will probably have had a period of **induction**, where you will have learned about:

- the policies and procedures of the organisation
- how the structures work
- the people who are your managers and supervisors.

Working for smaller private or voluntary organisations, or working as a personal assistant directly employed by the person you are supporting, may mean that your initial induction was less formal and you learned 'on the job'.

In each case, you will have been given an idea of the duties and responsibilities of your job and what your employer expects of you, and what you can expect in return.

However, the duties and responsibilities required by your employer are not the only requirements of working in social care. The **regulator** in the UK country in which

you work will require that you follow the **Code of Practice** (see page 87) that lays out the duties and expectations for everyone who works in the sector.

Key terms

Induction – a formal briefing and familiarisation for someone starting at an organisation

Regulator – someone who ensures compliance with laws, regulations and established rules

Code of Practice – a set of guidelines and regulations to be followed by members of an occupation or organisation

Having Codes of Practice is important in social care, because in this sector you work with some of the most vulnerable people in society. They have a right to expect a certain standard of work and a certain standard of moral and ethical behaviour.

In order to be employed in social work anywhere in the UK and in social care in some parts (soon to be all) of the UK, there is a requirement to be registered. This means having, or working towards, a certain minimum level of qualification and agreeing to work within the Code of Practice that sets out the required behaviour. Employers have to ensure that everyone who works for them is registered and eligible to work in social work or social care.

Case study

Dealing with theft

Joanne works as a personal assistant to Esme, who lives in Cardiff and has cerebral palsy. Esme is a regional organiser and fund-raiser for a large charity; she has a very busy and active life. She needs support workers to accompany her during all her business time in order to support her personal needs and to take notes at meetings. Esme has recruited a team of support workers and they work in shifts. Several months after Joanne started working for her, Esme noticed that items were going missing from her house. Initially they were just small things like CDs, then larger items, and money also started going missing from her purse. It always seemed to link in to when Joanne had been working. Esme confronted Joanne, who initially denied any involvement.

Eventually she broke down and admitted that she had been stealing the items because her boyfriend had a drug habit and he kept demanding more and more money.

Esme dismissed Joanne from her post and reported the matter to the police. She reported Joanne to the Care Council for Wales, where she was interviewed by a disciplinary panel and was banned from working in social care for three years.

1. Do you think that Esme took the right actions?
2. What else could she have done?
3. What would have been the consequences of these other courses of action?

1.2 Expectations about your work role as expressed in relevant standards

Your job may have come with a job description, but while that tells you *what* you need to do, it does not usually tell you *how* you need to do it. To find that out, you need to look at the Standards that apply to your work.

Standards, as with Codes of Practice, will vary depending on the UK country in which you work. Each UK country has **National Minimum Standards** that are used by inspectors to ensure that services are being delivered at an acceptable level (see page 32).

Finally, and most importantly in terms of how you carry out your work, there are the **National Occupational Standards** (NOS). These apply across the whole of the UK, and explain what you need to know and be able to do in order to work effectively in social care. The National Occupational Standards form the basis for all the qualifications in the social care sector, and are divided into units of competence. Some of these are mandatory, and everyone should be able to demonstrate competence in these areas. Other units are optional and you should be able to demonstrate competence in those units relevant to your job role.

Key terms

National Minimum Standards – these are used by the Commission for Social Care Inspection (CSCI) to inspect the quality of care in services

National Occupational Standards – UK standards of performance that people are expected to achieve in their work, and the knowledge and skills they need to perform effectively

Competence – demonstrating the skills and knowledge required by the National Occupational Standards

Competence

In performing your job role, **competence** means that you have been able to provide evidence that you can demonstrate the skills and the underpinning knowledge contained in the National Occupational Standards. It is important to understand that competence is not only about doing the job; it is also about understanding why you do what you do and the theoretical basis that underpins the work.

Activity 1

National Occupational Standards

Each of the units of assessment in the Level 3 Diploma is based on units of competence from the National Occupational Standards.

1. Choose any three of the units of assessment from your Diploma qualification and find the relevant units of competence.
2. Look at how the work you are doing for your Diploma links to the units of competence. Create a table showing these links.
3. How can you show that you have met the requirements set out in the National Occupational Standards?

Functional skills

English: Reading; Writing

Read through a minimum of three units from your Diploma and find the relevant units of competence. Look at how the work you are doing links to the units of competence. Use these texts to gather information and summarise these findings in a table. Ensure that the layout is clear and that spelling, punctuation and grammar are accurate.

2. Be able to reflect on practice

2.1 The importance of reflective practice in continuously improving the quality of service provided

The social care sector is one which constantly changes and moves on. New standards reflect the changes in the profession, such as the emphasis on personalised, quality services, the focus on tackling exclusion, and the influence of the culture of rights and responsibilities. There has been a huge increase in understanding in all parts of the sector, and a recognition of the satisfaction that comes from working alongside people so that they are directing their own support, rather than being passive receivers of services.

Developments in technology have made huge strides towards independence for many people, thus promoting a changing relationship with support workers. At the same time, these developments have brought different approaches to the way in which social care work and the administration and recording of service provision are carried out.

Legislation and the resulting guidelines are a feature of the work of the sector. Sadly, many of the new guidelines, policies and procedures result from enquiries and investigations that followed tragedies, errors and neglect.

Despite all this, much of what we do in the care sector will remain the same. The basic principles of supporting people and treating them with dignity and respect, and ensuring they have choice and control, will continue. This means that the skills of good communication remain as vital as ever.

Being aware of new developments

There are many ways in which you can keep up to date with new developments in the field of social care, and particularly those which affect your own area of work. You should not assume that your workplace will automatically inform you about new developments, changes and updates which affect your work. You must be prepared to be active in maintaining your own knowledge base and to ensure that your practice is in line with current thinking and new theories. The best way to do this is to incorporate an awareness of the need to update your knowledge constantly into all of your work activities. If you restrict your awareness of new developments to specific times, such as a monthly visit to the library, or a training course every six months, you are likely to miss out on a lot of information.

Case study

Researching sleep deprivation

Joe, a senior care assistant, has recently started to work nights on a rota system. Unfortunately, at first, things did not go as well as he had hoped. Everyone said he would get used to it, but that simply did not happen. At three o'clock in the morning, no matter how busy he was, he found himself getting light-headed and feeling quite nauseous. The other major problem was that he found sleeping during the day quite difficult. He managed to get through his first week, but dreaded the next time it was his turn on nights. He felt that the quality of his work might be unsafe if he did not learn to cope.

Joe mentioned his concerns to Maria, a nursing friend. It turned out that she had once researched sleep deprivation, and found that there are all sorts of ways of coping. She recommended that he look at one or two helpful websites, and also that he read some of the research on night working, at the local library. The websites she suggested were www.bbc.co.uk/science/humanbody/sleep and www.sleepeducation.com

Joe looked at the websites and the research. He found them very helpful and followed some of the advice given within them. He is now able to cope better and more safely with his night shifts.

1. Was Joe right to be concerned and to follow up his concerns? Why?
2. Why do you think Joe went to a friend rather than his manager for advice?
3. Should Joe have talked to his manager?
4. How could Joe share what he has learned with his colleagues?

Sources of information

The media

Health and care is always in the news, so it is relatively easy to find out information about new studies and research. You will need to pay attention when watching television, listening to radio news bulletins or surfing the net to find out about new developments, legislation, guidelines and reports related to people using health and care services and workers in this area.

Articles in newspapers and professional journals are excellent sources of information. When reporting on a recently completed study, they usually give information about where to obtain a copy of it.

Reports and reviews

You can read the findings of enquiries into the failures experienced within social work and health and social care. This might provide you with a focus for reflection. In the past there have been many cases where children and adults have been neglected or abused and social services have failed to protect vulnerable people adequately. Currently there is great national concern about the cleanliness and safety of hospital wards. While you may not be involved in policy-making decisions about these services, there may be many actions such as **whistle-blowing** that are relevant in your own work setting. Many past serious failings might have been preventable if people had been able to identify the issues and take action earlier.

Activity 2

Health and care in the news

For one week, keep a record of every item which relates to health and care services which you hear on a radio bulletin, see in a television programme, or read in a newspaper article. You may be surprised at just how many references you manage to find. For reference, note down where you found the information and which places are likely to be useful sources of information in the future.

Key term

Whistle-blowing – reporting concerns about practice in your workplace

---

How often do you check for current information?

As well as reflecting on failures of the service, it will be important to reflect on positive practice. The websites of the inspectorates and professional bodies contain many examples of good practice, as do those of the Sector Skills Council. For social care with adults this is Skills for Care (www.skillsforcare.org.uk) and for children and young people it is the Children's Workforce Development Council (CWDC, www.cwdcouncil.org.uk).

Conferences

Professional journals also carry advertisements for conferences and training opportunities. You may also find such information in your workplace. There is often a cost involved in attending these events, so the restrictions of the training budget in your workplace may mean that you cannot attend. However, it may be possible for one person to attend and pass on the information gained to others in the workplace, or to obtain conference papers and handouts without attending.

The Internet

The development of information technology, and in particular the Internet, has provided a vast resource of information, views and research. The use of computers in the social care sector is becoming increasingly widespread and important. If you have access to one, you may use the Internet on a daily basis.

However, you need to be wary of the information you obtain on the Internet. It provides free access to vast amounts of information, but it is an unregulated environment – anyone can publish information on the Internet, and there is no requirement for it to be checked or approved. People can publish their own views and opinions, which may not be based on fact. Make every effort to check the validity of what you are reading and do not assume anything to be factually correct unless it is from a reliable or **accredited** source, such as a government department, a reputable university or college, or an established research centre.

> **Key term**
>
> **Accredited** – given official recognition or approval

Treated with caution, though, the Internet can prove to be one of the speediest and most useful tools in obtaining up-to-date information. One of the simplest and most effective means of keeping up to date with all

Do you attend conferences for up-to-date information?

How often do you use the Internet to find out information?

the latest information is to subscribe to an RSS (Really Simple Syndication) news feed on your computer or phone. This will download headlines on any relevant news items, and you can then follow up any that look interesting.

Your supervisor and colleagues

Never overlook the obvious: one of the sources of information that may be most useful to you is close at hand – your own workplace supervisor and colleagues. They may have many years of experience and accumulated knowledge that they will be happy to share with you. They may also be updating their own practice and ideas, and may have information that they would be willing for you to use too.

Understanding new information

Reading and hearing about new studies and pieces of research is all very well, but you must understand what you are reading. It is important that you know how new theories are developed and how research is carried out.

Reliability and validity

There are specific methods of carrying out research to ensure the results are both reliable and valid. Research is judged on both of these factors, and you need to be able to satisfy yourself that the reports you read are based on reliable and valid research.

Reliability means the results would be the same if someone else were to carry out the same piece of research in exactly the same way. Validity means that the conclusions that have been drawn from the research are:

- consistent with the results
- consistent with the way in which the research was carried out
- consistent in the way in which the information has been interpreted.

The research process

You will need to understand some of the basic terms that are used when discussing research in any field.

Primary research refers to information or data that is obtained directly from the research carried out, not from books or previously published works.

Secondary research refers to information obtained from books, previously published research and reports, CD-ROMs, the Internet and so on — any information obtained from work carried out by others. For example, if you were asked to write an assignment, you would be most likely to find the information from secondary sources such as textbooks or the Internet, rather than carrying out a research project yourself in order to obtain the information you need.

The information obtained from research is often referred to as data — this is regardless of whether it is in numbers or in words.

There are two broad areas of approach to research and they determine both how the research is carried out and the type of results obtained. They are:

- **quantitative research**
- **qualitative research**.

Key terms

Primary research – the collection of data that does not already exist

Secondary research – the summary or gathering of existing research and data

Quantitative research – research that is measurable and in numeric form

Qualitative research – research that is based on attitudes, opinions and perceptions

Quantitative research

Quantitative research is about measuring. It produces hard facts and figures, and uses statistics and numbers to draw conclusions and make an analysis.

Many researchers in health and social care use quantitative approaches and produce quantitative data. They may carry out 'experiments' using many of the rules of scientific investigation. In general, if you are reading research that provides statistics and numerical information and is based purely on facts, it is likely to have used one of the quantitative approaches.

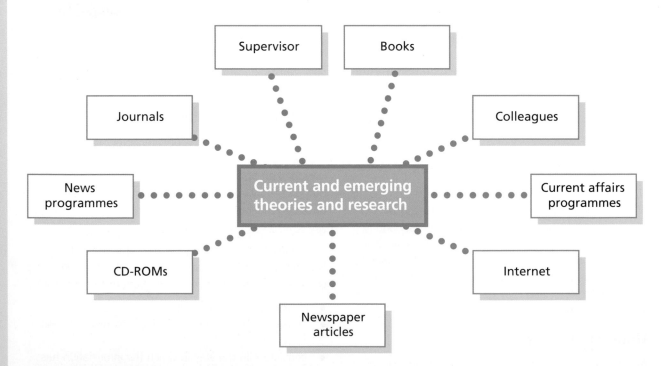

Are you making use of all the options for finding out up-to-date information?

Case study

Opportunities for self-directed training

Olesya works as a care worker at a big, busy day centre and meets many of the families of people who have chosen to use the centre as part of their support plan. One day she was chatting to the son of one of the older people using the centre and they ended up discussing the issue of teenage drug use and crime. Olesya was critical of the young people taking drugs until the man she was talking to mentioned that his son was an addict. He explained how it had taken a hold on his son's life, but he was trying to get better through a local drug programme. Olesya felt embarrassed, and decided she needed to know more about the drugs issue. She got in touch with the local drug programme and spoke to the manager, explaining that she would like to learn more about the drug rehabilitation services available to young people. She arranged to spend some time on a self-directed 'work experience' placement at the centre, and is now a volunteer there, helping to run the coffee bar. In her reflective diary she writes the following.

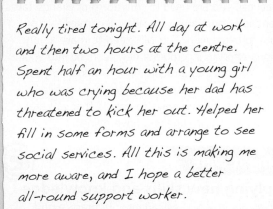

Really tired tonight. All day at work and then two hours at the centre. Spent half an hour with a young girl who was crying because her dad has threatened to kick her out. Helped her fill in some forms and arrange to see social services. All this is making me more aware, and I hope a better all-round support worker.

1. What benefits do you think will come from Olesya's self-directed training?
2. Who will benefit from her new experience?
3. How can training help to overcome prejudice?

Many government publications are good examples of quantitative research — they give statistics in relation to the National Health Service, for example, such as the numbers of patients on waiting lists, the numbers having a particular operation or the numbers of residents in nursing homes throughout the country.

Qualitative research

A qualitative approach looks at the quality rather than the quantity of something. It could be used, for example, to investigate the feelings of people who have remained on the waiting list for treatment, or people's attitudes towards residential care, or the relationships between those in residential care and those who care for them. Generally, qualitative data is produced in words rather than figures and will consist of descriptions and information about people's lives, experiences and attitudes.

Activity 3

Quantitative and qualitative research

Find two pieces of research (one quantitative and one qualitative) carried out within the past two years using any of the following sources:

- newspapers
- journals
- reports
- television
- the Internet
- textbooks.

Read the results of both pieces of research and make a note of the differences in the type of information provided.

Functional skills

Mathematics: Interpreting information

Conduct two pieces of quantitive research (figures should be given for a minimum of two years) on statistics relevant to your area of work. Extract the relevant data and use it to prepare a graph or diagram to show the changes in numbers for the period chosen. What are the chances of these numbers increasing or decreasing over the coming two years? Give reasons for your answers.

Your work practice should be updated and improved as a result of reading research articles, watching TV programmes and attending training days. It is often difficult to find time to keep up to date and to change the practices you are used to. Any form of change takes time and is almost always a little uncomfortable or unusual to begin with. You will need to make a very conscious effort to incorporate new learning into your practice. You need to allocate time to updating your knowledge, and incorporating it into your practice. You could try the following ways to ensure that you are using the new knowledge you have gained.

Doing it well

Applying new skills and knowledge
- Plan out how you will adapt your practice on a day-to-day basis, adding one new aspect each day. Do this until you have covered all the aspects of the new information you have learned.
- Discuss with your supervisor and colleagues what you have learned and how you intend to change your practice, and ask for feedback.
- Write a checklist for yourself and review it at the end of each day.
- Give yourself a set period of time, for example, one month, to alter or improve your practice, and review it at the end of that time.

New knowledge is not only about emerging theories. It is also often about day-to-day aspects of your practice, which are just as important and can make just as much difference to the quality of support you provide. It is also about taking your practice forward by developing your knowledge across a range of situations.

Do you talk to colleagues about day-to-day practice?

2.2 The ability to reflect on practice

Not all of the learning you do will take place on a course or a lecture, or through the latest textbook. A very large amount of your learning will take place while doing your job.

Everything you do at work is part of a process of learning. Even regular tasks are likely to be important for learning because there is always something new each time you do them. A simple task like taking someone a hot drink may result in a lesson — for example, you may find that the person tells you they do not want tea, but would prefer coffee this morning. You will have learned a valuable lesson about never making assumptions that everything will be the same.

Learning from working is also about using the huge amount of skills and experience that your colleagues and supervisor have. Not only does this mean they will be able to pass on knowledge and advice to you, but also you have the perfect opportunity to discuss ideas and talk about day-to-day practice in the service you are delivering.

Most supervision will take place at scheduled times but you may also be able to discuss issues in the course of hand-over meetings or team meetings, and other day-to-day activities. Use supervision time or quiet periods to discuss situations which have arisen, problems you have come across or new approaches you have noticed other colleagues using.

Using your mistakes

Everyone makes mistakes — they are one way of learning. It is important not to waste your mistakes, so if something has gone wrong, make sure you learn from it. Discuss problems and mistakes with your supervisor, and work out how to do things differently next time. You can use reflective skills in order to learn from situations that have not worked out the way you planned. It is important that you consider carefully why things turned out the way they did and think about how you will ensure that they go according to plan next time. Unfortunately, there are real people on the receiving end of any mistakes in social care, and learning how not to make mistakes again is vitally important.

Activity 4

Enhancing your practice through reflection

1. Plan a feedback session with your manager. You may have straightforward questions, or more complicated issues to do with appropriate decisions about rights and risks, such as, 'How did you make the decision that it was safe enough for Mr Jackson to go out to the shops by himself, when there are obvious risks?'

2. Try discussing such issues with different experienced colleagues – you may be surprised at what you learn.

Functional skills

English: Speaking and listening

Take part in a formal discussion with a minimum of three others about rights and risks of people in your workplace. Use notes from the meeting with your manager to take the discussion forward and ensure that you present all points clearly. Use your initiative to pick up points made from others in the group. You must use appropriate language and speak clearly at all times.

Using your successes

Talking to colleagues and supervisors is equally useful when things work out really well, as it is important to reflect on success as well as failure. If you reflect on why something worked, this will make it more likely that you can repeat it.

2.3 How your values, belief systems and experiences may affect working practice

Everyone has different values, beliefs and preferences. What you believe in, what you see as important and what you see as acceptable or desirable is an essential part of who you are.

The way in which you respond to people is linked to what you believe in, what you consider important and what interests you. You may find you react positively to people who share your values and less warmly to

people who have different priorities. When you develop friendships, it is natural to spend time with people who share your interests and values. However, the professional relationships you develop with people you support are another matter. As a professional, you are required to provide the same quality of support for all, not just for those who share your views and beliefs. This may seem obvious, but knowing what you need to do and achieving it successfully are not the same thing.

Working in the social care sector, you are bound to come across people whose views you do not agree with, and who never seem to understand your point of view. Awareness of differences, your reaction to them and how they affect the way you work is a crucial part of personal and professional development.

If you allow your own preferences to dominate your work with people, you will fail to perform to the standards of the Codes of Practice for social care workers set out by the UK regulating bodies. All the codes require care workers to respect and promote people's individual views and wishes. But how do you manage to make the right responses when there is a clash between your views and those of the people you are working for? The first step is to identify and understand your own views and values.

Have you noticed how you have friendships with people who reflect your own values, interests and beliefs?

Being aware of the factors that have influenced the development of your personality is not as easy as it sounds. You may feel you know yourself very well, but knowing who you are is not the same as understanding how your beliefs are influencing your reactions — understanding how you got to be you.

Activity 5

Exploring your values

1. Take a range of about six or seven items from a newspaper. Make a note of your views and your feelings on each one – does it shock or disgust you, make you sad or angry, or grateful that it has not happened to you?
2. Think about why you reacted in the way you did to each item. Think about what may have influenced you to feel that way – this may include complex factors such as your upbringing and background, experiences you had as a child and as an adult, and relationships you have shared with others.
3. Think about how your reactions could affect your work. Do any of the people you support share some of the views you disagree with? Have any of them been involved in situations you disapprove of? Do any of them annoy you? What about colleagues?
4. Make some notes about aspects of your attitudes or working practices that you may need to change.

Unravelling these influences is never easy, and you are not being asked to carry out an in-depth analysis of yourself. You simply need to begin to realise how your development has been influenced by a range of factors.

Factors that influence your development

Everyone's values and beliefs are affected to different degrees by the same range of factors. These include those shown in the diagram on page 53.

Each of us will be influenced to a greater or lesser degree by these layers of influence. As each person is different, the extent of the influences will be different for each person. It is therefore important that you have considered and reflected on the influences on your

development so that you understand how you became the person you are.

Reflect

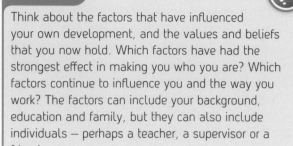

Think about the factors that have influenced your own development, and the values and beliefs that you now hold. Which factors have had the strongest effect in making you who you are? Which factors continue to influence you and the way you work? The factors can include your background, education and family, but they can also include individuals — perhaps a teacher, a supervisor or a friend.

This is not something you can do in ten minutes — take your time; think about it over a period of days or weeks if you need to.

Then try to find a colleague or a friend, preferably with a very different background, who is also prepared to do this exercise. Compare results and try to imagine what it would have been like to live their life and to have experienced the influences that they have.

Key influences on development

Table 1 on page 54 shows some of the key factors associated with differences between people — the factors that can result in different people having different values.

We are strongly influenced by our contact with other people. But different people live very different lives and mix with communities that have very different beliefs. People have different cultures, family values, religions, social class backgrounds and so on. Men often grow up with very different expectations and experience of life from women. Older people are likely to have had different life experiences than younger people. Some ways in which people are different from each other (or **diverse**) are shown in Table 1.

Key term

Diverse – being different; people are unique according to their own background, culture, personality, race, any disability, gender, religion/belief, sexual orientation and age

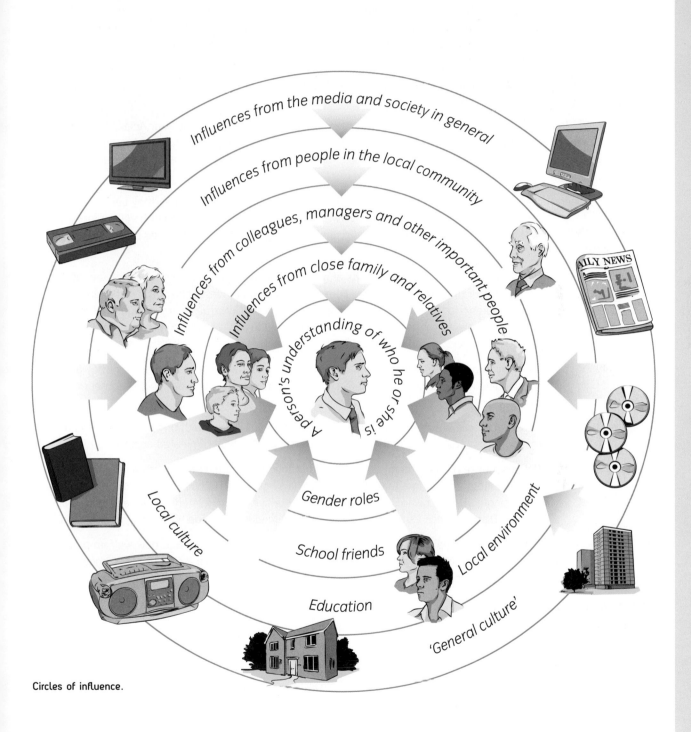

Circles of influence.

Area	How they differ
Age	People may be classified as being children, teenagers, young adults, middle-aged or old. **Discrimination** can creep into our thinking if we see some age groups as being 'the best', or if we make assumptions about the abilities of different age groups.
Gender	In the past, men often had more rights and were seen as more important than women. Assumptions about gender, such as what is women's or men's work, can still result in mistakes and discrimination.
Race	There are ethnic categories such as black or white, or European, African or Asian. Many people have specific national identities such as Polish, Nigerian, English or Welsh. Assumptions about racial characteristics and beliefs, or thinking that some groups are superior to others, result in discrimination.
Class	People differ in their upbringing, the kind of work they do and the money they earn. People also differ in their lifestyle and the views and values that go with different levels of income and spending habits. People may discriminate against others because their class or lifestyle is different.
Religion	People grow up in different traditions of religion. For some people, spiritual beliefs are at the centre of their understanding of life. For others, religion influences the cultural traditions that they celebrate; for example, many Europeans celebrate Christmas even though they might not see themselves as practising Christians. Discrimination can take place when people assume that their customs or beliefs should apply to everyone else.
Sexuality	Many people see their sexual orientation as very important to understanding who they are. Gay and lesbian relationships are often discriminated against. Heterosexual people sometimes judge other types of sexuality as 'wrong' or abnormal.
Ability	People may make assumptions about what is 'normal'. People with physical disabilities or learning difficulties may become labelled, stereotyped and discriminated against.
Relationships	People choose many different lifestyles and emotional commitments, such as marriage, having children, living in a large family, living a single lifestyle but having sexual partners, or being single and not being sexually active. People live within different family and friendship groups. Discrimination can happen if people start to judge that one lifestyle is 'right' or best.
Politics	People can develop different views as to how a government should act, how welfare provision should be organised and so on. Disagreement and debate are necessary; but it is important not to judge people as bad or stupid because their views are different from ours.

Table 1: Ways in which people differ.

Possible influences on your ideas and beliefs may include:

- ideas and ways of thinking that you developed with friends when you were a teenager
- ideas and beliefs that you developed from mixing with others in you local community
- ideas and beliefs associated with your religion
- ideas and beliefs you have developed from newspapers, magazines and TV programmes
- ideas and beliefs associated with your culture
- ideas and beliefs associated with your current network of friends and work colleagues
- the way your parents/carers taught you to behave as a child.

> **Key term**
>
> **Discrimination** – unfair treatment of a person or group on the basis of prejudice

Problems arise because our own culture and life experience may lead us to make assumptions as to what is 'right' or 'normal'. When we meet people who are different, it can be easy to see them as 'not right' or 'not normal'. Different people see the world in different ways. Look at the image below. If a person was used to seeing this cube in one way, they might be sure that view was the right one. In the same way, our culture may lead us to think that some habits are more 'normal' than others. However, in a multicultural, multifaith society such as the UK, it is more difficult to define what 'normal' is.

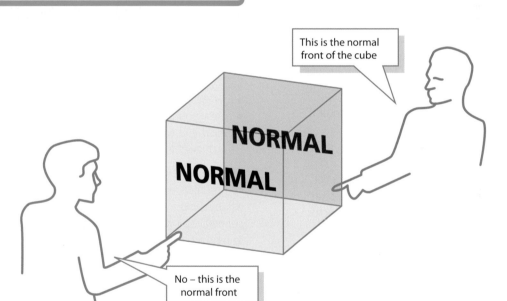

Which is the 'normal' front of the cube?

3. Be able to evaluate own performance

3.1 Evaluating your knowledge, performance and understanding against relevant standards

Once you have begun to identify the major factors that have influenced your development, the next stage is to look at how they have affected the way in which you work and relate to the people with whom you work. This is the basis of developing into a 'reflective practitioner' — someone who evaluates what they do.

When working in social care, to be effective and to provide the best possible service for those you support, you need to be able to think about and evaluate what you do and the way you work, and to identify your strengths and weaknesses. It is important that you learn to think about your own practice in a constructive way. Reflection and evaluation should not undermine your confidence in your own work; rather, you should use them in a constructive way to identify areas for improvement.

The ability to do this is an indication of excellent practice. Any workers in social care who believe that they have no need to improve their practice or to develop and add to their skills and understanding are not demonstrating good and competent practice, but rather an arrogant and potentially dangerous lack of understanding of the nature of work in the sector.

Becoming a thoughtful practitioner is not about torturing yourself with self-doubts and examining your weaknesses until you reach the point where your self-confidence is at zero. But it is important that you examine the work you have done and identify areas where you know you need to carry out additional development. A useful tool in learning to become a reflective practitioner is to develop a checklist which you can use, either after you have dealt with a difficult situation or at the end of each shift or day's work, to look at your own performance.

Doing it well

Checklist to evaluate practice

1. How did I approach my work?
2. Was my approach positive?
3. How did the way I worked affect the people I support?
4. How did the way I worked affect my colleagues?
5. Did I give my work 100 per cent?
6. Which was the best aspect of the work I did?
7. Which was the worst aspect of the work I did?
8. Was this work the best I could do?
9. Are there any areas in which I could improve?
10. If so, what are they, and how will I tackle them?

Your approach to professional development

A key factor is to be organised in your approach to professional development. You should know:

- what you are trying to achieve
- how you are you going to achieve it
- how you will be able to tell when you have achieved it.

If, for example, you were planning to develop your communication skills, you might have the aim of establishing a degree of trust with someone you support. You would not be able to plan a set strategy to produce trust — it is a feeling that might grow and develop within a supportive relationship. But you could list some of the skills you would be using in your communication that would contribute to the development of a supportive relationship.

You will need to have an understanding of relationships in order to be able to explain what you are planning. You should use theory during the planning stage of your work in order to identify how you will know if you have achieved your aim.

Thinking clearly about what you are doing can have benefits, as shown by the following diagram.

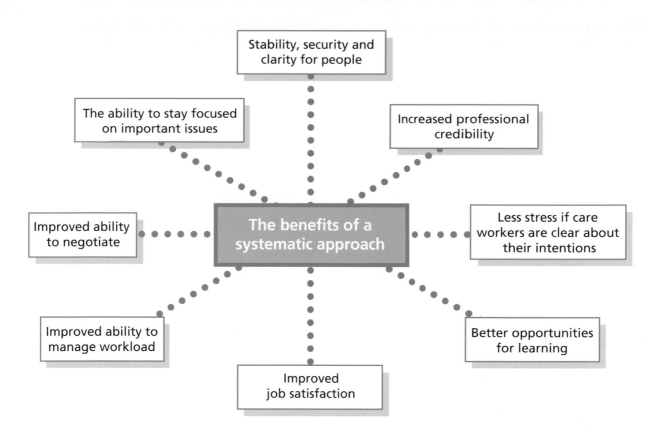

The benefits of a systematic approach.

Setting aims and objectives

Mr Gommer has been very unhappy since the death of his wife just over a year ago. He has stopped going out and has had no interest in meeting other people or becoming involved in activities. You provide support to Mr Gommer and he has asked you to help him in re-establishing contact with other people. You make a plan so that you can check how well this has worked.

This type of plan will help you see if you are achieving your aim at each stage, by checking your progress. You will then know at which point something has not worked and can ask for help if necessary from your colleagues and supervisor. It will also help you to know when something has gone well and if your plan has worked. Do not simply pat yourself on the back! Explore why your work went well. Use your supervision time and opportunities to talk with experienced colleagues.

What needs to be achieved (the aim):
Improve Mr Gommer's social contacts

Goals which help to measure success (objectives):
Mr Gommer to agree to meet local organiser of Age Concern
Mr Gommer to attend St Chad's luncheon club

How to do it (method):
1. Talk to him about meeting the organiser and secure his agreement
2. Arrange the meeting at his home
3. Be there for the meeting
4. Be positive and encouraging
5. Offer to accompany him for his first visit to the luncheon club
6. Arrange transport for his first visit
7. Go with him

Making good use of training and development opportunities

Personal development is to do with developing the personal qualities and skills that everyone needs in order to live and work with others, such as understanding, empathy, patience, communication and relationship-building. It is also to do with the development of self-confidence, self-esteem and self-respect.

If you look back on the ways in which you have changed over the past five years, you are likely to find that you are different in quite a few ways. Most people change as they mature and gain more life experience. Important experiences such as changing jobs, moving home, illness or bereavement can change people. It is inevitable that your **personal development** and your **professional development** are linked – your personality and the way you relate to others are the major tools you use to do your job. Taking advantage of every opportunity to train and develop your working skills will also have an impact on you as a person.

Key terms

Personal development – developing the personal qualities and skills needed to live and work with others

Professional development – developing the qualities and skills necessary for the workforce

Professional development is to do with developing the qualities and skills that are necessary for the workplace. Examples are:

- teamwork
- the ability to communicate with different types of people
- time management
- organisation
- problem solving
- decision making
- the skills specific to the job.

Continuing professional development involves regularly updating the skills you need for your work. You can achieve this through attending training sessions both on and off the job, and by making the most of the opportunities you have for training by careful planning and preparation.

How to get the best out of training

Your supervisor will work with you to decide on the types of training that will benefit you most. This will depend on the stage you have reached with your skills and experience. There would be little point, for example, in doing a course in advanced micro-surgery techniques if you were at the stage of having just achieved your first aid certificate! It may be that not all the training you want to do is appropriate for the work you are currently assigned to – you may think that a course in advanced therapeutic activities sounds fascinating, but your supervisor may suggest that a

Case study

Choosing appropriate training

Michelle is a health care support worker in a large hospital, on a busy ward. She was very aware of the fact that she lacked assertiveness in the way she dealt with both her colleagues and many of the people whom she supported. Michelle was always the one who agreed to run errands and to cover additional tasks that others should have been doing. She knew that she ought to be able to say no, but somehow she could not. She then became angry and resentful because she felt she was doing far more work than many others on her team.

Her supervisor raised the issue during a supervision session and suggested that Michelle should consider attending assertiveness training. Although initially reluctant, Michelle decided to take the opportunity. After six weeks of attending classes and working with the supportive group she met there, Michelle found that she was able to deal far more effectively with unfair and unreasonable requests from her colleagues. She was also able to deal in a firm but pleasant way with the people she supported.

1. What difference is Michelle's training likely to make:
   a) to the people she supports
   b) to herself?
2. Have you ever said 'yes' to extra work or additional responsibility when you wanted to say 'no'? How did this make you feel?
3. What could you have done about it?

Do you know about all the different types of training?

course in basic moving and handling is what you need right now. You will only get the best out of training and development opportunities if they are the right ones for you at the time. There will be opportunities for training throughout your career, and it is important that you work out which training is going to help you to achieve your goals.

Get the most out of training and development

You should work with your supervisor to prepare for any training you receive, and to review it afterwards. You may want to prepare for a training session by:

- reading any materials which have been provided in advance
- talking to your supervisor or a colleague who has attended similar training, about what to expect
- thinking about what you want to achieve as a result of attending the training.

Doing it well

Training

Make the most of training by:

- preparing well
- taking a full part in the training
- asking questions about anything you do not understand
- collecting any handouts and keeping your own notes of the training
- thinking about how to apply your learning to your work, by discussing the training with your supervisor later
- reviewing the ways in which you have benefited from the training.

Activity 6

Training session review

1. Think about the last training or development session you took part in and write a short report.
2. What preparations did you make beforehand so that you could benefit fully from it?
3. What did you do at the session? For example, what and how did you contribute, and what did you learn? Do you have a certificate to show that you participated in the session? Do you have a set of notes?
4. How did you follow up the session? Did you review the goals you had set yourself, or discuss the session with your supervisor?
5. Describe how you have used what you learned at the session. For example, how has the way you work changed, and how have the people you support and your colleagues benefited from your learning?

Functional skills

English: Writing

Write a short report on the last training or development session you took part in. Use a suitable format with appropriate headings to show your knowledge of report writing. This is a formal document and you need to check that spelling, puncutation and grammar are accurate.

Do you get the best from supervision by preparing well?

3.2 Using feedback to evaluate your performance and inform development

You will need to be prepared to receive feedback on your performance. It may be from your supervisor, your manager, your colleagues or the people you support. It is not always easy to welcome it and to use it to improve your practice, but you will need to work hard until you can do just that. While it is best for feedback to be given in a positive way, this does not mean that it will be uncritical. Many people have considerable difficulty in accepting criticism in any form, even where it is intended to be supportive and constructive. If you are aware that you are likely to have difficulty accepting criticism, try to prepare yourself to view feedback from any source as valuable and useful information that can add to your ability to reflect effectively on your work. This is not easy, but it is essential if you are to develop into a reflective and effective practitioner.

Your response to negative feedback should not be to defend your actions or to reject the feedback. You should try to accept and value it. A useful reply would be: 'Thank you, that's very helpful. I can use that next time to improve.' If you are able to do this, you are likely to be able to make the maximum use of opportunities to improve your practice.

On the other hand, if criticism of any kind undermines your confidence and makes it difficult for you to value your own strengths, you should ask your supervisor to identify areas in which you did well. Use this positive feedback to help you respond more constructively to the negative feedback.

Activity 7

Constructive criticism

1. Ask a colleague, or a friend or family member, to offer some constructive criticism on a task you have undertaken – for example, a practical activity such as cooking a meal, or work you have undertaken in the garden or in the house.
2. Work hard on accepting the criticism as constructive and helpful. Try to make a positive response.
3. How did the constructive criticism make you feel? If you found it hard to deal with, why do you think this was?

If you are able to practise receiving feedback on something that is relatively unthreatening, you are likely to be able to use the same techniques when considering feedback on your working practices.

4. Be able to agree a personal development plan

4.1 Sources of support for planning and reviewing your development

There are many sources of support that you can access and many different ways that you can help yourself, when developing your practice.

The appraisal or supervision system in your workplace can be a good starting point. This will help you to identify areas of your practice that need to be developed, and to plan to use opportunities for training and development. Some employers provide appraisal at six-monthly or 12-monthly intervals, but supervision should be at least once a month. This gives you a good opportunity to use the experience and knowledge of your supervisor to help you plan how to move forward in your practice.

Getting the most out of supervision

Make sure that you are well prepared for sessions with your supervisor so that you can get maximum benefit from them. This will mean bringing together your reflections on your own practice, using examples and case notes where appropriate. You will need to demonstrate to your supervisor that you have reflected on your own practice and that you have begun identifying areas for development. If you can provide evidence through case notes and records to support this, it will assist your supervisor greatly.

Your supervisor's role

Your supervisor's role is to support and advise you in your work and to make sure that you know and understand:

- your rights and responsibilities as an employee
- what your job involves and the procedures your employer has in place to help you carry out your job properly
- the approach to social care where you work — that is, the beliefs, values and attitudes of your employer regarding the way that people are supported, and how you can demonstrate values in the way you do your work
- your career development needs — the education and training requirements for the job roles you may progress into, as well as for your current job.

Working as a personal assistant

If you work as a personal assistant and the person who employs you is also the person you support, then you may not have formal supervision sessions. Alternatively, your employer may be linked into other employers and able to access a local scheme offering support and supervision through the Local Authority or through a Sector Skills Council. However, if there is no support, you will be on your own and will need to find ways to access training and development with the support of your employer. There are plenty of suggestions in this section as to where you can find information to make sure that your practice is up to date. You may want to find some opportunities for volunteering in order to gain work experience in areas of practice that you want to develop.

Activity 8

Supervision of staff

1. Ask your supervisor for a copy of the relevant policy or plan at work on the supervision of staff.
2. Read the plan and note down what it covers — for example:
   - how you will be supervised
   - how often you can expect to be formally supervised
   - what things your supervisor will be able to help you with in your work role and career.
3. If the plan is not clear, make a list of the things on which you would like your supervisor's support, and agree a time and place to discuss these items with them.
4. If you are working alone, work out how you are going to keep your practice up to date. How will you find out about any training and development programmes that may be useful?

Using informal networks

Informal support networks are likely to consist of your work colleagues. These can be major sources of support and assistance. Part of the effectiveness of many teams in many workplaces is their ability to provide useful ideas for improving practice, and their provision of support when things go badly.

Do you have any informal networks to support you?

Some staff teams provide a completely informal and ad-hoc support system, where people give advice, guidance and support as and when necessary. Other teams will organise this on a more regular basis, and they may get together to discuss specific situations or problems that have arisen for members of the team. These are often called **Action Learning Sets** and provide excellent opportunities to share issues and good practice with colleagues in similar roles to you. In order to develop and improve your practice effectively, you need to be sure that you are making maximum use of all opportunities to gain support, advice and feedback.

Key term

Action Learning Set – a group of between about four and seven people, who meet regularly to support one another in their learning in order to take purposeful action on work issues

Activity 9

Formal and informal support networks

1. Identify the formal and informal support networks in your workplace.
2. Note down the ways in which you use the different types of network and how they support your development.
3. Think about an occasion when you have used a network to improve your practice. How did you feel about being supported by colleagues? How useful was it? If you can, make some notes so that you can use the network again in the future. If you do not have access to a network, think about starting one.

4.2 Working with others to review and prioritise your learning needs, professional interests and development opportunities

Using training and development sessions

One of the formal ways of reflecting on your own practice and identifying strengths, weaknesses and areas for development is during training opportunities. On a course, or at a training day, aspects of your practice and areas of knowledge that are new to you will be discussed, and this will often open up avenues that you had not previously considered. This is one of the major benefits of making the most of all the training and education opportunities that are available to you.

Are you getting the most out of training days?

4.3 How to work with others to agree your personal development plan

A personal development plan is a very important document, as it identifies your training and development needs. Because the plan is updated when you have taken part in training and development, it also provides a record of participation.

You should work out a personal development plan with your supervisor. Remember that it is essentially *your* plan for *your* career. You need to think about what you want to achieve, and discuss with your supervisor the best ways of achieving your goals. If you do not work with a supervisor, you can still prepare a plan and follow it through for yourself.

There is no single right way to prepare a personal development plan. There are plenty of different models and styles; what matters is what is in the plan. It should include:

- different development areas, such as practical skills and communication skills
- the goals or targets you have set — such as learning to manage a team
- a timescale for achieving these goals or targets.

Timescales must be realistic; for example, if you decided that you needed to achieve competence in managing a team in six months, this would be unrealistic and unachievable. You would inevitably fail to meet your target and would run the risk of becoming demoralised and demotivated. But if your target was to attend a training and development programme on

Case study

Identifying opportunities to improve practice

Palvinder is a support worker in a unit for young adults with disabilities, run by a leading charity. He was aware that his knowledge of disability legislation was not as comprehensive as it ought to be. He felt uncertain about answering some of the questions that the young people put to him.

Palvinder raised this issue with his line manager, who immediately found that training days were provided by the Local Authority that would help Palvinder to learn about the relevant legislation. Following his training

days, Palvinder felt far more confident, as not only had he learned a great deal during the course itself, but he had also been given some handouts and been informed about useful textbooks and websites.

1. How will Palvinder benefit personally from taking this training?
2. How will the people Palvinder works with benefit?
3. Are you confident about your knowledge of legislation relating to your own work? If not, what steps are you taking to improve it?

team building during the next six months and to lead two team meetings by the end of the six months, those goals and targets would be realistic and you would be likely to achieve them.

When you have set your targets, you will need to review your progress towards achieving them — this should happen every six months or so. You need to look at what you have achieved and how your plan needs to be updated.

Development plans can take many forms, but the best ones are likely to be developed in conjunction with your manager or workplace supervisor. You need to consider the 'areas of competence' carefully and understand which ones you need to develop for your work role. Categorise each area as one of the following:

- you feel fully confident in this area
- there is room for improvement and development
- you have very limited current ability.

The headings in Table 2 are example suggestions only.

Development plan		
Area of competence	Goals	Action plan
Time management and workload organisation	Learn to use computer recording and information systems	Attend two-day training and use study pack. Attend follow-up training days. Use computer instead of writing reports by hand
Review date: 3 months		
Professional development priorities		
My priorities for training and development in the next 6 months	IT and computerised record systems	
My priorities for training and development in the next 6–12 months	As above, and assessor training	
Repeat this exercise in: 6 months and review the areas of competence and priorities		

Table 2: A sample development plan.

5. Be able to use learning opportunities and reflective practice to contribute to personal development

5.1 How learning activities have affected practice

Learning

When you have identified skills and knowledge you would like to improve, the next step is to set about learning. There are many theories about how people learn, and being able to understand how you learn is often helpful to the process of learning. A useful theory is the Lewin/Kolb cycle of experiential learning, as shown in the diagram below.

- **Concrete experience:** something happens to you or you do something; it can be an unusual event or something you do every day.

- **Reflective observation:** you think about it.

- **Abstract conceptualisation:** you work out some general rules about it, or you realise that it fits into a theory or pattern you already know about.

- **Active experimentation:** next time the same situation occurs, you apply your rules or theories.

This will make your experience different from the first time, so you will have different factors to think about and different things to learn — and this means the cycle continues. You never stop learning.

Imagine that you are working with a man who has a learning disability that means he does not speak. It is the first time you have met him and you are offering

him a drink at lunchtime. You offer a glass of orange squash by placing it in front of him. He immediately pushes the glass away with a facial expression that you take to express disgust.

Within Kolb's learning cycle you have had a concrete experience.

Stage 1

Stage 1 of the learning cycle is the experience that this person has rejected your offer of orange squash. But why has he reacted in this way?

Stage 2

Stage 2 involves thinking through some possible reasons for the reaction.

- Perhaps he does not like orange squash?
- Perhaps he does not like the way you put it in front of him?
- Perhaps he does not like to take a drink with his meal?
- Could it be that he prefers a hot drink?
- Could a cold drink make him feel he is being treated as a child?
- Does he see adult status as defined by having a hot drink?

Reflection on the non-verbal behaviour of the person may provide a range of starting points for interpreting his actions.

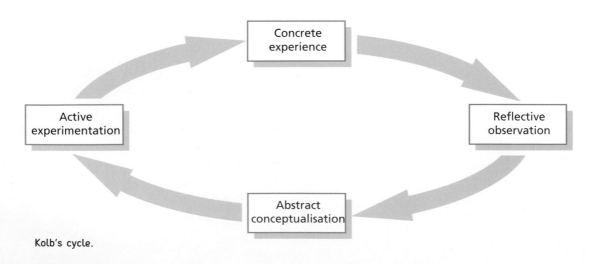

Kolb's cycle.

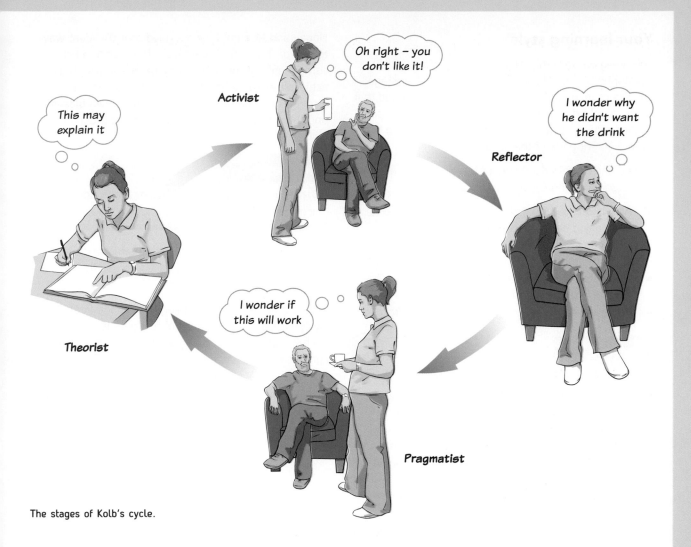

The stages of Kolb's cycle.

Stage 3

Kolb's third stage involves trying to make sense of your reflections. What do you know about different cultural interpretations of non-verbal behaviour? What are the chances that the way you placed the drink in front of the person has been construed as an attempt to control or dominate him? You did not intend to send this message, but he may have interpreted your behaviour on an emotional level as being unpleasant. The more you know about human psychology and social group membership, the more you can analyse his reaction. You need to choose the most likely explanation for his behaviour using everything you know about people.

Stage 4

Kolb's fourth stage involves experimenting, or checking out ideas and assumptions that you may have made. You could attempt to modify your non-verbal behaviour

to look supportive. You might show the person a cup and saucer to indicate the question: 'Is this what you would like?' If he responds with a positive non-verbal response, you would have been around the four stages of the cycle and would have solved the problem in a way that valued the individuality and diversity of the person.

You can expect to have to go round this learning cycle a number of times before you are able to understand and interpret a person's needs correctly.

How quickly can you work through these four stages? Would you be able to think through these issues while working with someone, or would you need to go away and reflect on practice? The answers to these questions might depend on the amount of experience you have had in similar situations.

Your learning style

Following on from this, Honey and Mumford (1982) developed a theory based on this idea of a four-stage process of learning from experience. They theorised that some people develop a preference for a particular part of the learning cycle. In other words, people learn better from different parts of the process.

Honey and Mumford's theory of learning styles fits the four-stage learning cycle as follows.

- **Activists** enjoy the activity of meeting new people and having new experiences.
- **Reflectors** mainly enjoy sitting down and thinking things through.
- **Theorists** enjoy analysing issues in terms of established theoretical principles.
- **Pragmatists** prefer trying out new ideas in practice.

Reflect

Think about the ways in which *you* learn new things. Do you tend to enjoy or use one part of the learning cycle more than others? How have you worked this out? Use some examples and try it out so that you are sure that you have got it right. Think about ways in which you could develop your skills in other parts of the cycle.

Honey and Mumford have argued that the ideal way to approach practical learning is to balance all the components of the learning cycle. Some people can achieve this more holistic approach. For other people it might be important to recognise their own **biases** and to try to compensate for relying too much on one style.

Key term

Bias – an unfair influence, whether positive or negative

You can test your own learning style preference or obtain further details of tests based on this theory at www.peterhoney.com

The 'four-stage' or 'cycle' theory of learning from experience is just one model of learning. It may be useful in practice, especially as a way of approaching complicated, non-routine problem solving. There are many other ways in which care workers might undertake personal development.

Stage 1: Activists
People who concentrate on experience

Stage 2: Reflectors
People who like to stand back and think about experience

Stage 3: Theorists
People who like to concentrate on analysis

Stage 4: Pragmatists
People who like to try things out

Honey and Mumford's theory of learning styles.

Activity 10

Reflective diary

Keep a reflective diary for a week. At the end of each working day, spend half an hour writing down one or two key issues that concerned you or irritated you, or that you dealt with well.

1. How did you respond to these issues?
2. How could you learn from this experience to take your own practice forward?

Different ways of learning

Formal training and development are not the only ways you can learn and expand your knowledge and understanding. There are plenty of other ways to keep up progress towards the goals you want to achieve.

Not everyone learns best from formal training. Other ways people learn are from:

- being shown by more experienced colleagues
- working and discussing issues as a team or group
- reading textbooks, journals and articles
- following up information on the Internet

- making use of local library facilities or learning resource centres
- asking questions and holding professional discussions with colleagues and managers.

Activity 11

Learning methods

1. Write down the different ways of learning that you have experienced. Ways of learning that you might find useful include:
    - watching other people
    - asking questions and listening to the answers
    - finding things out for yourself
    - going to college and attending training courses
    - studying a distance learning course or a course on the Internet.
2. Which have been the most enjoyable and most successful for you?
3. How could you use this information about how you best like to learn in order to update your workplace skills?

Do you make use of libraries and resource centres?

5.2 How reflective practice has led to improved ways of working

The purpose of reflective practice is to improve and develop your practice by thinking about what you are doing. Reflection involves taking time to consider how you are working and why you are doing things in a particular way.

Thinking and reflecting is like any other skill — you can learn it, and you can practise it until you become very good at it.

Becoming a reflective practitioner means thinking not only about your actions, but also about the people you support. Learning to reflect will help you to understand people better because learning to take the time to reflect helps you to consider why people behave in particular ways and what messages the behaviour is trying to convey. Spending time reflecting on the people you support will ultimately mean that you have a greater understanding of them and provide a better service.

The important thing is to think positively about areas of your work that you can improve. Reflection that does not identify areas for improvement is of little value — in fact, it can be highly destructive.

Reflective practice means that you need to use the learning cycle (see page 66) to consider:

- what your experience was
- what it has taught you
- how you can make use of what you have learned.

Thinking about your practice means that you keep learning, because there is always something new.

Earlier in this unit you looked at the factors that influence your practice; understanding all of this is part of being a reflective practitioner. You need to be able to see how and why your practice has developed and the factors that have influenced and shaped the development.

It is not possible to consider properly what you have been doing, if you do not understand what has influenced you to take the actions that you have. Reflecting on your practice means bringing together everything you have learned in this unit and using it to understand and improve every aspect of your professional practice.

Reflect

Think about an occasion when you have been able to look at an area of your own practice or knowledge that needed improvement, and the steps you took to make the changes. What did you do, and what factors made you choose a particular course of action? Consider where you looked for help and what you found to be the most and least useful actions you took. Finally, think about how you can use this experience to make future changes and improvements to your practice. Has looking back at a previous occasion made it easier to plan for the future? What does this tell you about how you work best?

Case study

Seeking constructive feedback

Lewis works in a large residential setting for elderly adults where one of the people he supports is Mrs Kaur, an Indian woman who speaks very little English. Mrs Kaur has many relatives who visit her regularly, and has long and animated conversations with them. But when she has no visitors, Mrs Kaur is very quiet. She hardly responds at all when Lewis tries to talk to her and is unwilling to talk to the other residents or to take part in any of the activities on offer. Lewis is concerned that Mrs Kaur may feel isolated. He would like to be able to communicate with her better and to improve his own practice.

1. What are the barriers to communication between Lewis and Mrs Kaur?
2. Whom could Lewis speak to about the situation?
3. What other actions could he take to improve his practice?

5.3 How to record progress in relation to personal development

Once you have completed your plan, you can identify the areas on which you need to concentrate. You should set some goals and targets, and your supervisor should be able to help you ensure they are realistic. This is a personal development programme for *you* and you must be sure that it reflects not only the objectives of your organisation and the job roles they may want you to fulfil, but also your personal ambitions and aspirations.

When you have identified the areas in which you feel competent and you have chosen your target areas for development, you will need to design a personal development log to keep a record of your progress. This can be put together in any way that you find effective.

Personal Development Plan
Name:
Workplace:
Supervisor:
Long-term goals (1–5 years)
Medium-term goals (6–12 months)
Short-term goals (next 6 months)
Areas of strength
Areas of weakness

Have you covered all aspects of a personal development plan?

In your plan, you may wish to include things as varied as:

- learning sign language
- learning a particular technique for working with people with dementia
- developing your potential as a manager by learning organisational and human resources skills.

You could also include areas such as time management and stress management. All of these are legitimate areas for inclusion in your personal and professional development plan.

Activity 12

Personal development plan

1. Prepare a personal development plan. You should use a computer to do this, even if you print out a hard copy in order to keep a personal portfolio. Use the model on the following pages to prepare your plan.
2. Complete the plan as far as you can at the present time. Note where you want your career to be in the short, medium and long term. You should also write down the training you want to complete and the skills you want to gain. You should do this on a computer if possible, otherwise complete a hard copy and keep it in a file.
3. Update the plan regularly. Keep on reviewing it with your supervisor.

Training and development

This section of your plan helps you to look at what you need to do in order to reach the goals you recorded in the first section. You should make a note of the training and development you need to undertake in order to achieve what you have identified.

Short-term goals	
Medium-term goals	
Long-term goals	

Table 3: Your goals.

Milestones and timescales

Here you should look at the development you have identified in the previous section and plan some timescales. Decide what the **milestones** will be on the way to achieving your goal. Make sure that your timescales are realistic.

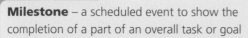

Key term

Milestone – a scheduled event to show the completion of a part of an overall task or goal

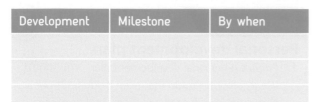

Development	Milestone	By when

Table 4: Your milestones.

Reviews and updates

This section helps you to stay on track and to make the changes that will be inevitable as you progress. Not all your milestones will be achieved on target — some will be later, some earlier. All these changes will affect your overall plan, and you need to keep up to date and make any alterations as you go along.

Milestone	Target date	Actual achievement/ revised target

Table 5: Reviewing your progress.

Getting ready for assessment

LO1

This assessment is knowledge-based. You are likely to have to prepare an assignment that shows how your job role is linked to the relevant standards, and how the duties and responsibilities of your role are reflected in the standards. This could be a written assignment or it could be in the form of a presentation.

LO2

This assessment is competence-based and requires you to show that you can evaluate your own performance. You need to be able to demonstrate that you can measure your own work against relevant standards. You may do this through a written evaluation or in a verbal presentation. To do this you will have to show how you can demonstrate where your practice meets the standards and where there are areas that need further development. The requirement to reflect on your own values and beliefs may be a written assignment or it may be in the form of a discussion with your assessor.

LO3

This assessment is focused on your personal development plan. The activities you review will need to be linked to one of the goals in the plan, and you will have to show how you have used the plan to record how well you are progressing towards your goals. The review of the development activities may be a written one, or you may be asked to provide a verbal presentation. In either case, you must provide a brief description of the activity and then show how it has assisted your progress towards the goals set out in your development plan.

LO4

This assessment is essentially competence-based. You are required to produce your own development plan, with the support of a supervisor, tutor or other colleague. You will need to show that you have considered what you want to achieve and identified the areas of your practice that require improvement.

LO5

This assessment requires you to demonstrate a mix of competence and knowledge. You may be required to prepare an assignment that explains how reflective practice is related to quality of service. Remember that this is an explanation, so do not just describe – use words and phrases like 'because', 'therefore', 'as a result of', so that' and 'in order to'. You also have to show that you are able to be a reflective practitioner and are able to think about your own practice and identify where developments are needed. You will have to do this in relation to a real work situation.

Further reading and research

The introduction to this section highlights your duty to make sure that the service provided is the best it can possibly be. In order to do this it is essential that you are constantly reflecting on your practice and striving to develop the way you work. Here are some suggestions of further reading and research to help you to do this.

- www.gscc.org.uk (General Social Care Council (GSCC) – training and learning)
- www.dh.gov.uk (Department of Health – human resources and training)
- www.skillsforcare.org.uk (Skills for Care – workforce development for UK social care sector)
- www.skillsforhealth.org.uk (Skills for Health – workforce development for UK health sector)
- www.cwdcouncil.org.uk (Children's Workforce Development Council)
- www.scie.org.uk (Social Care Institute of Excellence)
- Hawkins, R. and Ashurst, A. (2006) *How to be a Great Care Assistant*, Hawker Publications
- Knapman, J. and Morrison, T. (1998) *Making the Most of Supervision in Health and Social Care*, Pavilion Publishers
- Shakespeare, P. *Learning in Health and Social Care*, journal, Blackwell Publishing

Unit SHC 33

Promote equality and inclusion in health, social care or children's and young people's settings

This unit is all about ensuring that people are treated equally – this does not necessarily mean treating people the same. It involves valuing people's differences and working in a way that does not leave people out and that supports people to take part in whatever they want to do.

It is also about understanding the effects of being excluded and left out, and about the barriers that people have to overcome in order to participate fully in society. Working in social care and providing support for people so that they can live their lives as they wish means being able to value and understand the differences and to recognise the different contributions that everyone makes.

In this unit you will learn about:

- the importance of diversity, equality and inclusion
- how to work in an inclusive way
- how to promote diversity, equality and inclusion.

1. Understand the importance of diversity, equality and inclusion

1.1 What is meant by diversity, equality and inclusion

Diversity

Diversity is about difference, and its value is the richness and variety that different people bring to society.

'All apples are red.' That statement is clearly silly. Of course they are not – some are green, some are yellow. When it comes to people, everyone is different. There are so many ways in which people differ from each other, including, for example:

- appearance
- ability
- gender
- talent
- race
- beliefs.
- culture

Imagine how boring life would be if everyone was exactly the same. Whole societies of identical 'cloned' people have been the central theme of many films, and it is clear immediately how unnatural that seems. However, we are not always very good at recognising and valuing the differences in the people we meet.

Different sorts of diversity

You can think about diversity in different ways. There are specific differences between people, all of the features that make each of us an individual, and there are broader differences as you can see from the list above. Both of these are important and you need to take account of each of them, and value the contributions that are made by different perspectives, different ways of thinking and different approaches.

Generalisations and stereotypes

It is often easy to make broad, sweeping statements that you believe apply to everyone who belongs to a particular group. It is the exact opposite of valuing diversity, by saying that everyone is the same. This is the basis of prejudice and discrimination, and you need to be sure that you are not guilty of making generalisations and thinking about people in stereotypes. People are often discriminated against because of their race, beliefs, gender, religion, sexuality or age. Treating everyone the same will result in

---

---

discrimination because some people will have their needs met and others will not. In order to prevent discrimination, it is important to value diversity and treat people differently in order to meet their different needs.

Activity 2

Generalisations

Complete the following sentences.
- Police officers are…
- Teenagers are…
- Nurses are…
- Politicians never…
- West Indians are all…
- Asians always…
- Men all…
- Women are…
- Americans are…

You can probably think of plenty of statements that you make as generalisations about others. Think about how easy you found it to come up with statements for each of the examples. How do you think these generalisations could affect the way you work?

Stereotypes

One of the main causes of discrimination is the fear and lack of understanding of others that is spread because of **stereotyping**. Prejudice is what makes people think in stereotypes and, equally, stereotypes support prejudice. Stereotypes are an easy way of thinking about the world. Stereotypes might suggest that all people over 65 are frail and walk with a stick, that all black young people who live in inner cities are on drugs, that all Muslims are terrorists, or that all families have a mother, father and two children. These stereotypes are often reinforced by the media or by advertising. Television programmes will often portray violent, criminal characters as young and black, and older people are usually shown as being dependent and unable to make a useful contribution to society.

Key term

Stereotyping – making negative or positive judgements about whole groups of people based on prejudice and assumptions, rather than facts or knowledge about people

Activity 3

Stereotyping in adverts

Next time you watch television, note down the number of adverts for cars that show trendy, good-looking young business people with a wealthy lifestyle. The advertisers attempt to convince us into believing that buying that particular brand of car will make us good-looking and trendy and give us the kind of lifestyle portrayed.
1. How many people do you know with those particular makes of car that are anything like the people in the adverts?
2. How many do you know who wish they were?

What effect do stereotypes have?

The effect of stereotypes is to make you jump to conclusions about people. How many times have you felt uneasy seeing a young man with a shaved head walking towards you? You know nothing about him, but the way he looks has made you form an opinion about him. If you have a picture in your mind of a social worker or a police officer, think about how much the media influences that – do they really all look like that?

Labelling

Labelling is slightly more complex than stereotyping, and happens when someone thinks the factor which people have in common is more important than the hundreds of factors which make them different.

For example, the remark 'We should organise a concert for the elderly' makes an assumption that being older is what is important about the people concerned, and that somehow as you grow older your tastes become the same as those of all other people your age! It would be much better to say, for example, 'We should organise a concert for older people who like music from the shows' or 'We should organise a concert for older people who like opera'.

It's not funny

'Have you heard the one about…?'

Telling jokes at the expense of particular groups of people is just displaying prejudices. If someone has stereotypes about people being mean, stupid or dangerous because of their nationality, they fail to treat

What jobs and homes do you think these people have? Why do you think this?

people as individuals and fail to recognise that there are individuals everywhere and that all people are different. Of course, some people will be just as the stereotype portrays them – but a lot more will not be. Avoiding stereotypes and the discrimination that they promote is essential if you want to succeed in social care.

Challenging prejudice

Stop yourself every time you make a generalisation and look at the prejudice that is behind it. Think about why you think the way you do, and do something about it. The next time you hear yourself saying, for example, 'Social workers never understand what is really needed', 'GPs always take ages to visit' or 'People who live here wouldn't be interested in that', stop and think what you are really doing.

It is probably true that some social workers will not understand, maybe even all those you have met so far! But that does not necessarily apply to them all.

Perhaps most of the people you support would not be interested in whatever was being suggested, but some might. You cannot make that assumption. You need to ask. You need to offer people choices because they are all different. Do not fall into the trap of stereotyping people based on factors such as gender, age, race, culture, dress or where they live.

Avoiding stereotypes at work

It is a key part of your job to find out the personal beliefs and values of each person you support. Think about all the aspects of their lives, such as:

- diet
- clothing
- personal hygiene
- worship
- language
- relationships with others.

It is your responsibility to find out – not for the person to have to tell you. It will be helpful for you, and for other support workers, if this type of information is kept in the personal record.

Equality

How can you foster and encourage equality, which seems to be about everyone being equal, alongside diversity, which is about everyone being different?

It is not as impossible as it appears. The first key concept to understand is that what you are being asked to do is to promote 'equality' – and that is not necessarily the same thing as treating everyone the same.

Try thinking about a race. Everyone would agree that generally, for a race to be fair, all the competitors must be on the start line and start together. Before people have a chance to take part in the race, they have to reach the starting line. Yet many people in our society need considerable help just to reach the starting line before they can even begin to take part in the race.

If you are to support people in reaching the starting line, you have to be able to find out from them what additional support they are going to need. This is called **positive action**. It is not the same thing as **positive discrimination**, which is illegal.

Following the first 'women-only' shortlists in the 1997 election, the scene had been set for more women to enter politics and views had changed sufficiently to ensure that in the National Assembly for Wales and the Scottish Parliament, over 40 per cent of members elected were women.

Key terms

Positive action – ensuring that people are able to enter into fair competition with others

Positive discrimination – acting more favourably towards someone because of their perceived disadvantage – this is not legal in the UK

Reflect

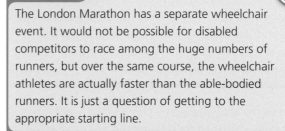

The London Marathon has a separate wheelchair event. It would not be possible for disabled competitors to race among the huge numbers of runners, but over the same course, the wheelchair athletes are actually faster than the able-bodied runners. It is just a question of getting to the appropriate starting line.

A competitor in the London Marathon wheelchair event.

Reflect

In planning for elections, political parties will have some 'women-only' shortlists for parliamentary candidates. This is a form of positive action that has resulted in a vast increase in the number of women MPs. In turn, this means that women MPs have the chance to begin at the same point as their male colleagues when it comes to being in posts of responsibility. Previously, so few women were selected as candidates to become MPs that even fewer were successfully elected or given government posts, which meant the waste of a wide range of skills and talents. This results in the self-fulfilling prophecy that women are not really 'cut out' for politics.

It is easy to apply the same principles to a job. Someone who has impaired vision or is in a wheelchair can do a job just as well, if not better, than someone who is able-bodied, provided that they are allowed the opportunity. That means removing physical barriers, such as steps or narrow doorways, and installing equipment that allows someone with impaired vision to 'read' documents.

Structure of society

The way in which people are grouped together and given status within all societies is called social stratification. This depends on the society — for example, in the American South before the US Civil War, this was carried out on the basis of racial grouping, where black communities existed only as slaves of white plantation owners. Many societies have used religion as a means of separating groups within society. In India, a caste system separates social groupings on the basis of the caste into which each person is born.

In most modern industrial societies, social stratification is not governed entirely by a pre-ordained group into which a person is born or only by land ownership, but it is defined quite clearly in terms of social class. In the UK, the government defines social class through the occupational area of the person concerned using the National Statistics Socio-Economic Classification (NS-SEC). This classifies people as shown in Table 1.

The government uses NS-SEC classes 1 to 8 when it carries out research into the trends in society, and also every ten years during the census population count. This provides the government with information that it can use to plan for the services and infrastructure which it will need over the next ten years and longer to meet the needs of the population effectively.

Classes	Operational categories and sub-categories	
1.1	L1 Employers in large organisations	
	L2 Higher managerial occupations	
1.2	L3 Higher professional occupations	L3.1 Traditional employees
		L3.2 New employees
		L3.3 Traditional self-employed
		L3.4 New self-employed
2	L4 Lower professional and higher technical occupations	L4.1 Traditional employees
		L4.2 New employees
		L4.3 Traditional self-employed
		L4.4 New self-employed
	L5 Lower managerial occupations	
	L6 Higher supervisory occupations	

3	L7 Intermediate occupations	L7.1 Intermediate clerical and administrative
		L7.2 Intermediate sales and service
		L7.3 Intermediate technical and auxiliary
		L7.4 Intermediate engineering
4	L8 Employers in small organisations	L8.1 Employers in small organisations (non-professional)
		L8.2 Employers in small organisations (agriculture)
	L9 Own account workers	L9.1 Own account workers (non-professional)
		L9.2 Own account workers (agriculture)
5	L10 Lower supervisory occupations	
	L11 Lower technical occupations	L11.1 Lower technical craft
		L11.2 Lower technical process operative
6	L12 Semi-routine occupations	L12.1 Semi-routine sales
		L12.2 Semi-routine service
		L12.3 Semi-routine technical
		L12.4 Semi-routine operative
		L12.5 Semi-routine agricultural
		L12.6 Semi-routine clerical
		L12.7 Semi-routine childcare
7	L13 Routine occupations	L13.1 Routine sales and service
		L13.2 Routine production
		L13.3 Routine technical
		L13.4 Routine operative
		L13.5 Routine agricultural
8	L14 Never worked and long-term unemployed	L14.1 Never worked
		L14.2 Long-term unemployed
*	L15 Full-time students	
	L16 Occupations not stated or inadequately described	
	L17 Not classifiable for other reasons	

Table 1: Social class defined according to the occupational area of a person.

Activity 4

Social class

From Table 1, work out what social class you believe that you are in. Do the same exercise for members of your family and neighbours who live in your area. Then try to fill in the gaps in all the other classes by putting down at least one person who you know, either personally or because they are a public figure, who fits into each category.

Functional skills

Mathematics

Conduct a survey on which class your friends, colleagues and family belong to using the following headings: working class, middle class and upper class. Use a minimum of 20 people as the basis for your analysis. Tabulate your findings under headings. Calculate the following ratios from your results:

- working class – upper class
- middle class – upper class
- middle class – working class.

Show all your calculations. Work out the percentage of those surveyed who are working class.

Social class

The government's definition of social class is important when it comes to planning services and running the country. However, there are many other ways of defining social class and it is unusual for the official government definitions of social class by occupation to be used in general day-to-day conversation. Most people will refer to the working class, middle class and upper class. You may hear people talk about lower classes or the aristocracy, but if you ask someone to define exactly what they mean by one of these classes, you are likely to receive a wide range of responses including accent, education, the area people live in, the amount of money they have or the job that they do. All of these factors can influence the social class into which a person believes that they fall.

Social mobility

The movement between social classes is called 'social mobility'. Unlike structures such as the caste system, it is possible within a social class system such as that in the UK for people to move between classes. The commonest way to do this is through education, thus enabling a move into a different job role. The most usual example of this is the child of a manual worker who goes to university, obtains a degree and other qualifications and becomes a professional such as a doctor or lawyer. There are other ways that people can move between social classes – for example, through establishing a successful business and making a large amount of money or through acquiring wealth by inheritance or good fortune.

Activity 5

Social mobility

In your own family, trace back through at least two previous generations and see if your family has been socially mobile during that time.

Causes of inequality

While social class is in itself a simple means of describing the living and working conditions of a particular person – their socio-economic status – it is also a valuable way of describing the conditions and living circumstances of many people and highlighting the kinds of inequalities which people suffer. For example, more people in the lower socio-economic groups are likely to experience the difficulties caused by poverty as a result of living on state benefit or by working in a job with low wages.

On a worldwide scale, poverty is defined by the World Health Organization as living on less than $1 a day. There is little doubt that in many third-world undeveloped countries, there are millions of people who suffer great hardship and live in very real poverty. This is 'absolute poverty'. In a society such as ours, poverty takes on a different meaning and in the UK it is 'relative poverty', which means that people are poorer than the majority of society.

People living in poverty are far more likely to experience the conditions which will lead to ill health and a greater need for the health and care services than those in higher social groups who are likely to live in better conditions. Some of the most obvious effects of poverty are poor housing, a poor diet and the likelihood of living in a poor area or neighbourhood with poor-quality local facilities. Socio-economic factors are a major cause of inequality, for example:

- infant and childhood death rates are significantly higher among children whose fathers are unskilled and in social classes 7 and 8
- children from classes 7 and 8 are four times as likely to die in accidents as those from class 1
- children in poverty have poorer attendance records at school and are less likely to continue into further education – this also reduces their opportunity for social mobility
- the highest incidence of mental health problems occurs among people who live in poverty and are in classes 7 and 8
- nutrition and eating habits show that people in lower socio-economic groups tend to eat less fruit and vegetables, and less food which contains dietary fibre. There seems to be evidence that the diets of those in lower social groupings tend to lack choice and variety and often contain inappropriate foods such as crisps, sweets and soft drinks
- only 44 per cent of babies born to mothers in social classes 7 and 8 are breastfed compared with 81 per cent of babies born to mothers in social class 1.

Poverty is not the only cause of inequality; it can also result from issues around race, gender or disability. For example, there is a much higher incidence of coronary heart disease and diabetes among the Asian population of the UK, where the death rate from heart disease can be up to twice as high as that of the general population. There also seems to be a link between race and educational achievement. Government figures show that Chinese and Indian students are over twice as likely to obtain five or more passes at GCSE than those from African-Caribbean or black African ethnic backgrounds (source: Office of National Statistics 2007).

Gender, disability and age can also be causes of inequality. This can be made significantly worse by the effects of poverty and the fact that very large numbers of older people live on very low incomes. Over 30 per cent of pensioners entitled to higher levels of income through income support fail to claim it, and as a result they exist in a lifestyle of severe **deprivation**.

Poverty and socio-economic deprivation are among the underlying causes of inequality in the UK. This is then reinforced by attitudes such as racism, sexism and discrimination against people with disabilities. If such attitudes go unchallenged, then inequality will continue.

1.2 Potential effects of discrimination

Effects of discrimination

Discrimination on the grounds of age, gender, race, sexuality or ability can damage a person's **self-esteem**, and reduce their ability to develop and maintain a sense of identity. When people are affected by discrimination they experience anger, humiliation, frustration and a feeling of hopelessness. They are made to feel worthless and of less value than others.

> **Key terms**
>
> **Deprivation** – a lack of something important, for example, a physical lack of money, shelter or clothing, or an emotional lack of loving, nurturing and caring
>
> **Self-esteem** – how you value yourself, and therefore how you believe the rest of the world sees you

Anti-discrimination means positively working to eliminate discrimination and to challenge it if you see it occurring in your place of work. For example, when weekly menus are being planned at a day centre, if no account is taken of the religious and cultural needs of people, you should challenge this and suggest changes.

Some obvious types of discriminatory practice are shown in the diagram on page 84. You should check your work to make sure that you are not falling into any of these behaviours. You also need to look at the way that colleagues are working and be prepared to challenge discrimination if you see it happening.

Your day-to-day practice and attitudes are important in how effective your inclusive practice will be. You should develop an interest in learning about other people's lifestyle, culture and needs. Even though you may hold a different set of values and beliefs from those of the people you support, you have to value them and respect people's rights to hold those values and beliefs. There may, in fact, be occasions when you will have to act as an advocate for someone's beliefs, even if you do not personally agree with them.

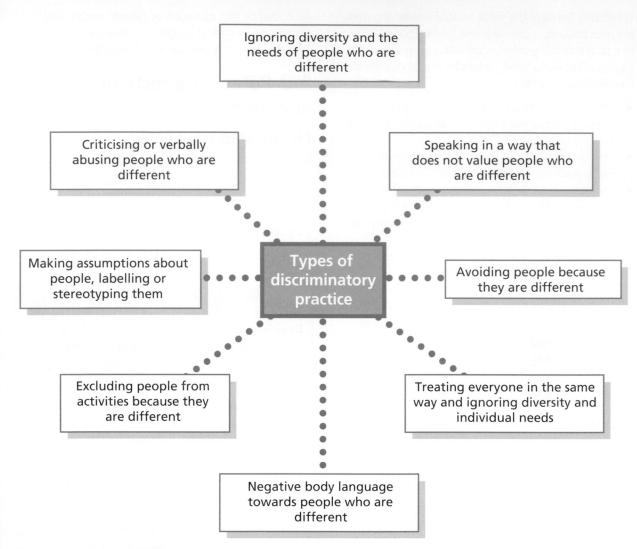

Types of discriminatory practice.

Reflect

Stereotypes can influence how you think about someone. Be prepared to challenge your own thinking and assumptions. Do not make judgements about people – try to learn about different cultures, beliefs and lifestyles. Everyone is entitled to their own beliefs and culture. If you do not know about someone's way of life, ask.

How well do you do this? Can you honestly say that you follow all of the points above?

What changes do we need to make so that everyone can be included?

1.3 How inclusive practice promotes equality and supports diversity

Definitions of inclusive practice are varied, but broadly, it is about ensuring that there are no barriers that would exclude people, or make it difficult for them to fully participate in society. People must be included in all aspects of life, not excluded from some of them because of an illness or a disability. Traditionally, we have developed separate worlds in order to meet people's needs — for example, separate workshops, education groups, living accommodation for people with mental health needs or any type of disability have kept people out of the mainstream of society. Older people have been separated with clubs, day centres and residential accommodation on the assumption that separate is best — but increasingly, we have come to see that separate is not equal, and we should have an inclusive society that everyone can enjoy.

Now, we ask a different question about how we organise society. We do not ask 'What is wrong with this person that means they cannot use the leisure centre or the cinema?' but 'What is wrong with the cinema or the leisure centre if people with disabilities can't use it?'

Inclusive practice is about providing the support that people want in order to live their lives as fully as possible. Examples of inclusive practice are:

- providing a ramp to give wheelchair access to a building
- providing information in a range of languages and in audio format
- ensuring that systems and processes for obtaining support are easy to use and that access allows people to work out the support that they need and find the best way to put it in place.

Overall, practising in an inclusive way means constantly asking 'What changes need to happen so that this person can participate?' and then doing whatever is within your area of responsibility to make those changes happen.

2. Be able to work in an inclusive way

2.1 How legislation and Codes of Practice relating to equality, diversity and discrimination apply to your work role

Laws, and Codes of Practice

Rights and responsibilities are a huge subject. In order to look at rights in terms of how they affect the people you support, it is helpful to discuss them under the following headings:

- rights under National Standards, Codes of Practice, guidelines and policies
- rights provided by law.

Responsibilities are the other side of the coin to rights – most of our responsibilities are about protecting, improving or not **infringing rights** of others. Responsibilities are the balance for rights, and it is impossible to consider one without the other.

> ### Key term
>
> **Infringing rights** – a situation where a person's entitlements have been disregarded and access to entitlements has been blocked through deliberate or accidental actions

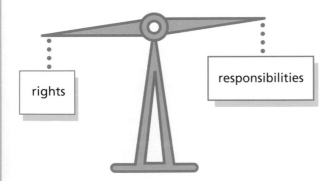

Have you thought about how rights and responsibilities balance each other?

Rights under National Standards, Codes of Practice, guidelines and policies

These are rights that do not have the force of law, but which are enforceable within social care and designed to improve the quality of services that people receive.

National Minimum Standards

Each of the countries of the UK has a body that is responsible for inspecting all social care facilities to make sure that they are complying with National Minimum Standards, and these are:

- the Care Quality Commission in England
- the Care Commission in Scotland
- the Care and Social Services Inspectorate in Wales
- the Regulation and Quality Improvement Authority in Northern Ireland.

Each of them uses a series of National Minimum Standards in order to inspect the quality of care. There are different sets of standards for different types of services. For example, there are separate standards for care homes for older people and for younger adults, for children's homes and for fostering services. The standards documents provide a detailed set of definitions that outline the minimum quality of care that a person may expect. All of the organisations also provide user-friendly information for people who are using the services about the levels of service that they can expect to receive.

Codes of Practice

The regulatory bodies in the UK have Codes of Practice for both employers in the social care field and for the social care workforce. The General Social Care Council in England, the Scottish Social Services Council, the Care Council for Wales and the Northern Ireland Social Care Council have similar codes covering key areas of practice. These require the workforce to:

- protect the rights and promote the interests of people and their carers – this includes respect for individuality and support for people to control their own lives, and respect for and maintenance of equal opportunities, diversity, dignity and privacy

- establish and maintain the trust and confidence of people and their carers – this means not abusing, neglecting or exploiting people, or forming inappropriate personal relationships, not discriminating or condoning discrimination, or placing oneself or others at unnecessary risk, and not abusing the trust of others in relation to confidentiality
- uphold public trust and confidence in social care services – this includes maintaining confidentiality, using effective communication, honouring commitments and agreements, declaring conflicts of interest and adhering to policies about accepting gifts
- promote the independence of people while protecting them from danger or harm – this means recognising the right to take risks, following risk

assessment policies, minimising risks and ensuring others are informed about risk assessments
- respect the rights of people while seeking to ensure that their behaviour does not harm themselves or other people – this includes maintenance of rights, challenging and reporting dangerous, abusive, discriminatory or exploitative behaviour, following safe practice, reporting resource problems, reporting unsafe practice of colleagues, following health and safety regulations, helping people to make complaints and using power responsibly
- be accountable for the quality of one's work and take responsibility for maintaining and improving your knowledge and skills – this means meeting standards, maintaining appropriate records and informing employers of personal difficulties.

All of the regulators have also developed a Code of Practice for employers.
Examples of the areas that are covered by all the Codes of Practice are as follows.

Code of Practice for Employers of Social Care Workers

1. Employers must make sure people are suitable to enter the social care workforce and understand their roles and responsibilities.

2. Employers must have written policies and procedures in place to enable social care workers to meet the Code of Practice for Social Care Workers. This includes written policies on:
   - confidentiality
   - equal opportunities
   - risk assessment
   - record keeping
   - acceptance of gifts
   - substance abuse.

   Employers must also provide:
   - effective systems of management and supervision
   - systems to report inadequate resources
   - support for workers to meet the Code of Practice.

3. Employers must provide training and development opportunities to enable social care workers to strengthen and develop their skills and knowledge, including:
   - induction
   - workplace assessment and practice learning

   - supporting staff to meet eligibility criteria
   - responding to workers who seek assistance.

4. Employers must put into place and implement written policies and procedures to deal with dangerous, discriminatory or exploitative behaviour and practice, including written policies and procedures on:
   - bullying, harassment and discrimination
   - reporting dangerous, discriminatory, abusive or exploitative behaviour
   - minimising the risk of violence and managing violent incidents
   - support for workers who experience trauma or violence
   - equal opportunities
   - assistance to care workers in relation to health needs.

5. Employers must promote the Codes of Practice to social care workers, individuals and carers, and co-operate with the Council's proceedings. This includes:
   - informing workers of the code
   - informing social care users
   - using the code to assist in decision making
   - informing the Council of any misconduct
   - co-operating with any investigations.

Activity 6

Codes of Practice

Take a look at the Codes of Practice and check whether you comply with the Code in your day-to-day practice. Check whether or not your employer complies with the Code. If you think that there are areas of your own practice that need improvement, think about how you are going to achieve this and include the plans in your Personal Development Plan (see page 64). If there are areas where you think your employer is not complying, discuss the issue with your manager.

By following professional Codes of Practice for social care workers, you are ensuring that the way you work will support the rights of people who use social care services.

Rights also involve responsibilities. Everyone has the responsibility not to infringe the rights of other people.

Some responsibilities linked to the rights in the diagram below are set out in Table 2. These apply to you and to the people you support. Understanding the balance between rights and responsibilities is important; it is easy to forget that sometimes one person exercising their rights may restrict the rights of others. For example, someone may claim the right of free speech to say that all non-British people should go back to where they came from. Clearly this is unacceptable because it infringes other people's fundamental rights to be respected and valued as individuals, and it is racist and discriminatory. Beware, because you will hear it said that it is a right of free speech for people to say whatever they wish — it is not.

You may also find that one person believes they have a right to enjoyment of their music at whatever volume they want to play it — but not if it affects the rights of others to enjoy peace and quiet.

Rights and responsibilities are always finely balanced. Table 2 shows some examples.

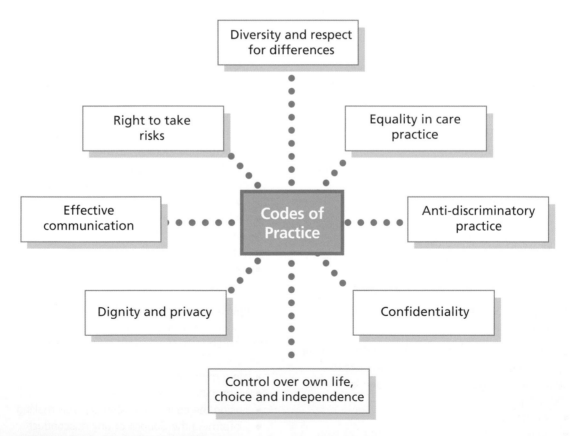

Rights covered by the Codes of Practice.

Right	Responsibility
Diversity and the right to be different	Respect for diversity in others
Equality and freedom from discrimination	Respect for the equality of others and valuing members of other social groups
Control over own life, choice and independence	Making choices that respect others' independence, choices and lifestyles
Freedom to choose lifestyle, self-presentation, diet and routine	The consequences of choices for the person and others around them
Dignity and privacy	Respect for the dignity and privacy of others
To be valued as an individual	Respect for the identity needs of others
Confidentiality	Respect for the confidentiality of others
To be safe and secure	To behave in a way that does not threaten or abuse the physical or emotional safety and security of others
To take risks, including taking risks as a matter of choice, in order to maintain the person's own identity or perceived well-being	Not to expose oneself or others to unacceptable risks, including a willingness to negotiate with respect to the impact of risk on others

Table 2: Rights and responsibilities of people.

Rights provided by law

Most of the provisions of the UK's Human Rights Act came into force on 2 October 2000. This means that residents of the United Kingdom – this Act applies in England, Scotland, Wales and Northern Ireland – are entitled to seek help from the courts if they believe that their human rights have been infringed.

Residential homes or nursing homes	These perform functions which would otherwise be performed by a local authority.
Charities	
Voluntary organisations	
Public services	This could include the privatised utilities, such as gas, electric and water companies.

Table 3: Organisations subject to the Human Rights Act 1998.

It is likely that anyone who works in health or social care will be working within the provisions of the Human Rights Act, which guarantees the rights to:

1. life
2. freedom from torture and inhuman or degrading treatment or punishment
3. freedom from slavery, servitude and forced or compulsory labour
4. liberty and security of person
5. a fair and public trial within a reasonable time
6. freedom from retrospective criminal law and no punishment without law
7. respect for private and family life, home and correspondence
8. freedom of thought, conscience and religion
9. freedom of expression
10. freedom of assembly and association
11. marry and found a family
12. the prohibition of discrimination in the enjoyment of convention rights
13. peaceful enjoyment of possessions and protection of property
14. access to an education
15. free elections
16. not be subjected to the death penalty.

Legislation about equality and rights

Discrimination is a denial of rights. Discrimination can be based on issues such as race, gender, disability or sexual orientation. The main Acts of Parliament and Regulations relating to equality and human rights in England, Scotland and Wales (Northern Ireland has its own equality legislation) were the:

- Equal Pay Act 1970
- Sex Discrimination Act 1975
- Race Relations Act 1976
- Disability Discrimination Acts 1995 and 2005
- Special Educational Needs and Disability Act 2001
- Employment Equality (Religion or Belief) and (Sexual Orientation) Regulations 2003
- Employment Equality (Age) Regulations 2006
- Racial and Religious Hatred Act 2006
- Equality Act 2006.

All of these Acts and Regulations have been superseded by a single Equality Act 2010. It came into force on 1 October 2010 and covers all the previous pieces of legislation and gives even more extensive protection by extending it to older people. The Act also gives protection to people not to be discriminated against on the grounds of their sexual orientation.

The Equalities Act 2010 provides a new Act to protect the rights of people and equality of opportunity. It makes the legislation simpler, as there is now just one Act. Broadly, the Act covers:

- the basic framework of protection against direct and indirect discrimination, harassment and victimisation in: services and public functions; premises; work; education; associations, and transport
- changing the definition of gender reassignment, by removing the requirement for medical supervision
- levelling up protection for people discriminated against because they are perceived to have, or are associated with someone who has, a protected characteristic, so providing new protection for people like carers
- clearer protection for breastfeeding mothers
- applying the European definition of indirect discrimination to all protected characteristics
- extending protection from indirect discrimination to disability
- introducing a new concept of 'discrimination arising from disability', to replace protection under previous legislation lost as a result of a legal judgement

- applying the detriment model to victimisation protection (aligning with the approach in employment law)
- harmonising the thresholds for the duty to make reasonable adjustments for disabled people
- extending protection from third-party harassment to all protected characteristics
- making it more difficult for disabled people to be unfairly screened out when applying for jobs, by restricting the circumstances in which employers can ask job applicants questions about disability or health
- allowing hypothetical comparators for direct gender pay discrimination
- making pay secrecy clauses unenforceable
- extending protection in private clubs to sex, religion or belief, pregnancy and maternity, and gender reassignment
- introducing new powers for employment tribunals to make recommendations which benefit the wider workforce
- harmonising provisions allowing voluntary positive action.

Activity 7

Equalities and Human Rights Commission

Research the work of the Equalities and Human Rights Commission and make notes about all the different ways it applies to the work you do and the organisation you work for. If you record this activity, it may contribute towards the assessment of this learning outcome and the achievement of functional or core skills.

Functional skills

English: Reading

Using a minimum of three sources, research the work of the Equalities and Human Rights Commission, and make notes on all the different ways it applies to the work you do.

Think about places you visit regularly where someone in a wheelchair would be unable to go — how many can you think of?

2.2 Respecting beliefs, culture, values and preferences

You also need to support your colleagues to work in ways that recognise and respect people's beliefs and preferences. Your work setting should be a place in which diversity and difference are acknowledged and respected. You need to set a good example and to make it clear that behaviour such as the following is unacceptable:

- speaking about people in a derogatory way
- speaking to people in a rude or dismissive way
- undermining people's self-esteem and confidence
- patronising and talking down to people
- removing people's right to exercise choice
- failing to recognise and treat people as individuals
- not respecting people's culture, values and beliefs.

If you find that you have colleagues who are regularly practising in a discriminatory way, you need to seek advice from your manager or supervisor.

Doing it well

Providing support for rights

- Hold regular staff meetings and have a regular item on your agenda about rights.
- Ensure that people are fully aware of complaints procedures and know how to follow them.
- Make sure that you know your organisation's policies and guidelines designed to protect and promote people's rights.
- Ensure that you share with your colleagues any information that relates to people's choices, preferences and rights.
- Make sure that you discuss choices and preferences with people.
- Support people to maintain independence together with other rights if necessary.
- Never participate in or encourage discriminatory behaviour.

How to recognise your own prejudices

One of the hardest things to do is to acknowledge your own prejudices and how they affect what you do. Prejudices are a result of your own beliefs and values, and may often come into conflict with work situations. There is nothing wrong with having your own beliefs and values – everyone has them, and they are a vital part of making you the person you are. But you must be aware of them, and how they may affect what you do at work.

Think about the basic principles that apply in your life. For example:

- you may have a basic belief that people should always be honest. Then think about what that could mean for the way you work – might you find it hard to be pleasant to someone who you found had lied extensively?
- you may believe that abortion is wrong. Could you deal sympathetically with a woman who had had an abortion?
- you may have been brought up to take great care of disabled people and believe that they should be looked after and protected. How would you cope in an environment that encouraged disabled people to take risks and promoted their independence?

Activity 8

Values

1. Make a list of the things you believe in as values, such as honesty, caring about others and so on. Then make a second list of how they could affect your work.
2. Examine whether they do affect your work – you may need the views of a trusted colleague or your supervisor to help you with this.

This exercise is very hard, and it will take a long time to do. It is often better done over a period of time. As you become more aware of your own actions, you will notice how they have the potential to affect your work.

Recording the results of this exercise over a period of time may be useful when you are being assessed on this unit.

Exploring your own behaviour is never easy, and you need good support from either your supervisor or close friends to do it. You may be upset by what you find out about some of your attitudes, but knowing about them and acknowledging them is the first step to doing something about them.

Can you value the differences in all the people you meet?

As a support worker, it will be easier to make sure that you are practising effectively if you are confident that you have looked at your own practice and the attitudes that underpin it. Remember that you can ask for feedback from people you support and colleagues too, not only from your supervisor.

Beliefs and values of others

Once you are aware of your own beliefs and values, and have recognised how important they are, you must think about how to accept the beliefs and values of others. The people you work with are all different, so it is important to recognise and accept that diversity.

Respect for people

If you are going to make sure you always respond to people in a respectful way which ensures they are valued, you need to understand what happens when people are not valued or respected. It is also important that you recognise the ways in which good practice helps to protect people from discrimination and exclusion.

People should make choices about how they want to live their lives. For some people, choices may be about things like how they will spend their Direct Payments or Individual Budget and the people they will choose to employ. For others, choices may be more limited, as in some of the suggestions in Table 4. The ability to make

choices of any sort is an important part of exercising rights and being valued.

Support service	Choices
Personal hygiene	• Bath, shower or bed bath • Assistance or no assistance • Morning, afternoon or evening • Temperature of water • Toiletries
Food	• Menu • Dining table or tray • Timing • Assistance • In company or alone

Table 4: Examples of choices available in support services.

As we have seen, promoting equality and rights is supported by the practical steps you can take in day-to-day working activities to give people more choice and more opportunities to take decisions about their own lives. Much of this will depend on your work setting and the particular needs of the people you support. Respecting people and valuing them as individuals is always going to be an important factor in promoting self-esteem and therefore well-being.

Case study

Dealing with prejudice

Garth is a care worker in a residential setting for adults with disabilities. He is gay but had never discussed his sexual orientation at work and it was not mentioned at the time of his appointment. His sexual orientation only became known when the parents of one of the residents spotted him in a photograph of a gay pride event printed in a national newspaper.

Garth had always been a popular member of staff and had an excellent work record, with appraisals which showed his skills and abilities were developing and progressing. However, following the discovery that he was gay, the atmosphere in the setting began to change. Two of the residents complained about being cared for by someone who was gay and said they were

not prepared to have Garth provide them with any personal care. Both of these residents were young men in their late 20s and their action was supported by their parents. Comments and jokes at Garth's expense began to circulate within the setting, particularly when Garth was on duty.

Garth felt that he was being unfairly discriminated against and intended to obtain the support of his trade union.

1. What are Garth's rights in this situation?
2. What are the rights of the residents in this sort of situation? How do rights and responsibilities balance here?
3. How could this be approached by management?

Doing it well

Valuing diversity

- The wide range of different beliefs and values that you will come across are examples of the rich and diverse cultures of all parts of the world.
- Value each person as an individual. The best way to appreciate what others have to offer is to find out about them. Ask questions. People will usually be happy to tell you about themselves and their beliefs.
- Be open to hearing what others have to say – do not be so sure that your values and beliefs and the way you live are the only ways of doing things.

- Think about the great assets which have come to the UK from people moving here from other cultures, including music, food and entertainment, and different approaches to work, relaxation or medicine.
- Think about language. The words and expressions you use are important. Avoid using language that might suggest assumptions, stereotypes or discrimination about groups (see Table 5).

Area	Examples of negative language
Disability	Some words such as 'handicapped' can suggest the discriminatory assumption that disabled people are damaged versions of 'normal' people. In general, people prefer to be called 'disabled people' rather than 'people with a disability'. The term 'disabled people' is used to show that people are disabled by the environment and the society in which they live and by the barriers that prevent them from participating.
Race	Some words and phrases may be linked to the discriminatory idea that certain ethnic groups (white groups) are superior to others. For example, the phrase 'play the white man' means to play fair, and there are words that are associated with slavery in the past.
Age	Some words and phrases make fun of older people. Do not address an older person as 'pop' or 'granddad' unless you are invited to do so. Terms such as 'wrinklies' or 'crumblies' are offensive.
Gender	Some words and phrases are perceived as implying that women have a lower social status than men. Addressing women as 'dear', 'petal' or 'flower' may be understood as patronising or insulting. There is also the instance of always referring to people in high status roles as 'he' – often heard when talking about doctors or lawyers.
Sexuality	Gay and lesbian people often object to being catalogued using the biological terminology of 'heterosexual' and 'homosexual'. Use the terminology that people would apply to themselves.

Table 5: Language that might suggest assumptions, stereotypes or discrimination.

3. Be able to promote diversity, equality and inclusion

3.1 Actions that model inclusive practice

The National Occupational Standards defines active support as 'Working in a way that recognises that people have the right to take part in the activities and relationships of everyday life as independently as they can, and so supports them by helping only with what they really cannot manage to do for themselves'.

All the key aspects are included in this definition. It is a right of people to participate in life, not a privilege. Social care has made massive steps forward in moving away from a 'gift model', where social care support was in the control of the provider and people who wanted to use the support had to accept what was on offer. We now recognise that control must be in the hands of the people who are using the support services and they must be able to make choices about how, when and at what level they want to be active participants in society.

Participate and achieve

There are major changes taking place in all parts of the UK about how people gain access to and use social care support services. Services are being transformed and the **personalisation agenda** is putting choice and control firmly in the hands of the people who are using social care support services. The development of Direct Payments and Individual Budgets has given people choice and control over how, when and by whom their support services are delivered.

> ### Key term
>
> **Personalisation agenda** – the process of putting people in control of the services they receive by giving them control over how the budget for their support is spent

This is a new experience for many people who use social care support, who have often been unable to make choices about their lives because of the inflexible way that support services were delivered.

> ### Activity 9
>
> #### Limited choices
> Make a list of four or five people you support, and think about five normal activities of living over which they have limited or no choices. These activities could include:
> - which music to listen to
> - access to shops or facilities
> - meals
> - entertainment
> - daily relationships
> - bath/shower time
> - dependence on a carer.
>
> Think about how you would feel if your choices were limited in the same way.
> 1. How would you rank these issues in order of importance?
> 2. How has this choice changed since people were placed in control of their own services?

The impact of powerlessness

In order to understand the importance of the effects of placing people in control, you must understand what can happen to people who feel that they are powerless in relation to their day-to-day activities. How much we value ourselves – our self-esteem – is a result of a combination of factors, but a very important one is the extent of control, or power, we have over our lives.

Of course, many other factors influence our self-esteem, such as:

- the amount of encouragement and praise we have had from important people in our lives, such as parents, partners and friends
- whether we have positive and happy relationships with other people, such as family and work colleagues
- the amount of stimulation and satisfaction we get from our work – paid or unpaid.

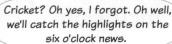

Come on Jack, the bus is ready – we're off to the Blue Skies Shopping Centre. We want to get there before the crowds.

Whose idea was this anyway? I wanted to watch the cricket.

Cricket? Oh yes, I forgot. Oh well, we'll catch the highlights on the six o'clock news.

How do you think this man is feeling as a result of what the care worker says to him?

People who are unable to exercise choice and control may very soon suffer lower self-esteem and lose confidence in their own abilities. Unfortunately, this means they may become convinced that they are unable to do many tasks for themselves, and that they need help in most areas of their day-to-day lives. This can result in people becoming dependent on others and less able to do things for themselves. Once this downward spiral has begun it can be difficult to stop, so it is far better to avoid the things that make it begin.

Reflect

Look at the illustration above. This situation is not untypical – there are more women in residential care than men, not everyone likes cricket and this care worker clearly had not bothered to remember Jack's needs.

1. What could she have done, even at the last moment, to support Jack?
2. How could this situation have been avoided in the first place?
3. Have you ever been guilty of the 'one size fits all' attitude towards the people you support?

Self-esteem has a major effect on people's health and well-being. Someone with a confident, positive view of themself, who believes that they have value and worth, is far more likely to be happy and healthy than

someone whose self-esteem is poor and whose confidence is low.

People who have a positive and confident outlook are far more likely to be interested and active in the world around them, while those lacking confidence and belief in their own abilities are more likely to be withdrawn and reluctant to try anything new. It is easy to see how this can affect someone's quality of life and reduce their overall health and well-being.

3.2 Supporting others to promote equality and rights

It used to be often the case that people were told the level of support they would receive and the days on which they would receive it. They may even have been told the times at which they would receive such help. In England, the White Paper 'Our health, our care, our say' in 2005 and the subsequent policy 'Putting people first' in 2007 set out to change these practices dramatically. Similar work is going on throughout the rest of the UK, but is at different stages of development.

Putting power and control in the hands of the people who use services was the key message. People are now encouraged to control their own support services through 'self-directed support', where the amount of budget available is agreed through self-assessment, but control over how it is spent is entirely in the hands of the

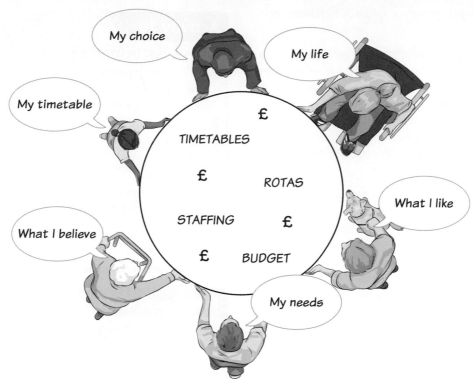

What is the most important priority here?

person. The concept of Individual Budgets is rather like Direct Payments, but without the requirement for a person to be an employer.

This places a whole new set of demands on organisations delivering services. The services that are commissioned must be flexible enough to meet the needs of people and to enable them to decide the outcomes they want to achieve and how they want to realise these. People are now able to choose when they want services and how and by whom they want them to be delivered.

Participation in positive outcomes

Outcomes are about results, so if someone decides that they would like to feel less isolated and have contact with more people, then your role is to work with them to find out what support they need in order to achieve that. It is not about you doing it for them, it is just about 'filling the gaps' in areas where people need some extra support.

For example, in order to feel less isolated, a person may decide to join a local singing group, join the pub quiz team or go to a lunch club. They may need support with particular aspects of the activity – possibly

transport, or support with eating or drinking – but the activity is something they do for themselves. With this active participation, support fills in the gaps, but does not take over.

It is not always easy for people to get used to controlling their own lives. Many have seen themselves as dependent on their support workers to organise appropriate daily activities to ensure their needs are met. Some older people may be disorientated, and people with dementia may feel unable to interpret and control their surroundings without appropriate support. However, as people experience taking control of their own services, they become more able to make their own choices about the help they need from social care support workers.

Achievements

Most achievements which give us pleasure are relatively small – for example, passing a driving test, finishing a run, clearing a garden, passing an exam, putting together a set of flat-pack bookshelves. Achievement does not have to mean reaching the North Pole or climbing Everest, or winning the World Cup. Achievements that are much smaller and closer to home are those that provide a sense of fulfilment for most people.

Supporting people to have a sense of achievement is a key part of supporting. It is tempting to undertake tasks for people you work with, because you are keen to support them and because you believe that you can make their lives easier. Often, however, you need to hold back from directly providing care or carrying out a task, and look for ways you can enable someone to undertake the task for themselves.

For example, it may be far easier, less painful and quicker for you to put on people's socks or stockings for them. However, this would reinforce the fact that they are no longer able to undertake such a simple task for themselves. Time spent in providing a sock aid, and showing them how to use it, means that they can put on their own clothing and have a sense of achievement and independence.

Sometimes you need to realise that achievement is relative to someone's circumstances. What may seem an insignificant act can actually be a huge achievement. Someone recovering from a stroke who succeeds in holding a piece of cutlery for the first time may be achieving something that has taken weeks or even months of physiotherapy, painful exercise and huge determination. The first, supported steps taken by someone who has had a hip replacement represent a massive achievement in overcoming pain, fear and anxiety.

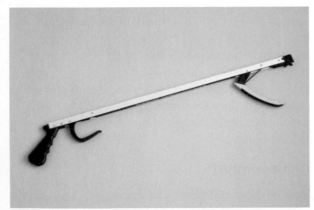

Can you see how equipment gives people control rather than being dependent?

Activity 10

Active participation

1. Think about a person with whom you work regularly, and identify a task or activity that is carried out for them.
2. Why are they unable to do this task themselves?
3. Draw up a plan of active participation to improve on this situation. This could involve enabling them to carry out the task themselves or to have more say in the way they are supported. If possible, include the person in writing this plan.

If you record this activity, it may be useful for the assessment of this unit.

Functional skills

English: Writing

Identify a task or activity that is done by others for somebody you work with. In writing, review why they are unable to carry out the task themselves. Devise an action plan whereby the person could carry out the task independently or with support from others. You may find it helpful to discuss this with them before formulating your plan. In the plan, set short-, medium- and long-term goals that will enable the person to work towards doing the task or activity independently. Ensure that the plan is laid out appropriately, that the language used is appropriate for the setting and that you have checked spelling, punctuation and grammar for accuracy.

What you need to do

Supporting people's rights by encouraging and recognising their achievements is one of the best parts of being a support worker. Sometimes you may need to spend time encouraging people in order for them to achieve a goal.

- You may need to steady someone's hand while they write a thank-you note, but it is far better to spend time doing this rather than write it for them.
- You could accompany someone who is overcoming agoraphobia on many trips round the supermarket, and eventually wait in the car park while they go in alone.

Why is recognition of achievements important?

- You could demonstrate to someone with poor **motor control** how to create pictures by painting with the fingers.

Make sure you always recognise and celebrate achievements. Think about it — whenever you achieve something, you usually want to share it with someone. Your enthusiasm and recognition are important to the people you support.

Supporting people to access information

Knowledge is power, and giving a person information **empowers** them to make choices and take control. Working as a professional support worker means that you will often work with people who are vulnerable and who have no confidence or power. Many people you work with will not have the information they need, because:

- they are unaware that the information exists
- they do not know how to find it

- there are physical barriers to accessing information
- there are emotional barriers to seeking information.

If you are going to provide people with access to information, there are certain basic rules you must observe.

Key terms

Motor control – the ability to control body movements. Gross motor control is the ability to make large movements, such as waving, and fine motor control is the ability to make more complex movements, such as holding a pencil

Empower – to enable people who had previously depended on others to make decisions and take control of their own lives. People can be empowered through finding access to information and knowledge, or through growing and developing confidence in their own abilities

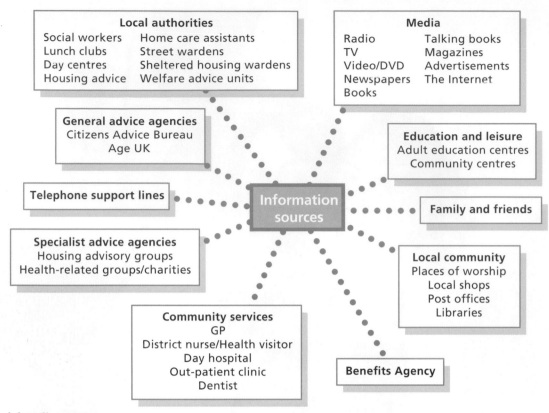

Local authorities
Social workers   Home care assistants
Lunch clubs   Street wardens
Day centres   Sheltered housing wardens
Housing advice   Welfare advice units

Media
Radio   Talking books
TV   Magazines
Video/DVD   Advertisements
Newspapers   The Internet
Books

General advice agencies
Citizens Advice Bureau
Age UK

Education and leisure
Adult education centres
Community centres

Telephone support lines

Information sources

Family and friends

Specialist advice agencies
Housing advisory groups
Health-related groups/charities

Local community
Places of worship
Local shops
Post offices
Libraries

Community services
GP
District nurse/Health visitor
Day hospital
Out-patient clinic
Dentist

Benefits Agency

Information sources.

Doing it well

Accessing information

- Make sure that your information access points are up to date. You may have to contact quite a few places to make sure you have the most accurate information possible. Check the dates on any leaflets you have and contact the producer to see whether they have been replaced.
- Go to the most direct source, wherever possible. For example, for information about benefits, contact the DWP (Department for Work and Pensions).
- Advice services such as the Citizens Advice Bureau are excellent and provide a wide range of information. Make use also of the specialist organisations such as Age UK or Scope.
- Check whether the information you are providing has local, regional and national elements. For instance, if you are providing information about Age UK's services for older people, it is important to provide the local as well as national contact points.

- The information you provide must be in a format that the person it is for can use. For example, there is little value in providing an ordinary leaflet to a person with impaired vision. Obtain a large-print, audio or Braille version depending on the way in which the person prefers to receive information.
- Consider the language used and provide information in a language that the person can easily understand. Information is of no value if it is misunderstood.
- Provide access to information at an appropriate time when the person can make use of it. For example, a man who has just had a leg amputated, following an accident, will not be ready to receive information about the latest design in wheelchairs or how to join in sports for disabled people. He may be interested in 12 months' time, but initially he is going to need information about support groups, and practical information such as how prosthetic limbs work, and how to manage to use the toilet.

3.3 Describe how to challenge discrimination in a way that promotes change

There may be occasions when you have identified a person's rights and given them access to the information needed. However, they may not be able to exercise those rights effectively. There can be many reasons why people miss out on their rights, and these are:

- their rights may be infringed by someone else
- there may be physical barriers
- there may be emotional barriers.

Advocates

When you need to support people to maintain a right to choice, control and independence, it may be important to involve an outside **advocate**. An advocate is someone who argues a case for another person. An advocate tries to understand the person's perspective and argues on their behalf. Your organisation may have procedures and advice to assist you in gaining the services of people who will act as advocates for people.

> **Key term**
>
> **Advocate** – a person responsible for acting and speaking on behalf of somebody who is unable to do so.

You may also need to defend people's rights in a more informal way during your normal work. For example, people have a right to privacy, and you may need to act to deal with someone who constantly infringes upon that by discussing other people's circumstances in public. You will have to balance the rights of one person against another, and decide whose rights are being infringed. You may decide that a right to privacy is more important than a right to free speech.

> **Reflect**
>
> A person's right to rest may be infringed by someone who shouts all night. How would you balance the rights of one person not to be disturbed against the rights of another not to be given medication that only benefits others?

Overall, the key to active participation is ensuring that you:

- do as much as possible to support only the parts of people's lives that they really cannot manage for themselves
- provide support that will encourage them to take control and make decisions that enable the maximum possible participation in every aspect of their lives.

Case study

The right to make choices

Mrs Sullivan lives alone on just her state pension. She has never claimed any pension credit, although there is no doubt she would be entitled to it. She struggles to survive on her pension and, by the time she has paid all her bills and fed the cat, there is little left for herself. She eats very little and is reluctant to turn the heating on. Despite being given all the relevant information by her home care assistant, Mrs Sullivan will not claim any further benefits. She always says, 'I shall be fine. There are others worse off than me – let it go to them.'

1. What are Mrs Sullivan's rights?
2. Should action be taken on her behalf?
3. Would the situation be different if she had a son with a learning disability who lived with her? Would her rights and responsibilities still be the same?
4. What would your responsibilities be if you were a support worker for Mrs Sullivan?

Getting ready for assessment

LO1

This learning outcome requires you to show that you understand what is meant by diversity, equality and inclusion. You may be asked to prepare an assignment or perhaps to make a presentation. Be sure that you use clear explanations, using words and phrases like 'so', 'therefore', 'because', 'in order to' and 'as a result of', to show that you understand the concepts you are being asked to explain. You are also asked or describe the effects of discrimination. A description needs to be more than a list, so you must make sure that you give plenty of details about how discrimination can affect people.

LO2

This is about how you are able to work with people and interact with them in a way that shows respect for them as individuals. You may need to show your assessor how you ensure that you ask people what they want rather than making assumptions, that you always record information about people's culture, beliefs and preferences, and that you speak to people in a respectful way. You will also need to show that you have thought about any prejudices of your own and considered how they may affect your work. An assessor may observe you working with people and you may also have to answer questions about why you did things in a particular way.

Further reading and research

Providing care for vulnerable people can be challenging and difficult, while at the same time rewarding. The more support you receive and information you gather, the better equipped you will be to cope with the demands and responsibility.

- www.ageuk.org.uk (Age UK)
- www.citizensadvice.org.uk (Citizens Advice Bureau)
- www.crb.gov.uk (Criminal Records Bureau)
- www.cqc.org.uk (Care Quality Commission – guidance related to the social care services you are researching)
- www.dh.gov.uk (Department of Health, including No Secrets – Guidance on Developing and Implementing Multi-Agency Policies and Procedures to Protect Vulnerable Adults from Abuse)
- www.dwp.gov.uk (Department for Work and Pensions)
- www.elderabuse.org.uk (Action on Elder Abuse)
- www.everychildmatters.gov.uk (Working Together to Safeguard Children – Every Child Matters)
- www.gscc.org.uk (General Social Care Council – Codes of Practice)
- www.justice.gov.uk (Ministry of Justice)
- www.nspcc.org.uk (National Society for the Prevention of Cruelty to Children)
- www.pcaw.co.uk (Public Concern at Work, tel: 020 7404 6609)
- www.scope.org.uk (Scope)
- www.unison.org.uk (Unison – guides to POVA (Protecting of Vulnerable Adults) and PoCA (Protection of Children Act), including a leaflet called 'Reported')
- www.valuingpeople.gov.uk (Valuing People: A New Strategy for Learning Disability in the 21st Century)
- Arroba, T. and Ball, L. (2001) *Staying Sane; Managing the Stress of Caring*, Age Concern
- Maclean, S. and Maclean, I. (2001) *Social Care and the Law*, Kirwin Maclean Associates
- Maclean, S. and Maclean, I. (2005) *Supporting You: Supporting Others: Health and Social Care* (Level 3), Kirwin Maclean
- Moore, R. and Maclean, I. (2004) *Cultural Sensitivity in Social and Health Care*, Kirwin Maclean

Unit SHC 34

Principles for implementing duty of care in health, social care or children's and young people's settings

In this unit you will learn about your responsibilities as a professional care and support worker. You will also learn how to get the balance right between exercising your professional responsibilities and people's rights to make choices and decisions about their own lives. It is a small unit, but understanding your duty of care is a big matter and it is essential for your own professional development that you understand the implications in your own work setting.

In this unit you will learn about:

■ how duty of care contributes to safe practice

■ how to address conflicts or dilemmas that may arise between an individual's rights and the duty of care

■ how to respond to complaints.

1. Understand how duty of care contributes to safe practice

1.1 What it means to have a duty of care in your work role

A duty of care is the requirement that all health and social care professionals, and organisations providing health and care services, must put the interests of the people who use their services first. They also have to do everything in their power to keep people safe from harm.

Your duty of care underpins everything that you do; it is what underlies the Codes of Practice and it should be built into your practice on a day-to-day level. Exercising your duty of care is also a legal requirement, and would be tested in court in the event of a case of negligence or malpractice.

People have a right to expect that when a professional is providing support, they will be kept safe and not be neglected or exposed to any unnecessary **risks**. The expression is that we 'owe' a duty of care to the people we work with. 'Owe' is a useful word to describe the nature of the duty of care because it is just like a debt. It is something that you must pay as a part of choosing to become a professional in the field of social care.

> **Key term**
>
> **Risk** – the likelihood of a hazard's potential being realised (a hazard is anything that has the potential to cause harm)

You always have a duty of care, even when out and about.

Having a duty of care towards the people you work with is not unique to social care; all professions who work with people have a duty of care. This includes doctors, teachers, nurses, midwives and many others.

Thinking about the duty of care that you owe to people is helpful when you are planning your work. It makes you consider whether what you were planning to do is in the best interests of the person you are working with. This is not only about physical risks; you also have a duty of care to treat people with dignity and respect.

Activity 1

Duty of care scenarios

Consider the following scenarios. What is your duty of care in each situation?

- You help someone to take a bath.
- You accompany someone on a shopping trip.
- You support someone to complete their benefit claim forms.
- You pass on a message to someone's relative.
- You are on duty in a residential setting when the fire alarm goes off.
- You organise a theatre trip for a group of people.

Make notes about your duty of care in each situation. You will probably find that there is more than one aspect that you need to cover.

Functional skills

Mathematics: Add, multiply and divide whole numbers

Plan a trip for the people you support. Consider:

- transport costs
- insurance costs
- the cost of the venue, for example, the theatre
- the cost of carers.

Work out the costs under headings for eight people. Then work out the total cost for the whole trip. Show all your calculations.

Each of the regulators in the UK countries requires that professionals working in social care exercise a duty of care towards everyone for whom they work. All four of the regulators have agreed a joint Code of Practice that sets out very clearly the expectation that each person who undertakes a role as a professional in social care will follow the Code of Practice and will be held to account by the regulator if they fail to do so. The key section of the Code of Practice is section 3:

As a social care worker you must promote the independence of service users while protecting them as far as possible from danger or harm. This includes:

3.1 promoting the independence of service users and assisting them to understand and exercise their rights

3.2 using established processes and procedures to challenge and report dangerous, abusive, discriminatory or exploitative behaviour and practice

3.3 following practice and procedures designed to keep you and other people safe from violent and abusive behaviour at work

3.4 bringing to the attention of your employer or the appropriate authority resource or operational difficulties that might get in the way of the delivery of safe care

3.5 informing your employer or an appropriate authority where the practice of colleagues may be unsafe or adversely affecting standards of care

3.6 complying with employers' health and safety policies including those relating to substance abuse

3.7 helping service users and carers to make complaints, taking complaints seriously and responding to them or passing them to the appropriate person

3.8 recognising and using responsibly the power that comes from your work with service users and carers.

Each of the subsections identifies the behaviours that are expected of professionals. This is not just a set of ideas that sound like a good thing. This is the basis on which your professional conduct will be judged.

If there were to be a problem, or a complaint or an accident of some sort, then your behaviour would be considered using this Code of Practice as a benchmark. Make sure that you read and understand what you need to think about when you are working. Can you say that you have always followed the Code of Practice in your day-to-day work? Do you think that you will now?

1.2 How duty of care contributes to the safeguarding or protection of individuals

Knowing that you must exercise your duty of care towards everyone you work with provides a clear guide to how you should behave, and how you must consider those you work with. Following a Code of Practice and thinking about your duty of care means that your practice will be safer because you will stop to think if you are working in the best interests of the person you are supporting and if you are keeping them from harm.

The concept of safeguarding, whether it is children or vulnerable adults, is broader than protection. Safeguarding is also about keeping children or vulnerable adults safe from any sort of harm, such as illness, abuse or injury. This means all agencies and families working together and taking responsibility for the safety of children and vulnerable adults, whether it is by promoting health, preventing accidents or protecting children or vulnerable adults who have been abused.

Protection is about what you do when someone has been harmed, or is at imminent risk of harm. Your response in order to provide protection is of vital importance and this subject is covered in more detail in Unit HSC 024. Your duty of care is closely linked to protection and safeguarding, because you have a responsibility to keep people safe from harm.

2. Know how to address conflicts or dilemmas that may arise between an individual's rights and the duty of care

2.1 Potential conflicts or dilemmas between the duty of care and an individual's rights

Exercising a duty of care is not about wrapping people in cotton wool or preventing them from taking any risks. Just participating in everyday life involves risks – for example, crossing the road is a risky business. There has to be a balance and you need to consider risks.

You do have a duty of care for the people you support, but they also have the right to make their own choices and to reach decisions about actions they want to take. Sometimes these two areas may present you with a dilemma or a conflict, and how it is resolved depends to a large extent on the legal position of the person you are supporting.

The vast majority of people that you work with will be in a position to take their own decisions about what they do in their lives. In order to exercise your duty of care, you must ensure that any decisions and choices people make are based on understanding the consequences and potential risks of what they want to do. Your role is not to prevent people from doing what they want, but making sure that they know the possible results.

This can result in some very finely balanced decisions, especially where there are concerns about someone's **capacity** to understand the possible risks and consequences from their actions. The question of capacity to make decisions is highly complex and you must consider it carefully. It is very easy to make the assumption that because someone has dementia, a learning disability or a long-term mental health problem, for example, they lack the capacity to make decisions about important issues affecting their own life.

If you think about it, the capacity to make a decision can often depend on how much help we have. For example, if a government minister has to choose between two different highly advanced fighter aircraft to commission for the RAF, they will ask for help from:

- experts across the aviation industry
- experienced civil servants from the relevant departments
- the pilots and senior officers who are going to use the aircraft.

The minister will make the final decision – but lacks the capacity to make the decision alone, and so uses lots of help and support.

Similarly, most of us, if asked to make a choice between two different types of central heating system, would need to ask for help from experts before deciding – we would lack the capacity to make the decision without advice and help.

So remember – capacity is relative to what has to be decided and depends on the circumstances.

Mental Capacity Act 2005

The Mental Capacity Act sets out a framework for supporting people to make decisions, and lays out the ways in which people can be supported. The Act is underpinned by five key principles, which are:

1. a presumption of capacity – every adult has the right to make their own decisions and must be assumed to have capacity to do so unless it is proved otherwise
2. the right for people to be supported to make their own decisions – people must be given all appropriate help before anyone concludes that a person cannot make their own decisions

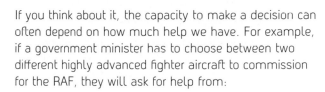

Key term

Capacity – the necessary requirements to do, or achieve, something

3. that people must retain the right to make what might be seen as eccentric or unwise decisions

4. best interests – anything done for or on behalf of people without capacity must be in their best interests

5. least restrictive intervention – anything done for or on behalf of people without capacity should be the least restrictive of their basic rights and freedoms.

The Act sets out clearly how to establish if someone is incapable of making a decision. The 'incapacity test' is only in relation to a particular decision. No one can be deemed 'incapable' in general simply because of a medical condition or diagnosis. The Act introduces a new criminal offence of ill treatment or neglect of a person who lacks capacity. A person found guilty of such an offence may be liable to imprisonment for a term of up to five years.

Reflect

Think about decisions you have had to make. Which ones have you needed help or advice on before making your decision?

This is obviously risky, but other activities can carry risks too.

Case studies

Backpacking in Australia

Kevin is 24. He has a learning disability and has always been protected by his parents. He wants to go backpacking around Australia with a friend whom he has met at the restaurant where he works. His parents are opposed to it, but his brother and sister are supportive.

1. What are the issues for you as Kevin's support worker?
2. What should you do?
3. What is your duty of care here?
4. Can anything be done to stop Kevin? Should it be?

Stopping medication

George has a long history of schizophrenia. He has been living in the community for over ten years and is doing well with regular medication. He has now decided that he does not want to continue with his medication, because he has read that putting chemicals into your body may be harmful.

1. What is your duty of care here?
2. Who else may have a duty of care?
3. What can you do?

Buying a scooter

Olga is 75 years old. She has severe osteoarthritis, poor vision and uses a hearing aid. She has recently decided to purchase a mobility scooter in order to be able to get out more. You are concerned about her safety and the safety of others if she takes the scooter out on the road.

1. What can you do?
2. What is your duty of care?

The three scenarios in the case studies opposite are very different and you can see that your role would be very different in each of the circumstances. They are each quite extreme situations, but they illustrate some of the difficulties and dilemmas that you may face.

The underlying principle is that you can give people information so that they understand the potential risks and consequences of their actions, but, apart from exceptional circumstances, you cannot stop people from doing something they have decided to do.

There are some circumstances in which you can and should take action, and these are if someone is planning to do something that:

- is criminal or illegal
- will deliberately harm them
- represents a serious risk to others.

In any of these circumstances, you must seek advice from your manager quickly.

2.2 Managing risks associated with conflicts or dilemmas between an individual's rights and the duty of care

The purpose of risk assessment is not to remove risks, but to take reasonable steps to reduce them. The process involves looking at the risk, and considering what can be done to make it less likely that the risk will develop into a reality. Assessing risks is always about achieving a reasonable balance and reducing the potential impact of activities.

Risk	Protecting factor
Kevin will get lost in Australia	He is going with a trusted friend
George will develop acute symptoms if he does not take his medication	Increase monitoring visits so that he is seen every day
Olga will fall off her scooter	She is accompanied for the first few times she uses it

Table 1: Risks and protecting factors.

None of the protecting factors in Table 1 make the risk go away, but they do reduce the chances of it becoming a reality. An important part of promoting rights, choice and control is that people are encouraged to take the risks that come with day-to-day living, but have an understanding of the potential consequences and have taken all possible steps to reduce the possibility of harm to themselves or others.

The way in which you can exercise your duty of care in a risky situation is not to take steps to stop someone doing what they want, but to assess the risks carefully and to look at the protecting factors. You may need to think about what other protecting factors you can put in place so that the risk is managed effectively. For example, thinking about the case studies, you could accompany Olga when she uses her scooter or increase monitoring visits to George.

2.3 Where to get additional support and advice about conflicts and dilemmas

Your first port of call if you are unsure about what to do and if you are exercising your duty of care is to consult your manager. They should be able to advise you about the best approaches to take.

You could also contact your Regulator for advice about how to implement the Code of Practice. All of the Regulators produce guidance about how to implement the Code of Practice. These guidance documents can be very helpful in looking at the implications for day-to-day work.

If you are a member of a professional association or a trade union, they will also be able to offer advice about any uncertainties you have about whether you are exercising a duty of care towards the people you support effectively.

Doing it well

Exercising your duty of care
- Remember that this is not about stopping people from doing what they want.
- Make sure people have information about risks.
- Assess risks.
- Look at protecting factors and how they can be strengthened.
- Ask for advice if you are unsure.

3. Know how to respond to complaints

3.1 How to respond to complaints

Complaints to an organisation are an important part of the monitoring process and they should be considered as part of every review of service provision. If everyone simply put up with poor service and no one complained, they would never be aware of where the service needs improvement. Similarly, if complaints are not responded to appropriately, services will never improve.

All service providers or organisations commissioning services will have a system for complaints. There will be clear information about how and to whom a complaint should be made, and timescales for it to be dealt with.

Most important, though, is what happens to complaints after they have been resolved with the people concerned. An effective complaints system will analyse all complaints and feed them into service reviews. This way management can identify:

- poor-quality services
- services being delivered in the wrong way or place
- services that are needed but not currently provided.

This helps with service planning and gives organisations the opportunity to identify changes and new developments that are needed.

3.2 The main points of agreed procedures for handling complaints

Your organisation should have a complaints policy. This should be publicised and information on it should be readily available in the form of leaflets, posters and a complaints form, both web-based and printed. All public service organisations are required to have a complaints procedure and to make the procedure readily available for people to use. Part of your role may be to support people in making complaints or in handling complaints made to you. You may support people:

- directly, by supporting them in following the complaints procedure
- indirectly, by making sure that they are aware of the complaints procedure and are able to follow it.

Case study

Complaints about a daycare facility

Julie is an Assistant Director with responsibility for commissioning services for older people. She has recently been receiving a series of complaints about a particular daycare facility. The complaints are different: one or two have been about lateness of transport, a couple about the quality of the food and most recently one about the attitude of staff. This has made Julie decide to ask the Service Manager to carry out a review of the facility and to look at what is going wrong. Seen separately, these few isolated complaints may have gone unnoticed, but when put together, they suggest a provision that is not working as it should.

1. Why do you think these complaints suggest that the daycare facility is not working as it should?
2. Which complaints are the most serious?

Functional skills

English: Writing

You are an assistant director in Social Services and have received a number of complaints about a daycare facility in your area. Write a letter to the manager to find out what her opinions are and to arrange a meeting to discuss solutions. The points to raise in the letter are:
- lateness of transport
- the quality of food
- attitude of staff
- possible dates of meeting.

Remember to check the letter for layout, use of language and the accuracy of spelling, punctuation and grammar.

Meeting the needs of carers

Sahid is Operations Director in a large voluntary organisation. Lately he has been receiving complaints that the outreach support team will not work in the evenings or at weekends. Sahid understands this as the team are employed to provide in-home, short-term care for a few hours on Monday to Friday from nine till five. However, he identifies that the complaints are showing the need for a rethink of the service, so that carers can get out and have a social life. He decides to sit down with his carers' panel and staff from the outreach support team to work out how the service can better meet the needs of carers.

1. What consequences do you think there might be to the outreach support team not being available in the evenings or at weekends?
2. Can you think of any ways in which the service might be adapted to meet the needs of the carers better?

You also need to learn to respond openly and appropriately to any comments or complaints you receive from people about their support. Most complaints procedures will involve an informal stage, where complaints are discussed before they become more formal issues.

If a complaint is made to you, then you should:

- make sure the person understands how to use the complaints procedure
- explain to them how it works and when they can expect to receive a response
- offer support in following the complaints procedure if necessary
- advise your manager that the complaint is being made.

Do not:

- attempt to resolve complaints yourself
- discuss the complaint with the person it is about
- discourage people from making complaints
- promise that you will 'sort it out'
- discuss the complaint with colleagues or anyone other than your manager.

Your duty of care is wide ranging and it forms the basis of your professional role. As a social care worker, you have a position of great responsibility for some of the most vulnerable people in society. Your responsibility to exercise a duty of care is their protection.

Legislation

- Mental Capacity Act 2005

Further reading and research

- www.gscc.org.uk (General Social Care Council – Codes of Practice)

Getting ready for assessment

LO1

This learning outcome requires that you explain your understanding of the duty of care. You may be asked to prepare an assignment or you may have to do a presentation. This is mainly about how the duty of care helps to make practice safer and ensures that people's safety is always considered. You will need to be able to give examples of the sort of situations where your duty of care is important and show how the duty of care is linked to safeguarding people from harm. Remember that as this requires you to explain, you must use words and phrases such as 'because', 'so that', 'in order to' and 'as the result of', to show that you have a clear understanding.

Unit HSC 024

Principles of safeguarding and protection in health and social care

In this unit you will look at some of the most difficult issues that support workers face. Working in social care means coming to terms with the fact that some people will be subjected to abuse by those who are supposed to care for them. Knowing what you are looking for, and how to recognise it and how to respond, is the best possible contribution to protecting people from harm and abuse. You need to know how society handles abuse, how to recognise it, and what to do about it.

If you can learn always to think about the risks, always to be alert to potentially abusive situations and always to listen and believe when you are told of harm and abuse, then you will provide the best possible protection for people you support.

In this unit you will learn about:

- how to recognise signs of abuse
- how to respond to suspected or alleged abuse
- the national and local context of safeguarding and protection from abuse
- ways to reduce the likelihood of abuse
- how to recognise and report unsafe practices.

1. Know how to recognise signs of abuse

Recognising risks

Many different factors will place people at risk, and it will not always be possible for you to protect everyone from everything, neither is it desirable. There are many situations in which you will have to consider the rights of someone to place themselves in potential danger in order to take control over their own lives. This does not necessarily mean that every disabled person you work with will want to take up wheelchair rock climbing, but the element of risk can equally apply to a vulnerable adult with deteriorating memory function who wants to go out alone on a shopping trip. There is undoubtedly a significant risk, but this needs to be balanced against the importance of empowerment, dignity and control.

There are vital differences between danger, harm and abuse. You need to know how each relates to what you do.

- **Danger** is about the possibility or risk of abuse.
- **Harm** is about the results and consequences of abuse.

Have you thought about the balance between protection and restriction?

Whether your job role means that you are responsible only for your own work, or whether you have some responsibility for the work of colleagues, you will need to give some thought to your role in protection. There are also likely to be differences depending on your working environment, for example, the dangers and risks presented in somebody's home will be different from those in a residential or health care setting. Clearly, the three concepts of abuse, danger and harm are interlinked; someone who is abused may be in danger and will be suffering harm — but not everyone who is exposed to danger is being abused, and people can be harmed through accident or carelessness rather than deliberate abuse.

Abusive situations

Abuse may happen just once, or it can be ongoing — either situation should be viewed just as seriously. If abuse has happened once, the risks of it happening again are far higher. It may be physical, sexual or emotional abuse. Deliberate neglect or a failure to act is also abuse, as is a vulnerable person persuaded to enter into a financial arrangement, or a sexual act to which they have not given or cannot give informed consent.

A wide range of people, including family members, friends, professional staff, care workers, volunteers or other people, may abuse vulnerable adults.

Abuse may take place within the person's own home, nursing, residential or day care facilities or hospitals. Incidents of abuse can be either to one person or to a group of people at a time. Some instances of abuse will constitute a criminal offence — for example, assault, rape, theft or fraud. This can then be prosecuted, but not all abuse falls into this category.

1.1 Different types of abuse

Abuse can take many forms. These are usually classified under five main headings:

- physical
- sexual
- psychological
- financial
- institutional.

1.2 Signs and symptoms of abuse

Warning signs of harm or abuse

The following are indications for which you should consider harm or abuse as a possible cause. However, each of them can be the result of something other than abuse – so they are far from being foolproof evidence, but they do act as pointers to make you look at the option of abuse being the answer. You and your colleagues will need to use other skills, such as observation and communication with other professionals, in order to build up a complete picture.

Different types of abuse have different remedies in law, and some have no legal remedies, but are dealt with through other policies, procedures and guidelines.

Signs of possible abuse in adults

Abuse can often show as physical effects and symptoms. These are likely to be accompanied by emotional signs and changes in behaviour, but this is not always the case.

Any behaviour changes could indicate that the person is a victim of some form of abuse, but remember that they are only an indicator and will need to be linked to other factors to arrive at a complete picture.

Physical abuse

Physical abuse includes:

- hitting
- slapping
- pushing
- pinching
- force feeding
- kicking
- burning
- scalding
- misuse of medication or restraint
- catheterisation for the convenience of staff
- inappropriate sanctions
- a carer causing illness or injury to someone in order to gain attention for themselves (this might be associated with a condition called fabricated and induced illness or FII)
- refusing access to toilet facilities
- leaving people in wet or soiled clothing or bedding.

Potential indicators of physical abuse include the following. Any of these factors are not evidence of abuse – they are a warning indicator only.

- Multiple bruising or finger marks (especially in well-protected areas such as eye sockets, inner arms or thighs).
- Fractures – especially twisting fractures – and dislocations – especially when accompanied with bruising or finger marks.
- Scratches or cuts.
- Pressure ulcers and sores or rashes from wet bedding/clothing.
- Black eyes or bruised ears.
- Welt marks – especially on the back or buttocks.
- Scalds or cigarette burns.
- A history of unexplained minor falls or injuries or a history of accidental overdoses/poisonings.
- Explanations not consistent with the injuries.
- Clinical interventions without any clear benefit to the person.
- Deterioration of health without obvious cause.
- Loss of weight.
- Inappropriate, inadequate or soiled clothing.
- Withdrawal or mood changes.
- Carer's resistance to allowing people to visit.
- Reluctance by the vulnerable adult to be alone with the alleged abuser.

Sexual abuse

Sexual abuse, whether of adults or children, can also involve abuse of a position of power. Children can never be considered to give informed consent to any sexual activity of any description. For some adults, informed consent is not possible because of a limited capacity to understand its meaning. In the case of other adults, consent may not be given and the sexual activity is either forced on someone against their will or the person is tricked or bribed into it.

Sexual activity is abusive when informed consent is not freely given. This might involve one person using services who is abusing another more vulnerable person. It is important to recognise the difference between the freely consenting sexual activity of adults who also happen to be supported by social care services, and those situations where abuse is taking place because someone is exploiting their position of relative power. The key is the capacity to give informed consent to any sexual activity.

Sexual abuse includes:

- rape and sexual assault
- masturbation
- indecent exposure
- penetration or attempted penetration of intimate areas
- sexual harassment
- involving a vulnerable adult in pornography
- enforced witnessing of sexual acts or sexual media
- participation in sexual acts to which the vulnerable adult has not consented, or could not consent, or was pressured into consenting.

Physical signs	Behavioural signs
• Bruises, scratches, burns or bite marks on the body	• Provocative sexual behaviour, promiscuity
• Scratches, abrasions or persistent infections in the anal/genital regions	• Prostitution
	• Sexual abuse of others
• Pregnancy	• Self-injury, self-destructive behaviour including alcohol and drug abuse, repeated suicide attempts
• Recurrent genital or urinary infections	• Behaviour that invites exploitation and further physical/sexual abuse
• Blood or marks on underwear	• Disappearing from home environment
• Abdominal pain with no diagnosable cause	• Aggression, anxiety, tearfulness
	• Reluctance by the vulnerable adult to be alone with the alleged abuser
	• Frequent masturbation
	• Refusal to undress for activities such as swimming/bathing

Table 1: Potential indicators of sexual abuse (any of these factors are not evidence of abuse — they are a warning indicator only).

Psychological abuse

All forms of abuse also have an element of psychological abuse. Any situation which means that a person becomes a victim of abuse at the hands of someone they trusted is, inevitably, going to cause emotional distress. However, some abuse is purely psychological — there are no physical, sexual or financial elements involved.

Psychological abuse includes:

- emotional abuse
- bullying
- threats of harm or abandonment
- ignoring
- shouting
- swearing
- deprivation of contact with others
- humiliation
- blaming
- controlling
- intimidation
- coercion
- harassment
- verbal abuse
- deprivation of privacy or dignity
- lack of mental stimulation.

Potential indicators of psychological abuse include the following. Any of these factors are not evidence of abuse — they are a warning indicator only.

- Carer seeming to ignore the vulnerable person's presence and needs.
- Reports from neighbours of shouting, screaming, swearing.
- Reluctance by the vulnerable adult to be alone with the alleged abuser.
- Cared-for person fearful of raised voices, distressed if they feel they may be 'in trouble'.
- A culture of teasing or taunting which is causing distress and humiliation.
- Referring to the cared-for person in a derogatory way.
- No valuing of basic human rights, for example, choice, opinion, privacy and dignity.
- Cared-for person being treated like a child — infantilisation.

Financial abuse

Many adults are very vulnerable to financial abuse, particularly those who may have a limited understanding of money matters. Financial abuse, like all other forms of abuse, can be inflicted by family members and even friends as well as care workers or informal carers, and can take a range of forms.

Financial or material abuse includes:

- theft
- fraud
- exploitation
- pressure in connection with wills, property, inheritance or financial transactions
- the misuse or misappropriation of property, possessions or benefits.

What consequences do you think financial abuse could have?

Potential indicators of financial abuse include the following. Any of these factors are not evidence of abuse — they are a warning indicator only.

- People not being allowed to manage their own financial affairs.
- No information being given where consent has been given to act.
- Family unwilling to pay, from person's funds, for services, although person has sufficient money.
- Person not made aware of financial matters.
- Enduring power of attorney set up without consulting a doctor where the vulnerable adult is already confused.
- Other people moving into person's property.

- Family regularly asking for money from personal allowance.
- Very few or no personal possessions.
- Unusual and unexplained change in spending pattern.
- Unexplained shortage of money despite a seemingly adequate income.
- Unexplained disappearance of personal possessions or property.
- Sudden changing of a will.

Neglect

Neglect happens when care is not given and a person suffers as a result. There are broadly two different types of neglect: self-neglect and neglect by others.

Self-neglect is different from abuse by others, but it is still a situation that can place people at risk of harm and, potentially, place them in danger. People neglect their own care for a range of reasons; the commonest are:

- increasing infirmity
- physical illness or disability
- memory and concentration problems
- sensory loss or difficulty
- mental illness and mental health problems
- learning difficulties/disabilities
- alcohol and drug misuse problems
- a different set of priorities and perspectives.

However, what may appear as self-neglect may be an informed lifestyle choice, and it is important that you do not attempt to impose your standards and values on people who have made a decision to live in a particular way. Decisions in these situations are very difficult and a balance must be achieved between safeguarding and protecting people who are vulnerable, and making sure that you are not removing people's ability to choose to live as they wish. Obviously, where someone has a deteriorating mental or physical condition, then you can, and should, act in order to protect them. A deliberate choice to follow a particular way of living is an entirely different matter.

Neglect by others occurs when either a support worker or a family or friend carer fails to meet someone's support needs. Neglect can happen because those responsible for providing the support do not realise its importance, or because they cannot be bothered, or choose not, to provide it. As the result of neglect, people can become ill, hungry, cold, dirty, injured or deprived of their rights. Neglecting someone you are supposed to be supporting can result from failing to undertake support services, for example:

- not providing adequate food
- not providing assistance with eating food if necessary
- not ensuring that someone receives support with personal care
- not ensuring that someone is adequately clothed
- leaving someone alone
- not supporting someone with mobility or communication needs
- failing to maintain a clean and hygienic living environment
- failing to obtain necessary medical/health-care support
- not supporting social contacts
- not taking steps to provide a safe and secure environment.

In some social care situations, support workers may fail to provide some support services because they have not been trained, or because they work in a setting where the emphasis is on cost saving rather than service provision. In these circumstances it becomes a form of institutional abuse. Unfortunately, there have been residential care homes and NHS trusts where people have been found to be suffering from malnutrition as the result of such neglect. Individual workers who are deliberately neglecting people in spite of receiving training and working in a quality caring environment are, fortunately, likely to be spotted very quickly by colleagues and supervisors.

However, family and friend carers are in different circumstances, often facing huge pressures and difficulties. Some may be caring for a relative reluctantly because they feel they have no choice; others may be barely coping with their own lives and may find caring for someone else a burden they are unable to bear. Regardless of the many possible reasons for the difficulties that can result in neglect, it is essential that any suspicions or concerns are investigated and followed up so that help can be offered and additional support provided if necessary.

As with self-neglect, it is important that lifestyle decisions made by people and their carers are respected. Full discussions should take place with people and their carers where there are concerns about possible neglect. Neglect and failure to care includes:

- ignoring medical or physical care needs
- failure to provide access to appropriate health, social care or educational services

- withholding of the necessities of life, such as medication, adequate nutrition and heating.

Potential indicators of neglect include the following. Any of these factors are not evidence of abuse – they are a warning indicator only.

- Medical condition deteriorating unexpectedly or not improving as expected.
- Hypothermia or person cold or dressed inadequately.
- Cared-for person is hungry.
- Living environment is dirty and unhygienic.
- Risks and hazards in the living environment are not dealt with.
- Person has sores and skin rashes.
- Unexplained loss of weight.
- Clothes or body dirty and smelly.
- Reluctance by the vulnerable adult to be alone with the alleged abuser.
- Delays in seeking medical attention.

Discriminatory abuse

Discriminatory abuse includes:

- racist and sexist abuse
- abuse based on a person's disability
- harassment, slurs or similar treatment
- abuse related to age, gender or sexual orientation
- abuse directed towards religion.

It is also the case that discriminatory abuse can underpin other forms of abuse – particularly physical or psychological abuse.

Potential indicators of discriminatory abuse include the following. Any of these factors are not evidence of abuse – they are a warning indicator only.

- Exclusion from activities based on inadequate justifications.
- Restricted or unequal access to health care and medical treatment.
- People are not supported in challenging discrimination.
- Unnecessary barriers restrict participation.
- People experience fear, withdrawal, apathy, loss of self-esteem.
- Many of the emotional indicators are similar to other forms of abuse.

Institutional abuse

Institutional abuse is not only confined to large-scale physical or sexual abuse scandals of the type that have been publicised regularly in the media. Of course this type of systematic and organised abuse has happened in residential and hospital settings, and must be recognised and dealt with appropriately so that people can be protected. However, people can be abused in many other ways in settings where they could expect to be supported, cared for and protected.

Abuse is not only carried out by individuals; groups, or even organisations, can also create abusive situations. It has been known that groups of care workers in residential settings can abuse people in their care. Often people will act in a different way in a group than they would alone. Think about teenage 'gangs', which exist because people are prepared to do things jointly which they would not think to do if they were alone. Many of the types of abuse described here can also be identified in their individual categories of physical, sexual or psychological abuse.

Abuse in a care setting may not just be at the hands of members of staff. There is also abuse which comes about because of the way in which an establishment is run, where the basis for planning the systems, rules and regulations is not the welfare, rights and dignity of the residents or patients, but the convenience of the staff and management. This is the type of situation where people can be told when to get up and go to bed, given communal clothing, only allowed medical attention at set times and not allowed to go out.

The key factor in identifying institutional abuse is that the abuse is accepted or ignored by the organisation, or that it happens because an organisation has systems and processes that are designed for its own benefit and not those of the people using the service. For example:

- people in residential settings are not given choice over day-to-day decisions such as mealtimes or bedtimes
- freedom to go out is limited by the institution
- privacy and dignity are not respected
- personal correspondence is opened by staff
- the setting is run for the convenience of the staff
- excessive or inappropriate doses of sedation/medication are given
- access to advice and **advocacy** is restricted or not allowed
- complaints procedures are deliberately made unavailable.

Activity 1

Researching abuse cases and risk factors

Research a case of abuse of a vulnerable adult. Ask your supervisor or line manager about any situations they can tell you about from their own experience. Otherwise look at a case study, or a report into an incident that took place in another workplace. See how many risk factors you can identify. Before you start thinking that people should have seen the potential risk – remember that hindsight is always 20:20 vision!

Functional skills

English: Reading

When researching for a case study, select a variety of texts to identify a range of risk factors. By doing this you will use relevant information and compare sources.

Key term

Advocacy – acting and speaking on behalf of a person who is unable to do so

Patterns and nature of abuse

Patterns and the nature of abuse vary and can take place in different ways.

Serial abuse is where the perpetrator seeks out and 'grooms' vulnerable adults (sexual abuse and some forms of financial abuse usually fall into this pattern). These are often, but not always, criminal offences and are committed by people who deliberately prey on vulnerable people. This can range from the confidence trickster who poses as an official in order to gain entry to an older person's home to the abuser who will 'befriend' someone with mental health problems through an Internet chat room, and later subject them to abuse or assault. It can also include those criminals who attempt to commit fraud or threaten vulnerable people in connection with wills, property inheritance or other financial assets.

How vulnerable do you think some people could be to strangers visiting?

Situational abuse is a result of pressures building up and/or because of difficult or challenging behaviour. This type of 'acute' and immediate abusive situation normally results in physical abuse, although it can result in verbal or emotional abuse and sometimes in neglect where a carer no longer seeks out necessary medical treatment or other support.

Long-term abuse may occur in the context of an ongoing family relationship, for example, domestic violence, or where a family member with a physical or a learning disability is humiliated and belittled, or where an older relative has all their money and belongings gradually taken from them over a period of time. Neglect of somebody's needs because others are unable or unwilling to take responsibility for their care is also likely to take place over a long period of time.

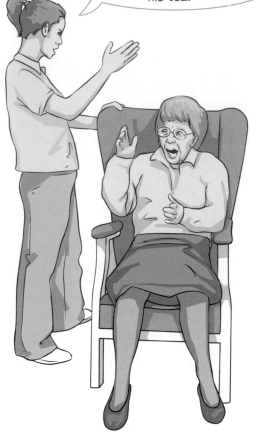

I've told you six times already, Dad's been dead for twenty years, you don't have to go and cook his tea.

Can you see how stress builds up in some situations?

Institutional abuse arises from poor standards of care, inadequate staffing, lack of response to people's complex needs, staff with inadequate knowledge, skills, understanding and expertise. This can also involve unacceptable treatment programmes including overmedication, unnecessary use of restraint, and withholding food, drink or medication.

Caring at home

Sunita, aged 48, has Parkinson's disease, which has recently begun to develop very rapidly. Her mobility has become very limited and she cannot be left alone because she falls frequently. The number of personal care tasks she can carry out has decreased significantly, and she is almost totally dependent on her husband for care.

Sunita has two grown-up sons who live and work considerable distances away. They both visit as often as they can, but are not able to offer any regular caring support. Sunita's husband has given up his career as a ranger in the local country park, a job he loved, in order to look after Sunita. She is very reluctant to go out because she feels people are looking at her. She is very angry about the way Parkinson's has affected her, and has alienated many of the friends who tried to help initially, by being uncooperative and refusing much of the help they offered.

1. How could you try to relieve some of the pressures in this situation?
2. Are there any warning signs in this situation that would make you aware of the possibility of abuse? If so, what are they?
3. Can you think of a situation where you may have missed some signs like these?

1.3 Risk factors

People can be abused for many reasons, and it is important in highlighting any contributing factors to make it clear that the factors alone do not mean that abuse is taking place. It is quite possible to have any or several factors in place and for there to be no abuse – equally, there may be no obvious factors but, nonetheless, abuse is happening.

Some of the factors that are known to contribute to the risk of harm and abuse of adults by family and friend carers are:

- poor communication between cared-for person and carer – this could be because of a medical condition, or a social/relationship issue
- challenging behaviour by the cared-for person
- carer being young or immature
- carer feeling unable to carry on
- strong feelings of frustration on the part of the carer
- carer and cared-for person having a history of a troubled relationship
- carer having an alcohol or drug dependency
- carer believing that the cared-for person is being deliberately difficult or ungrateful
- caring role not having been taken on willingly
- carer having had to make major lifestyle changes
- carer having more than one caring responsibility – for example, young children and an older relative
- cared-for person being violent towards the carer
- carer having disturbed sleep
- carer and cared-for person being socially isolated
- financial or housing pressures
- delays or insufficient resources to provide adequate support
- isolated older people without family support or contact – particularly in relation to financial abuse.

Reflect

Look at your workplace. Do any of the factors that are known to contribute to the risk of harm and abuse by professional support workers apply? If so, you need to be aware that people can be put under so much stress that they behave abusively. Remember that abuse is not just about physical cruelty.

If none of the factors happen in your workplace, then try to imagine what work would be like if they did. Sit down with a colleague, if you can, and discuss what you think the effects of any two of the items in the list would be. If you cannot do this with a colleague, you can do it on your own by making notes.

Functional skills

English: Speaking and listening

Use the list above to initiate a group discussion. Choose a minimum of two points as a basis for the discussion. You will need to take an active role as a participant and to present your ideas clearly.

Abuse by professionals

Some of the factors which are known to contribute to the risk of harm and abuse by professional support workers can include:

- poor-quality staff training
- lack of knowledge and understanding by staff
- inadequate staffing numbers
- lack of investment in continuing professional development
- little or no staff support or supervision
- low staff morale
- lack of opportunity for care workers to form relationships with people they support
- organisational culture which fails to treat people with dignity and respect as individuals
- culture of bullying of staff members by management.

Recognising the signs

You have looked at several tables showing possible signs and symptoms that may alert you to abuse or harm. One of the most difficult aspects of dealing with abuse is to admit that it is happening. If you are someone who has never come across deliberate abuse before, it is hard to understand and to believe that it is happening. It is not the first thing you think of when someone has an injury or displays a change in behaviour. However, you have to accept that abuse does happen, and is relatively common. Considering abuse should be one of the options when someone has an unexplained injury or a change in behaviour that has no obvious cause. That does not mean that it will be abuse, or that you should start formal reporting procedures — it means that you should always consider it as a real possibility.

Victims of abuse often fail to report it for a range of reasons. They:

- are too ill or too frail
- do not have enough understanding of what is happening to them
- are ashamed and believe it is their own fault
- have been threatened by the abuser or are afraid
- do not think that they will be believed
- do not believe that anyone has the power to stop the abuse.

Given the fact that relatively few victims report abuse or harm without support, it is essential that those who are

Doing it well

Recognising abuse

If you want to be effective in helping to stop abuse, you will need to:

- believe that abuse happens
- recognise abusive behaviour
- be aware of when abuse can happen
- understand who abusers can be
- know the policies and procedures for handling abuse
- follow the person's plan of care
- recognise likely abusive situations
- report any concerns or suspicions.

working in care settings are alert to the possibility of abuse or harm and are able to recognise possible signs and symptoms.

Abuse can take place at home or in a formal care setting. At home, it could be a family or friend carer who is the abuser, or it could be a neighbour or regular visitor. It can also be a professional support worker who is carrying out the abuse. This situation can mean that abuse goes undetected for some time because of the unsupervised nature of a support worker's visits to someone's home.

In a residential social care setting, abuse may be more likely to be noticed, although some of its more subtle forms, such as humiliation, can sometimes be so commonplace that they are not recognised as abusive behaviour.

Up to this point, we have looked at abuse by professional support workers and by family and friend carers. But remember that in residential or hospital settings, abuse can occur between residents or patients, and it can also happen between visitors and residents or patients. People can also abuse themselves.

Self-harm

The one abuser it is very hard to protect someone from is the person themselves. People who self-harm should have the risk identified in their plan of care, and responses to their behaviour will be recorded. You must ensure that you follow the agreed plan for provision of care to someone who has a history of self-harm. It is usual that somebody who is at risk of self-harm will be closely supported and you may need to contribute towards planned activities or therapies.

Case study

Appropriate ways to care

Julie, aged 43, had been a senior support worker in a residential unit for people with a learning disability for the past five years. Julie loved her job and was very committed to the residents in the unit. She was very concerned for the welfare of the people she supported and did everything she could for them. Many of them had been in the unit for many years and Julie knew them well. The unit was not very large and had only a small staff who were able to work very closely with the resident group.

Julie and the other staff were concerned that the residents could easily be taken advantage of, as some were not able to make effective judgements about other people and potentially risky situations.

Regular mealtimes were arranged so that everyone could share the day's experiences and talk together, and bedtimes and getting-up times were also strictly adhered to. The staff found that this was a good way of keeping the residents organised and motivated.

Residents did not go out into the local town in the evenings because of the potential safety risk, but the staff would plan evenings of TV watching, choosing programmes that they thought would interest the residents. Sometimes simple games sessions or walks in the local park were arranged.

A new manager was appointed to the unit, and Julie and the other staff were very surprised to find that the new manager was horrified by many of these practices, and wanted to make major changes.

1. What changes do you think the manager may have suggested?
2. Why do you think those changes may be needed?
3. Do you consider that Julie and the other staff members were practising in the best way for the residents?
4. Think about, or discuss, whether this situation was abusive.

2. Know how to respond to suspected or alleged abuse

2.1 and 2.2 What to do if you suspect or someone alleges that they are being abused

If someone makes an allegation of abuse to you, the first and most important response is that *you must believe what you are told*. One of the biggest fears of those being abused is that no one will believe them – do not make this fear into a reality.

This is often harder than it sounds. If you have never been involved with an abusive situation before, it is hard to believe that such cases arise and that this could really happen.

You must reassure the person that you believe what you have been told. Another common fear of people who are being abused is that it is somehow their fault. You must therefore also reassure them that it is not their fault and that they are in no way to blame for what has happened to them.

When someone tells you about abuse or neglect, try not to get into a situation where you are having to deal with a lot of detailed information. After reassuring the person that you believe them, you should report the allegation immediately to a senior colleague and hand over responsibility. This may not always be possible because of the circumstances or location in which the allegation takes place, or because the person wants to tell you everything once they have begun to talk. If you do find yourself in the position of being given a great deal of information, you must be careful not to ask any leading questions – for example, do not say, 'And then did he punch you?' Just ask, 'And then what happened?' Use your basic communication and listening skills so that the person knows they can trust you and that you are listening. Make sure you concentrate and try to remember as much as possible of what you are told so that you can record it accurately.

Remember that people tell you about abuse because they want it to stop. They are telling you because they want you to help make it stop. You cannot make it stop if you keep it secret.

Confidentiality

In general, of course, the right of every person to confidentiality is a key part of good practice. However, abuse is one of the few situations where you may have to consider whether or not it is possible to maintain this. You will always need to be clear, when someone alleges abuse, that you cannot promise to keep what they tell you confidential. This is not always easy; very often, when someone tells you about abuse they have suffered, they will start by saying, 'If I tell you something, will you promise not to tell anyone?' You cannot guarantee this, so do not make this promise – it is one you cannot keep. It is never acceptable to tell someone one thing and do another, so you must be clear from the start about what your responsibilities are, and make it clear that you may have to share what you are told with others. You can, however, reassure someone by saying, 'I can't promise not to say anything to anyone, but I can promise you that I will only tell people who will help you.' You can also promise that although some information may have to be shared, it will be shared on a 'need to know' basis, and only among those agencies directly involved in any investigation.

However, vulnerable adults are not children, and if they absolutely refuse to allow you to share information, it is very difficult for you to do so – beyond the absolute necessity to share the information with your manager. All efforts then have to go into trying to encourage the person to agree to sharing the information and pursuing an investigation. However, if there is no question of capacity (see page 107), then you may have to accept that you can only monitor matters carefully.

There can be some circumstances in which it is necessary for you to break confidentiality; for example, if someone discloses that an officer in charge in a residential care home is systematically stealing from the people living there. You would be justified in breaking the confidentiality of one person in order to protect other vulnerable people. However, this must only be done in discussion with your line manager, and any decisions taken must be fully recorded, giving reasons why it is necessary. You must also make sure that the person concerned knows to whom you have talked and why.

Speech bubble (left): Promise you won't tell anyone?

Speech bubble (right): I can't promise that, but I promise I will only tell people who can help you.

Why is it important for you to be clear that you may have to share what you are told with others?

The Data Protection Act 1998 (see page 31) requires you to ensure that any written information is kept securely. Information about abuse or potential abuse is very sensitive and it is important that people have their right to privacy and confidentiality respected. Information must be kept in a secure situation, password protected if it is kept electronically and with any hard copies filed securely in a locked cabinet. Make sure that only essential and necessary information is kept, and that it is used for the abused person's benefit and in their best interests.

How do you respond?

According to organisations promoting good practice in safeguarding vulnerable adults, there are four key priorities in responding to concerns or allegations of abuse:

- Priority 1: Protect
- Priority 2: Report
- Priority 3: Preserve
- Priority 4: Record and refer.

Priority 1: Protect

The first and most important concern is to ensure that the abused person is safe and protected from any further possibility of abuse. Make sure that any necessary medical treatment is provided, and give plenty of reassurance and comfort so that the person knows that they are now safe. Even if the abuse happened a long time ago, or has been going on for a long period, the process of making an allegation can be very distressing as well as being a huge relief, so lots of warm, kind and caring support is vital. When you find out, or suspect, that someone is being abused or neglected, you have a responsibility to take action immediately. Concerns, suspicions or firm evidence all require an immediate response.

Action to protect may mean taking someone to a safe place, or removing the alleged perpetrator. It may mean getting medical assistance or contacting trusted family or friends to provide support.

Priority 2: Report

You must report any abusive situation you become aware of to your line manager, or the named person in your workplace procedures for the Protection of Vulnerable Adults. You may have formal reporting procedures in place in your organisation, or you may simply make an initial verbal referral. However, it will be essential that you make a full, written report as soon as you can after the event. In the meantime, the checklist on the next page may help you to recall details you will need later, and make sure that you have done everything you need to.

Functional skills

English: Writing – formal report
You will be practising your skills of writing and presenting information in a logical and concise way. Proofread your work to ensure accuracy of punctuation, spelling and grammar. By producing a report you will be using a range of sentence structures, including complex ones, and ordering paragraphs to communicate effectively.

Priority 3: Preserve

Preserve any evidence. If this is a potential crime scene, you must be very careful not to destroy any potential evidence. If an incident of physical or sexual abuse is recent and there is likely to be forensic evidence, then you must preserve it carefully until the police arrive and take over. For example:

- do not clear up
- do not wash or clean any part of the room or area in which the alleged abuse took place

Checklist

Disclosure/observation made by ....

Date ....

How? ....

To whom? ....

Action taken by ....

What action? ....

If no action, reasons ....

Vulnerable adult seen?   Yes / No

When seen? (date and time) ....

Who saw the vulnerable adult? – list all ....

Consultations/information sharing/notification – health

GP?   Yes / No

District nurse?   Yes / No

CPN?   Yes / No

Consultations/information sharing/notification – Social Services

Community team?   Yes / No

Hospital team?   Yes / No

Police?   Yes / No

Housing/supporting people?   Yes / No

Provider agencies?   Yes / No

Other ....

Medical examination?   Yes / No

When? ....

Where? ....

By whom? ....

All action recorded?   Yes / No

Reasons for non-action recorded?   Yes / No

Telephone conversations confirmed in writing?   Yes / No

Strategy meeting?   Yes / No

Date of meeting ....

- do not remove bedding
- do not remove any clothes the abused person is wearing
- do not allow the person to wash, shower, bathe, brush their hair or clean their teeth
- keep other people out of the room or area.

If financial abuse is alleged or suspected, ensure that you have not thrown away any papers or documents that could be useful as evidence. Try to preserve as much as possible, in order to hand it over to those investigating the allegations.

The evidence for other types of abuse is different. Sadly, neglect speaks for itself, but it will be important to preserve living conditions as they were found until they can be recorded and photographed. This does not include the person concerned; bearing in mind Priority 1, any treatment and medical attention needed must be provided immediately. Make sure that you explain to any doctor or paramedic in attendance that the situation may result in a prosecution, so they should record any findings carefully in case they are later required to make a statement.

Psychological or discriminatory abuse is likely to be dependent on witnesses and disclosure from the abused person, rather than physical evidence.

Priority 4: Record and refer

Any information you have, whether it is simply concerns, hard evidence or an allegation, must be carefully recorded. You should write down your evidence or, if you are unable to do so for any reason, you should record it on audio tape and have it transcribed (written down) later. It is not acceptable to pass on your concerns verbally without backing this up with a recorded report. Verbal information can be altered and can have its meaning changed very easily when it is passed on. Think about the children's game of Chinese Whispers — by the time the whispered phrase reaches the end of its journey, it is usually changed beyond all recognition.

Your workplace may have a special report form for recording causes for concern or allegations. If not, you should write your report, making sure you include:

- everything you observed
- anything you have been told — but make sure that it is clear that this is not something you have seen for yourself
- any previous concerns you may have had
- what has raised your concerns on this occasion.

Record what has happened. This is vitally important, as you may need, at some stage, to make a formal statement to police, or other investigation team. Initially, however, you should make sure that you have recorded all the key details for your own organisation. You may also need to make a referral to another agency, for example, the police or social services. You will need to record all of the following information carefully, including a detailed account of what actually

> **Activity 2**
>
> ### Concerns about an abuse situation
> Write a report on concerns about an abuse situation that could occur in your workplace. If you are aware of abuse situations that have happened, you could report on one of them, making sure you do not use people's real names or any other information that could identify them. If not, make up the details. State to whom, in your workplace, you would give the report.

happened, what you saw or were told, and who said or did what.

Be clear that you do not mix fact and opinion, and make sure that you state clearly what you actually know because you have seen or heard it yourself. Also identify what you have heard from others as this is hearsay, or third party evidence, and it is important that others know how reliable your information is. For example:

Mrs James was crying when I arrived.

This is a fact.

Mrs James should not have been living there with him — everyone is aware of his bad temper.

This is an opinion.

Mrs James had been upset earlier in the morning when her neighbour had visited.

This is hearsay from the neighbour, and not a fact that you have witnessed first hand. This type of information can be useful in a report, but you must identify it as hearsay, for example: 'Mrs James's neighbour told me that she had been upset earlier in the morning when he had visited.'

If you do have to make a formal statement, or produce a report that will be used in court, you cannot include hearsay, and must only report facts which you know because you have seen or heard them for yourself.

If you need to make a referral to another agency you will need to include all the following information:

Referral information

Details of abused person

- Name
- Address
- Telephone number
- Date of birth
- Gender
- Ethnic background (including principal language spoken)
- Details of any disability (including any communication needs)
- GP
- Details of carers and any significant family members, neighbours, friends
- Details about home/accommodation
- Reasons for concerns with details of any incidents, etc.
- Details of alleged abuse including information about suspicions, specific information
- Details of any immediate action taken to make safe and protect
- Details of any medical examination/treatment
- Whether the person has agreed to/is aware of referral being made
- The mental capacity of the person — how this has been decided
- Details of any other professional/agency involved
- Details of other agencies copied in to referral (Commission for Social Care Inspection, Police, Primary Care Trust, Hospital Trust, etc.)
- Details of the alleged abuser
- Background information or history

How to reduce individual risks

The kinds of attitude changes needed before whole communities see that taking responsibility for the well-being of their vulnerable members are going to take time. In the meantime, vulnerable people still need to be safeguarded and protected. Whatever your role, and regardless of your work setting, you will be able to have an impact in reducing the risks of harm and abuse for vulnerable adults.

No one can guarantee to prevent abuse from happening — human beings have always abused each other in one form or another. However, using the information you have about possible abusive situations, you are now able to work towards preventing abuse by recognising where and how it can happen.

Working with carers

The 2001 census identified that there were six million carers in the UK. This was 12 per cent of the adult population. The increasing number of older people, along with the policy of empowering people to remain active in the community for longer, means that the number of carers is forecast to rise by over 50 per cent to almost nine and a half million by 2037.

Try to ensure that people in stressful situations are offered as much support as possible. A carer is less likely to resort to abuse if they feel supported, acknowledged and appreciated. Showing caring and understanding of a person's situation can often help to defuse potential explosions. If you work directly with carers, you might express this by saying, 'It must be so hard caring for your mother. The demands she makes are so difficult. I think you are doing a wonderful job.' Such comments, although simple and straightforward, can often help a carer to feel that they do have someone who understands and has some interest in supporting them. So many times the focus is on the person in need of care and the carer is ignored. If your role involves the management and support of colleagues who are working directly in the community, you can ensure that there is an awareness and focus on carers and meeting their needs.

How carers are supported in law

The first National Strategy for carers — Caring for Carers — was introduced in 1999. Since April 2001, carers have had further rights under a new law: the Carers and Disabled Children Act 2000. This entitles carers to an assessment of their needs if they wish. This can be done when the person they care for is being assessed, or separately. The carer can, with guidance from a social worker or care manager, assess themselves.

The Carers (Equal Opportunities) Act 2004 came into force in England on 1 April 2005. The Act gives carers new rights to information and ensures that work, life-long learning and leisure are considered when a carer is assessed. The Work and Families Act 2006 extends the right of carers to request flexible working.

Working alongside carers is an essential part of protecting vulnerable adults. Even if there are no immediate concerns, working with carers to make sure that they are accessing their rights and the support they are entitled to reduces the risks that an abusive incident can develop out of anger and frustration.

Supporting carers in the community

Some situations require much more than words of support, and giving practical, physical support to a carer or family may help to reduce the risk of abuse. The extra support provided by a professional carer can do this in two ways: firstly, it can provide the additional help which allows the carer to feel that they are not in a hopeless never-ending situation; and secondly, it can provide a regular opportunity to check somebody where abuse is suspected or considered to be a major risk.

When resources are provided within the community rather than at home, this also offers a chance to observe someone who is thought to be at risk. Day centres and training centres also provide an opportunity for people to talk to staff and to feel that they are in a supportive environment where they can talk about any fears and worries and they will be believed and helped.

Situation	Solution
Carer needs to be able to access breaks when necessary	Either regular or flexible breaks can be arranged. Some areas operate voucher schemes so carers can organise breaks when it suits them; others have regular planned breaks.
Carer needs aids, equipment and adaptations	Physical environment can be adapted to make caring easier. Hoists, ramps, accessible bathrooms, electronic equipment can all make the caring task easier.
Carer needs support to work or undertake training	Carers can be provided with support for the cared-for person while they are at work and they can be helped to undertake training courses in order to return to work.
Carers need some time and interests for themselves	Carers can be provided with support while they are involved in leisure activity. Advice and information about opportunities as well as practical support is available.

Table 2: Identifying situations where carers need support.

Vulnerable carers

Identifying vulnerable people

Mrs Clarke is 75 years old. She is quite fit, although increasingly her arthritis is slowing her down and making her less steady on her feet. She has been a widow for 15 years and lives with her only son, Ronnie, who is 51. When Ronnie was 29, he was involved in a motorcycle accident that caused brain damage, from which he has never fully recovered. His speech is slow and he sometimes has problems communicating. His coordination and fine motor skills have been affected, so he has problems with buttons, shoelaces and writing. Ronnie also suffers from major mood swings and can be aggressive. Mrs Clarke is Ronnie's only carer. He has never worked since the accident, but he goes to a day centre three days each week. Mrs Clarke takes the opportunity to go to a day centre herself on those three days because she enjoys the company, the outings and activities.

Recently, Mrs Clarke has had an increasing number of injuries. In the past two months she has had a grazed forehead, a black eye, a split lip and last week she arrived at the day centre with a bruised and sprained wrist. She finally admitted to the centre staff that Ronnie had inflicted the injuries during his periods of bad temper. She said that these were becoming more frequent as he became more frustrated with her slowness.

Despite being very distressed, Mrs Clarke would not agree to being separated from Ronnie. She was adamant that he did not mean to hurt her. She would not consider making a complaint to the police. Finally, Mrs Clarke agreed to increasing both her and Ronnie's attendance at their day centres, and to having some assistance with daily living.

1. What action can be taken?
2. What action should be taken?
3. Whose responsibility is this situation?

Mrs Clarke and Ronnie

Imagine that you are the support worker to Mrs Clarke and Ronnie. Your work involves regular visits to their house to monitor the effectiveness of the care package and provide support. One day you arrive to find Ronnie screaming at Mrs Clarke and hitting her.

1. What would your immediate actions be?
2. Write a report covering the incident, including your actions.
3. To whom would you give your report?
4. Who else would need to be informed of this incident?

Never forget that sometimes, the carer can be the person who is vulnerable. For example, an older parent caring for a son or daughter with mental health problems, or who exhibits challenging behaviour, may be very much at risk. It is important to look at the whole picture when looking at a risk assessment, and to offer support and protection to any vulnerable adult who is at risk.

Consent

A key issue in the protection of vulnerable adults is one of consent. Vulnerable adults have a fundamental human right to decide how and with whom they live. A person who is able to make decisions for themselves is entitled to refuse protection and to limit what you are able to do. In general, any action you take in relation to protecting a vulnerable adult must be with their consent.

The issue of gaining consent before taking any action does not only apply to reporting abuse, it also applies to providing evidence for any prosecution and to having any medical examination to record and confirm any injuries or other forensic evidence. If you are faced with a situation where it is clear that abuse has taken place and the vulnerable person is refusing to make a complaint, or to undergo a medical examination, then your only way forward is to try to give them as much clear information as possible and then to refer the situation to your line manager for consideration as to whether any further action is possible.

The steps you can take are limited; there is no legislation that gives vulnerable adults a right of protection as there is for children.

Reasons for refusing consent

There are many reasons why people refuse to agree to any further action being taken. If you can find out the reason, you may be able to provide the information and support that people need. Some of the reasons include those shown in Table 3.

Important difference

A refusal to undergo medical treatment following injuries is an entirely different situation to refusing to undergo a medical examination. If you are faced with someone who has been injured and is refusing treatment, then you must refer the matter to a doctor immediately, so that a decision can be made on the best way forward depending on the nature and severity of the injuries. This is not a decision for you to make without medical support.

Reason for refusal	Information to give
Fear of reprisals from the abuser	Reassure that it will be possible to make sure that there is no need to have contact with the abuser, and the person can be protected.
Belief that it is own fault	Emphasise that it is **never** the fault of the survivor, give information and reassurance about rights and that abuse is against the law. Confirm that abusers are bullies and criminals.
Fear that services will be withdrawn	Reassure that a complaint against a professional is taken very seriously, and that services are a right. No one will remove services because of a complaint. Assure that service provider is on the side of the survivor, not the abuser — even if the abuser is the employee.
Fear of medical examination	Ask medical staff to explain procedure and to reassure. Explain why it is important to provide evidence, and show types of evidence that can be found from examination.
Fear of police investigation/court appearance	Explain support available for police interviews and for court appearances.

Table 3: Possible reasons for refusing consent, and how to respond to these.

3. Understand the national and local context of safeguarding and protection from abuse

3.1 National policies and local systems

Both nationally and locally, the protection of vulnerable adults forms part of the Safeguarding Adults agenda. Local authorities now have Safeguarding Adults Boards; these mirror the Local Safeguarding Children Boards, except that they do not have the statutory basis and powers of the Children's Boards. The local boards are responsible for delivering a multi-agency response to safeguarding adults and exist to ensure that all the partner agencies are recognising and acting on safeguarding issues at a strategic and an individual level. For example, late-night transport or street lighting may be a strategic issue for safeguarding adults, but it is equally important that systems are in place to deal with individual allegations. The local boards will have members from social services, the voluntary sector, police, housing and health as a minimum, and possibly other areas such as leisure, transport and highways. They are also responsible for conducting Serious Case Reviews when someone has died as the result of abuse and there are lessons to be learned.

Empower and protect

Current thinking in relation to policy for vulnerable adults is to focus less on the person as 'having a problem' which needs to be resolved, and more on empowering vulnerable people in their role as citizens. If people are contributors to decision making and are a valued and recognised vital part of a community, then abuse is less likely to occur, or if it does people feel more able to report it and to take steps to stop it. Even the term 'vulnerable adults' tends to make people sound as if they have no power and are a target for bullies. It also sounds as if people need to be protected from harm and risk — and they do.

This type of policy change will take time to come into effect; if you have been around in the sector for many years you may remember a time when rights, dignity, choice and anti-discriminatory practice were unheard of. Now all of these form a vital part of good practice and everyone understands how essential they are. The same thing will happen to the concept of empowerment as a

means of protection, and it will become the basis for reducing the incidence of abuse and protecting vulnerable people from it.

If you take a direct comparison with child abuse, you can see that for over 20 years, the focus was on risk analysis, individual intervention and the removal of children into 'care'. Sadly, this often replaced one type of abuse with another. The 'Quality Protects' initiative in the late 1990s began a change in attitude and professionals began to recognise that improving the quality of children's services was an effective means of safeguarding against abuse, but it was the introduction of Sure Start and Connexions which really made it clear that children and young people are an integral part of society and that there has to be a 'whole system' — rather than separate parts just working together. The 2007 White Paper 'Our Health Our Care Our Say', quickly followed by 'Putting People First', set out the agenda for empowering people to take control of their services and support. This is moving rapidly and by 2011, everyone who uses social care services will have the option to choose what services they want and how and by whom they want them delivered.

Being strong, informed and active citizens is a good protection against abuse.

Information is power

Giving people information and making sure that they are aware of their rights is very important. It is surprising how often a vulnerable adult who has been in an abusive situation did not even realise that they were being abused, or that there was anything that could be done about it.

After all, you have to be able to recognise abuse before you can report it!

Information

Awareness   *Recognition*

Access to help   *How to report*

One-stop shop   *Single phone number*

Involvement in decisions   *Publicity*

Knowledge is power — it makes people strong and less vulnerable.

Ways to empower vulnerable adults

For people to feel that they are able to take control and deal with difficulties, they need to have the means to do so. Many of the changes that need to be made will be outside your area of responsibility, and need to be undertaken by organisations at a strategic level. However, your own practice can make a huge contribution and you can make suggestions and gain agreement to make improvements.

- Awareness of abuse of vulnerable adults must be part of all information that goes out. It should be available in a wide range of formats — print, audio, Braille, appropriate languages, in picture format, large print and plain language.
- Information should be available about what abusive behaviour is, how to recognise it and how and where to report it.

Case study

Reporting concerns

Kathy works in a post office in a small Midlands market town. She has known Mrs Morris for many years and always stops for a chat when she collects her pension. Kathy also sees her at the local church every week. Mrs Morris has always been active in the local community and is very friendly and sociable.

Mrs Morris's son and daughter-in-law have recently moved into her house. They have just moved from another part of the country and are not working. Mrs Morris had never spoken much about her son Paul, and Kathy was quite surprised when she mentioned he was moving in — Mrs Morris just said that he had had a bit of trouble where he was, but did not seem keen to talk about it. After Paul moved in, Mrs Morris did not come to church or to the post office for a few weeks. Eventually Paul came in to collect his mother's money. When Kathy asked how she was, Paul said that she was very confused and unable to look after herself any more. Kathy was surprised and sad, as Mrs Morris had always been so well and such an active person.

A few weeks later, Kathy was walking past Mrs Morris's house and saw Paul and his wife carrying boxes out of the house. Mrs Morris was watching through the window and crying, obviously unhappy about what they were doing. Kathy was very concerned and asked what was going on. Paul shouted at her that he was having to cope with looking after his mother who was too confused to communicate and was unable to go out, and that he was doing his best and that Kathy should mind her own business.

Kathy left because she was quite frightened by his aggression, but she still felt that something should be done.

1. Should Kathy report her concerns and if so, to whom?
2. How could she find out what Mrs Morris wants?
3. Is abuse everyone's business?

- Information should be available everywhere, leaflets in all communications sent out by the agency, posters in libraries, leisure centres, schools, hospitals, churches, community centres, cinemas, pubs as well as in places providing services for vulnerable adults.
- Reporting of abuse must be easily accessible – one easily remembered free telephone number or a 'one-stop shop' in a central place.
- Publicity could be carried out through local newspapers, television programmes and radio programmes.
- Involvement of survivors of abuse in policy making forums can assist in looking at how to improve responses.
- Involvement of vulnerable adults in decisions about how services are planned and commissioned can raise their profile.

Legislation

There are laws that provide the basis for dealing with abuse of vulnerable adults. The legislation is not as clear-cut as it is for the protection of children, and there are not specific laws in England that deal exclusively with abuse, although the situation is different in Scotland.

Table 4 identifies some of the laws, regulations and guidelines that can be used in abusive situations.

Act of Parliament/ regulation/guideline	Use	Type of abuse
Criminal Justice Act 1998	Criminal prosecution by police for assault.	Physical
Civil action by the victim	For assault, battery or false imprisonment.	Physical
Care Standards Act 2000	Regulation of residential and nursing homes – Ss10 – cancellation of Registration, S11 – emergency cancellation, for breach of regulations. However, it is the driving up of quality as a result of this act which offers the best protection against abuse.	Institutional
Sexual Offences Act 2003	Police prosecution for rape, indecent assault and other sexual offences. This Act has greatly increased the protection for people with a learning disability or mental health problems because it has defined 'consent'.	Sexual
Family Law Act 1996	Can provide injunctions and non-molestation orders.	Physical, sexual, psychological
Offences Against the Person Act 1861	Prosecution by the police for more serious offences of actual bodily harm or grievous bodily harm.	Physical
No Secrets (England) and In Safe Hands (Wales)	Guidance documents that set out how local authorities must work jointly with other agencies to make local arrangements to safeguard and protect vulnerable adults.	All
Safeguarding Vulnerable Groups Act 2006	Sets up vetting and barring scheme for people who work with children and vulnerable adults in England and Wales.	All
Protections of Vulnerable Groups Act 2007	Sets up a vetting and barring scheme for people who work with vulnerable adults in Scotland.	All in Scotland
Adult Support and Protection (Scotland) Act (ASPA) 2007	Gives local authorities in Scotland the power to enter premises where they suspect abuse is taking place, and there are also powers to remove perpetrators and ban them from returning to the premises.	Physical, sexual

Act of Parliament/ regulation/guideline	Use	Type of abuse
Criminal Injuries Compensation scheme	Can provide payments for survivors of abuse that was the result of a criminal act.	Physical, sexual, financial if criminality proven
Mental Capacity Act 2005	A criminal offence to ill treat or neglect a person who lacks capacity.	Physical, sexual, neglect
Police and Criminal Evidence Act 1984 S17	Gives police emergency powers to enter premises if they believe there is danger to 'life and limb'.	Physical
Mental Health Act 1983	S37 is about the powers of a local authority, relative or court to take out guardianship of a vulnerable adult. S115 is about the powers of entry and inspection for Approved Social Workers. S117 is about providing after care for people with mental health problems. S135 is about powers to remove people to a 'place of safety'. S127 is about the ill-treatment of patients with mental health problems.	All
Protection from Harassment Act 1997	Provides protection from harassment and from fear of violence.	Psychological
Theft Act 1968	Police prosecution for theft.	Financial
National Assistance Act 1984 S47	Local authority has responsibility for matters to do with protection of property.	Financial
Fraud Act 2006	Has made it an offence to abuse a position of trust.	Financial
Office of the Public Guardian	Supports and promotes decision making for people who lack capacity.	Financial

Table 4: Acts of Parliament that relate to abusive situations.

Vetting and barring

Both England and Scotland now have legislation that sets up vetting and barring schemes that are designed to ensure that people who are unsuitable to work with vulnerable adults, or with children, are prevented from doing so.

In England, the Act set up the Independent Safeguarding Authority (ISA) which oversees the registration of people working, or who want to work, with vulnerable adults or children. There are different levels of activity, for those who work or volunteer occasionally with vulnerable groups and those who work with them

on a day-to-day basis. Criminal records checks are undertaken on everyone who works or volunteers and anyone found to have a record of offences will be barred from working with vulnerable groups.

Information about people who have been barred is circulated to employers so that they do not take on someone unsuitable. Under the Act it is an offence for an employer to employ someone they know has been barred. For more information, see www.isa-gov.org.uk

Recognise the importance of whistleblowing

Abuse by professional carers

Responding to an abusive situation in your own or another workplace can be very difficult. There may be many reasons why you feel that you should not intervene.

- It will mean problems with colleagues — you will make yourself unpopular.
- It could jeopardise promotion — no one will trust you again.
- You might be wrong.

You may feel that you should leave matters to sort themselves out. You should not and they will not.

'Blowing the whistle' about an abusive situation among colleagues is never easy, but you have an absolute duty to do so; there are no ifs and buts.

The government has recognised this, and following several well-publicised cases, passed the Public Interest Disclosure Act 1998. This protects whistleblowers and ensures that you cannot be victimised by your employer for reporting abuse, or any other illegal acts. The Act protects people making disclosures about:

- a criminal offence
- the breach of a legal obligation
- a miscarriage of justice
- a danger to the health or safety of any person
- damage to the environment
- deliberate covering up of information lending to show any of the above five matters.

The basis for being protected by the Act is that the worker is giving information that they 'reasonably believe tends to show that one or more of the above matters is either happening now, took place in the past, or is likely to happen in the future'.

It is important to realise that you must have reasonable belief that the information tends to show one or more of the offences or breaches listed above. You actually may not be right — it might be discovered on investigation that you were wrong — but as long as you can show that you believed it to be so, and that it was a reasonable belief in the circumstances at the time of disclosure, then you are protected by the law.

If you believe that your line manager will not take action, either because of misplaced loyalty or an unwillingness to confront or challenge difficult situations, then you must make a referral to a more senior manager. You must keep moving through the management chain until you reach the person you consider able and willing to take action. If there is no one within your own organisation, then you must make a referral to an outside agency. Contact your local authority and make the referral to the social services department.

Case study

Abuse by a care professional

Mr Patel is 89 years old and has lived alone in his three-bedroomed house since his wife died several years ago. He has impaired sight and hearing, and mobility is limited after a recent fall in which he hurt his back. He has had twice-weekly visits from a physiotherapist from the local Primary Care Trust, for the past month. Mr Patel has social care support daily from a private provider contracted by social services.

Selina has been Mr Patel's support worker for the past year. She has noticed that over the past few weeks he is losing weight and that his meals, which are delivered daily, are largely uneaten. Mr Patel will only say that he is feeling a bit down and has not felt very hungry recently.

One day, Selina arrives at the door and hears someone shouting, 'Get on with it — you are not trying at all, you are so lazy.' As Selina walks into the hall, the physiotherapist looks shocked to see her and says that she is just leaving. After she leaves, Selina tackles Mr Patel and asks if everything is going well with the physio's visits. He says that there is a long waiting list for physio and he is very lucky to have anyone.

1. What can Selina do?
2. What barriers may she face in trying to deal with this issue?
3. Is this abusive behaviour?
4. How would you try to empower Mr Patel?

If you believe that the abuse you are aware of is potentially a criminal offence, such as physical or sexual assault, theft or fraud, then you should refer the matter to the police. At the same time, you should refer to the Care Quality Commission or inspectorate for the UK country in which you work.

How is this investigated?

Each local authority must have a multi-agency Local Safeguarding Adults Board for the protection of vulnerable adults. This committee is responsible for setting out procedures and policies, identifying and protecting those at risk, and ensuring each agency has an appropriate response to abuse. It is likely that the procedure for your workplace in relation to abuse by a professional carer will involve:

- immediate suspension of the person accused
- investigation by police if appropriate
- investigation led by an independent agency
- disciplinary procedures following the outcome of any police or protection investigation.

When the organisation abuses

You may want to blow the whistle about the way an organisation is run, or the quality of a service. You could find yourself working in an organisation where standards are not being met and vulnerable people are being abused because of the policies and procedures of the organisation rather than through the behaviour of any particular person. There may be a policy of overmedication, or vulnerable people may not be given sufficient food. People could be left in wet or soiled clothing or bedding, or the organisation may have a policy of restricting rights or freedoms. There is further information about institutional abuse on page 118. In this situation, you should contact your local Inspectorate or the Local Safeguarding Adults Board.

Public Concern at Work is a national organisation that provides legal advice to people concerned about malpractice at work. The service is free and strictly confidential. For more information, see www.pcaw.co.uk

Challenging the potential for abuse

All abusive behaviour is unacceptable. However, there are other sorts of behaviour which you may come across which you may not be able to define directly as abusive, but which is certainly close to it — or could lead to an abusive situation if not dealt with.

Generally you can define behaviour as unacceptable if:

- it is outside what you would normally see in that situation
- it does not take into account the needs or views of others
- people are afraid or intimidated
- people are undermined or made to feel guilty
- the behaviour is likely to cause distress or unhappiness to others
- someone is threatening violence
- someone is subjecting another person to unwelcome sexual harassment
- someone is playing loud music in a quiet area, or late at night
- there is verbal abuse, racist or sexist innuendo
- a person is spreading malicious gossip about someone
- someone is attempting to isolate another person.

Unacceptable behaviour from colleagues

You may come across unacceptable and oppressive behaviour in your colleagues or other professionals in your workplace. While you may see or hear a colleague behaving in a way which is not abusive as such, it may be oppressive and unacceptable. This can take various forms such as:

- speaking about people in a derogatory way
- speaking to people in a rude or dismissive way
- humiliating people
- undermining people's self-esteem and confidence
- bullying or intimidation
- patronising and talking down to people
- removing people's right to exercise choice
- failing to recognise and treat people as individuals
- not respecting people's culture, values and beliefs.

In short, the types of behaviour that are unacceptable from workers in care settings are those which fail to meet the standards required of good-quality practitioners. Any support worker who fails to remember that all people they support are individuals, and that all people have a right to be valued and accepted, is likely to fall into behaving in an oppressive or unacceptable way.

All of these types of behaviour are oppressive to others and need to be challenged, whether it is behaviour by colleagues, visitors, carers or others. You can probably think of many other situations in your own workplace that have caused unhappiness. You may have had to deal with difficult situations, or have seen others deal with them, or perhaps you have wished that you had done something to challenge unacceptable behaviour.

Activity 4

Unacceptable behaviour

Ask three colleagues in your workplace to state one behaviour that they would find unacceptable in:

a) someone who was being supported

b) a colleague.

Compare the six answers and see if they have anything in common. Find out from your supervisor about the type of behaviour that is challenged in your workplace, and behaviour which is allowed.

The effects of abuse

Abuse can devastate those who experience it. It causes people to lose their self-esteem and their confidence. Many adults and children who have been abused become withdrawn and find it hard to communicate. Anger is a common emotion among people who have been abused. It may be directed against the abuser, or at those people around them who failed to recognise the abuse and stop it happening.

One of the greatest tragedies is when people who have been abused turn their anger against themselves, and blame themselves for everything that has happened. These are situations that require expert help, and this should be available to anyone who has been abused, regardless of the circumstances.

Some of the behaviour changes that can be signs of abuse can become permanent, or certainly long-lasting. There are very few survivors of abuse whose personality remains unchanged, and for those who do conquer the effects of abuse, it is a long, hard fight.

The abuser, or perpetrator, also requires expert help, and this should be available through various agencies, depending on the type and seriousness of the abuse. People who abuse, whether their victims are children or vulnerable adults, receive very little sympathy or understanding from society. There is no public recognition that some abusers may have been under tremendous strain and pressure, and abusers may find that they have no support from friends or family. Many

abusers will face the consequences of their actions alone.

Support workers who have to deal with abusive situations will have different emotional reactions. There is no 'right way' to react. Everyone is different and will deal with things in their own way. If you have to deal with abuse, these are some of the ways you may feel, and some steps you can take that may help.

Shock

You may feel quite traumatised if you have witnessed an abusive incident. It is normal to find that you cannot get the incident out of your mind, that you have difficulty concentrating on other things, or that you keep having flashbacks and re-enacting the situation in your head. You may also feel that you need to keep talking about what happened.

Talking can be very beneficial, but if you are discussing an incident outside your workplace, you must remember the rules of confidentiality and never use names. This way of talking does become second nature, and is useful because it allows you to share your feelings about things that have happened at work while maintaining confidentiality.

These feelings are likely to last for a fairly short time, and are a natural reaction to shock and trauma. If at any time you feel that you are having difficulty, you must talk to your manager or supervisor, who should be able to help.

Anger

Alternatively, the situation may have made you feel very angry, and you may have an overwhelming urge to inflict some damage on the perpetrator of the abuse. While this is understandable, it is not professional and you will have to find other ways of dealing with your anger. Again, your supervisor or manager should help you to work through your feelings.

Everyone has different ways of dealing with anger, such as taking physical exercise, doing housework, punching a cushion, writing feelings down and then tearing up the paper, crying or telling your best friend. Whatever you do normally to express your anger, you should do the same in this situation (just remember to respect confidentiality if you need to tell your best friend – miss out the names). It is perfectly legitimate to be angry, but you cannot bring this anger into the professional relationship.

Distress

The situation may have made you distressed, and you may want to go home and have a good cry, or give your own relatives an extra hug. This is a perfectly normal reaction. No matter how many years you work, or how many times you have to deal with abuse, you may still feel the same way.

Some workplaces will have arrangements in place where workers are able to share difficult situations and get support from each other. Others may not have any formal meetings or groups arranged, but colleagues will offer each other support and advice in an informal way. You may find that work colleagues who have had similar experiences are the best people with whom to share your feelings.

There is, of course, the possibility that the situation may have brought back painful memories for you of abuse you have suffered in your own past. This is often the most difficult situation to deal with, because you may feel as if you should be able to help because you know how it feels to be abused, but your own experience has left you without any room to deal with the feelings of others. There are many avenues of support now available to survivors of abuse. You can find out about the nearest support confidentially, if you do not want your workplace colleagues or supervisor to know. Try www.stopitnow.org or www.abuse-survivors.org.uk. Organisations such as your local Citizens Advice Bureau, health centre or library will also have contact details on posters and leaflets in case you do not want to ask.

There is no doubt that dealing with abuse is one of the most stressful aspects of working in social care. There is nothing odd or abnormal about feeling that you need to share what you have experienced and looking for support from others. In fact, most experienced managers would be far more concerned about a worker involved in dealing with abuse who appears quite unaffected by it than about one who comes looking for guidance and reassurance.

Dealing with abuse is difficult and demanding for everyone, and it is essential that you receive professional supervision from your manager. This may be undertaken in a regular supervision or support meeting if you have one. If not, it will be important that you arrange to meet with your supervisor, so that you can ensure you are working in the correct way and in accordance with the procedure in your setting.

Overview

Much of what you read about dealing with abuse may give you the impression that this is an area full of rules and procedures. It is, and for very good reasons. Abuse is extremely serious — it is potentially life-threatening. Systems and rules have been developed by learning from the tragedies that have happened in the past. Many of these tragedies occurred because procedures either were not in place, or were not followed. You must make sure that you and any staff you supervise know what the procedures are in your workplace and follow them carefully.

Working through this unit may make you feel as though abusive behaviour is all around you and that vulnerable people are being hurt and frightened by carers all around you. Thankfully, the majority of carers and support workers do not abuse, but provide a good standard of care, and most vulnerable adults are not subjected to harm. However, while that may be comforting to know, it is the case that as more professionals develop understanding of abuse and are aware of how to recognise and respond to abuse, the less likely it is that abusers will be able to continue to harm vulnerable people.

Doing it well

Dealing with abuse
- Feeling upset is normal.
- Talk about the incident if that helps, but respect the rules of confidentiality and miss out the names.
- Being angry is OK, but deal with it sensibly — take physical exercise, do the housework, cry.
- Do not be unprofessional with the abuser.
- If you are a survivor of abuse and you find it hard to deal with, ask for help.

Legislation

- Adult Support and Protection (Scotland) Act (ASPA) 2007
- Care Standards Act 2000
- Carers and Disabled Children Act 2000
- Carers (Equal Opportunities) Act 2004
- Criminal Justice Act 1998
- Data Protection Act 1998
- Family Law Act 1996
- Fraud Act 2006
- Mental Capacity Act 2005
- Mental Health Act 1983
- National Assistance Act 1984 S47
- No Secrets (England) and In Safe Hands (Wales)
- Offences Against the Person Act 1861
- Police and Criminal Evidence Act 1984 S17
- Protection from Harassment Act 1997
- Protections of Vulnerable Groups Act 2007
- Public Interest Disclosure Act 1998
- Safeguarding Vulnerable Groups Act 2006
- Sexual Offences Act 2003
- Theft Act 1968
- Work and Families Act 2006

Further reading and research

- www.abuse-survivors.org.uk (Abuse Survivors, support and information)
- www.cqc.org.uk (Care Quality Commission)
- www.isa-gov.org.uk (Independent Safeguarding Authority)
- www.pcaw.co.uk (Public Concern at Work)
- www.stopitnow.org (Stop It Now, an organisation fighting sexual abuse against children)

Getting ready for assessment

Some parts of this unit require you to demonstrate that you have some of the necessary skills and knowledge to safeguard vulnerable people and to protect them from harm. The nature of abuse means that your assessor will not be able to observe you in dealing with abusive situations, but you will have to show that you do know and understand what has to be done. You will also need to show that you are clear about the legislation and the processes around safeguarding and protection and that you understand how to recognise and reduce the risk of abuse. You may have to complete an assignment, or you could be asked to do role plays or to describe what you would so in relation to a series of scenarios.

Unit HSC 025

The role of the health and social care worker

This unit looks at your role as a professional care and support worker. The way in which you perform your role can have a major impact on a person's well-being and how they experience the services they need.

As a support worker, you have a range of responsibilities; primarily you are responsible for delivering a quality service to the person you are supporting. You must do this by working in ways that your employer expects – of course, it may be that your employer is the person whom you support. You will also need to work in partnership with others, both professional colleagues and family or friends who are also providing support.

In this unit you will learn about:

- **working relationships in health and social care**
- **how to work in ways that are agreed with the employer**
- **how to work in partnership with others.**

1. Understand working relationships in health and social care

1.1 Working relationships and personal relationships

Different types of relationships

Everyone has a wide range of relationships with different people in different aspects of their lives. Relationships range from family to work colleagues. Each of the different types of relationship is important and plays a valuable role in contributing to the overall well-being of each of us as an individual. However, the needs and demands of different types of relationships are varied, as are the effects that relationships can have on a person's view of themselves and the confidence with which they deal with the world.

Family relationships

Family relationships are usually those that influence people most. For most children the type of relationship they have within the family where they grow up influences the rest of their lives and the kind of people they become. Primarily it is the relationship with their parents or main carers that is the most influential during childhood. For a growing child, relationships with parents and other extended family members, such as grandparents and siblings, provide the emotional security that is important in establishing a positive self-image and in developing confidence. As children grow through adolescence and into early adulthood, family relationships become less dominant as an influence; however, they remain significant for most people throughout their lives. It is notable that most major occasions in people's lives, such as weddings, christenings and coming-of-age birthdays, are regarded as 'family occasions', when members of the immediate and extended family are usually involved and invited to join the celebrations.

Sexual relationships

Most people who have a long-term sexual relationship would probably view that as being the most significant relationship in their lives. Even short-term sexual

Types of relationships	Features of relationship
Family relationships	These are relationships with parents, grandparents, siblings and children. Depending on the type of family, they can be close or distant.
Sexual relationships	These relationships can be long term or short term, with a spouse or permanent partner, or shorter term non-permanent relationships. The impact of sexual relationships is different from family relationships and more intense than the demands of a friendship.
Friendships	Friendships can be long term or can be short term but quite intense. Most people have a few close friends and a much larger circle of friends who are not quite so intimate or close. These may be friends who are part of a wide social circle but perhaps not close enough to share intimate details of someone's life. Close friends, on the other hand, are often the ones who are an immediate source of support in times of difficulty and the first person with whom good news is shared.
Working relationships	These can be relationships with employers or with work colleagues. Some may stray over the boundaries into friendships, but for most people the colleagues with whom they work are related in a different way to that in which they would relate to friends. For example, work colleagues may share very little information about someone's personal life even though they may have very close and regular day-to-day contact. It is perfectly possible to spend a great deal more time with work colleagues than with friends, but not be as close.

Table 1: Types and features of different relationships.

relationships can have a huge effect on people and how they regard themselves and their general health and well-being. The physical closeness of a sexual relationship means that the dynamics involved are significantly different from other family relationships. Sexual partners are often close emotionally as a result of their intimate physical relationship. Sexual relationships can be long or short term, can be with an opposite or same sex partner, and can be exclusive – with just one partner – or non-exclusive – where partners also have sexual relationships with others. These types of sexual relationships will obviously have different effects and will meet the needs of different people, possibly at different stages in their lives. For example, many teenagers and young adults have short-term and non-exclusive sexual relationships with quite a number of partners, but many will eventually develop a long-term exclusive relationship with one partner with whom they may remain for many years.

Friendship

Friends become increasingly significant as children grow. For very young children, pre-school individual friendships with other children, while important for their social development, are relatively insignificant as influences on their lives. Their relationships with other members of their family or their main carer are far more important. As children progress through school and into adolescence their friendships become more important and have a huge influence on their behaviour. The ability to form friendships with others is an important skill and is a need that most human beings have. An inability of a child or young person to make friends or to be in a situation in which they feel they do not have friends, or are being bullied or excluded by others with whom they had hoped to be friends, can be extremely distressing and have a serious effect on the child's self-image and self-confidence. Adults too find it difficult to cope with being excluded and being unable to relate to others as friends. Most people, regardless of circumstances, need to have a close relationship with another person, through which they can share confidences, worries and joy.

Family structures

As recently as the early part of the last century, family structures were very different than they are now. Less than a hundred years ago the most common family structure was an extended family with mother, father,

grandparents, aunts and uncles living close to one another, if not in the same house. Children would move between different members of the family regularly and would be equally at home being cared for by a range of relations. Fifty years ago the most common family structure was a nuclear family, with mother, father and children living in the same house but not necessarily living close to other members of their family. While both nuclear and extended families are still quite common, there is now a much wider range of family structures and, as a result, a wider range of relationships and patterns of communication within families. Table 2 shows family structures and relationships within them.

Type of family	Features
Traditional extended family	Parents, grandparents, aunts, uncles, sisters, brothers, children, nieces and nephews living together or in close proximity.
Traditional nuclear family	Two parents and children living together. May or may not be close contact with other members of the family, but less likely than in an extended family.
Reconstituted family	Parents both with children from previous relationships.
Step-parent family	Families where one parent has children from a previous relationship and the other takes a step-parenting role.
Lone parent family	One parent bringing up children without a partner.
Cohabiting family	Unmarried partners who may also come into any of the categories above.
Same-sex family	Same-sex partners with or without children.

Table 2: Different types of family structures.

Families can be structured in different ways.

Working relationships

Effective working relationships are extremely important both to people and to the organisations for whom they work. Businesses use techniques designed to encourage work colleagues to work well and effectively together. Usually, establishing good working relationships with colleagues requires an effective use of communication skills and a recognition of the value and significance of work undertaken by colleagues. For most people, having a good working relationship with colleagues is important, as it contributes significantly to overall job satisfaction. There are significant differences in a working relationship and the kind of personal relationships you may have with your friends or family. A working relationship is different because of:

- specific objectives and purpose
- boundaries
- professional codes of conduct
- employer policies and procedures
- time limits
- being in some cases a one-way relationship.

In a working relationship the reasons why you are involved with a particular person are clear. They will be in the outcomes of the support plan. This is different from choosing to be someone's friend, or having been born into a family. In a professional relationship, you are in a relationship with someone because it is your job. You will also have working relationships with colleagues and other professionals. In the same way, these are relationships that are necessary because they are part of your job and are in the interests of the people you support.

Professional relationships have clear boundaries; there are lines that you must not cross. For example, you should never invite someone you support to your home, nor should you visit them socially. You must not accept gifts or any payments, nor should you take gifts or give any of your own money to someone you are supporting. Sharing personal information can be difficult sometimes, especially as you will have a great deal of information about the people with whom you work. This can be especially difficult if you see them very regularly and they are friendly and show an interest in you. If people ask questions, it is almost impossible not to give some information. Sharing some basic information about yourself with someone who has a genuine interest is acceptable, but it is not acceptable to discuss any significant personal details about your life.

For example, telling someone that your daughter is sitting her GCSE exams is fine – even telling them the results if they ask is acceptable – but telling them about problems with your partner or that you think your son may be getting in with a bad crowd is not.

Taking gifts is not permitted.

Reflect

Have you ever felt that you would like to become a personal friend of someone you support? Has there been somebody with whom you have got on really well? How did you handle it? Do you honestly feel on reflection that you were totally professional and did not allow your personal feelings to cross the line a little? Think about what lessons you can learn from that experience.

Professional Codes of Conduct set down by the regulators in each of the UK countries (see Unit 038) spell out how relationships are to be conducted. Following your Code of Conduct is a requirement of being a professional, and it is expected that everyone will practise in a way that stays within the Code.

There is no written Code of Conduct for personal friendships or families, even though you may sometimes think that there should be! The way we conduct our personal relationships follows an unwritten code about how people behave towards each other, but it is not monitored by a regulator nor a requirement of holding a professional position.

Your employer will have policies and procedures around what is acceptable; these are likely to follow the Codes of Conduct. However, if your employer is the person you support, it may be a little less formal and they may choose to have a more personal relationship.

In general, professional relationships are 'one-way' in that you are not looking for anything back from the person you are supporting. There is no expectation that they will be supportive to you in return as you would expect from a friend or family member.

You are the person who is offering support; you are not looking for anything in return. In reality, of course, there are benefits that you will get, but they are in the area of job satisfaction, not personal friendship or support.

Information sharing is also one-way in the other direction, as you are likely to know a great deal more information about the person you are supporting than they do about you.

1.2 Different working relationships

You have just been looking at how the relationship works with people that you support, but they are not the only working relationships that you need to understand. You will also have relationships with colleagues both in your own organisation and in other organisations.

In any setting, it is not only the people using the services who have to be together for long periods of time – the staff have to learn to get along with each other too! This may be the first time you have worked in a team with other colleagues, or it may be that you have moved to a new team that will function differently from the last place you worked – each team is different.

Teams take time to work well; they go through various stages as they settle down and every time a new team member arrives, things change. Not everyone will share the same views about how tasks should be undertaken and the right course of action on every occasion, and much will depend on how well the team is managed. However, some ground rules to make sure that you can work well with others can be used in most situations.

- Find out the ways in which decisions are reached and the team members who should be included.
- Always ask for advice and clarify anything you are not sure about.

- Do not assume that everything is the same in every workplace.
- Recognise that every team member, regardless of their role and status, has an essential contribution to make.
- Value the input of all colleagues and recognise its importance.
- Make sure that the way you work is not increasing the workload of others or hindering them in carrying out their work.

Most workplaces have a means of decision making – this could be planning and review meetings where decisions are made about service provision, staff meetings may be the forum for making decisions about general practice matters or there may be specific staff development and training meetings for sharing best practice. Organised staff meetings run by a line manager or supervisor are the best place for airing differences about practice.

Supporting colleagues

'Supportive working relationships' is a very general term and can mean a great many things depending on the context and the purpose of the support. In the context of relationships with a work colleague in a team, support could mean:

- recognising when somebody is having difficulty in a particular area of work
- recognising when somebody is having difficulty in their personal life which may be affecting their work
- recognising and acknowledging when a colleague has worked particularly well
- noticing when people are overloaded with jobs to do and offering to lend a hand
- telling colleagues about information you have discovered or something you have seen or read which you know would be of interest to them
- making sure colleagues know of opportunities for training courses which you think are likely to interest them
- noticing when a colleague is nervous or unsure of a new task or procedure and offering help and encouragement
- noticing if a colleague is being made uncomfortable by the way in which they are being spoken to or treated by someone and offering to help if it is needed.

This list will make a contribution towards effective and supportive working relationships with other members of your team. If your team is working well, your colleagues will be doing the same thing for you and supporting you in your role.

Functional skills

Maths

Use statistical methods to investigate situations. Keep a tally chart of the number of times you give support to others over a four-week period. Carry out calculations to show the different amounts of support given weekly and at the end of the four-week period. Find the mean and range of the weekly and four-week results.

Activity 1

Receiving and giving support

Keep a calendar for a week or two, or even a month. For each day, draw a stick figure which represents yourself. At the end of each working shift, draw arrows:

- outward from you for support which you have given to others in your team
- inward for the occasions when support has been offered to you.

None of the items may seem large, but a series of small actions of support are what is likely to contribute most effectively to successful teams.

At the end of each week, count up the arrows inward and the arrows outward. They should be in proportion to the people who work on the team and you should be giving and receiving support in equal measure. If there are more arrows in than out, then you need to explore for yourself additional ways in which you can support colleagues. If there are more arrows out than in, then this is an item that could usefully be placed on the agenda at a team meeting.

2. Be able to work in ways that are agreed with the employer

2.1 The scope of the job role

Working within the boundaries of your job is important. There are many different roles within social care, and your job should have a clear job description so that you know the areas for which you are responsible.

Usually, when an employer advertises a job, regardless of whether it is placed by a large local authority, a voluntary organisation, a private sector company or a person, there will be a job description that explains the requirements of the job. The job description will form part of your contract with your employer and is likely to include information about:

- the responsibilities of the role
- where the work is to be done
- who will supervise the work
- who the line manager is for the work
- any staff you will be responsible for.

It will also tell you the rate of pay for the job and the hours you will need to work. The job description will vary depending on the employer, but will probably look something like the one below, which is for a care assistant in day services for people with a learning disability.

JOB DESCRIPTION: Senior Care Assistant

Employer: Everywell Residential Care Home

Reporting to: Registered Manager

MAIN OBJECTIVES OF THE POST
- To support the Management in all aspects of the Home's running.
- To work as part of a team providing and maintaining high standards of care to suit the individual needs of each resident as directed by the Line Manager or delegated Deputy. To foster an atmosphere whereby residents are encouraged to maintain and further develop their independence as fully as possible.

PRINCIPAL DUTIES
1. To participate in the working rotas, including evenings, weekends and Bank Holidays as necessary, for the efficient provision of care for all residents in a way that respects the dignity of the individual at all times.
2. To participate in the emotional and physical care of residents seeking to provide as far as possible, a happy stimulating and stable environment.
3. Help to ensure that all junior and domestic staff contribute to the best of their ability to the efficient running of the Home and the creation of a homely atmosphere.
4. To assist in the formulation of care plans for new residents and the review of care plans for established residents.
5. To assist when authorised by the Person in Charge with the administration and issue of medications for which the Home has taken responsibility and to maintain the necessary records.
6. To care for residents by:
   - washing and bathing residents and assisting with dressing and undressing
   - assisting with toileting requirements of residents, especially those who are physically, mentally frail or confused
   - assisting residents with their mobility by the use of mobility aids provided for their use.
7. Participate in the development of activities and day care programme for residents in which they can join and will enhance their quality of life.

---

8. To monitor the preparation, cooking and serving of food to ensure standards are met in respect of nutrition, environmental health, special diets etc.

9. Reporting observations of alterations in behaviour, physical conditions eg. changes in skin state, body fluids etc to Line Manager or delegated Deputy.

10. To help care for residents who are dying.

11. Recording and monitoring care charts and observations.

12. To act as Keyworker to a number of residents and be responsible for the care of those persons' rooms, clothing, emotional needs etc.

13. Assist with ensuring that bedrooms and communal areas are properly cleaned and maintained and adequately heated in accordance with requirements.

14. To be fully involved in the social activities and outings with residents.

15. To attend and participate in training and staff development programmes as identified in the annual staff appraisal system.

16. To support the Business Services Manager and Matron in their duty as 'responsible officers' for the Home under the Health and Safety at Work Act 1974 and the Fire Regulations.

17. To help the Business Services Manager and Matron maintain such log books and records as may be required by the Registering Authority or the Association.

18. To undertake on call or sleep in duties when designated.

19. To participate in other duties which may be required from time to time.

PERSON SPECIFICATION: SENIOR CARE ASSISTANT
ESSENTIAL
DESIRABLE
QUALIFICATIONS
NVQ Level 3 in health and Social Care or willing to work towards it
Manual Handling First Aid

WORK EXPERIENCE
A minimum of two years' experience of working in a care setting.
Caring for the elderly

SKILLS
Proficient verbal and written communication skills Ability to undertake training to obtain minimum NVQ Level 3
Strong inter-personal skills
Well organised
Planning
Knowledge of the administration of medication Knowledge of lifting techniques

SPECIAL APTITUDES
Ability to work without supervision Practical approach Aptitude towards learning and personal development.
Teamworker Commitment to providing a quality service Responsive to individual needs

Job description for a care assistant in day services for people with a learning disability.

This sets out very clearly what the employer expects of the person doing the job. If you applied for this job, you would be in no doubt as to what the job entailed and what you would be required to do. Some jobs may be a little less formal. If you are working as a personal assistant for somebody managing their own support, a job description may be more like the following.

Job Description for Personal Assistant for D. F.

A Personal Assistant is employed to help me live my life the way I choose. Getting the right assistance when I need it allows me to lead my life independently. A Personal Assistant will enable me to do this by listening to what I want and following my instructions. It is therefore vital that an employee has good communication and listening skills.

The job involves assisting me with a variety of tasks. As for most people, my day varies, so it is difficult to list every task that is expected of a Personal Assistant.

After a period of familiarisation with the duties, you will be required to assist me with the following tasks, sometimes without close supervision. The post holder will therefore need to be able to work on their own initiative while at the same time being respectful of my wishes.

The post holder will work as part of a team and work on a rota so that I have support for 18 hours each day. This will involve evening and weekend working, and the ability to work well with other team members is essential as is the willingness to be flexible with working patterns.

The job involves moving and assisting/use of a hoist, etc. Previous experience is preferred, but training will be given if necessary. You do not have to be strong to do the job well, but general good health is important.

The job requires providing assistance with the following.

Personal tasks
- Assistance with getting in and out of bed
- Assistance with showering/bathing
- Assistance with dressing and undressing
- Assistance with brushing hair and teeth
- Assistance with eating and drinking

Social tasks
- Helping to go to pubs, cinema, theatre with or without friends
- Assistance when going out for a walk
- Helping to shop for pleasure
- Assistance with correspondence – phone calls/letter writing
- Assistance with other leisure activities, such as board games, music, reading

Domestic tasks
- Preparing and cooking food
- Washing dishes and general cleaning of kitchen
- Laundry and ironing
- General cleaning and tidying of house
- Assistance with shopping

Other tasks
- Assistance to maintain upkeep of equipment, such as wheelchairs
- Assistance with gardening
- Driving
- Any other reasonable task

Pay: £7.56 per hour

Hours: 38 per week

Job description for a personal assistant to somebody managing their own support.

Functional skills

Maths: Calculations and solving problems

Calculate the cost of employing a care worker for 18 hours a day at £7.56 per hour. Care is needed for 365 days a year – calculate the total amount needed to fund this care. This activity will develop skills in using whole numbers.

Both of the examples show how employers make the scope of the job clear from the outset. There are good reasons for this; when an employer is planning how to deliver services, they will work out:

- what needs to be done
- how much of it needs to be done
- who needs to do it
- where they need to do it.

The answers to these questions give employers what they need to plan their workforce and make sure that there are enough people doing the right jobs at the right level in order to be able to deliver services. You will have been recruited to do a particular job at a particular level, and other people will have been recruited to do different jobs at different levels. Everyone has their own area of responsibility and is accountable for what they do. If everyone started doing other people's jobs, there would be chaos.

The other reason for working within the agreed scope of your job is that you are working at the level for your experience and qualifications. Other job roles may require specialist knowledge or training, and you would not be able to do these jobs until you had been given the right training and gained relevant experience.

Activity 2

Your job description

Find the job description for your job. If you no longer have it, ask your line manager for a copy. Look at the information on your job description and see how well it matches up to the job that you do. Make notes about any differences and discuss the reasons for this with your manager.

Functional skills

English: Reading; Speaking and listening

Select, read, understand and compare texts to gather information on your job description and the actual job you do. Use the information to have a discussion with your line manager about the differences between your job role and the written description of it. This can then be used as a basis for a wider discussion with other members of staff who have a similar role to the one you are doing.

2.2 and 2.3 Agreed ways of working

Your employer identifies what you are to do in your job description, but sets out how it is to be done in the policies and procedures of the organisation you work for.

Policies will cover all the key areas of practice, such as the examples in Table 3.

These examples of policies are just a few of the many that most employers will have in place. Policies will provide the broad outlines for the way you should work; they set out the boundaries rather than fill in the detail.

Detail is more likely to be found in procedures. Every employer will have procedures to go along with the policies. The procedures set out the detail of how to carry out day-to-day activities. For example, you are likely to find procedures for how to:

- deal with disciplinary issues
- deal with allegations of abuse
- assess and manage risk
- allocate resources
- respond to emergencies
- administer medication
- deal with a death
- handle an admission.

Policies and procedures are an important way of knowing that you are working in the way that your employer requires. Working within policy guidelines and following the laid-down procedures is a good indication that you are carrying out your job in the right way.

Policy area	Sets out...
Equal opportunities	how the organisation makes sure that there is no discrimination in the way it works
Bullying and harassment	how the organisation will deal with staff found to be bullying or harassing other staff or others
Confidentiality	the steps to be taken to ensure that people's information is kept as confidential as possible and only shared on a need-to-know basis
Data protection	how information will be handled to ensure compliance with the law
Supervision	how staff are to be given professional support and supervision
Environmental policy	how practice must look at the environmental impact of activity

Table 3: Key areas covered by policies.

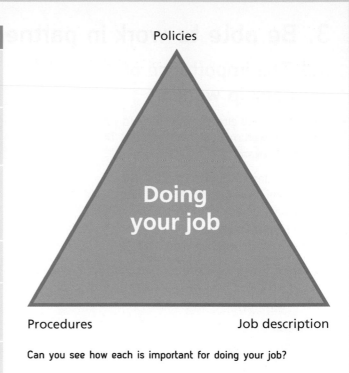

Can you see how each is important for doing your job?

3. Be able to work in partnership with others

3.1 The importance of partnership working

In doing your job effectively, you could work in partnership with many different people. These may include, for example:

- colleagues in your workplace
- other professional colleagues from other organisations
- the person you are supporting
- their informal support network.

Effective partnerships are about good teamwork, and in order to work well, they require some basic ground rules. These need to include agreements on:

- purpose/objectives
- communication
- roles and responsibilities
- decision making
- resolving conflicts
- sharing information.

Partnerships matter in delivering good-quality social care, because there are so many aspects involved in supporting people that no one person or organisation can deliver them alone. A support plan that will meet someone's needs requires cooperation and working together.

Having a shared purpose is a key part of good partnership working. Usually, the shared purpose will be the support of the person at the centre of the plan. Regardless of whether the partnership is all professionals in a multidisciplinary team or involves family and friends, an agreement on a shared purpose is the starting point

A team has an agreed purpose. What other teams can you think of?

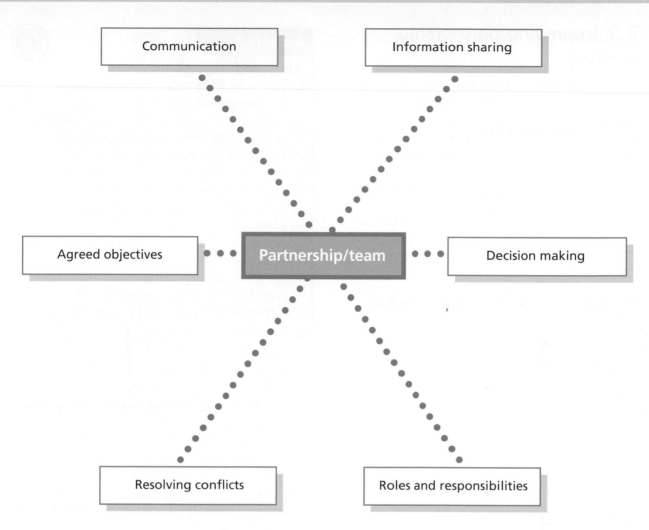

Can you see how there are many important aspects to effective team or partnership working?

The circumstances in which groups can form are almost endless. However, if a group of people have a specific purpose that they are setting out to achieve, then that group becomes a team. For example, a group of friends who are a group because they all drink in a particular pub become a team when they enter the annual tug-of-war contest and attempt to win. Similarly the quiz team develops or the football team develops. If people are a group because they all go to the same gym and talk to each other, but then decide to take on a neighbouring gym in a squash match, then they become a team.

Reflect

What is the difference between a gang and a team? Does a gang ever become a team?

3.2 Improving partnership working

There are certain key steps that will help to ensure that any partnership is able to work effectively.

Good communication

This is essential. Failure to maintain communication is fatal to partnership working. Having a partner find out about a course of action long after everyone else is likely to cause anger and mistrust, and a loss of the good will that is so important for partnerships to work well. Ensure you keep everyone informed about actions and decisions that may be of interest or importance to the partnership.

Respecting and valuing the work of others

Nothing is more likely to make people fed up with working in partnership than feeling that they are not appreciated or that their contribution to the partnership is not valued. Remember that all partners are essential; each person brings different skills, knowledge and experience. Make sure that you find out about the contribution of all of the partners and its importance to achieving the team objectives. Always acknowledge and demonstrate that you respect and value what people have to say.

Making clear decisions

All partners should feel confident that decisions being made within the team are following the agreed process. There is likely to be serious concern if partners feel that some decisions are being taken outside of the team and that not everyone is being involved in the process. If people are not involved, then they will not take responsibility for the decisions and they may not be prepared to abide by them. If there is an agreed procedure for making decisions, then use it.

Activity 3

Aims and objectives

1. Make a list of the aims and objectives of the organisation you work for. They should be contained in your organisation's mission statement or policy documents, or possibly a public plan or charter that your organisation has developed.
2. Then make a list of your own aims and objectives in your work. They may include things such as wanting to give the best possible service to people, wanting to be of use to the people you support, or wanting to improve your skills and understanding of the area you work in.
3. Look at the people you support and what they want from the service and what their aims are in terms of their own lives, and how they see that your support can assist them. Make a list of these aims.

When you have completed all three lists compare them and see to what extent they match. You should check particularly how well the list of your aims and objectives fits with those of your organisation. Do not compare simply the words on the list, but look at the overall effect of what you want to achieve and what your organisation wants to achieve, and see how far they match.

3.3 and 3.4 Resolving issues and difficulties and getting support for working relationships

When you have begun to consider your relationship with the people in your team, you will need to work out how you deal with any problematic relationships. There are inevitably people in any team who do not get on with each other. Bear in mind that a working relationship does not require the same commitment or sharing of ideals, values and understanding as a personal friendship. In order to work with someone, it is sufficient that you recognise and value their contribution to the team performance and that you always communicate effectively and courteously when working. Although many teams socialise together, this is not an essential requirement for a successful team. The loyalty and camaraderie that is built up among good team members can be based purely on their performance at work and does not necessarily have to carry over into their personal lives.

Remember – everyone working at the same time is not the same thing as everyone working together.

Asking for advice and support

Your manager or supervisor is your first line of support for partnership working. Your organisation may have set policies and procedures for setting up and working in a partnership. If so, these will need to be followed.

It is also likely that your manager will have experience of partnership working and will be able to share advice and their own experience. It is a sign of a mature and reflective worker that they know when to ask for advice and recognise when they need help. You will be working in the best interests of the people you support by making sure that you have the best possible guidance to work alongside others.

Functional skills

English: Writing
Communicate your ideas clearly and effectively using complete sentences that are checked for accuracy in spelling, punctuation and grammar.

Activity 4

Improving working relationships

If you have to work with people with whom you feel you have little in common, try the following checklist to try to view them in a more positive light.

1. List all the positive things and only the positive things about your colleague. For example…
   - Do they have a nice smile?
   - Are they good with people?
   - Do they have a particular skill in one area of practice?
   - Are they good in a crisis?
   - Are they willing to accommodate swaps in shifts?
   - Are they good at organising?
   - Do they make good coffee?

2. Make a positive comment to your colleague at least once each day. This could range from 'Your hair looks nice today' to 'I have learned such a lot from watching you deal with…'

3. Ask questions about your colleague and try to find out more about them. This does not have to be on a personal level. Questions could be about their professional skills. You could try something like, 'Where did you learn to move people so well?' or take the trouble to find their opinions on current issues. Perhaps you could ask, 'What do you think about the new set of proposals for the shift rotas?'

4. Pick up on any comments that may lead to areas of common interest. For example, your colleague may comment about something they have done over the weekend, or they may make a reference to reading something or seeing a film or a play that you know something about. You should follow up on any of these potential leads which may allow you to find out more about the person.

5. Learn what you can, either by listening to others or by asking questions about the person's background, and look at where their ideas and influences have come from. If you understand their culture, beliefs and values, it will be easier to see how and why they hold the opinions and views that they do.

6. Make a list of the positives that this particular colleague brings to the team.

Doing it well

Team working

- Agree and share a common purpose, aims and objectives.
- Work on building relationships which value and respect all team members.
- Contribute to the planning process for all the team activities.
- Make sure that all team members are involved in decision making.
- Respect and value diversity of each team member.
- Value working together and recognise the difference between working at the same time and working together.
- Support the goals which have been agreed by the team.
- Praise and give credit to the work of all team members.
- Use your communication skills effectively when working with other members of the team.
- Ensure the team has dialogue and not debate.
- Work to identify and resolve conflicts within the team.
- Examine the way the team is operating and do not be afraid to initiate constructive and supportive criticism.
- Contribute to the growth and development of the team as a whole, the members of the team and yourself as an individual.

Further reading and research

- www.gscc.org.uk (General Social Care Council (GSCC))
- www.dh.gov.uk (Department of Health)
- www.skillsforcare.org.uk (Skills for Care)
- www.skillsforhealth.org.uk (Skills for Health)
- www.cwdcouncil.org.uk (Children's Workforce Development Council)
- Hawkins, R., Ashurst, A. (2006) *How to be a Great Care Assistant*, Hawker Publications
- Knapman, J., Morrison, T. (1998) *Making the Most of Supervision in Health and Social Care*, Pavilion Publishers
- Shakespeare, P. (2007) *Learning in Health and Social Care*, Blackwell Publishing

Getting ready for assessment

The first learning outcome of this unit requires that you demonstrate that you understand the importance of working relationships. Your assessor will need to be sure that you know about different types of relationships and the important aspects of working with colleagues and the features that make working together successful. You may be asked to develop an assignment or a presentation. Your assessor will also want to see that you can actually work with other people and will probably want to observe how you interact with colleagues and follow your employer's policies while you are in a real work situation. Assessors may decide to look at these aspects of your practice while they are observing other aspects of your practice.

Unit HSC 036

Promote person-centred approaches in health and social care

This unit looks at how person-centred approaches have changed the way we deliver social care and support. Planning and delivering services with the person at the centre of social care has given people more control over how their support services are delivered and more say in how they are planned.

Building services around a person rather than offering them the 'best fit' available to meet their needs has made a real difference to people's lives.

In this unit you will learn about:

- the application of person-centred approaches in health and social care
- how to work in a person-centred way
- how to establish consent when providing care or support
- how to implement and promote active participation
- how to support the individual's right to make choices
- how to promote individuals' well-being
- the role of risk assessment in enabling a person-centred approach.

1. Understand the application of person-centred approaches in health and social care

1.1 Person-centred values in all aspects of health and social care work

Some of the key values that underpin work in this sector include:

- treating people as individuals
- supporting people to access their rights
- supporting people to exercise choice
- making sure people have privacy if they want it
- supporting people to be as independent as possible
- treating people with dignity and respect
- recognising that working with people is a partnership rather than a relationship controlled by professionals.

It is important that you apply these values in every aspect of the work you do. It is easy to learn about them, complete an assessment about them and then forget them! These values are the basis for all the work you do, and you need to think about how they impact on the work you do every day.

Person centred means exactly what it says — building everything you do around the person you are working with. This is not just about consulting people, it is also about people taking control of the planning and delivery of their own support and care services.

Aspects of work

It is important to think about how person-centred working affects everything you do. The key areas of practice break down into the broad areas of:

- practical/physical support
- emotional support
- social support
- intellectual/cognitive support.

If we look at each area in turn, you can see how to make sure that you are putting the values into practice in your day-to-day work.

Practical and physical support

This is a major area of work and includes support for day-to-day living such as bathing, dressing, personal hygiene, preparing meals, shopping and general domestic tasks. Remembering person-centred values when carrying out these tasks will help to keep you on track. For example, providing services at a time and in a way that suits the person — not you, or the system. If someone decides that they want a bath, even though you have gone to their home with the intention of supporting them to prepare a meal, they are quite within their rights to change their mind. Think about how often you change your mind and end up doing something completely different. Just because someone needs some additional support to accomplish something does not mean that they lose control over that part of their lives.

Fortunately, the way we deliver social care and support services has changed and is continuing to do so. So if someone wants a bath, and you have enough support available to comply with the risk assessment, then they should have a bath.

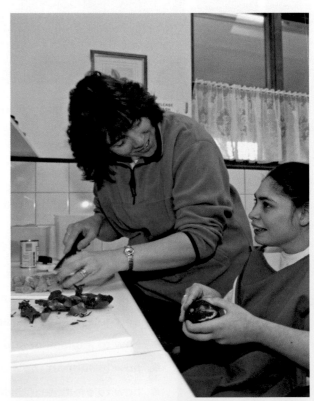

How does person-centred working put people in control of their own lives?

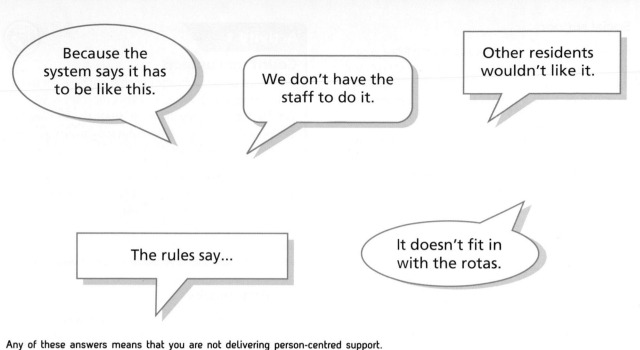

Any of these answers means that you are not delivering person-centred support.

Putting the person at the heart of delivering social care support has a big influence on how you work. Think about how you might make changes in other areas of practical support that will ensure you always put the person you support at the centre of everything you do. Doing this means asking 'Why am I doing this?' or 'Why am I doing it this way?' The answer to both of those questions must be, 'Because this is what the person wants.'

If the answer is, 'Because the system says it has to be like this', 'Because the rules say…', 'Because we don't have the staff to do it', 'Because it doesn't fit in with the rotas' or 'Because other residents wouldn't like it', then you are not working in a person-centred way.

Emotional support

You may be working with someone to support them to cope with mental health problems, or because they are dealing with losing someone close to them. You may be working with someone in order to offer other kinds of support, but there is often an element of emotional support involved in your relationship.

In Unit SHC 31 you looked at developing effective working relationships and how to use skills to do this. Now you need to look at how person-centred values are important to your relationships with the people you support. In relationships and when providing emotional support, person-centred working means:

- taking an interest in what they have to say
- offering empathy and understanding
- supporting and encouraging people in the choices they make
- listening effectively
- giving someone time to express how they feel
- respecting someone's feelings — even if you do not understand them
- encouraging people to look for positive outcomes
- providing support to overcome challenges and barriers.

Social support

If one of the outcomes someone has identified is to have more social contacts, or to maintain contact with friends or family, you may be involved in supporting people to make new friends or to become involved in new networks.

In general, human beings are sociable; we will attempt to relate to other people and develop relationships with them. Relationships are hugely varied in nature, level of importance and how intense they are, but interaction with other people is part of what makes us human.

Sometimes people will need support in relating to others – this can be for a range of reasons. Illness or social circumstances may have meant that someone has lost contact with other people, others may have had issues in making relationships and some may have had difficult or painful experiences which have made them wary of becoming involved with others.

Everyone has a wide range of relationships with different people in different aspects of their lives. Relationships range from family to work colleagues. Each of the different types of relationship is important and plays a valuable role in contributing to the overall well-being of each of us as an individual. However, the needs and demands of different types of relationships are varied, as are the effects that relationships can have on someone's view of themselves and the confidence with which they deal with the world.

Some people may need social support to make contacts with others. They may have become socially isolated because of illness, a location change, bereavement or increasing frailty and may welcome support to begin making contacts with others and expanding their social networks. Loss of contact can also happen because of social factors such as an abusive past, bullying or discrimination that has resulted in low self-esteem and no confidence. Learning or re-learning how to reach out to others and make initial contact is an important part of people developing self-esteem and growing in confidence as they make contacts and get good, positive responses. People who never make contact with anyone never get the chance to become a part of a wider social network and to develop relationships. Humans live in groups and communities; very few of us are able to function well in isolation and maintain our emotional health and well-being.

Activity 1
Count up contacts
Make a list of the number of people you have contact with each day for a week. You will probably be surprised at how many there are. These do not have to be close relationships – simply contact – any interaction at all should be included.

Then try making a similar list with a person who is using your support to help them to develop social links. You will probably find that the list is very much shorter. Try to see where the key differences are and see if that gives you a starting point to work on.

Social networks

The growth of social networking on the Internet has enabled people in all kinds of circumstances to maintain and develop contacts with others. Of course, this is not suitable for everyone and learning how to use the Internet is not something that everyone wants to do. However, more and more people of all ages are very comfortable using the Internet and it can provide an excellent way for people to make contact with others across the world and to share views, interests and issues. However, there are always precautions to be taken when people are making contact with others through chat rooms or social networking sites. You should advise people to be cautious and follow some basic precautions.

- Never give your real name or address or any other contact details to someone you have met on the Internet.
- If you decide to meet them, make sure it is in a public place and take someone with you.
- Never give money or any of your financial details to anyone you have met through the Internet.
- Be cautious if you are asked for photos or personal information.

Making sure that you apply person-centred values means that you provide advice and information about risks such as those posed by the Internet, but you do not impose your own ideas or tell people what to do. It also means supporting people to feel confident to try new ways of doing things and using all the current options for social networking.

In what ways does the Internet help people to stay in touch?

Intellectual/cognitive support

You may be involved in working with someone to help them to achieve outcomes around learning and development. They may need assistance with undertaking learning programmes, or it may simply be that they are looking for someone to support them with activities that maintain intellectual activity. These can be complex activities such as advanced learning or research, or simpler activities such as chess, crosswords, Sudoku or other games.

Intellectual support is not just about learning and education, it is about keeping people's minds and brains active and alert. Games and quizzes can be useful as can reading groups and discussion sessions. These activities can be undertaken with groups of people, but they can also be used on a one-to-one basis. For example, a regular discussion about what has been in the newspaper today over a cup of coffee can be very useful for someone who has always had an interest in current affairs, but is now living a fairly solitary life. There is a wide range of activities that support different aspects of work in health and social care, and you must remember that the person is at the centre of all of them, but it may be useful for you to be able to suggest activities that will link into the outcomes that people want to achieve.

Type of activity	Examples	Possible outcome supported
Social activities	<ul><li>Birthday parties</li><li>Social events</li><li>Joint events with local community</li><li>Visits to places of interest</li><li>Luncheons</li><li>Family outings</li></ul>	<ul><li>Prevents isolation</li><li>Gives opportunity to have variety in life</li><li>Promotes joy/happiness</li><li>Provides support and companionship</li><li>Improves health and well-being</li><li>Helps meet emotional and social needs</li><li>Maintains contact with outside activities</li><li>Provides opportunities to maintain/increase social contacts</li><li>Provides interest and stimulation</li></ul>
Intellectual activities	<ul><li>Word games</li><li>Chess</li><li>Current events</li><li>Using Internet and other IT</li><li>Academic classes</li><li>Health care groups</li></ul>	<ul><li>May help to improve verbal ability</li><li>Stimulates thought processes</li><li>Stimulates those with cognitive impairment</li><li>Provides intellectual challenges</li><li>Maintains contact with the outside world</li><li>Helps orientation level</li><li>Maintains intellectual/cognitive level</li></ul>
Spiritual activities	<ul><li>Attending religious service</li><li>Attending prayers shabbat</li><li>Shalom</li><li>Nature sounds and sights</li></ul>	<ul><li>Meets need for pastoral/spiritual care</li><li>Improves comfort level</li><li>Maintains religious/cultural beliefs</li><li>Helps with mood and behaviour</li><li>Boosts self-esteem</li><li>Provides opportunities to socialise</li></ul>
Speciality activities	<ul><li>Sensory integration</li><li>Re-motivation</li><li>Twenty-four-hour reality orientation</li><li>Handwriting classes</li></ul>	<ul><li>Maintains or increases alertness</li><li>Decreases anxiety</li><li>Improves or maintains orientation</li><li>Increases motivation</li><li>Helps with mood</li><li>Maintains or improves skills</li><li>Prevents withdrawal/regression</li><li>Increases attention span</li><li>Increases independence</li></ul>
Creative activities	<ul><li>Resident council</li><li>Craft, art, poetry or creative writing classes</li><li>Knitting</li><li>Needlework</li></ul>	<ul><li>Maintains or improves cognitive skills</li><li>Improves self-esteem</li><li>Improves motor control/coordination</li><li>Provides intellectual stimulation</li></ul>
Physical activities	<ul><li>Walking</li><li>Exercise programmes</li><li>Competitive sports</li><li>Swimming</li><li>Gardening</li><li>Golf</li></ul>	<ul><li>Maintains or improves cardiovascular fitness</li><li>Tones muscles</li><li>Promotes feeling of well-being</li><li>Improves self-esteem</li><li>Maintains/improves mobility</li></ul>

Table 1: Activities and the outcomes they support.

1.2 The use of support plans in applying person-centred values

Support or care plans are the basis for how social care and support services are delivered. The most important part of the plan is the outcomes that people want to achieve; the whole of the plan is geared to making progress towards those outcomes.

Inputs or outcomes

One of the key ways in which support/care plans reflect person-centred values is that we do not structure services around what we, as the social care workforce, do in order to ensure that people receive services. Instead, we structure services around 'outcomes' – in other words, what is achieved by the people receiving the services.

Think of it like this. You spend three hours taking Emily on a shopping trip. You:

- worked with her to plan the trip, as she has not been out of the house since she had a bad fall six months ago
- accompany her to the local shops
- spend time while she chooses her shopping
- go back home with her
- talk through the trip with her and discuss what went well and any areas she was not so confident about
- discuss plans for the next outing with her.

Your three hours and everything you do during that time is your 'input'. This can include:

- time
- planning
- professional skill
- health care
- daily living aids
- physiotherapy
- domiciliary support.

In order to find the 'outcome', you need to look at what Emily has got out of it. The trip has helped to increase her confidence, raise her self-esteem and increase her general well-being; it has helped to achieve some physical exercise and improved her mobility. It has also contributed to increasing her independence. These are the achievements that have resulted from your 'input'. These achievements are called 'outcomes' and can include:

- increased confidence
- improved health
- feeling valued
- becoming active
- independence
- feeling involved.

This means that when we plan for delivering services using person-centred values, we need to think about the outcomes the person wants to achieve and work with them to make sure that the services are helping to achieve these.

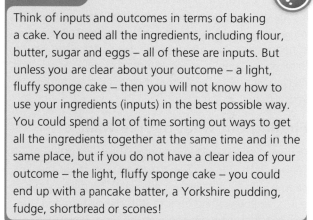

Reflect

Think of inputs and outcomes in terms of baking a cake. You need all the ingredients, including flour, butter, sugar and eggs – all of these are inputs. But unless you are clear about your outcome – a light, fluffy sponge cake – then you will not know how to use your ingredients (inputs) in the best possible way. You could spend a lot of time sorting out ways to get all the ingredients together at the same time and in the same place, but if you do not have a clear idea of your outcome – the light, fluffy sponge cake – you could end up with a pancake batter, a Yorkshire pudding, fudge, shortbread or scones!

Doing it well

Person-centred planning

- The person is at the centre.
- Family and friends are full partners.
- Person-centred planning reflects the person's capacities, what is important to the person (now and for their future) and specifies the support they require to live their life in the way they wish.

2. Be able to work in a person-centred way

2.1 Finding out people's history, preferences, wishes and needs

Person-centred working means that the wishes of the person are the basis of planning and delivering support and care services. Therefore, you must find out exactly what people want and expect from the care and support they are planning. Service provision has moved a long way from the time when we would find out what people would like and then tried to work out the 'best fit' with what was available. Person-centred working means that service provision fits around the person – not the other way around.

If you are going to work with someone, it is important that you know as much about them as possible.

You have looked at ways to find out information about people in earlier units. There are various ways of doing this, but the most effective is always to ask the person concerned about whatever you want to know. Try to find time to sit down with someone and ask about their life. If they are able to tell you about their own history, you will learn a great deal and it will help you to offer support in the most appropriate ways. It is often easy to think about people, especially older people, as you see them now and to forget that their lives may have been very different in the past.

Finding out what people want

Person-centred working is about putting people in control of their lives. This may be a new experience for people who have been using services for many years, but have always had to fit in with the system and the services that were available at the time. People often find it hard to think about what they want and you can help by offering prompts such as, 'Remember when you said you wanted to...', 'What sort of time do you want to get up?' or 'What about going out and meeting more people?'

Most workplaces will have a format for undertaking assessments where people have the opportunity to identify:

- the goals they want to achieve
- what they are able to do for themselves
- areas where they need support.

Reflect

This poem is said to have been found, after her death, in the locker of Kate, a geriatric patient in the early 1970s.

What do you see, nurses, what do you see?
What are you thinking when you look at me?
A crabbit old woman, not very wise,
Uncertain of habit with far-away eyes
Who dribbles her food and makes no reply
When you say in a loud voice, 'I do wish you'd try.'
Who seems not to notice the things that you do
And forever is losing a stick or a shoe
Who, unresistingly or not lets you do as you will,
With bathing and feeding – the long day to fill.
Is that what you're thinking? Is that what you see?
Then open your eyes nurse – you're looking at me.
I'll tell you who I am as I sit here so still
As I use at your bidding, as I eat at your will
I'm a small child of ten with a father and mother,
Brothers and sisters who love one another.
A young girl of sixteen with wings on her feet,
Dreaming that soon a lover she'll meet
A bride soon, at twenty my heart gives a leap
Remembering the vows that I promised to keep.
At twenty-five now I have young of my own
Who need me to build a secure, happy home
A young woman of thirty, my young now grow fast
Bound to each other with ties that should last.
At forty my young ones now grown will soon be gone
But my memory stays beside me to see I don't mourn
At fifty, once more babies play round my knee
Again, we know children, my loved one and me.
Dark days are upon me – my husband is dead
I look at the future, I shudder with dread.
For my young are all busy rearing young of their own
And I think of the years and the love I have known.
I'm an old woman now and nature is cruel
The body it crumbles, grace and vigour depart
There is now a stone where I once had a heart
But inside this old carcass a young girl still dwells
And now and again my battered heart swells
I remember the joys, I remember the pain
And I'm loving and living life over again
I think of the years – all too few – gone too fast
And accept the stark fact that nothing can last
So open your eyes, nurses, open and see
Not a crabbit old woman ....look closer, see ME.

Forms will vary between local areas, but are likely to cover:

- personal care
- nutritional needs
- practical aspects of daily life
- physical health, mental health and well-being
- relationships and social inclusion
- choice and control
- risk
- work, leisure and learning
- travelling
- caring/parenting
- social support
- unpaid carer support.

2.2 and 2.3 Putting person-centred values into practice

People and their needs should be at the centre of the support process. Your role is to make sure that people have every opportunity to state exactly how they wish

their needs to be met, and this is especially important when the issues are difficult, sensitive or complex. Some people will be able to share this information personally; others will need an advocate who will support them in expressing their views.

People who are distressed

If people are in sensitive or complex situations as the result of an outside event, such as the death of a close friend or relative, or because they have received some other bad news, there is probably little you can do to prevent the distress, but the way you handle the situation is important. Make sure that the person still

retains control and is able to make choices about what they want to do. It is tempting to take over when someone is very upset, but you need to check carefully that you are following the choices that people make. You must be careful not to pressurise people to discuss more than they want to. You could also offer them a choice of talking to another member of staff or a relative or friend, if they appear to be unwilling to discuss their worries with you.

Situations may be complex or sensitive because of family pressures; sometimes the views of the person you are supporting and those of their family carers may not be the same. In this situation, you should not forget that your priority is the person you are supporting. You must make sure that you are working with their choices and preferences, although it is not always easy to deal with the responses from a strong-minded family carer who believes that they are acting in the best interests of the person concerned.

Doing it well

Putting person-centred values into practice

- Your key focus is the person you support.
- Services revolve around the person, not the other way around.
- Even in complex or difficult situations, always keep the person at the centre.
- Always treat people with dignity and respect.
- Make sure that people have all the support they need in order to make choices.
- Make arrangements for an advocate if necessary.

Case study

Acting in somebody's best interests

Dennis is 27 years old; he has a learning disability and is in a work placement supported by a job coach. He likes sports and wants to spend more time playing football and doing athletics, which he enjoys. He has put together a support plan, but his parents think that it will all be too much for him and that he needs to come home and rest after a day at work.

Father: This plan is hopeless, he'll never do all this – you don't understand, it's just what he thinks he'd like to do.

Dennis: No, this is what I want, I like playing football and doing running. I'm not tired.

Father: You're just being silly son, I know it sounds good now, but you won't be able to do it. You know you like your evenings at home with me and your mum.

Dennis: No I don't.

Father: Don't be rude, Dennis. Do you see what I mean – he doesn't really know what he wants. I don't know why you people want to let him decide, it's just irresponsible.

Support worker: What do you think about that, Dennis?

Dennis: I want to do my plan.

Support worker: Mr Smith, this is about Dennis making decisions for himself and us helping him to do what he wants to with his life. I'm sorry if you don't agree, but I do think that Dennis has to try things his way. I think that your support is very important to him and it would be good if he could try this plan with your help.

Father: Well, we don't want to stand in his way – but I don't think you people really understand what he's like. We'll give it a go, but I'm not convinced.

Support worker: No, I understand that, but it has a better chance of working if you are backing it. What do you think, Dennis?

Dennis: Thanks Dad.

1. How do you think the initial response of the father would have made Dennis feel?
2. How does the support worker help the father to understand why doing things Dennis's way is preferable?
3. How do you think you would have acted in this scenario?

3. Be able to establish consent when providing care or support

3.1 The factors that influence capacity

The question of capacity to make decisions is highly complex and must be considered carefully. It is very easy to assume that because someone has dementia, a learning disability or a long-term mental health problem, they lack the capacity to make decisions about important issues affecting their own life. If you think about it, the capacity to make a decision can often depend on how much help we have.

For example, imagine you are a local councillor and you have to choose between two different types of road surface for a new by-pass in your town. Unless you have a good knowledge of road construction, you are going to need advice and information from civil engineers, highways experts and road safety experts to support you in making a decision. You will have to make the decision, but you do not have the capacity to make it without support.

In the same way, if you were having your roof repaired, it is quite likely that you would have to take advice if you were offered the choice between two different types of roofing tiles. So you can see that capacity is relative to the decision that is being made.

Legal position

With this in mind, Parliament passed the Mental Capacity Act in April 2005. This sets out a framework for supporting people to make decisions, and lays out the ways in which people can be supported. The Act is underpinned by five key principles, which are:

1. a presumption of capacity — every adult has the right to make their own decisions and must be assumed to have capacity to do so unless it is proved otherwise
2. the right for people to be supported to make their own decisions — people must be given all appropriate help before anyone concludes that they cannot make their own decisions

3. people must retain the right to make what might be seen as eccentric or unwise decisions
4. anything done for or on behalf of people without capacity must be in their best interests
5. anything done for or on behalf of people without capacity should be the least restrictive of their basic rights and freedoms.

The Act sets out clearly how to establish if someone is incapable of taking a decision; the 'incapacity test' is only in relation to a particular decision. No one can be deemed 'incapable' in general simply because of a medical condition or diagnosis. The Act introduces a new criminal offence of ill treatment or neglect of a person who lacks capacity. A person found guilty of such an offence may be liable to imprisonment for a term of up to five years.

> **Reflect**
>
> Think about decisions you have had to make. When have you needed help or advice to make them?

3.2 How to establish consent for an activity or action

As a broad principle, consent should be obtained before carrying out any kind of activity. Even something as simple as moving somebody or plumping their pillows should always be preceded by the question, 'Would you like me to plump your pillows?' In general, people will need to provide consent for the provision of personal care. An overall agreement to the provision of care and support cannot be taken as a blanket consent to all activities; someone may not want the planned care on a particular day, so consent must always be obtained: 'Are you ready for your hair to be brushed?' or 'Do you want to go in the shower now?' are essential questions where agreement indicates consent.

Informed consent

In a clinical setting, consent has a very specific meaning and assumes a great deal of importance. It is essential that people not only consent, but understand what it is they are consenting to and the implications of this. This is informed consent. Informed consent means that the person has full information about:

- what is to happen
- why it is to happen
- the possible effects, both positive and negative.

All the risks should have been explained so that a person is in a position to make a judgement about whether or not they wish to go ahead. Informed consent can be written, as in the case of somebody undergoing surgery, or it can be a verbal consent – for example, if somebody is having blood taken, then the procedure, the purpose of the blood test and what will be found out from the blood test would be explained to them before they agreed to it.

Implied consent

It is reasonable to assume that someone implies their consent to you taking their blood pressure if they present their arm when they see you arriving and taking out the blood pressure cuff. If somebody opens their mouth when you appear with a thermometer, it is reasonable for you to assume that they are implying consent to you taking their temperature. If people raise themselves up as you come to help them from a chair, you may assume that they consent. For these relatively minor and non-invasive procedures, implied consent is perfectly acceptable, as it would be very overcomplicated if consent to these types of activities had to be recorded on every occasion.

Written consent

This is most likely to be used in a clinical setting where there will be a form for written consent. This requires patients, or their relatives in the case of an emergency, to sign to say that they are willing for the named clinical procedure to be undertaken. Generally, written consent is likely to also be informed consent as on most occasions the procedures will have been explained carefully before signing.

Verbal consent

Verbal consent is normally understood to exist when a person requests that a procedure be undertaken. For example, in a hospital, someone asking for pain relief who has been told, 'Yes, we will give you an injection for pain but it will make you sleepy', and the response is, 'Yes, give it to me anyway', is taken to be verbal consent for the procedure and this consent must be recorded in the case notes. This could also apply, for example, to someone who is severally constipated and has asked for an enema, or to somebody who has requested that they be moved from the bed to the chair using lifting equipment.

Why consent is important

It is vital that consent is always obtained. This is not only in order to protect care providers against legal challenge, it is also because of the growth in recognition and understanding of the rights of the person and the importance of recognising that people should determine what happens to them. Historically, areas of clinical practice have always 'acted in the best interests' of patients, and there are still many older people who believe that 'doctor or nurse knows best', and would not presume to question any medical suggestions about the way their treatment should proceed. As the traditional view of medical practitioners being more powerful has changed and it has become more common to question and challenge the opinions of doctors, nurses and other health workers, people have become more comfortable with the idea of being asked for their views and their consent.

If you are asked to obtain client consent for an activity, you must take great care that you:

- answer any questions honestly and as fully as you can
- never attempt to answer a question that you are not sure of and that you always refer the question on to somebody who has the knowledge to give the person a full answer
- direct your information wherever possible to the person concerned, even if there is a relative or friend with them.

In most cases it is the person's consent that you must obtain, not that of their friend or relative. Where there is an issue of capacity to understand the information, then you should explain the procedure carefully to the person who is acting as their advocate. This could be a relative, friend or possibly a social worker. It could also be a representative of the court if the person is subject to guardianship or a court order.

If, however, the person is capable of understanding but has difficulty with communications, then you must use the communication skills that you have learned (see Unit SHC 31) to provide the necessary information in order for them to make a decision. People who have sensory impairments should not be prevented from making their own decisions and asking their own questions by the limitations of either your time or your communication skills.

Where there are language difficulties, an interpreter should be used as appropriate. You should always consider the nature of the consent being sought before a decision is made about whether or not to use a member of the person's family. It may be that due to either confidentiality or the nature of the procedure being discussed, it may not be appropriate and the use of an interpreter may be preferable.

3.3 What to do if consent cannot be obtained

You must not proceed with any care or clinical activity without consent. If someone refuses their agreement or changes their mind after having said yes, you must stop what you are doing.

It may be useful to repeat the information again just to be sure that any queries and concerns have been answered, but it is not your job to persuade someone or to put pressure on them to agree.

You must immediately report any refusal of consent or any reservations expressed by the person to your supervisor or to the clinical practitioner responsible for the procedure.

4. Be able to implement and promote active participation

4.1 Active participation and individual needs

The feeling of having achieved something is a feeling everyone can identify with — regardless of the size of the achievement or its significance when viewed from a wider perspective. Most achievements which give us pleasure are relatively small — passing a driving test, finishing a run, clearing a garden, passing an exam, putting together a set of flat-pack bookshelves... Achievement does not have to mean reaching the North Pole or climbing Everest, or winning the World Cup. Achievements that are much smaller and closer to home are those that provide a sense of fulfilment for most people.

Working with people to help them have a sense of achievement is a key part of caring. It is tempting to undertake tasks for people you work with because you are keen to care for them and because you believe that you can make their lives easier. Often, however, you need to hold back from directly providing care or carrying out a task, and look for ways you can enable people to undertake the task for themselves, to enable **active participation**.

> ### Key term
>
> **Active participation** – when a person participates in the activities and relationships of everyday life as independently as possible; they are an active partner in their own care or support, rather than a passive recipient

For example, it may be far easier and quicker for you to put on people's socks or stockings for them. But this would reinforce the fact that they are no longer able to undertake such a simple task for themselves and remove the motivation to find a way to do it independently. Time spent in providing a 'helping hand' sock aid, and showing them how to use it, means that they can put on their own clothing and, instead of feeling dependent, have a sense of achievement and independence.

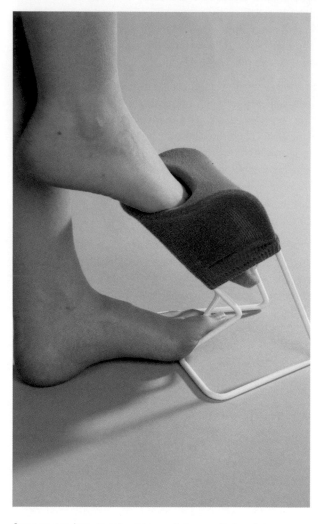

Can you see how simple aids can help people to retain independence?

Sometimes you need to realise that achievement is relative to a person's circumstances. What may seem an insignificant act can actually be a huge achievement. Someone recovering from a stroke who succeeds in holding and eating using a piece of cutlery for the first time may be achieving something that has taken weeks or even months of physiotherapy, painful exercise and huge determination. The first, supported steps taken by someone who has had a hip replacement represent a massive achievement in overcoming pain, fear and anxiety.

4.2 Agreeing how active participation will be implemented

Supporting people's independence by encouraging and recognising their achievements is one of the best parts of providing professional care and support. Sometimes you may need to spend time guiding and encouraging people in order for them to achieve something.

- You may need to steady someone's hand while they write a thank-you note, but it is far better that you spend time doing this rather than write it for them.
- You could accompany someone on many trips round the supermarket, and eventually wait in the car park while they go in alone.
- You could demonstrate to someone with poor motor control how to create pictures by painting with their fingers.

Make sure you always recognise and celebrate achievements. Think about it — whenever you achieve something, you usually want to share it with someone. Your enthusiasm and recognition are important to the people you work with.

How does celebrating your achievements make you feel?

4.3 Holistic needs

One of the essential aspects of planning care services is to have a **holistic** approach to supporting people's needs and preferences. This means recognising that all parts of someone's life will have an impact on care and support needs and preferences. It will also put people's achievements into the proper perspective.

> **Key term**
>
> **Holistic** – looking at the whole person or situation

> **Activity 2**
>
> **Promoting active participation**
> Think about someone with whom you work regularly, and identify a task that is carried out for them.
>
> 1. Why are they unable to do this task themselves?
> 2. Work with the person to draw up an active participation plan to improve on this situation. This could be enabling them to carry out the task themselves or having more say in the way they are supported.

4.4 Promoting understanding of active participation

You may understand the importance of people being active participants in their care and support, but not everyone will. You may have to work to support colleagues, but the people most likely to need to think differently about how care and support is delivered may be the person themselves, or their family.

Many people have been used to having care and support provided in a way where they had little choice and no control, so moving to a situation where they are an active participant can be difficult for some people. You need to be sensitive to the fact that some people may never have made a choice about what they wanted and that they may not immediately be comfortable with taking control.

The following conversation is typical of some that you are likely to have.

Ingrid (support worker): Have you thought about when you would like to have your support service?

George: When is it available?

Ingrid: We can try to arrange it for times that suit you — it depends what you would like your support service to do.

George: Well... I'm just grateful for anything they do for me, just tell me what's available and I'll fit in.

Ingrid: What do you think you will need most help with?

George: Getting a bath would be good — I can't do that on my own.

Ingrid: OK — what about getting out and about?

George: I'd love to go out sometimes, but I'm scared of falling after that last time.

Ingrid: Would you like someone to go out with you?

George: They won't do that, will they?

Ingrid: You decide on what support you need, George, so that you can live your life the way you want.

George: You mean I can choose what I want to do?

Ingrid: Yes — and when you want to do it.

George: That'll take some thinking about — will you help me?

Families

Families may want to protect people who they see as vulnerable and in need of care, and may have many concerns about the growing independence of loved ones who have always been dependent. Do not jump to the conclusions that families are being difficult or obstructive; usually people believe that they are doing their best for their relatives by protecting them and by reducing the risks. Working in partnership with people and their families to help them get used to new approaches and to see the benefits of active participation may be a slow process that needs to be taken gently, but the long-term benefits of people being able to participate in society as full citizens is worth the effort.

5. Be able to support the individual's right to make choices

5.1 Supporting an individual to make choices

Where people want to make choices about their lives, you should ensure that you do your best to help them identify any barriers they may meet and then offer support in overcoming these. If you are working with someone living in their own home, it is likely to be easier for them to make day-to-day choices about their lives. In some situations they may require help and support in order to achieve the choice, but it is generally less restrictive than a residential or hospital setting, where the needs of many other people also have to be taken into account.

For many people living in their own homes, the development of direct payments and individual budgets has meant a far higher level of choice and empowerment than was possible previously. This system means that payments for the provision of services are made to the person, who then employs support workers directly and determines their own levels and types of service. This changes the relationship between the person and the support workers, and puts people in a position of power as an employer. Individual and personal budgets also give people the chance to control their lives. Here they have control over how resources are used and how money is spent, but do not have to be employers. You may need to offer some help initially, so people can get used to directing their own services.

The process of making choices can also be about simple things — it can just be a matter of checking with the person as you work, as in the example below.

The worker in our example has offered Mrs Jones a choice about clothes. Mrs Jones has indicated that she is not happy with the choice offered, and she has also identified the possible barrier to having the clothes she wants. The care worker has looked for a way that the barrier may possibly be overcome. This process can be used in a wide range of situations.

How do you think this interaction will have made Mrs Jones feel?

Doing it well

Supporting people to make choices

- Always ask people about their needs, wishes and preferences – whether this is the service they want and if this is the way they want to receive it.
- Ask if they prefer other alternatives, either in the service or the way it is delivered.
- Look for ways you can actively support people in achieving the choice they want.

We looked at the issue of capacity on page 107 when considering questions of consent. You also need to think about capacity in relation to choice. You may be working with someone who is not able to participate fully in all decisions about their day-to-day life because they have a different level of understanding. This could, for example, include people with a learning disability, dementia or a brain injury. In this situation, it may be that the person has an advocate who represents their interests and is able to present a point of view about choices and options. The advocate may a professional one such as a solicitor, social worker or a rights worker, or they could be a relative or friend. It is essential that you include the advocate in discussions, to make sure that the person's wishes are followed.

Sometimes people are not able, because of the nature of a particular condition or illness, to identify choices or to take part directly in decision making. In these circumstances, it is important that you make every effort to involve them as far as they are able. The most effective way is through the use of an advocate to ensure that people can make their wishes known.

There are also some ways that you can make day-to-day communication easier and support active participation. For example, if somebody communicates differently from you as the result of a particular condition, or there are language differences, it is important that you ensure the communication differences are reduced as far as possible so that the person can take part in discussions and decisions. This may involve using specific communication techniques, or arranging to have help from an appropriate specialist.

For example:

- if you are communicating with someone who has a sensory impairment, you may need to write things down or you may need to arrange for a sign language interpreter
- if you are communicating with someone who has speech difficulties following a stroke, you may need to use visual communication, or use cards that show a range of pictures such as food and drink
- if you are communicating with someone whose first language you do not speak, you will need to use an interpreter
- some people with a learning disability communicate more easily using images and graphics.

Informed choices

Earlier in this unit you looked at how to ensure that people are able to give informed consent. Making informed choices is similar.

One of your key roles is to provide information to the person and their family about the choices that they need to make. For example, it is not reasonable to expect a person to agree to 'attendance at a project' unless they have full information to make a choice. This will include information about:

- the exact nature of the project
- the location of the project
- the type of activities
- the general atmosphere and ethos of the project
- the number of people who will be attending
- what the transport arrangements will be.

These are just a few of the questions that someone may have about what will be provided. Informed choice requires full information. This same principle applies to any choices that people have to make about, for example:

- accommodation
- money
- medical treatment
- support plans
- relationships
- leisure activities
- aids and adaptations
- education and learning.

All of us have the right to make informed choices about all aspects of our lives. For example, you would not purchase a house simply because the estate agent said,

'Oh, I have got a nice house for you.' You would want a great deal of information and to visit and look at the house for yourself, and to carry out extensive planning and questioning before you finally made that decision. Similarly you would not buy a holiday simply because somebody said to you, 'I have got a nice holiday here that I am sure would suit you.' You would want to ask questions about where, when, how much, what type of accommodation and so on.

Would you make a choice to buy this without finding out full information?

Activity 3

Providing choice

Think about a person with whom you have recently worked. Consider all of your actions and whether or not they were given a choice about how to live their lives. If you believe that they were given every possible choice, then list the ways in which you ensured that that happened. If you believe that their choice was restricted in some way, identify the reasons why this happened and the steps you can take to ensure that it is not repeated.

Doing it well

Supporting people to make choices

- Communicate all information to people and their families clearly and in a way that can be understood.
- Make sure that their views are clearly represented at any forum where decisions are being taken or proposals are being formulated.
- Support people to put forward their own views wherever possible.
- Clearly record information and options, and ensure that all of the relevant people involved receive them.
- Make sure that people and their families receive information in a form that they can access and understand.
- Ensure that the person has the opportunity to comment in their own time about options and in an atmosphere where they feel able to make adverse comments if necessary.
- Always provide people with the information they need to make informed choices, even if that is restricted by their circumstances.

Exactly the same applies to people making choices about their lives. Your role is to make sure that they have the information they need, and either get it for them or signpost them to where to find it.

5.2 How your own role can support choices

Sometimes you may be in a position to support people in making choices because your own role may place you in a position of being able to promote people's rights, or even to direct others to do so. For example, you may be able to ensure that someone is able to exercise their rights in relation to access to records because your position gives you information on how to go about it.

Your job role may enable you to support people by advocating on their behalf in order to support them in making choices and exercising their rights. More unusually, you may be in a position of being able to direct staff for whom you have responsibility to take steps to support people in making choices and exercising rights. This may be over seemingly minor issues such as meals, clothes, going out or decisions about entertainment and leisure, but these are important parts of people's lives and it is your responsibility to ensure that people have the opportunity to make choices and take control of their lives.

5.3 Risk management and choices

It may sound like a contradiction to talk about risk management and choices. It is easy to use 'risk management' as a reason to restrict or even prevent people from making choices. Of course there will always be risks, but life is risky and people have the right to take risks in order to live as they wish and enjoy life.

Managing risk is important. Putting measures in place to reduce risks and make it possible for people to choose to do the things they want to is a key part of your role. Your job is not to restrict what people can do because of the risks they may face. Table 2 gives some examples of how risks can be managed so that people are still able to make their own decisions.

Later in this unit, we will look at how risk assessments are linked to choice and putting people at the centre of all activities.

5.4 Challenges and complaints

An important part of exercising rights is being able to complain if services are poor or do not meet expectations. All public service organisations are required to have a complaints procedure and to make the procedure readily available for people to use. Part of your role may be to assist people in making complaints, either directly, by supporting them in following the procedure, or indirectly, by making sure that they are aware of the complaints procedure and are able to follow it. Most complaints procedures will involve an informal stage, where complaints are discussed before they become more formal issues.

Complaints or challenges to an organisation are an important part of the monitoring process and they should be considered as part of every review of service provision. If everyone simply put up with poor service and no one complained to an organisation, people would never be aware of where the service needs improvement.

Activity	Possible risk	Protective factor
Using direct payments to pay a neighbour for support	• No CRB check – possible risk of abuse/exploitation • No training – risk of poor manual handling or food hygiene	• Supportive family • Long-standing neighbour been helping voluntarily for long period • Provide information about how to deal with worries or concerns
Moving to independent living	• Will not cope with day-to-day tasks • Will be vulnerable to exploitation • Will have accident/fall	• Regular support visits • Encourage links to local community • Supportive friends/family
Taking solo shopping trip	• May get lost • Will be robbed • Will not manage checkout • Will lose money	• Plan trip in advance • Rehearse trip with support • Advise about security

Table 2: Managing risks in activities.

Challenging decisions

People who use care services can find themselves the subject of decisions made by professionals. They may not agree with the decisions, but may not always feel able to challenge the decisions. Decisions could be about:

- accommodation
- the support plan
- changes in service provision
- assessment
- medication
- development activities
- personal care
- leisure time.

Functional skills

English: Speaking and listening

Take part in a group discussion about somebody you support. Ensure that you take an active role in the discussion, give your opinions clearly and use relevant terminology.

Give a presentation lasting for a minimum of five minutes on your chosen person. Ensure that you have prepared for this thoroughly by organising your notes in a logical way. Speak clearly and adapt your use of language to suit the audience.

Case study

Dealing with comments and complaints

Sunny Ridge is a care home for older people. Many of the people in the setting are from a Chinese background and Chinese is regularly spoken, particularly during social activities like Mahjong tournaments, which are very popular.

Gerry, a new care worker, became key worker to Mr Wong. Mr Wong's English was limited and he sometimes forgot that Gerry could not speak Chinese. There were a number of misunderstandings where Mr Wong became frustrated because Gerry did not understand him. Gerry also felt at a disadvantage because he could not take part in the social activities that were conducted in Chinese.

One day Mr Wong's family came to complain to the supervisor that Gerry could not speak Chinese and would not try. They wanted Mr Wong to have a Chinese-speaking key worker.

Gerry's response was that he was employed as a care worker, not an interpreter, and as they were in the UK they should all be speaking English anyway.

1. What are the communication issues here?
2. What are Mr Wong's rights in this situation?
3. What are Gerry's rights?
4. How could the supervisor resolve this situation while promoting choice and independence for the residents and the care workers?

Decisions can be made in all aspects of people's lives.

Although good practice is that people should always be in control of decisions, this is not always the case. Sometimes events just happen, such as the closure of a facility or financial spending decisions, or changes in family circumstances.

On other occasions it may be that the type of decision does not put the person in control, such as decisions on benefits, immigration status or employment issues. Or, of course, it could just be poor practice!

People can find it hard to challenge a decision that has been made for them. It can be difficult for a range of reasons — for example, people:

- feel intimidated
- lack the confidence to make a challenge
- do not believe that they have the right to challenge the decisions of professionals
- may have had poor experiences in the past when they challenged decisions unsuccessfully
- may simply not know how to go about it.

You can support people to overcome all of these barriers. You may be able to provide encouragement and also practical help and advice. The following case studies show two different ways that people can be supported in exercising their rights to question and challenge decisions.

Case study

Reviewing Tony's medication

The doctor decided to change Tony's medication. Tony was unhappy about this, but did not feel that he could argue with the doctor. Carole, his support worker, spent time with Tony to talk through his worries and encouraged him to write some notes explaining his concerns. She then agreed to go with Tony to see the doctor, but only as a support while he raised the issues. In the event, Carole did not need to say a word; Tony used his notes to explain to his doctor why he was unhappy and disagreed with the change. Even when the doctor got quite cross, Tony was still able to make his point.

1. How do you think Carole's method of supporting affected Tony's confidence?
2. If you were Tony's care worker, would you have been tempted to speak up when the doctor got cross? When do you think you should intervene in that sort of situation?

Case study

May's Attendance Allowance

May has been told that she will only be eligible for Attendance Allowance at the lower rate. She thinks this is unfair as her daughter has to help her in the night sometimes. Davinda, her support worker, explained that May could appeal against the decision. She told May where to get the forms to do this and explained that she could get help from the Welfare Rights office if she needed someone to support her to make the appeal.

May and her daughter visited the office and were very pleased at how helpful the officers were, but May did say to Davinda that she was sure that they could not have managed the appeal on their own without support, as the process seemed pretty daunting.

1. What barriers was May facing?
2. How did Davinda support May to overcome these barriers?

6. Be able to promote individuals' well-being

6.1 Identity, self-image and self-esteem

The concept of self is usually described in terms of **self-image** — the person we think we are — and **self-esteem** or self-worth, which is concerned with the worth we attach to that self-image.

Self-image

Self-concept is about how people see themselves — self-image. 'Who am I?' This is one of the fundamental questions that philosophers and psychologists have sought to answer. How would you answer this question about yourself? Would you describe who you are in terms of what you do, for example, a support worker? Or perhaps in terms of your relationships with others, for example, a wife, a parent or a child? Have you ever described yourself as 'So-and-so's mum', or 'So-and-so's daughter'? You might think of yourself in terms of your hopes, dreams or ambitions. Or it is perhaps more likely that all of these ways of thinking about yourself contribute to your self-image.

Self-concept is about what makes people who they are. Everyone has a concept of themselves; it can be a positive image overall or a negative one, but a great

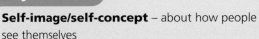

> **Key terms**
>
> **Self-image/self-concept** – about how people see themselves
> **Self-esteem** – how people value themselves

> **Activity 4**
>
> ### Your self-image
> Think about the number of different ways you could describe yourself. List them all. See how many relate to:
> * other people – for example, someone's mum, sister, friend
> * what you do – for example, care worker, volunteer at the youth club, gardener
> * what you believe – for example, honest, loyal, a Christian, a Muslim
> * what you look like – for example, short, brown hair, blue eyes.
>
> You may be surprised when you see the greatest influences on how you view yourself.

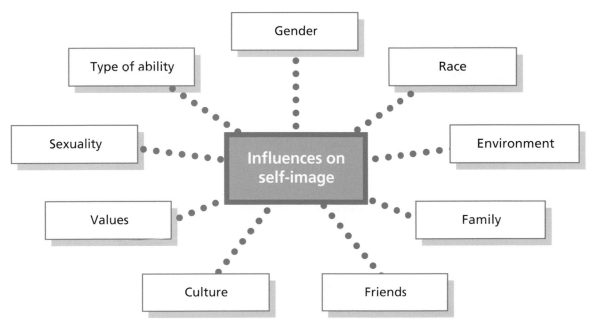

Do you see the factors that can influence how someone sees themselves?

many factors contribute to an individual sense of identity. These will include: gender, race, language/accent, values and beliefs, religion and sexual orientation.

All of these are aspects of our lives that contribute towards our idea of who we are. As a support worker, it is essential that you take time to consider how each of the people you support will have developed their own self-image and identity, and it is important that you recognise and promote this.

You should make sure you recognise that the values, beliefs, tastes and preferences which people have are what makes them who they are, and must be supported, nurtured and encouraged, and not ignored and disregarded because they are inconvenient or do not fit in with the care system.

Reflect

Think about just one person you have worked with. Note down all the influences on their sense of identity. Have you really thought about it before? Think about the difference it may make to your practice now that you have spent some time reflecting about the influences that have made a person who they are.

Self-esteem

Self-esteem is about how people value themselves — self-worth. Self-esteem results from the way people feel about themselves. It is important that people feel that they have a valuable contribution to make, whether it is to society as a whole or within a smaller area such as their local community, workplace or own family.

Feeling good about yourself also has a great deal to do with your own experiences throughout your life and the kind of confidence that you were given as you grew up. All human beings need to feel that they have a valuable place and a valuable contribution to make within society.

The reasons why people have different levels of self-esteem are complex. The way people feel about themselves is often laid down during childhood. A child who is encouraged and regularly told how good they are and given a lot of positive feelings is the sort of person who is likely to feel that they have something to offer and can make a useful contribution to any situation. But a child who is constantly shouted at, blamed or belittled is likely to grow into an adult who lacks belief in themselves, or finds it difficult to go into new situations and to accept new challenges.

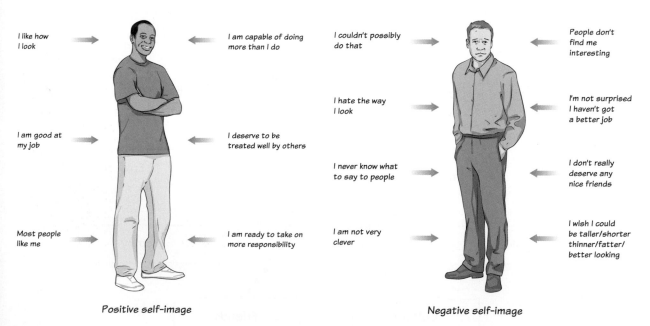

I like how I look

I am capable of doing more than I do

I am good at my job

I deserve to be treated well by others

Most people like me

I am ready to take on more responsibility

Positive self-image

I couldn't possibly do that

People don't find me interesting

I hate the way I look

I'm not surprised I haven't got a better job

I never know what to say to people

I don't really deserve any nice friends

I am not very clever

I wish I could be taller/shorter thinner/fatter/ better looking

Negative self-image

Do you see the factors that can influence how someone values themselves?

Not all the reasons for levels of self-confidence and self-image come from childhood. There are many experiences in adult life that can affect self-confidence and how people feel about themselves, for example:

- being made redundant
- getting divorced
- the death of somebody close
- the loss of independence, possibly having to go into residential care or into hospital
- the shock of being burgled
- having a bad fall, which results in a feeling of helplessness and a lack of self-worth
- being the subject of discriminatory or stereotyping abusive behaviour
- being the victim of violent or aggressive behaviour.

All of these experiences can have devastating effects. Very often, people will become withdrawn and depressed as a result, and a great deal of support and concentrated effort is needed to help them through these very difficult situations. People can be very vulnerable at these low points in their lives, and it is important that you make sure you have followed the procedures in your organisation for assessing and managing the risk of self-harm where you are aware that someone is going through a period of very low self-esteem.

Activity 5

Identifying criteria that trigger a risk assessment

Check your organisation's policies and procedures to identify the key criteria which will trigger a risk assessment for someone who has been showing low self-esteem and feelings of worthlessness.

Functional skills

English: Reading

Read formal documents within your organisation to gather information. Identify the key components within the text and summarise them in written notes to help you form the basis of a risk assessment.

Self-esteem is also very closely tied into the culture we live in, and the values which that particular culture has about what is important. For example, among a group of young car thieves, the person most admired might be the one who has stolen most cars, and the self-esteem of that person is likely to be really high because of this admiration and approval; these are not values that would be shared by other people in the community! So never forget the influences of values and culture on self-esteem and on self-concept.

6.2 Influences on well-being

Well-being concerns all aspects of a person's life including physical and mental health, emotional and intellectual fulfilment, and overall contentment. Overall well-being is far more than just not being ill – it is about meeting different kinds of needs from basic physical needs like food and shelter through intellectual fulfilment. Only when someone has their needs met are they likely to feel contented and happy with their lives.

Can you think of ways to encourage healthy eating?

Physical and mental health

Physical health is important and people who do have physical health issues can find it difficult to feel happy and contented. Promoting good health is always an important part of your support role; encouraging healthy eating and appropriate exercise and activity is valuable in supporting the well-being of people you support. This does not mean delivering lectures or organising marches! It does mean thinking about a balanced diet that is appropriate for the level of activity that people can undertake, and supporting people during an activity within their abilities.

Mental health can have a major impact on people's lives and their well-being. If someone is suffering from depression, the whole world will seem dark and they will feel hopeless and helpless. People who are feeling stressed or anxious will also not be able to feel contented and happy. Mental health problems can be the result of external factors such as the demands and stresses of life, but some serious types of psychotic illness are also the result of chemical imbalances that require ongoing medication and treatment.

Do not expect that anyone who has a mental health problem will be able to 'pull themselves together' or 'just get on with it'. They are not able to do that — if they could, they would have already done so — people do not generally choose to be unhappy.

Meeting needs

People have all sorts of needs, but making sure that they are met is a key part of support plans and the services you deliver.

Physical needs

These are things like food and drink, warmth, shelter, sleep and exercise.

Physical needs are usually very basic, and it is impossible to survive without them. The needs will vary with the age of the person and their stage of life, but generally, human beings have a greater range of physical needs at the start of their lives and in old age. These tend to be the times when physical needs are greater than just food, drink, warmth and shelter. At the beginning of life a baby needs help with moving, feeding and cleaning of body waste. In the later stages of life, or because of a disability or accident, people may also need help to meet some, or all, of these needs.

Intellectual needs

This is not about being clever! Intellectual needs are about mental stimulation and having varied interests. Everyone needs to keep their brain active — all humans need to have something which holds their interest or makes them think. Like physical needs, intellectual needs change to fit the life stage: a baby will be stimulated by colours and simple shapes or by new sounds, whereas an older child or adolescent requires considerably more to prevent boredom. An adult will benefit from having interests and outlets which offer a challenge and a change. Later adulthood is a vital time to ensure that intellectual needs are met, as maintaining interests and having access to mental stimulation become increasingly important if physical abilities decline.

Emotional needs

The keys to emotional fulfilment are being clear about who you are, and liking who you are. If people are confused about their own identity or are unhappy with themselves, then it will always be difficult for them to reach out to others and develop good relationships. Most people like to be liked; most people like to love and be loved. At the various stages of our lives, the needs will be different, but basically everyone needs to feel secure, nurtured and loved. A newborn child needs to feel safe and secure, or they will become distressed and unhappy. As children grow, they benefit from receiving love and caring, as well as having boundaries, limits and routines which provide security. As adolescents progress into adulthood, emotional fulfilment is likely to come from developing a close emotional bond with another person.

Social needs

Social needs are about relationships with other people. Humans have always sought to meet their social needs by living in groups alongside others. All cultures have a history of people grouping together in villages and towns, or simply in tribes or families.

Activity 6

Your needs

Think about the different needs you have. Make a list, including at least five needs under each of the headings above. Ask a friend or colleague to do the same, then compare and see how many are different and how many are the same.

6.3 and 6.4 Supporting identity, self-image and self-esteem

There are also many practical ways in which people's needs can be met through the way in which you provide the services they need. Being recognised and valued as an individual is hugely important for people's self-esteem. When somebody either requests, or is referred, for a service, the assessment and planning cycle begins. Throughout the consultation and planning which follows, the person and their needs should be at the centre of the process. You will need to make sure that the person has every opportunity to state exactly how they wish their needs to be met. Some will be able to give this information personally, while others will need an advocate who will support them in expressing their views.

Feeling valued as an individual is vital to increasing self-esteem and confidence, and making people feel good about themselves. After all, it is very hard to feel good about yourself, if you do not believe that anyone else thinks much of you. If you are able to feel that people respect and value you, then you are more likely to value yourself.

As a care worker, you will come across situations where a little thought or a small change in practice could give greater opportunities for people to feel that they are valued and respected as individuals. For example, you may need to find out how someone likes to be addressed – do they consider that 'Mr' or 'Mrs' is more respectful and appropriate, or are they happy for a first name to be used? This, particularly for some older people, can be one of the ways of indicating the respect that is important for anyone who uses care services.

You will need to give thought to the values and beliefs which people may have, for example:

- religious or cultural beliefs about eating specific foods
- values about forms of dress which are acceptable
- beliefs or preferences about who should be able to provide personal care.

This will mean that you need to make sure that people have been asked about religious, cultural or personal preferences and that those preferences are recorded so that all care workers and others providing care are able to access them.

There may already be arrangements in your workplace to ask for and record this information. If so, you must ensure that you are familiar with the process and that you know where to find the information for everyone you work with. If your workplace does not have arrangements in place to find out about people's choices and preferences, you should discuss with your line manager ways in which you can help to find this out.

Simple, open questions, asked politely are always the best way: 'Excuse me, Mr Khan, the information I have here notes that you are vegetarian. Can you tell me about the foods you prefer?'

Why do you think looking good can help self-esteem and confidence?

Some information you can obtain by observation – for instance, looking at someone can tell you a lot about their preferences regarding dress. Particular forms of dress which are being worn for religious or cultural reasons are usually obvious; a turban or a sari, for instance, are easy to spot, but other forms of dress may also give you some clues about the person wearing them. Consider how dress can tell you about how much money people have or what kind of background they come from. Clothes also tell you a lot about someone's age and the type of lifestyle they are likely to have had. Beware, however – any information you think you gain from this type of observation must be confirmed by checking your facts. Otherwise it is easy to be caught out – some people from wealthy backgrounds wear scruffy clothes, and some people in their seventies wear the latest fashions and have face lifts!

Equally, be careful that you do not resort to thinking in stereotypes, rather than working with people as individuals. Avoid making assumptions about people based on any of the factors that make them similar to others, such as:

- age
- gender
- race
- culture
- skin colour
- job
- wealth
- where they live.

All of these factors are important in giving you information about what may have influenced the development of each person – but they will never, on their own, tell you anything else about a person. The impact of stereotypical assumptions about people can result in very low self-esteem and a negative self-image. After all, if everyone assumes that just because you are 85 years old, you are too old to be interested in current affairs, or the latest sports news, you may decide that perhaps you are too old to bother; or, if employers keep refusing to give you a job because you live in an inner city, are 16 years old, male and black, you may well decide that it is not worth bothering to try any more.

Activity 7

Filling in a form

Look at the form, or other means of recording information, which is used in your workplace. Fill it in as if you were the person using the service. Now note down all the factors which make you who you are. For example, think about your:

- gender
- age
- background
- economic and social circumstances
- nationality
- culture
- religion
- sexual orientation
- food preferences
- entertainment preferences
- relaxation preferences
- reading material preferences.

Look at the form you have completed – would it tell anyone enough about you so that they could ensure that all your needs were met and you did not lose parts of your life that were important to you? If not, think about what other questions you need to ask, note them down and make sure that you ask them to the people you support!

Functional skills

English: Writing

You will practise completing a form. The information must be fit for purpose and punctuation, spelling and grammar should be accurate. Information on the form should be clear and concise.

7. Understand the role of risk assessment in enabling a person-centred approach

7.1 Risk assessment in health and social care

Risk assessments are used in several different ways in order to deliver safe and effective services that have people at the centre. Table 3 shows some examples.

Activity	Purpose of risk assessment
Moving and handling	Reduce risk of injury to worker and person being moved
Development activities	Reduce risk of injury to person undertaking the activity
Invasive treatment, managing open wounds	Reduce risk of infection
Finding appropriate resources for someone	Reduce risk of harm and abuse
Planning changes in support arrangements	Reduce risk of distress or concern

Table 3: Risk assessments for different activities.

As you can see from the table, risk assessments are carried out for various reasons, but they are always used in order to protect either the person using the services or the support worker, or both. Risk assessments should never be used as a reason to prevent people from making choices; they are there to protect and to ensure that risks are reduced.

7.2 How risk-taking and risk assessment relate to rights and responsibilities

Everyone is entitled to take risks. We all take risks in our daily lives. Every time we get on a plane or cross the road, put money in a bank, take part in a sporting activity or plug in a toaster, we are taking risks.

All of these risks we assess and make sure that they are managed. For example, we know that there are stringent safety procedures in place for aircraft, we know that there are regulations for banks, we take steps to maintain the electrical wiring in our houses so that we can reduce the risk of disaster when we use appliances.

Taking risks is part of being able to choose and being in control of your life, so you need to ensure that concern about risks is not getting in the way of people living their lives in the way they want to. Many times, a risk assessment can make it possible for someone to do something that may seem unlikely in the first instance.

Case study

Alice's risk assessment

Alice, who has a learning disability, wants to move into a flat with a friend she has met at her work placement. A risk assessment will look at ways of reducing the risks to Alice from her move. The assessment may look at the steps that can be taken for Alice to increase her independence in the way she wants to. There could be a drop-in from a support worker and a link set up with a local supported living unit where Alice could go if she feels she needs support. It may be possible for a flat to be found through a housing association so that there

are no concerns about the safety and the maintenance of the property. With all the steps in place to reduce the risks, it makes it possible for those who are concerned for Alice's safety and well-being to feel more confident and it means that Alice can live her life as she wishes.

1. What risks do you think the risk assessment might pick up?
2. How do you think Alice will feel, knowing the risk assessment has been carried out?

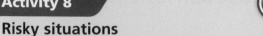

Activity 8

Risky situations

Think about a time when you have said 'no' or advised against something because you thought it was too risky. If you are honest, could you have done a risk assessment? Think about people you currently support who may like to change their lives or get involved in something that might be risky. Plan out how the risks can be reduced so that it may be able to happen.

7.3 Why risk assessments need to be regularly revised

People's circumstances do not remain the same for ever – everything changes. It could be someone's condition that improves or deteriorates, it could be their situation that changes or it could be that the risks change because of new developments. For example, the development of telecare and telehealth has reduced the risks for many people with long-term health conditions who want to remain at home.

Changes mean that people's risk assessments need to be revised regularly and updated. The most likely time to do this would be at the regular review when the risk

assessment can be reviewed along with all other aspects of service provision. If people's circumstances change, then a review of the risk assessment is essential – all changes to a person's life will mean that the risk profile has changed and needs to be looked at again.

Overall, putting people at the centre of all your work is about never forgetting that it is their life, hopes, dreams and plans that should remain the focus, and it is your job to make sure that they are able to make the most of their lives and achieve as much as they possibly can.

Legislation

● Mental Capacity Act 2005

Further reading and research

● www.bild.org.uk (British Institute of Learning Disabilities)
● www.dh.gov.uk (Putting People First Department of Health (2007))
● www.valuingpeoplenow.dh.gov.uk (Valuing people now)

Getting ready for assessment

You will need to demonstrate your knowledge and understanding. You may have to prepare an assignment or a presentation that will show that you understand the ways in which person-centred values are at the heart of the way you work. The assessment criteria require that you explain and evaluate; this means that you must be sure to give reasons and answer the question 'why'?

An evaluation means that you should be able to present evidence about the use of care plans and then reach some conclusions about how they can be used. Using examples is important; if possible, use examples of people with whom you work (with their agreement). If not, use examples from case studies or from a television programme, a film or a book.

Unit HSC 037

Promote and implement health and safety in health and social care

This unit is about how you can contribute to making your workplace a safe, secure and healthy place for people who use it to meet their care needs, for those who work alongside you, and for yourself. Your workplace may be a home environment or any other health or care facility. This unit provides you with the basic knowledge and skills to work safely and to ensure that others are aware of the importance of always being aware of the health and safety issues, regardless of where support is being provided.

In this unit you will learn about:

- **your responsibilities, and the responsibilities of others, relating to health and safety**
- **how to carry out your responsibilities for health and safety**
- **procedures for responding to accidents and sudden illness**
- **how to reduce the spread of infection**
- **how to move and handle equipment and other objects safely**
- **how to handle hazardous substances and materials**
- **how to promote fire safety in the work setting**
- **how to implement security measures in the work setting**
- **how to manage stress.**

1. Understand own responsibilities, and the responsibilities of others, relating to health and safety

1.1 Legislation relating to health and safety in a health or social care work setting

The settings in which you are likely to provide support are generally covered by the Health and Safety at Work Act 1974 (HASAWA). This Act is like the overall 'umbrella' that has been updated and supplemented by all the regulations and guidelines which extend it, support it or explain it. The regulations most likely to affect your workplace are shown in the diagram below.

1.2 and 1.3 Health and safety policies and procedures and responsibilities in the work setting

There are many regulations, laws and guidelines dealing with health and safety. You do not need to know the detail, but you do need to know where your responsibilities begin and end.

The laws place certain responsibilities on both employers and employees. For example, it is up to the employer to provide a safe place in which to work, but the employee also has to show reasonable care for their own safety.

Employers have to:

- make the workplace safe
- prevent **risks** to health
- ensure that machinery is safe to use, and that safe working practices are set up and followed
- make sure that all materials are handled, stored and used safely
- provide adequate first aid facilities
- tell you about any potential **hazards** from the work you do, chemicals and other substances used by the organisation, and give you information, instructions, training and supervision as needed
- set up emergency plans

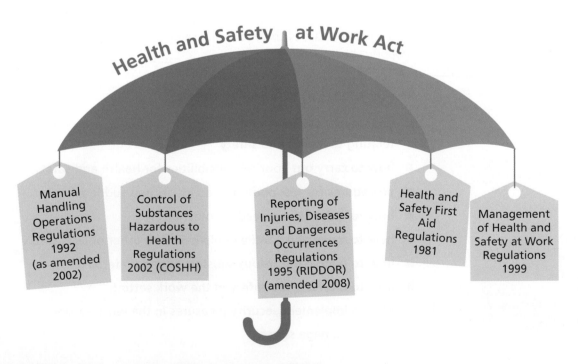

Do you see how the Health and Safety at Work Act is like an umbrella?

- make sure that ventilation, temperature, lighting, and toilet, washing and rest facilities all meet health, safety and welfare requirements
- check that the right work equipment is provided and is properly used and regularly maintained
- prevent or control exposure to substances that may damage your health
- take precautions against the risks caused by flammable or explosive hazards, electrical equipment, noise and radiation
- avoid potentially dangerous work involving manual handling and, if it cannot be avoided, take precautions to reduce the risk of injury
- provide health supervision as needed
- provide protective clothing or equipment free of charge if risks cannot be removed or adequately controlled by any other means
- ensure that the right warning signs are provided and looked after
- report certain accidents, injuries, diseases and dangerous occurrences to either the Health and Safety Executive (HSE) or the local authority, depending on the type of business.

Key terms

Risk – the likelihood of a hazard causing harm
Hazard – something that could possibly cause harm

As an employee you have both rights and responsibilities in the workplace. Your rights are:

- as far as possible, to have any risks to your health and safety properly controlled
- to be provided, free of charge, with any personal protective and safety equipment
- if you have reasonable concerns about your safety, to stop work and leave your work area, without being disciplined
- to tell your employer about any health and safety concerns you have
- to get in touch with the Health and Safety Executive (HSE) or your local authority if your employer will not listen to your concerns, without being disciplined by them
- to have rest breaks during the working day, to have time off from work during the working week and to have annual paid holiday.

Your responsibilities are:

- to take reasonable care of your own health and safety
- if possible, to avoid wearing jewellery or loose clothing if operating machinery or using equipment
- if you have long hair or wear a headscarf, to make sure it is tucked out of the way (it could get caught in equipment or machinery)
- to take reasonable care not to put other people – fellow employees and members of the public – at risk by what you do or do not do in the course of your work
- to cooperate with your employer, making sure that you get proper training and that you understand and follow the company's health and safety policies
- not to interfere with or misuse anything that has been provided for your health, safety or welfare
- to report any injuries, strains or illnesses you suffer as a result of doing your job (your employer may need to change the way you work)
- to tell your employer if something happens that might affect your ability to work (for example, becoming pregnant or suffering an injury). Because your employer has a legal responsibility for your health and safety, they may need to suspend you while they find a solution to the problem, but you will normally be paid if this happens
- if you drive or operate equipment or machinery, to tell your employer if you take medication that makes you drowsy – they should temporarily move you to another job if they have one for you to do.

Both the employee and employer are jointly responsible for safeguarding the health and safety of anyone using the premises.

Each workplace which has five or more workers must have a written statement of health and safety policy. The policy must include:

- a statement of intention to provide a safe workplace
- the name of the person responsible for implementing the policy
- the names of any other people responsible for preventing particular health and safety hazards
- a list of identified health and safety hazards and the procedures to be followed in relation to them
- procedures for recording accidents at work
- details for evacuation of the premises.

Health and safety policy

Find out where the health and safety policy is for your workplace and make sure you read it.

Health and Safety Commission and Executive

The Health and Safety Commission (HSC) and the Health and Safety Executive (HSE) are responsible for the regulation of almost all the risks to health and safety arising from work activity in Britain. The Health and Safety Commission is sponsored by the Department for Work and Pensions and is accountable to the Minister of State for Work. The HSE's job is to help the Health and Safety Commission ensure that risks to people's health and safety from work activities are properly controlled.

The Health and Safety Executive (www.hse.gov.uk) states:

> 'Our mission is to protect people's health and safety by ensuring risks in the changing workplace are properly controlled.

> 'The HSC [Health and Safety Commission] believes that prevention is better than cure, and two key roles are providing information and support to ensure that workplaces are safe and enforcement in order to ensure that legislation is adhered to. The HSE has the power to prosecute employers who fail in any way to safeguard the health and safety of people who use their premises.'

English: Reading; Writing

Read the policy on health and safety within your organisation. Find health and safety policies from two other organisations and compare their contents. In note form, summarise the key differences between the three policies.

1.4 Specific tasks in the work setting that should not be carried out without special training

All manual handling needs to be carried out by people who have had training to do it. Employers are obliged to provide training in manual handling, and you have to attend it once a year. Training is not a one-off; it is important to be up to date with the latest techniques and equipment, as well as any changes in regulations. This area of work is very tightly controlled by legislation and regulations for very good reasons; moving people without proper training is dangerous both for them and for you. You will also need training for specific pieces of equipment — for example, if a new hoist is to be used in your workplace, no one will be able to operate it without training. You may think that it looks very similar to the last one you used and may be sure that it probably works in the same way — but you must have specific training on that particular hoist before using it. This applies to any piece of equipment that you have not used before.

Clinical tasks including taking measurements such as temperature or blood pressure will require training as will changing dressings or giving medication. There is more information about each of these in Unit HSC 3047.

2. Be able to carry out own responsibilities for health and safety

2.1 Using policies and procedures that relate to health and safety

What is safety?

It sounds very simple and straightforward: make sure that the place in which you work is safe and secure. But for whom does it need to be safe, and from whom does it need to be safe? Do people need to be safe from tripping over things, hazardous fumes, infection, intruders, work-related injuries? You can begin to see that this is a wide and complex subject. It may help if you think about safety and security in respect of the areas of responsibility shown in Table 1.

There is no point having policies and procedures if they are not followed. You must be clear about the areas that are your responsibility and make sure that you are carrying out your work in line with the policies and procedures laid down by your employer.

2.2 Ways to support others to understand and follow safe practices

Support and care environments are places where accidents can quite often happen – not necessarily because staff are careless or fail to check for hazards, but because of the vulnerability of the people who are using support.

As people become frail or develop physical conditions that affect mobility such as arthritis or Parkinson's disease, they become susceptible to falls and trips because they are unsteady, and the slightest change in surface or level can upset their balance. Increasing age can also result in less flexibility of muscles and joints, meaning that people are less able to compensate for a loss of balance or a slip, and are more likely to fall than younger people, who may be better able to save themselves by reacting more quickly.

Age is not the only factor to increase risk. Other factors, such as impaired vision, multiply the risks of accidents from trips, falls, touching hot surfaces and knocking into objects. Hearing loss can increase the risk of accidents where people have not heard someone, or perhaps something such as a trolley, approaching around a corner. Dementia can increase risks because people fail to remember to take care when they move about. They can also forget where they have put things down or no longer remember the consequences of actions such as touching hot liquids or pulling on cupboard doors.

Supporting people to take steps about their own safety

It is important that you recognise that people you are supporting need to be able to ensure their own health and well-being as far as possible. To support this, you should encourage and assist people to:

- talk about the steps they would prefer to take in relation to health and safety
- understand and take responsibility for promoting their own health and care
- assess and manage risks to their health and well-being
- identify and report any factors that may put themselves or others at risk.

It is very difficult if you are the only person in your workplace following good practice. You may be able to encourage others by:

- always showing a good example yourself
- explaining why you are following procedures
- getting some health and safety leaflets from your trade union or environmental health office and leaving them in the staffroom for people to see
- bringing in any information you can about courses or safety lectures
- asking your supervisor if they can arrange a talk on health and safety.

Challenging inappropriate practice

You may have to deal with a situation where one of your colleagues is misusing equipment or behaving towards people in a way that fails to minimise risks to health, safety or security.

If you are faced with the situation where a colleague is behaving inappropriately or bad practice is being

Employer's responsibilities	Employee's responsibilities	Shared responsibilities
Planning safety and security	Using the systems and procedures correctly	Safety of people using the facilities
Providing information about safety and security	Reporting flaws or gaps in the systems, equipment or procedures in use	Safety of the environment
Updating systems and procedures		

Table 1: Responsibilities for safety and security in the workplace.

allowed to occur, you can respond in several ways. Depending on the severity of the problem, you should:

- challenge the behaviour, or the source of the bad practice
- have a one-to-one discussion with the colleague in question
- act as a mentor with whom your colleague can share problems and difficulties
- act as a role model of good practice.

Reflect

Working with your colleagues or alone, think about how inappropriate practice is challenged in your workplace. Have you ever challenged anything you have seen? Have you ever thought that you should? If you know that you should have acted, try to think about what stopped you. Spend some time thinking about how you could improve your practice.

2.3 Monitoring and reporting potential health and safety risks

You share responsibility with your employer for the safety of all the people who use your service. This means that you need to be alert all the time — risks and hazards are constantly changing and you need to make sure that you are aware of these changes. Just because you checked something six months ago, do not assume that it is still working well; a hoist that worked last week may not work today, a carpet that was fine three months ago may now be worn. Stay vigilant.

There are many hazards that can present risks of injury to people, especially if they are older, ill, have limited capacity or are disabled. You need to be aware of and monitor the following types of hazards regularly.

Environmental hazards

These include:

- wet or slippery floors
- cluttered passageways or corridors
- rearranged furniture
- worn carpets or rugs
- electrical flexes.

Hazards connected with equipment and materials

Examples of such hazards include:

- faulty brakes on beds
- worn or faulty electrical or gas appliances
- worn or damaged lifting equipment
- worn or damaged mobility aids
- incorrectly labelled substances, such as cleaning fluids
- leaking or damaged containers
- faulty waste-disposal equipment.

Hazards connected with people

This category of hazards includes:

- handling procedures
- visitors to the building
- intruders
- violent and aggressive behaviour.

If you become concerned that there are risks in your workplace, or relating to the people that you support or to colleagues, then you cannot ignore them. You need to take active steps to make sure that these risks are dealt with. Taking action means telling someone. There is little point in making a note in a file that you know your manager or employer is unlikely to see. Of course you will have recorded it and, yes, that will technically mean that you have taken the appropriate action. But if you know that your note is not going to result in a risk being reduced, then you have a duty to take more positive steps to ensure that the risk is dealt with.

Reporting risks

Reporting risks to your manager or employer is important if you feel that, even after a risk assessment and control measures, the risk is still not reduced sufficiently. When you inform your manager, the hazard and the management of the associated risk becomes an organisational responsibility. You should report hazards that are beyond your role and competence, such as:

- faulty equipment – for example, fires, kettles, computers
- worn floor coverings
- loose or damaged fittings
- obstructions too heavy for you to move safely
- damaged or faulty aids – for example, hoists, bed brakes, bathing aids
- people acting suspiciously on the premises
- fire.

As well as your responsibility to report risks and hazards to your employer, all employers have to report certain events to the Health and Safety Executive or environmental health department.

Reporting of Injuries, Diseases and Dangerous Occurrences (RIDDOR) Regulations 1995 (amended 2008)

Reporting accidents and ill-health at work is a legal requirement. All accidents, diseases and dangerous occurrences should be reported to the Incident Contact Centre. The Centre was established on 1 April 2001 as a single point of contact for all incidents in the UK. The information is important because it means that risks and causes of accidents, incidents and diseases can be identified, and any necessary risk assessments carried out. All notifications are passed on to either the local authority environmental health department, or the Health and Safety Executive, as appropriate.

Your employer needs to report:

- deaths
- major injuries (see Table 2)
- accidents resulting in more than three days off work
- diseases
- dangerous occurrences.

Dangerous occurrences

If something happens which does not result in a reportable injury, but which clearly could have done, then it may be a dangerous occurrence that must be reported immediately.

Activity 2

Reportable major injuries and diseases

Check that you understand fully all the terms used in Table 2. If there are any that you are unsure about, ask your supervisor or research them online or in the library.

Accidents at work

If accidents or injuries occur at work, either to you, other staff or to someone you are supporting, then the details must be recorded. For example, someone may have a fall, or slip on a wet floor. You must record the incident regardless of whether there was an injury.

Functional skills

Maths: Use statistical methods to investigate a situation

Find government statistics on accidents at work. Choose a minimum of two sets of data (these could be over two separate years) and devise a chart to show your findings under headings.

In your workplace, find the statistics for accidents/injuries over the last two years for employees and calculate the proportion/ratio of people who have had accidents to those who have not. What percentage of the workforce have had accidents? Show all calculations clearly.

Your employer should have procedures in place for making a record of accidents, either an accident book or an accident report form. This is not only required by the RIDDOR regulations, but also, if you work in a residential or nursing home, by the Inspectorate for the country in which you work.

Any accident book or report form must comply with the requirements of the Data Protection Act 1998 by making sure that the personal details of those involved

Reportable injuries	Reportable diseases
Fracture other than to fingers, thumbs or toes	Certain poisonings
Amputation	Some skin diseases such as occupational dermatitis, skin cancer, chrome ulcer, oil folliculitis acne
Dislocation of the shoulder, hip, knee or spine	Lung diseases including occupational asthma, farmer's lung, pneumoconiosis, asbestosis, mesothelioma
Loss of sight (temporary or permanent)	Infections such as leptospirosis, hepatitis, tuberculosis, anthrax, legionellosis (legionnaires' disease) and tetanus
Chemical or hot metal burn to the eye or any penetrating injury to the eye	Other conditions such as occupational cancer, certain musculoskeletal disorders, decompression illness and hand-arm vibration syndrome
Injury resulting from an electric shock or electrical burn leading to unconsciousness or requiring resuscitation or admittance to hospital for more than 24 hours	
Any other injury which leads to hypothermia (getting too cold), heat-induced illness, or unconsciousness; requires resuscitation; or requires admittance to hospital for more than 24 hours	
Unconsciousness caused by asphyxia (suffocation) or exposure to a harmful substance or biological agent	
Acute illness requiring medical treatment, or leading to loss of consciousness, arising from absorption of any substance by inhalation, ingestion or through the skin	
Acute illness requiring medical treatment where there is reason to believe that this resulted from exposure to a biological agent or its toxins or infected material	

Table 2: Reportable major injuries and diseases.

cannot be read by others using the book. This can be ensured by recording personal details on a tear-off part of the form so that only an anonymous description of the accident is left, or by using individual, numbered and recorded forms that are then logged at a central point. However it is done, it is a legal requirement that people's personal details are not available for others to see unless consent has been given.

Make sure you know where the accident report forms or the accident book are kept, and who is responsible for recording accidents. It is likely to be your manager. You must report any accident in which you are involved, or which you have witnessed, to your manager or supervisor. It may be useful to make notes, as in the example on the following page, as soon as possible after the incident so that details on the accident report form can be complete and accurate.

Any medical treatment or assessment that is necessary should be arranged without delay. If someone has been involved in an accident, you should check if there is anyone they would like to be contacted, perhaps a relative or friend. If the accident is serious, and you cannot consult the person — because they are unconscious, for example — you should inform their next of kin as soon as possible.

Date: 24.1.11   **Time:** 14.30 hrs   **Location:** Main Lounge

Description of accident:

PH got out of her chair and began to walk across the lounge with the aid of her stick. She turned her head to continue the conversation she had been having with GK, and as she turned back again, she appeared not to have noticed that MP's handbag had been left on the floor. PH tripped over the handbag and fell heavily, banging her head on a footstool.

She was very shaken and although she said that she was not hurt, there was a large bump on her head. PH appeared pale and shaky. I asked S to fetch a blanket and to call Mrs J, deputy officer in charge. Covered PH with a blanket. Mrs J arrived immediately. Dr was sent for after PH was examined by Mrs J.

Dr arrived after about 20 mins and said that PH was bruised and shaken, but did not seem to have any injuries.

PH wanted to go and lie down. She was helped to bed.

Incident was witnessed by six residents who were in the lounge at the time: GK, MP, IL, MC, CR and BQ.

Signed: **Name:**

Notes like these would help you to get all the details right in a later accident report.

Complete a report, and ensure that all witnesses to the accident also complete reports. You should include the following in any accident report:

- date, time and place of accident
- person/people involved – bearing in mind the Data Protection Act
- circumstances and details of exactly what you saw
- anything that was said by the people involved
- the condition of the person after the accident
- steps taken to summon help, time of summoning help and time when help arrived
- names of any other people who witnessed the accident
- any equipment involved in the accident.

2.4 Risk assessments in health and safety

Risk assessment in health and social care is important for everyone whether they are employers, self-employed or employees, who are required by law to identify and assess risks in the workplace. This includes any situations where potential harm may be caused. There are many regulations that require risks to be assessed and some are covered by European Community directives. These include:

- Management of Health and Safety at Work Regulations 1999
- Manual Handling Operations Regulations 1992 (amended 2002)
- Personal Protective Equipment at Work Regulations 1992

- Health and Safety (Display Screen Equipment) Regulations 1992 (amended 2002)
- Noise at Work Regulations 1989
- Control of Substances Hazardous to Health Regulations 2002 (COSHH)
- Control of Asbestos at Work Regulations 2002
- Control of Lead at Work Regulations 2002.

There are other regulations that deal with very specialised risks such as major hazards and ionising radiation. However, these are not common risks in health or social care workplaces.

There are five key stages to undertaking a risk assessment, which involve answering the following questions.

1. What is the purpose of the risk assessment?

2. Who has to assess the risk?

3. Whose risk should be assessed?

4. What should be assessed?

5. When should the risk be assessed?

The Management of Health and Safety at Work Regulations 1999 state that employers have to assess any risks which are associated with the workplace and work activities. This means all activities, from walking on wet floors to dealing with violence. Having carried out a risk assessment, the employer must then apply **risk control measures**. This means that actions must be identified to reduce the risks. For example, alarm buzzers may need to be installed or extra staff employed, as well as steps taken such as providing extra training for staff or written guidelines on how to deal with a particular hazard.

> **Key term**
>
> **Risk control measures** – actions taken in order to reduce an identified risk

Risk assessments are vitally important in order to protect the health and safety of both you and the people you support. You should always check that a risk assessment has been carried out before you undertake any task, and then follow the steps identified in the assessment in order to reduce the risk.

However, do not forget that you must balance the individual wishes and preferences of each person who uses a service with your own safety and the safety of others. Some examples of this principle are discussed in the section on manual handling on page 213.

Risks in someone's home

Of course, the situation is somewhat different if you work in a person's own home. Your employer can still carry out risk assessments and put risk control measures in place, such as a procedure for working in twos in a situation where there is a risk of violence. What cannot be done is to remove environmental hazards such as trailing electrical flexes, rugs with curled-up edges, worn patches on stair carpets or old equipment. All you can do is to advise the person whose home it is of the risks, and suggest how things could be improved. You also need to take care!

Dilemmas

It may be your workplace, but it is the person's home. If you work in somebody's home or long-term residential setting, you have to balance the need for safety with the rights of people to have their living space the way they want it. You are entitled to expect a safe place in which to work, but remember people's rights to choose how they want to live. Concerns for security can also create difficult situations. Of course people have a right to see whomever they wish, but there can be situations where there may be concerns about vulnerable people being exploited or placed at risk of harm. You cannot insist on the levels of security that people adopt in their own homes, but you can advise people of the risks of opening doors to strangers or inviting unknown people in.

People also need to assess the risks involved in doing the things they wish to do safely and without placing themselves at undue risk of harm. For example, someone with dementia may wish to go out shopping alone. This is potentially risky as they may become disoriented and be unable to find their way back. A risk assessment will help to look at the risks and the control measures that can be put in place in order to reduce the risks of the activity; for example, suggesting that a friend accompany the person, or cards with details of address and contact numbers be placed in pockets and bags and simple instructions with key landmarks are practised with the person prior to the trip.

Risks can be reduced through a risk assessment.

Effective risk assessments make it possible for people to do things. Risk assessments are not about restricting what people do, they are about making sure that it is done safely. The potential for health and safety concerns to limit people's activities and restrict their rights can be greatly decreased by good risk assessments that put sensible control measures in place to reduce the risks. Life is full of risks, and all people, regardless of age or ability, have the right to take risks in order to live as they wish. But a well carried-out risk assessment can make it less likely that any harm will result.

A person with a visual impairment may be intending to take up a new exercise regime at a local gym. A risk assessment carried out with the person can identify any control measures needed such as liaison with the gym to ensure that it can provide the necessary support on using the equipment, offering a support worker if necessary and a review of travel arrangements.

2.5 Minimising potential risks and hazards

It is important that you develop an awareness of health and safety risks, and that you are always aware of any risks in any situation you are in. If you get into the habit of making a mental checklist, you will find that it helps. You can also use this to support people to think about their own health and safety, and to make them aware of the need to be constantly vigilant to avoid accidents and injury. The checklist will vary for each person or workplace, but could look like the one in Table 3.

Your role

Your responsibility to contribute to a safe environment means more than simply being aware of these potential hazards. You must take steps to check and deal with any sources of risk. If you are supervising staff, you must also ensure that they are aware of the possible risks and hazards and know how to deal with them, or how to ask for help or advice from a senior member of staff. Although it is ultimately your employer's responsibility, you have a duty to ensure the safety of any staff you supervise.

Dealing with the hazard

This means you have taken individual responsibility. It will probably apply to obvious hazards such as:

- trailing flexes — roll them up and store them safely
- wet floors — dry them as far as possible and put out warning signs
- cluttered doorways and corridors — remove objects and store them safely or dispose of them appropriately; if items are heavy, use assistance or mechanical aids
- visitors to the building — challenge anyone you do not recognise; asking 'Can I help you?' is usually enough to establish whether a person has a good reason to be there
- fire — follow the correct procedures to raise the alarm and assist with evacuation.

After washing floors, dry them as much as possible, and set out warning signs.

Alternatively, you can inform your manager about hazards that you are unable to deal with directly. Once you inform your manager, the hazard becomes your employer's responsibility.

Area	Hazards	Check
Environment	Floors	Are they dry?
	Carpets and rugs	Are they worn or curled at the edges?
	Doorways and corridors	Are they clear of obstacles?
	Electrical flexes	Are they trailing?
Equipment	Beds	Are the brakes on? Are they high enough?
	Electrical or gas appliances	Are they worn? Have they been safety checked?
	Lifting equipment	Is it worn or damaged?
	Mobility aids	Are they worn or damaged?
	Substances such as cleaning fluids	Are they correctly labelled?
	Containers	Are they leaking or damaged?
	Waste disposal equipment	Is it faulty?
People	Visitors to the building	Should they be there?
	Handling procedures	Have they been assessed for risk?
	Intruders	Have the police been called?
	Violent and aggressive behaviour	Has it been dealt with?

Table 3: A hazard checklist.

How many hazards can you find — can you identify the risks?

3. Understand procedures for responding to accidents and sudden illness

3.1 Types of accidents and sudden illness that may occur in a health or social care setting

It is important that you are aware of the initial steps to take when dealing with the commonest health emergencies. You may be involved with any of these emergencies when you are at work, whether you work in a residential, hospital or community setting. There are major differences between the different work situations.

- If you are working in a hospital where skilled assistance is always immediately available, the likelihood of your having to act in an emergency, other than to summon help, is remote.
- In a residential setting, help is likely to be readily available, although it may not necessarily be the professional medical expertise of a hospital.
- In the community, you may have to summon help and take action to support a casualty until the help arrives. It is in this setting that you are most likely to need some knowledge of how to respond to a health emergency.

This section gives a guide to taking initial action in a number of illnesses or accidents that you may come across in your work. There are many others, but the general guidance given here may assist you in taking initial action until further assistance arrives in instances of:

- severe bleeding
- cardiac arrest
- shock
- loss of consciousness
- epileptic seizure
- choking and difficulty with breathing
- fractures and suspected fractures
- burns and scalds
- poisoning
- electrical injuries.

3.2 What to do following an accident or sudden illness

Severe bleeding

Severe bleeding can be the result of a fall or injury. The most common causes of severe cuts are glass, as the result of a fall into a window or glass door, or knives from accidents in the kitchen.

Symptoms

There will be apparently large quantities of blood from the wound. In some very serious cases, the blood may be pumping out. Even small amounts of blood can be very frightening, both for you and the casualty. Remember that a small amount of blood goes a long way, and things may look worse than they are. However, severe bleeding requires urgent medical attention in hospital. Although people rarely bleed to death, extensive bleeding can cause shock and loss of consciousness.

Aims

- To bring the bleeding under control
- To limit the possibility of infection
- To arrange urgent medical attention

Action for severe bleeding

You will need to apply pressure to a wound that is bleeding. If possible, use a sterile dressing. If one is not readily available, use any absorbent material, or even your hand. Do not forget the precautions (see 'Protect yourself' below). You will need to apply direct pressure over the wound for ten minutes (this can seem like a very long time) to allow the blood to clot.

If there is any object in the wound, such as a piece of glass, *do not* try to remove it. Simply apply pressure to the sides of the wound. Lay the casualty down and raise the affected part if possible. Make the person comfortable and secure.

In a residential care setting, call for the senior registered nurse to assess the severity of the injury. They will make a decision regarding whether the wound is severe enough to call a paramedic.

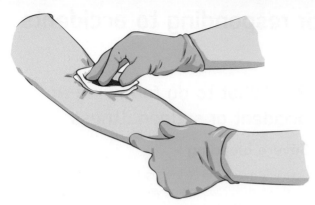

Would you know how to apply pressure to bleeding in an emergency situation?

Protect yourself

You should take steps to protect yourself when you are dealing with casualties who are bleeding. Your skin provides an excellent barrier to infections, but you must take care if you have any broken skin such as a cut, graze or sore. Seek medical advice if blood comes into contact with your mouth or nose, or gets into your eyes. Blood-borne viruses (such as HIV or hepatitis) can be passed only if the blood of someone who is already infected comes into contact with broken skin.

Ideally, wear disposable gloves. If this is not possible, cover any areas of broken skin with a waterproof dressing. If possible, wash your hands thoroughly in soap and water before and after exposure to blood. Take care with any needles or broken glass in the area. Use a mask for mouth-to-mouth resuscitation if the casualty's nose or mouth is bleeding.

Cardiac arrest

Cardiac arrest occurs when a person's heart stops. Cardiac arrest can happen for various reasons, the most common of which is a heart attack, but a person's heart can also stop as a result of shock, electric shock, a convulsion or other illness or injury.

Symptoms

- No pulse
- No breathing

Aims

- To obtain medical help as a matter of urgency

It is important to give oxygen, using mouth-to-mouth resuscitation, and to stimulate the heart, using chest compressions. This procedure is called cardio-pulmonary resuscitation – CPR. You will need to attend a first aid course to learn how to resuscitate; you cannot learn how to do this from a book. Giving CPR is very hard work and correct positioning is important, so you need the opportunity to try this out with supervision. On the first aid course you will be able to practise on a special dummy.

Action for cardiac arrest

Check whether the person is breathing. If not, take the following steps.

- If you have someone with you, send them to dial 999 (or 112) for an ambulance immediately.
- If you are alone, dial 999 (or 112) for an ambulance immediately and then return to help the casualty.

Give 30 chest compressions.

- Place heel of your hand in the centre of the chest.
- Place other hand on top and interlock fingers.
- Keeping your arms straight and your fingers off the chest, press down by four to five centimetres, then release the pressure, keeping your hands in place.
- Repeat the compressions 30 times, at a rate of 100 per minute.

Give 2 rescue breaths.

- Ensure the airway is open.
- Pinch the casualty's nose firmly closed.
- Take a deep breath and seal your lips around the casualty's mouth.
- Blow into the mouth until the chest rises.
- Remove your mouth and allow the chest to fall.
- Repeat once more.

Continue resuscitation, 30 compressions to 2 rescue breaths.

Do not stop unless:

- emergency help arrives and takes over,
- the casualty breathes normally, or
- you become so exhausted that you cannot carry on.

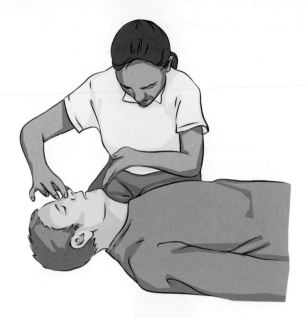
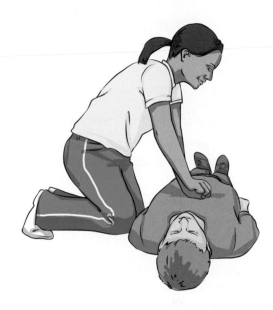

Rescue breaths (a) and chest compressions (b).

Shock

Shock occurs because blood is not being pumped around the body efficiently. This can be the result of loss of body fluids through bleeding, burns, severe vomiting or diarrhoea, or a sudden drop in blood pressure or a heart attack.

Symptoms

The signs of shock are easily recognised. The person:

- will look very pale, almost grey
- will be very sweaty, and the skin will be cold and clammy
- will have a very fast pulse
- may feel sick and may vomit
- may be breathing very quickly.

Aims

- To obtain medical help as a matter of urgency
- To improve blood supply to heart, lungs and brain

Action for shock

Summon expert medical or nursing assistance. Lay the person down on the floor. Try to raise the feet off the ground to help the blood supply to the important organs. Loosen any tight clothing.

Watch the person carefully. Check the pulse and breathing regularly. Keep the person warm and

comfortable, but do not warm the casualty with direct heat, such as a hot-water bottle.

Do not allow the casualty to eat or drink, or leave the casualty alone, unless it is essential to do so briefly in order to summon help.

Keep the casualty warm.

Loss of consciousness

Loss of consciousness can happen for many reasons, from a straightforward faint to unconsciousness following a serious injury or illness.

Symptom

A reduced level of response and awareness. This can range from being vague and woozy to total unconsciousness.

Aims

- To summon expert medical help as a matter of urgency
- To keep the airway open
- To note any information which may help to find the cause of the unconsciousness

Action for loss of consciousness

Make sure that the person is breathing and has a clear airway. Maintain the airway by lifting the chin and tilting the head backwards.

Look for any obvious reasons why the person may be unconscious, such as a wound or an ID band telling you of any condition they may have. For example, many people who have medical conditions that may cause unconsciousness, such as epilepsy or diabetes, wear special bracelets or necklaces giving information about their condition.

Place the casualty in the recovery position (see below), *but not if you suspect they have a back or neck injury*, until expert medical or nursing help or the emergency services arrive.

Do not:

- attempt to give anything by mouth
- attempt to make the casualty sit or stand
- leave the casualty alone, unless it is essential to leave briefly in order to summon help.

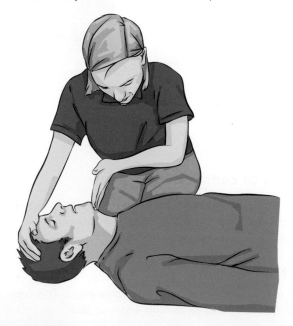

Open the airway.

The recovery position

Many of the actions you need to take to deal with health emergencies will involve you in placing someone in the recovery position. In this position a casualty has the best chance of keeping a clear airway, not inhaling vomit and remaining as safe as possible until help arrives. You should not attempt this position if you think someone has back or neck injuries, and it may not be possible if there are fractures of limbs.

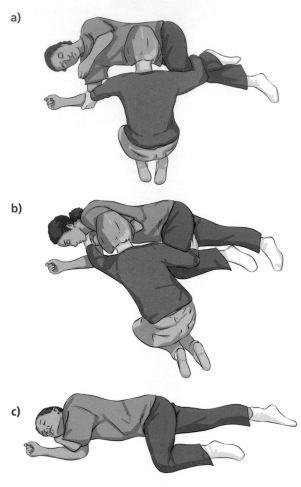

The recovery position.

- Kneel at one side of the casualty, at about waist level.
- Tilt back the person's head — this opens the airway. With the casualty on their back, make sure that limbs are straight.
- Bend the casualty's near arm as in a wave (so it is at right angles to the body). Pull the arm on the far side over the chest and place the back of the hand against the opposite cheek (**a** in the diagram).

- Use your other hand to roll the casualty towards you by pulling on the far leg, just above the knee (**b** in the diagram). The casualty should now be on their side.
- Once the casualty is rolled over, bend the leg at right angles to the body. Make sure the head is tilted well back to keep the airway open (**c** in the diagram).

Epileptic seizure

Epilepsy is a medical condition that causes disturbances in the brain, which result in sufferers becoming unconscious and having involuntary contractions of their muscles. This contraction of the muscles produces the fit or seizure. People who suffer with epilepsy do not have any control over their seizures, and may do themselves harm by falling when they have a seizure.

Aims

- To ensure that the person is safe and does not injure themselves during the fit
- To offer any help needed following the fit

Action for epileptic seizure

Try to make sure that the area in which the person has fallen is safe. Loosen all clothing.

Once the seizure has ended, make sure that the person has a clear airway and place them in the recovery position. Make sure that the person is comfortable and safe. Particularly try to prevent head injury.

If the fit lasts longer than five minutes, or you are unaware that the casualty is a known epileptic, call an ambulance.

Do not:

- attempt to hold the casualty down, or put anything in their mouth
- move the casualty until they are fully conscious, unless there is a risk of injury in the place where they have fallen.

Choking and difficulty with breathing

This is caused by something (usually a piece of food) stuck at the back of the throat. It is a situation that needs to be dealt with, as people can quickly stop breathing if the obstruction is not removed.

Symptoms

- Red, congested face at first, later turning grey

- Unable to speak or breathe, may gasp and indicate throat or neck — this is severe choking and requires immediate action

If a person can speak in answer to a question such as 'are you choking?' then this is regarded a mild choking and they should be encouraged to cough.

Aims

- To remove obstruction as quickly as possible
- To summon medical assistance as a matter of urgency if the obstruction cannot be removed

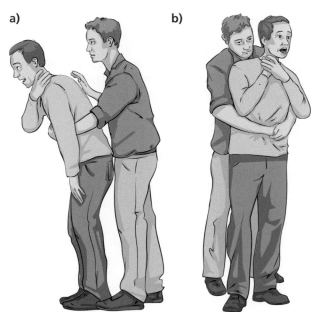

Dealing with an adult who is choking.

Action for choking

1. Ensure any dentures are removed. Sweep the mouth with one gloved finger to clear any food, vomit or anything else from the mouth.

2. Try to get the person to cough. If that is not immediately effective, move on to step 3.

3. Bend the person forwards. Use the heel of the hand to give five blows sharply on the back between the shoulder blades up to five times (**a** in the diagram).

4. If this fails, use the Heimlich manoeuvre — also called 'abdominal thrusts' — *if you have been trained to do so*. Stand behind the person with your arms around them. Join your hands just below the breastbone. One hand should be in a fist and the other holding it (**b** in the diagram).

5. Sharply pull your joined hands upwards and into the person's body at the same time. The force should expel the obstruction.

6. You should alternate backslaps and abdominal thrusts until you clear the obstruction.

Fractures and suspected fractures

Fractures are breaks or cracks in bones. They are usually caused by a fall or other type of injury. The casualty will need to go to a hospital as soon as possible to have a fracture diagnosed correctly.

Symptoms

- Acute pain around the site of the injury
- Swelling and discoloration around the affected area
- Limbs or joints may be in odd positions
- Broken bones may protrude through the skin

Action for fractures

The important thing is to support the affected body part. Help the casualty to find the most comfortable position. Support the injured limb in that position with as much padding as necessary — towels, cushions, pillows or clothing will do.

Take the person to hospital or call an ambulance. Do not:

- try to bandage or splint the injury
- allow the casualty to have anything to eat or drink

Burns and scalds

There are several different types of burn; the most usual are burns caused by heat or flame. Scalds are caused by hot liquids. People can also be burned by chemicals or by electrical currents.

Symptoms

Depending on the type and severity of the burn, skin may be red, swollen and tender, blistered and raw or charred. The casualty is usually in severe pain and possibly suffering shock.

Aims

- To obtain immediate medical assistance if the burn is over a large area (as big as the casualty's hand or more) or is deep

- To send for an ambulance if the burn is severe or extensive. If the burn or scald is over a smaller area, the casualty could be transported to hospital by car
- To stop the burning and reduce pain
- To minimise the possibility of infection

Action for burns and scalds

For major burns, summon immediate medical assistance.

Cool down the burn. Keep it flooded with cold water for ten minutes. If it is a chemical burn, this needs to be done for 20 minutes. Ensure that the contaminated water used to cool a chemical burn is disposed of safely.

Remove any jewellery, watches or clothing which is not sticking to the burn. Cover it if possible, unless it is a facial burn, with a sterile or at least clean non-adhesive dressing. If this is not possible, leave the burn uncovered. For a burn on a hand or foot, a clean plastic bag will protect it from infection until an expert can treat it.

Doing it well

Stop, drop, wrap, roll

If a person's clothing is on fire, STOP – DROP – WRAP – ROLL.

- *Stop* them from running around.
- Get them to *drop* to the ground – push them if you have to and can do so safely.
- *Wrap* them in something to smother the flames – a blanket or coat, anything to hand. This is better if it is soaked in water.
- *Roll* them on the ground to put out the flames.

Do not:

- remove anything which is stuck to a burn
- touch a burn, or use any ointment or cream
- cover facial burns — keep pouring water on until medical help arrives.

Poisoning

People can be poisoned by many substances, drugs, plants, chemicals, fumes or alcohol.

Symptoms

Symptoms will vary depending on the poison.

- The person could be unconscious.
- There may be acute abdominal pain.
- There may be blistering of the mouth and lips.

Aims

- To remove the casualty to a safe area if they are at risk, and it is safe for you to move them
- To summon medical assistance as a matter of urgency
- To gather any information which will identify the poison
- To maintain a clear airway and breathing until medical help arrives

Action for poisoning

If the casualty is unconscious, place them in the recovery position to ensure that the airway is clear, and that they cannot choke on any vomit. Dial 999 for a paramedic.

Try to find out what the poison is and how much the casualty has taken. This information could be vital in saving a life.

If a conscious casualty has burned mouth or lips, they can be given small frequent sips of water or cold milk. *Do not* try to make the casualty vomit.

Electrical injuries

Electrocution occurs when an electrical current passes through the body.

Symptoms

Electrocution can cause cardiac arrest and burns where the electrical current entered and left the body.

Aims

- To remove the casualty from the current when you can safely do so
- To obtain medical assistance as a matter of urgency
- To maintain a clear airway and breathing until help arrives
- To treat any burns

Action for electrical injuries

There are different procedures to follow, depending on whether the injury has been caused by a high- or low-voltage current.

Move the casualty away from the current.

Injury caused by high-voltage current

This type of injury may be caused by overhead power cables or rail lines, for example.

Contact the emergency services immediately. *Do not* touch the person until all electricity has been cut off.

If the person is unconscious, clear the airway. Treat any other injuries present, such as burns. Place in the recovery position until help arrives.

Injury caused by low-voltage current

This type of injury may be caused by electric kettles, computers, drills, lawnmowers and so on.

Break the contact with the current by switching off the electricity, at the mains if possible. It is vital to break the contact as soon as possible, because if you touch a person who is 'live' (still in contact with the current), you too will be injured. If you are unable to switch off the electricity, then you must stand on something dry which can insulate you, such as a telephone directory, a rubber mat or a pile of newspapers, and then move the casualty away from the current as follows.

Do not use anything made of metal, or anything wet, to move the casualty from the current. Try to move them with a wooden pole or broom-handle, even a chair. Alternatively, drag them with a rope or cord or, as a last resort, pull by holding any of the person's dry clothing that is *not* in contact with their body.

Once the person is no longer in contact with the current, you should follow the same steps as with a high-voltage injury.

Tasks that need training

The guidance above identifies situations where training is necessary, for example, carrying out CPR. This is important because you can do further damage to a casualty by attempting to carry out tasks you have not been trained for. Helping following an accident or sudden illness is about first aid, and you need to understand the actions you should take if such an emergency arises.

The advice in this unit is not a substitute for a first aid course, and will only give you an outline of the steps you need to take. Reading this part of the unit will not qualify you to deal with these emergencies. Unless you have been on a first aid course, you should be careful about what you do, because the wrong action can cause more harm to the casualty. It is always preferable to get suitably trained assistance if possible.

Only attempt what you know you can safely do. Do not attempt something you are not sure of. You could do further damage to the ill or injured person. Do not try to do something outside your responsibility or capability — summon help and wait for it to arrive.

What you can safely do

Most people have a useful role to play in a health emergency, even if it is not dealing directly with the ill or injured person. It is also vital that someone:

- summons help as quickly as possible
- offers assistance to the competent person who is dealing with the emergency
- clears the immediate environment and makes it safe — for example, if someone has fallen through a glass door, the glass must be removed as soon as possible before there are any more injuries
- offers help and support to other people who have witnessed the illness or injury and may have been upset by it. Clearly this can only be dealt with once the ill or injured person is being helped.

Summon assistance

In the majority of cases this will mean telephoning 999 and requesting paramedic assistance. It will depend on the setting in which you work and clearly is not required if you work in a hospital! But it may mean calling for a colleague with medical qualifications, who will then be able to make an assessment of the need for further assistance. Similarly, if you work in the residential sector, there should be a medically qualified colleague available. If you are the first on the scene at an emergency in the community, you may need to summon an ambulance for urgent assistance.

If you need to call an ambulance, try to keep calm and give clearly all the details you are asked for. Do not attempt to give information until it is asked for — this wastes time. Emergency service operators are trained to find out the necessary information, so let them ask the questions, then answer calmly and clearly.

Follow the action steps outlined in the previous section while you are waiting for help to arrive.

Assist the person dealing with the emergency

A second pair of hands is invaluable when dealing with an emergency. If you are assisting someone with first aid or medical expertise, follow all their instructions, even if you do not understand why. An emergency situation is not the time for a discussion or debate — that can happen later. You may be needed to help to move a casualty, to fetch water, blankets or dressings, or to reassure and comfort the casualty while they receive treatment.

Make the area safe

An accident or injury may have occurred in an unsafe area — and that was probably precisely why the accident occurred there! Sometimes, it may be that the accident has made the area unsafe for others. For example, if someone has tripped over an electric flex, there may be exposed wires or a damaged electric socket. Alternatively, a fall against a window or glass door may have left shards of broken glass in the area, or there may be blood or other body fluids on the floor. You may need to make the area safe by turning off the power, clearing broken glass or dealing with a spillage.

It may be necessary to redirect people away from the area of the accident in order to avoid further casualties.

Case study

Dealing with a health emergency

On the way to lunch one Tuesday, Miss Shaw, who sometimes experiences incontinence, had a little accident in the main hallway. Another resident coming along behind called out, 'Oh look! She's done a puddle!' and stopped to stare. Miss Shaw, feeling embarrassed and distressed, turned quickly to go back to her room and slipped on the wet floor, falling heavily on her hip. The first staff member on the scene was Maria.

1. List the actions that Maria should take, in order.
2. Could this accident have been prevented? If so, how?
3. What follow-up actions or discussions would you recommend to the management?

Maintain the privacy of the casualty

You may need to act to provide some privacy for the casualty by asking onlookers to move away or stand back. If you can erect a temporary screen with coats or blankets, this may help to offer some privacy. It may not matter to the casualty at the time, but they have a right to privacy and dignity if possible.

Make accurate reports

You may be responsible for making a report on an emergency situation you have witnessed, or for filling in records later. Concentrate on the most important aspects of the incident and record the actions of yourself and others in attendance in an accurate, legible and complete manner.

How to deal with witnesses' distress – and your own

People who have witnessed accidents can often be very distressed by what they have seen. The distress may be as a result of the nature of the injury, or the blood loss. It could be because the casualty is a friend or relative, or simply because seeing accidents or injuries is traumatic. Some people can become upset because they feel helpless and do not know how to assist, or they may have been afraid and then feel guilty later.

You will need to reassure people about the casualty and the fact that they are being cared for appropriately. However, do not give false reassurance about things you may not be sure of.

You may need to allow people to talk about what they saw. One of the commonest effects of witnessing a trauma is that people need to repeat over and over again what they saw.

What about you?

You may feel very distressed by the experience you have gone through. You may find that you need to talk about what has happened, and that you need to look again at the role you played. You may feel that you could have done more, or you may feel angry with yourself for not having a greater knowledge about what to do.

If you have followed the basic guidelines in this element, you will have done as much as could be expected of anyone at the scene of an emergency who is not a trained first aider.

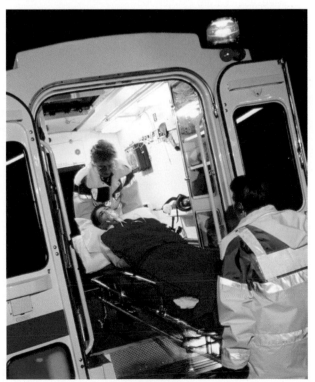

Witnessing accidents is often distressing.

4. Be able to reduce the spread of infection

Before you can show that you know how to reduce the spread of infection, you need to understand how infection gets into the body and how it spreads. Depending on your role, you may have responsibility for other people and for making sure that they understand the risks from infection and how to reduce them. Even if you are not responsible for the work of other staff, you may be able to share useful information with people that you support and assist them to reduce the risks from infection through following good practice in maintaining hygiene and avoiding infections risks.

How infection gets into the body

Infections are caused by micro-organisms (bacteria or viruses) known as pathogens. There are three sources of pathogens:

- within a person's body — called endogenous (for example, some micro-organisms from the gut can cause infections in other parts of the body)
- from other people through touching, coughs or sneezes — called exogenous
- from contaminated equipment or elements such as dust or water — known as environmental.

Chain of infection

A useful way of understanding how infections happen is to think of the 'chain of infection'. The purpose of infection control is to break one or more links in the 'chain' and thus stop the spread of infection.

The chain consists of four links: the first is the source of the micro-organism — that could be in any of the three categories above. The second link is the route of transmission — in other words, how the micro-organism gets from the source into the host. The third link is a susceptible host; people who are unwell or whose immune systems are not functioning very well are much more likely to get an infection. The final link in the chain is the point of entry — how the micro-organism gets into the host.

Micro-organisms can be transmitted through several different routes, which include:

- direct or indirect contact
- airborne
- **anthropods.**

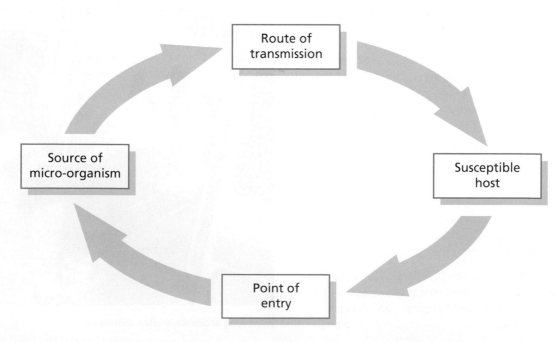

Can you see how breaking just one link will stop the chain?

Direct contact is through contact with infected body fluids such as sexually transmitted diseases or babies who are infected before birth. Indirect contact is the most usual form of transmission; this can include pathogens passed on from the hands or clothing of another person, those passed from animals, and pathogens in water or from objects such as equipment, bedding or surfaces people have touched.

Airborne transmission means pathogens travel through the air on airborne particles. These can result from the respiratory droplets expelled in coughs and sneezes or from dust particles.

Each of these droplets could carry infection.

Susceptible host

A range of factors can result in someone being susceptible, or more vulnerable, to infections. Older people and young babies are susceptible, as immune systems do not work as effectively when they are immature or older. General health and well-being can also affect immune systems and some diseases such as diabetes can also reduce a system's effectiveness. Medical interventions such as steroids, chemotherapy or surgery can also make people more susceptible.

Point of entry

Pathogens enter the body through:

- natural orifices such as mouth, nose, ears, rectum, vagina, urethra
- artificial orifices such as colostomy, ileostomy, tracheostomy
- mucous membranes that line most natural orifices
- breaks in the skin, whether accidental or because of medical intervention. The skin is one of the human body's best barriers against infection.

4.1 The recommended method for hand washing

Numbers of studies have shown that hands are the commonest way of spreading infection from one person to another. Working in health and social care means that you are likely to be working with more than one person and moving between people. Washing hands properly has been shown to be one of the most effective ways of reducing the spread of infection.

When	Before and after carrying out any procedure which has involved contact with a person, or with any body fluids, soiled linen or clinical waste. You must wash your hands even though you have worn gloves. You must also wash your hands before you start and after you finish your shift, before and after eating, after using the toilet and after coughing, sneezing or blowing your nose.
Why	Because hands are a major route to spreading infection. When tests have been carried out on people's hands, an enormous number of bacteria have been found.
How	Wash hands in running water, in a basin deep enough to hold the splashes and with either foot pedals or elbow bars rather than taps, because you can re-infect your hands from still water in a basin, or from touching taps with your hands once they have been washed. Use the soaps and disinfectants supplied. Make sure that you wash thoroughly, including between your fingers. This should take between 10 and 20 seconds.

Table 4: Washing your hands.

How

1. Wet your hands thoroughly under warm running water and squirt liquid soap onto the palm of one hand.

2. Rub your hands together to make a lather.

3. Rub the palm of one hand along the back of the other and along the fingers. Then repeat with the other hand.

4. Rub in between each of your fingers on both hands and round your thumbs.

5. Rinse off the soap with clean water.

6. Dry hands thoroughly on a disposable towel.

Alcohol hand rub

Alcohol hand rubs can be good for use when hands are **socially clean** and if you are not near a source of water. A small amount should be used and rubbed into the hands using the same technique as for washing with water. The hand rub should be rubbed in until the hands are completely dry.

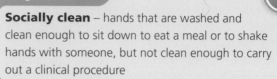

> **Key term**
>
> **Socially clean** – hands that are washed and clean enough to sit down to eat a meal or to shake hands with someone, but not clean enough to carry out a clinical procedure

Alcohol hand rub is not an alternative to hand washing and is only to be used alongside the proper hand-washing technique. It is not effective against bacteria with a spore phase, such as *Clostridium difficile*, so hand washing is essential.

4.2 Ways to ensure that your health and hygiene do not pose a risk to others

What you wear

There are several reasons why what staff wear has an impact on health and safety, and why many employers issue uniforms to their employees. The uniform should be comfortable and well fitting with plenty of room for movement. Inappropriate clothing can be restrictive and prevent free movement when working.

High-heeled or poorly supporting shoes are a risk to you in terms of foot injuries and very sore feet! They also present a risk to people you are supporting, because if you overbalance or stumble, so will they.

You should tie up long hair if you have it. Hair can contain substantial amounts of bacteria, which could cause infection. In addition, loose long hair could be a safety hazard. Someone who is agitated or confused may grab hair, or it might get caught in equipment.

There may be restrictions on wearing jewellery or carrying things in your pocket which could cause injury. This can also pose a risk to you — you could be stabbed in the chest by a pair of scissors or a ball-point pen! You should not wear a wrist watch. Apart from the possibility of scratching someone when providing personal care, wearing a watch can prevent good hand-washing practice. Fob watches that pin on to the uniform are convenient and easily obtainable.

Many workplaces do not allow the wearing of rings with stones. Not only are these a possible source of infection, but they can also scratch people or tear protective gloves.

The very nature of work in a care and support setting means that great care must be taken to control the spread of infection. You will come into contact with a number of people during your working day – an ideal opportunity for **cross-infection**. If you work in the community, cross-infection is difficult to control. However, if you work in a residential or hospital setting, infection control is essential. There are various steps that you can take in terms of the way you carry out your work (wherever you work) which can help to prevent the spread of infection.

> **Key term**
>
> **Cross-infection** – infection that spreads from one person to another

You do not know what viruses or bacteria may be present in any person, so it is important that you take precautions when dealing with everyone. The precautions are called 'standard precautions' precisely because you need to take them with everyone you deal with. You must ensure that all staff are familiar with standard precautions and adhere to them.

When	Any occasion when you will have contact with body fluids (including body waste, blood, mucus, sputum, sweat or vomit), or when you have any contact with anyone with a rash, pressure sore, wound, bleeding or any broken skin. You must also wear gloves when you clear up spills of blood or body fluids, or have to deal with soiled linen or dressings.
Why	Because gloves act as a protective barrier against infection.

Table 5: Wear gloves.

How

1. Check gloves before putting them on. Never use gloves with holes or tears. Check that they are not cracked or faded.

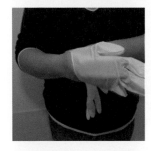

2. Pull gloves on, making sure that they fit properly. If you are wearing a gown, pull them over the cuffs.

3. Take them off by pulling from the cuff – this turns the glove inside out.

4. Pull off the second glove while still holding the first so that the two gloves are folded together inside out.

5. Dispose of them in the correct waste disposal container and wash your hands.

Personal protective clothing

When	You should always wear a gown or plastic apron for any procedure that involves bodily contact or is likely to deal with body waste or fluids. An apron is preferable, unless the procedure is likely to be very messy, as gowns can be a little intimidating to the person you are working with.
Why	Because it will reduce the spread of infection by preventing infection getting on your clothes and spreading to the next person you come into contact with.
How	The plastic apron should be disposable and thrown away at the end of each procedure. You should use a new apron for each person you come into contact with.

Table 6: Wear protective clothing.

Why	Because if it hangs over your face, it is more likely to come into contact with the person you are working with and could spread infection. It could also become entangled in equipment and cause a serious injury.

Table 7: Tie up hair.

Why	Because infection can spread from one person to another on instruments, linen and equipment just as easily as it can on hands or hair.
How	By washing large items like trolleys with antiseptic solution. Small instruments must be sterilised. Do not shake soiled linen or dump it on the floor. Keep it held away from you. Place linen in the proper bags or hampers for laundering.

Table 8: Clean equipment.

Why	Because it can then be processed correctly, and the risk to others working further along the line in the disposal process is reduced as far as possible.
How	By placing it in the proper bags. Make sure that you know the system in your workplace. It is usually: clinical waste – yellow soiled linen – red recyclable instruments and equipment – blue.

Table 9: Deal with waste.

When	There may be occasions when you have to deal with a person who has a particular type of infection that requires special handling. This can involve things like hepatitis, some types of food poisoning or highly infectious diseases.
How	Your workplace will have special procedures to follow. They may include such measures as gowning, double gloving or wearing masks. Follow the procedures strictly. They are there for your benefit and for the benefit of the people you support.

Table 10: Take special precautions.

Activity 3

Spreading infection
Make notes of three ways in which infection can be spread at your workplace. Then note down three effective ways to reduce the possibility of cross-infection.

5. Be able to move and handle equipment and other objects safely

5.1 Main points of legislation about moving and handling

Lifting and handling people is the single largest cause of injuries at work in health and care settings. One in four workers take time off because of a back injury sustained at work.

The Manual Handling Operations Regulations 1992 (amended 2002) require employers to avoid all manual handling where there is a risk of injury 'so far as it is reasonably practical'. Where manual handling cannot be avoided, then a risk assessment must be undertaken and all appropriate steps must be taken to reduce risks. Everyone from the European Commission to the Royal College of Nursing has issued policies and directives about avoiding hazardous lifting.

Provision and Use of Work Equipment Regulations 1998 (PUWER)

These regulations require employers to ensure that all equipment used in the workplace is:

- suitable for the intended use and for conditions in which it is used
- safe for use, maintained in a safe condition and, in certain circumstances, inspected so that it continues to be safe
- used only by people who have received adequate information, instruction and training
- accompanied by suitable safety measures, for example, protective devices, markings, warnings.

The regulations also mean that where the risk assessment has shown that there is a risk to the workers from using the equipment, employers must ensure that the equipment is inspected by suitably qualified people at regular intervals.

Lifting Operations and Lifting Equipment Regulations (1992) (LOLER)

These regulations came into effect on 5 December 1998 and apply to all workplaces. An employee does not have any responsibilities under LOLER, but under the Management of Health and Safety at Work Regulations 1999, employees have a duty to ensure

that they take reasonable care of themselves and others who may be affected by the actions that they undertake.

Employers do have duties under LOLER. They must ensure that all equipment provided for use at work is:

- sufficiently strong and stable for the particular use and marked to indicate safe working loads
- positioned and installed to minimise any risks
- used safely – that is, the work is planned, organised and performed by competent people
- subject to ongoing thorough examination and, where appropriate, inspection by competent people.

In addition, employers must ensure:

- lifting operations are planned, supervised and carried out in a safe way by competent people
- equipment for lifting people is safe
- lifting equipment and accessories are thoroughly examined
- a report is submitted by a competent person following a thorough examination or inspection.

Equipment designed for lifting and moving loads must be inspected at least annually, but any equipment that is designed for lifting and handling people must be inspected at least every six months.

If employees provide their own lifting equipment, this is covered by the regulations.

> **Doing it well**
>
> ### Manual handling
> - Manual handling is a joint activity between you and the person being moved.
> - Always use lifting and handling aids wherever possible.
> - There is no such thing as a safe lift, so always be alert to risks.

5.2 and 5.3 Safe moving and handling

On the rare occasions when it is still absolutely necessary for manual lifting to be done, there has to be a risk assessment and procedures put in place to reduce the risk of injury to the employee. This could involve ensuring that sufficient staff are available to lift or handle someone safely, which can often mean that four people are needed, or it may require the provision of specific equipment in order that the move can take place safely for all concerned.

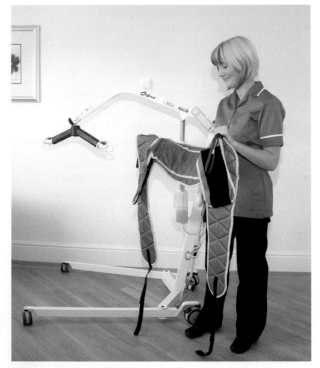

Using the right equipment reduces the risk of harm for everyone.

Reflect

Are you confident that your own moving and handling skills are up to date? If not, what steps are you taking to improve them?

The Health and Safety Executive is clear that manual lifting should be carried out jointly with the person concerned wherever possible and that there must be a balance between safety and the rights of the person. While you and your employer need to make sure that you and other staff are not put at risk by moving or lifting, it is also important that the person you are supporting is not caused pain, distress or humiliation. Groups representing people with disabilities have pointed out that blanket policies excluding any lifting may infringe the human rights of a person needing mobility assistance. For example, people may in effect be confined to bed unnecessarily and against their will by a lack of lifting assistance. A High Court judgement (A & B versus East Sussex County Council, 2003) found in favour of two women with disabilities who had been denied access to lifting because the local authority had a 'blanket ban' on lifting, regardless of circumstances. Such a ban was deemed unlawful under the Disability Discrimination Act 1995. It is likely that similar cases will be brought under the Human Rights Act 1998, which gives people protection against humiliating or degrading treatment.

Doing it well

Moving someone

- Decisions about the best way to move someone must be taken jointly with the person concerned wherever possible.
- Encourage and support people to do as much as possible for themselves; only provide the minimum manual handling required.
- Make maximum use of aids to support people to move themselves.
- Your employer has a statutory duty to provide lifting and handling equipment, but it is your responsibility to use the equipment that is provided.
- You have a right to work safely, but people have rights to be moved with dignity and as safely as possible.

6. Be able to handle hazardous substances and materials

6.1 Types of hazardous substances that may be found in the work setting

Control of Substances Hazardous to Health (COSHH) Regulations

What are hazardous substances? There are many substances hazardous to health – nicotine, many drugs, even too much alcohol! The Control of Substances Hazardous to Health (COSHH) Regulations apply to substances that have been identified as toxic, corrosive or irritant. This includes cleaning materials, pesticides, acids, disinfectants and bleaches, and naturally occurring substances such as blood, bacteria and other bodily fluids. Workplaces may have other hazardous substances that are particular to the nature of the work carried out.

The Health and Safety Executive states that employers must take the following steps to protect employees from hazardous substances.

Step 1: Find out what hazardous substances are used in the workplace and the risks these substances pose to people's health.

Step 2: Decide what precautions are needed before any work starts with hazardous substances.

Step 3: Prevent people being exposed to hazardous substances, but where this is not reasonably practicable, control the exposure.

Step 4: Make sure control measures are used and maintained properly, and that safety procedures are followed.

Step 5: If required, monitor exposure of employees to hazardous substances.

Step 6: Carry out health surveillance where assessment has shown that this is necessary, or COSHH makes specific requirements.

Step 7: If required, prepare plans and procedures to deal with accidents, incidents and emergencies.

Step 8: Make sure employees are properly informed, trained and supervised.

Every workplace must have a COSHH file, which should be easily accessible to all staff. This file should list all the hazardous substances used in the workplace. It should detail:

- where they are kept
- how they are labelled
- their effects
- the maximum amount of time it is safe to be exposed to them
- how to deal with an emergency involving one of them.

Reflect

Hazardous substances are not just things like poisons and radioactive material – they are also substances such as cleaning fluids and bleach.

6.2 Safe practices for storing, using and disposing of hazardous substances and materials

From April 2005, employers are required to focus on the following eight principles of good practice in the control of substances hazardous to health.

1. Design and operate processes and activities to minimise emission, release and spread of substances hazardous to health.

2. Take into account all relevant routes of exposure – inhalation, skin absorption and ingestion – when developing control measures.

3. Control exposure by measures that are proportionate to the health risk.

4. Choose the most effective and reliable control options which minimise the escape and spread of substances hazardous to health.

5. Where adequate control of exposure cannot be achieved by other means, provide, in combination with other control measures, suitable personal protective equipment.

6. Check and review regularly all elements of control measures for their continuing effectiveness.

7. Inform and train all employees on the hazards and risks from the substances with which they work and the use of control measures developed to minimise the risks.

8. Ensure that the introduction of control measures does not increase the overall risk to health and safety.

Activity 4

COSHH

You must ensure that you and all staff know the location of the COSHH file in your workplace. Read the contents of the file, especially information about the substances you use or come into contact with, and what the maximum exposure limits are. You do not have to know the detail of each substance but the information you need should be contained in the COSHH file, which must be kept up to date.

If you have to work with hazardous substances, make sure that you take the precautions detailed in the COSHH file. This may be wearing gloves or protective goggles, or it may involve limiting the time you are exposed to the substance or only using it in certain circumstances.

The COSHH file should also give you information about how to store hazardous substances. This will involve using the correct containers as supplied by the manufacturers. All containers must have safety lids and caps, and must be correctly labelled.

Never use the container of one substance for storing another, and *never* change the labels.

The symbols in Table 11 indicate hazardous substances. They are there for your safety and for the safety of those you care for and work with. Before you use any substance, whether it is liquid, powder, spray, cream or aerosol, take the following simple steps.

* Check the container for the hazard symbol.
* If there is a hazard symbol, go to the COSHH file.
* Look up the precautions you need to take with the substance.
* Make sure you follow the procedures, which are intended to protect you.

If you are concerned about a substance being used in your workplace that is not in the COSHH file, or if you notice incorrect containers or labels being used, report

Symbol	Abbreviation	Hazard	Description
	E	explosive	Chemicals that explode
	F	highly flammable	Chemicals that may catch fire in contact with air, only need brief contact with an ignition source, have a very low flash point or evolve highly flammable gases in contact with water
	T (also Carc or Muta)	toxic (also carcinogenic or mutagenic)	Chemicals that at low levels cause damage to health and may cause cancer or induce heritable genetic defects or increase the incidence of these
	Xh or Xi	harmful or irritant	Chemicals that may cause damage to health, especially inflammation to the skin or other mucous membranes
	C	corrosive	Chemicals that may destroy living tissue on contact
	N	dangerous for the environment	Chemicals that may present an immediate or delayed danger to one or more components of the environment

Table 11: Identifying hazardous substances.

this to your supervisor or manager. They then have a responsibility to deal with the issue.

Dealing with hazardous waste

As part of providing a safe working environment, employers have to put procedures in place to deal with waste materials and spillages. There are various types of waste, which must be dealt with in particular ways. The types of hazardous waste you are most likely to come across are shown in Table 12, alongside a list of the ways in which each is usually dealt with. Waste can be a source of infection, so it is very important that you follow the procedures your employer has put in place to deal with it safely, in order to reduce the risks to you and to the people you support.

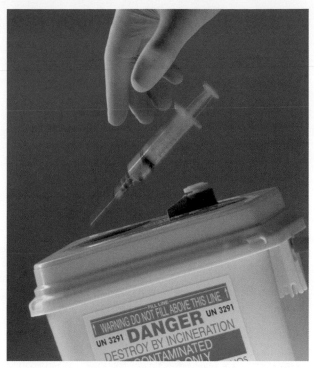

Are you familiar with sharps boxes and other forms of waste disposal?

Reflect

Other people will have to deal with the waste after you have placed it in the bags or containers, so make sure it is properly labelled and in the correct containers.

Type of waste	Method of disposal
Clinical waste – used dressings	Yellow bags, clearly labelled with contents and location. This waste is incinerated.
Needles, syringes, cannulas ('sharps')	Yellow sharps box. Never put sharps into anything other than a hard plastic box. This is sealed and incinerated.
Bodily fluids and waste – urine, vomit, blood, sputum, faeces	Cleared and flushed down sluice drain. Area to be cleaned and disinfected.
Soiled linen	Red bags, direct into laundry; bags disintegrate in wash. If handled, gloves must be worn.
Recyclable instruments and equipment	Blue bags, to be returned to the Central Sterilisation Services Department (CSSD) for recycling and sterilising.

Table 12: Types of waste and their disposal.

7. Be able to promote fire safety in the work setting

7.1 How to prevent fires from starting and spreading

Your workplace will have procedures that must be followed in the case of an emergency. All workplaces must display information about what action to take in case of fire. The fire procedure is likely to be similar to the one shown below.

Fire Safety Procedure

Raise the alarm.

Inform the telephonist or dial 999.

Ensure that everyone is safe and out of the danger area.

If it is safe to do so, attack the fire with the correct extinguisher.

Go to the fire assembly point (this will be stated on the fire procedure notice).

Do not return to the building for any reason.

Make sure that you know where the fire extinguishers or fire blankets are in your workplace, and also where the fire exits are.

Do you know what each fire extinguisher is for and where fire exits are?

Reflect

Do not be a hero! Never attempt to tackle a fire unless you are confident that you can do so safely, for example:

- you have already raised the alarm
- you have a clear, unobstructed route away from the fire in case it grows larger
- you are confident of your ability to operate the extinguisher
- you have the correct type of extinguisher.

Your employer will have installed fire doors to comply with regulations – never prop them open.

Your employer must provide fire lectures each year. All staff must attend and make sure that they are up to date with the procedures to be followed.

The Regulatory Reform (Fire Safety) Order 2005 requires that all businesses must have a person responsible for fire safety and for carrying out a risk assessment. The government recommends a five-step approach to a fire risk assessment.

1. Identify hazards: anything that could start a fire, anything that could burn.

2. Identify who could be at risk and who could be especially at risk.

3. Evaluate the risks and take action to reduce them.

4. Record what has been found out about hazards and the actions taken. Develop a clear plan of how to prevent fire and how to keep people safe if there is a fire. Train staff so they know what to do in the case of fire.

5. Keep the assessment under regular review and make changes if necessary.

Which extinguisher?

There are specific fire extinguishers for fighting different types of fire. It is important that you know this. You do not have to memorise them as each one has clear instructions on it, but you do need to be aware that there are different types and make sure that you read the instructions before use.

All new fire extinguishers are red. Each one has its purpose written on it. Each one also has a patch of the colour previously used for that type of extinguisher.

Type and patch colour	Use for	Danger points	How to use
Water Red	Wood, cloth, paper, plastics, coal, etc. Fires involving solids.	Do **not** use on burning fat or oil, or on electrical appliances.	Point the jet at the base of the flames and keep it moving across the area of the fire. Ensure that all areas of the fire are out.
Multi-purpose dry powder Blue	Wood, cloth, paper, plastics, coal, etc. Fires involving solids. Liquids such as grease, fats, oil, paint, petrol, etc. but **not** on chip or fat pan fires.	Safe on live electrical equipment, although the fire may re-ignite because this type of extinguisher does not cool the fire very well. Do **not** use on chip or fat pan fires.	Point the jet or discharge horn at the base of the flames and, with a rapid sweeping motion, drive the fire towards the far edge until all the flames are out.
Standard dry powder Blue	Liquids such as grease, fats, oil, paint, petrol, etc. but **not** on chip or fat pan fires.	Safe on live electrical equipment, although does not penetrate the spaces in equipment easily and the fire may re-ignite. This type of extinguisher does not cool the fire very well. Do **not** use on chip or fat pan fires.	Point the jet or discharge horn at the base of the flames and, with a rapid sweeping motion, drive the fire towards the far edge until all the flames are out.
AFFF (Aqueous film-forming foam) (multi-purpose) Cream	Wood, cloth, paper, plastics, coal, etc. Fires involving solids. Liquids such as grease, fats, oil, paint, petrol, etc. but **not** on chip or fat pan fires.	Do **not** use on chip or fat pan fires.	For fires involving solids, point the jet at the base of the flames and keep it moving across the area of the fire. Ensure that all areas of the fire are out. For fires involving liquids, do not aim the jet straight into the liquid. Where the liquid on fire is in a container, point the jet at the inside edge of the container or on a nearby surface above the burning liquid. Allow the foam to build up and flow across the liquid.

Foam Cream	Limited number of liquid fires.	Do **not** use on chip or fat pan fires. Check manufacturer's instructions for suitability of use on other fires involving liquids.	Do not aim jet straight into the liquid. Where the liquid on fire is in a container, point the jet at the inside edge of the container or on a nearby surface above the burning liquid. Allow the foam to build up and flow across the liquid.
Carbon dioxide CO_2 Black	Liquids such as grease, fats, oil, paint, petrol, etc. but **not** on chip or fat pan fires.	Do **not** use on chip or fat pan fires. This type of extinguisher does not cool the fire very well. Fumes from CO_2 extinguishers can be harmful if used in confined spaces: ventilate the area as soon as the fire has been controlled.	Direct the discharge horn at the base of the flames and keep the jet moving across the area of the fire.
Fire blanket	Fires involving both solids and liquids. Particularly good for small fires in clothing and for chip and fat pan fires, provided the blanket **completely** covers the fire.	If the blanket does not completely cover the fire, it will not be extinguished.	Place carefully over the fire. Keep your hands shielded from the fire. Take care not to waft the fire towards you.

Table 13: Fire extinguishers.

7.3 Emergency procedures in the event of a fire in the work setting

In an extreme case it may be necessary to help evacuate buildings if there is a fire, or for other security reasons, such as:

- a bomb scare
- the building has become structurally unsafe
- an explosion
- a leak of dangerous chemicals or fumes.

The evacuation procedure you need to follow will be laid down by your workplace. The information will be the same whatever the emergency is: the same exits will be used and the same assembly point. It is likely to be along the following lines.

- Stay calm, do not shout or run.
- Do not allow others to run.
- Organise people quickly and firmly without panic.
- Direct those who can move themselves and assist those who cannot.
- Use wheelchairs to move people quickly.
- Move a bed with a person in, if necessary.

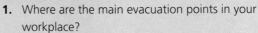

Activity 5

Emergency situations

1. Where are the main evacuation points in your workplace?
2. Which people use each one?
3. Do any of them need assistance to reach evacuation points? If so, of what kind?
4. Who is responsible for checking your workplace is cleared in an emergency?
5. What are your personal responsibilities in an emergency situation?

8. Be able to implement security measures in the work setting

8.1 Checking identity
and
8.2 Measures to protect security

Most workplaces where care is provided are not under lock and key. This is an inevitable part of ensuring that people have choice and that their rights are respected. However, they also have a right to be secure. Security in a care environment is about:

- security against intruders
- security in respect of people's privacy and decisions about unwanted visitors
- security against being abused
- security of property.

If you work for a large organisation, such as an NHS trust, it may be that all employees are easily identifiable by identity badges with photographs. Some of these even contain a microchip which allows the card to be 'swiped' to gain access to secure parts of the building. This makes it easier to identify people who do not have a right to be on the premises.

In a smaller workplace, there may be a system of issuing visitors' badges to visitors who have reasons to be there, or it may simply rely on the vigilance of the staff.

Some workplaces operate electronic security systems, like those in the NHS where cards are swiped to open doors. Less sophisticated systems in small workplaces may use a keypad with a code number known only to staff and those who are legitimately on the premises. It is often difficult to maintain security with such systems, as codes are forgotten or become widely known. In order to maintain security, it is necessary to change the codes regularly, and to make sure everyone is aware.

Some workplaces still operate with keys, although the days of staff walking about with large bunches of keys attached to a belt are fast disappearing. If mechanical keys are used, there will be a list of named keyholders and there is likely to be a system of handover of keys at shift change. However, each workplace has its own system and you need to be sure that you understand which security system operates in your workplace.

How does your workplace identify visitors?

The more dependent people are, the greater the risk. If you work with high-dependency or unconscious patients, people with a severe learning disability or multiple disabilities, or people who are very confused, you will have to be extremely vigilant in protecting them from criminals.

Doing it well

Protecting against intruders

- Be aware of everyone you come across. Get into the habit of noticing people and thinking, 'Do I know that person?'
- Challenge anyone you do not recognise.
- The challenge should be polite. 'Can I help you?' is usually enough to find out if a visitor has a reason to be on the premises.
- If a person says that they are there to see someone, do not give directions – escort them. If the person is a genuine visitor, they will be grateful. If not, they will disappear pretty quickly!
- If you find an intruder on the premises, do not tackle them – raise the alarm.

Protect the security of yourself and others

Workplaces where most or all people are in individual rooms can also be difficult to make secure, as it is not always possible to check every room if people choose to close the door. A routine check can be very time consuming, and can affect people's rights to privacy and dignity.

Communal areas are easier to check, but can present their own problems; it can be difficult to be sure who is a legitimate visitor and who should not be there. Some establishments provide all visitors with badges, but while this may be acceptable in a large institution or an office block, it is not compatible with creating a comfortable and relaxed atmosphere in a residential setting. Extra care must be taken to check that you know all the people in a communal area. If you are not sure, ask. It is better to risk offending someone by asking, 'Can I help you?' or 'Are you waiting for someone?' than to leave an intruder unchallenged.

Protecting people

If very dependent people are living in their own homes, the risks are far greater. You must try to impress on them the importance of finding out who people are before letting them in. If they are able to use it, the 'password' scheme from the utilities (water, gas and electricity) companies is helpful. There are many security schemes operated by the police in partnership with local authority services and charities such as Age UK, for example, 'Safe as Houses' and 'Safer Homes'. These provide security advice and items such as smoke alarms and door chains to older people.

Every time you visit, you may have to explain again what the person should do when someone knocks. Give the person a card with simple instructions. Obtain agreement to speak to the local 'homewatch' scheme and ask that a special eye is kept on visitors. Contact your local crime prevention officers and make them aware that a vulnerable person is living alone.

Restricting access

People have a right to choose who they see. This can often be a difficult area to deal with. If there are relatives or friends who wish to visit and the person does not want to see them, you may have to make this clear. It is difficult to do, but you can only be effective if you are clear and assertive. You should not make excuses or invent reasons why visitors cannot see the person concerned. You could say something like: 'I'm sorry, Mr Price has told us that he does not want to see you. I understand that this may be upsetting, but it is his choice. If he does change his mind we will contact you. Would you like to leave your phone number?'

Do not allow yourself to be drawn into passing on messages or attempting to persuade – that is not your role. Your job is to respect the wishes of the person you are caring for. If you are asked to intervene or to pass on a message, you must refuse politely but firmly.

There may also be occasions when access is restricted for other reasons, possibly because someone is seriously ill, or because of a legal restriction such as a court order. In either case, it should be clearly written on the person's record and your supervisor will advise you about the restrictions. If you are working in a supervisory capacity, it will be part of your role to ensure that junior staff are aware of these restrictions.

Case study

Checking visitors

Fitzroy works in a secure residential unit for older people with dementia. All the entry and exit doors to the unit are operated by a swipe card, and all staff and visitors are required to wear their identity pass visibly at all times. The visitor passes cannot open the doors. One day Fitzroy sees Mrs Gregory, a resident, standing at the exit door with a man Fitzroy does not recognise. The man has a swipe card and is about to open the door. Fitzroy quickly approaches and politely asks the man to identify himself. The man says he is Mrs Gregory's nephew and has come to take her out for a drive in his new car. It is a cold day but Mrs Gregory is not wearing a coat.

1. Was Fitzroy right to challenge the man?
2. What should Fitzroy do next?
3. What might have happened if Fitzroy had not challenged the man?
4. What are the management issues in this case study?

I'm sorry, that is not something I can do. If your uncle does decide he wants to see you, I will let you know right away. I will tell him you have visited, but I can't do anything else.

Have you ever been asked to make an intervention that is outside your role?

Activity 6

Restricting access

You need a colleague or friend to try this role play. One of you should be the person who has come to visit and the other the care worker who has to say that a friend or relative will not see them. Try using different scenarios – angry, upset, aggressive and so on. Try at least three different scenarios each. By the time you have practised a few, you may feel better equipped to deal with the situation when it happens in reality.

If you cannot find anyone to work with you, it is possible to do a similar exercise by imagining three or four different scenarios and then writing down the words you would say in each of the situations.

Security of property

Property and valuables belonging to people in care settings should be safeguarded. It is likely that your employer will have a property book in which records of all valuables and personal possessions are entered.

There may be particular policies within your organisation, but as a general rule you are likely to need to:

- make a record of all possessions on admission
- record valuable items separately
- describe items of jewellery by their colour, for example, 'yellow metal' not 'gold'

- ensure that people sign for any valuables they are keeping, and that they understand that they are liable for their loss
- inform your manager if a person is keeping valuables or a significant amount of money.

It is always difficult when items go missing in a care setting, particularly if they are valuable. It is important that you check all possibilities before calling the police.

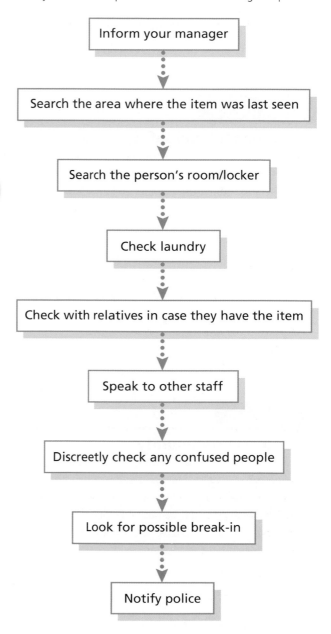

Inform your manager

Search the area where the item was last seen

Search the person's room/locker

Check laundry

Check with relatives in case they have the item

Speak to other staff

Discreetly check any confused people

Look for possible break-in

Notify police

Action stages for when property goes missing.

8.3 Making sure people know where you are

There is always an element of risk in working with people. There is little doubt that there is an increase in the level of personal abuse suffered by workers in the health and care services. There is also the element of personal risk encountered by workers who visit people in the community, and have to deal with homes in poor states of repair and an assortment of domestic animals!

However, there are some steps that you can take to assist with your own safety.

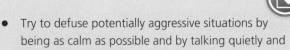

Doing it well

Steps to personal safety

- If you work alone in the community, always leave details of where you are going and what time you expect to return. This is important in case of accidents or other emergencies, so that you can be found and that someone will raise concerns if you are late returning.
- Carry a personal alarm, and use it if necessary.
- Ask your employer to provide training in techniques to combat aggression and violence. It is foolish and potentially dangerous to go into risky situations without any training.

- Try to defuse potentially aggressive situations by being as calm as possible and by talking quietly and reasonably. But if this is not effective, leave.
- If you work in a residential or hospital setting, raise the alarm if you find you are in a threatening situation.
- Do not tackle aggressors, whoever they are – raise the alarm.
- Use an alarm or panic button if you have it; otherwise yell – very loudly.
- Your employer should have a written 'lone-working' policy that identifies steps to be taken to protect staff working alone. Make sure that you have read and understood the policy.

Case study

Risk in the community

Karinda was a home-care assistant on her first visit to a new person, Mr West. She had been warned that his house was in a poor condition and that he had a large dog. She also knew that he had a history of psychiatric illness and had, in the past, been admitted to hospital compulsorily under the Mental Health Act.

When Karinda arrived on her first morning, the outside of the house was in a very poor state – the garden was overgrown, and it was full of rubbish and old furniture. The front door was half open and she could see that half the floorboards in the hallway appeared to be missing – there were simply joists and a drop into the

cellar below. Mr West's dog was in the hallway growling and barking, and Mr West was at the top of the stairs shouting, 'Who are you? You won't get me out of here – I'll kill you first!'

1. What should Karinda do?
2. When should she go back?
3. What sort of risks need to be assessed?
4. If Mr West refuses to allow a risk assessment, or his house to be repaired, should Karinda go back in anyway?
5. Who should carry out the risk assessment?

9. Know how to manage stress

9.1 and 9.2 Common signs and indicators of stress

All of us know somebody who appears to manage a workload and demands on their time that most of us would simply be unable to cope with; however they appear to manage and in many cases to thrive very happily with what is apparently an extremely stressful situation. While the responses to stress are individual, so are (to a large extent) the effects. Stress can show itself in a number of ways.

Emotionally, stress can cause people to feel:

- tense, uptight, angry
- depressed, anxious, tearful, worthless
- unable to cope, concentrate or make decisions
- tired and stretched to the limit
- uninterested in everything, including sex
- the effects of respiratory disorders such as asthma and chest pains.

Stress can cause:

- disturbance of sleep patterns
- disturbance or change in normal appetite
- feelings of anxiety
- loss of concentration
- a quick temper or irritation
- low tolerance of disruption, noise or other disturbance.

Physically, stress can cause:

- tensing of the muscles
- headaches, migraines
- circulatory disorders such as high blood pressure, heart attacks, strokes
- digestive disorders such as ulcers
- menstrual problems
- increases in infections, such as cold sores, colds.

9.3 Triggers for stress

Stress means different things to different people. The sorts of things that can cause stress include:

- work pressures
- debt
- relationship problems
- interrupted sleep.

Stress is believed to be one of the major causes of time off work and of staff turnover. Stress at work can be caused by:

- poor working relationships
- the type of work that has to be carried out, especially in social care
- the hours spent at work, especially for shift workers
- a lack of career progression opportunities
- a fear of redundancy or retirement.

Activity 7

Experiencing stress
Think of an occasion when you felt very stressed. Make a list of the feelings/emotions and physical symptoms you had at the time.

9.4 Ways of managing stress

Stress is dealt with in a range of ways, depending on the underlying causes. It can be dealt with by physical means – that is, an immediate removal from the cause of the stress such as taking a break from work or respite from caring for a difficult, very ill or demanding relative – or by medical means such as the prescribing of drugs to reduce the physical effects of stress on the body and alter mood and responses. Another way would be to undertake a programme of relaxation exercises in order to physically relax the body.

Everyone has their own way of coping with stress but sometimes coping mechanisms can make the situation worse! Things to avoid are:

- drinking
- smoking
- compulsive eating.

Behaviours like these might make matters feel better at the time, but in the long run can be very damaging to your health.

Positive ways to deal with stress include:

- physical activity, for example, going for a walk, doing some gardening, punching a pillow – physical activity uses up the extra energy bodies produce when stressed
- talking things over, for example, with a friend or your supervisor – chatting about a problem often helps to identify what the real issues are and how to deal with them
- doing something to take your mind off the problem, for example, going to the cinema, reading a magazine, pampering yourself – escaping from a problem enables you to come back to it with a clear head and be more able to tackle things
- learning relaxation techniques – activities in which you learn to control your breathing can help to release the muscular tension that goes hand-in-hand with stress
- organising your time – do not take on more than you can handle and do things in order of their importance
- learning to shrug things off – raising your shoulders and lowering them uses up energy, leaving you feeling more relaxed; it also helps you get things into perspective – how important is what is causing the stress anyway?

Accessing support, advice and guidance

Anyone suffering from symptoms of stress which persist and who can see no way forward, should seek help.

Family and friends are usually the first people to look to for support. They have either 'got the T-shirt' or know someone who has been in your position and can offer support and help.

If your stress is associated with work, talk things through with your supervisor. Some organisations employ people whose role includes talking people through their problems and guiding them in finding solutions. Often stressful situations at work can be improved by training to manage time more effectively, or in how to be more assertive so that it is easier to refuse to take on too much work or to deal with situations in which people feel that they have no control.

If the symptoms of your stress are seriously affecting your life, or if they have gone on for a long time, you should see your GP, who could treat your physical symptoms and perhaps refer you on to a suitably qualified therapist or counsellor.

Alternative therapies such as reflexology and aromatherapy can also help relieve stress.

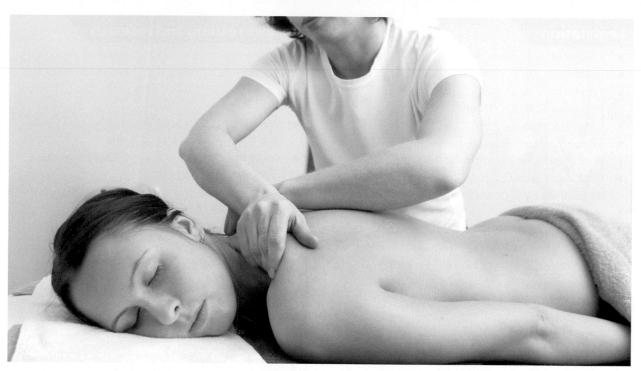

Do you know anyone who has tried massage, aromatherapy or reflexology to deal with stress?

Getting ready for assessment

This is a large unit, but it is very practical. You will have to show that you understand the legislation and regulations around health and safety, and that you know what your own responsibilities are. This may be done through an assignment, or though your assessor asking questions during an assessment. You will need to show that you know how to respond to emergencies, but you may choose to undertake a first aid course to demonstrate your skills. You will have to demonstrate that you are able to move and position people, and equipment safely, and that you can handle hazardous substances. You will also have to either demonstrate or answer questions to show that you know how to deal with security and fire safety. Your assessor will want to know that you understand the effects of stress and the best ways to avoid it. You may be asked to do an assignment or presentation on this, or your assessor may ask you questions about things that you find stressful and how you deal with them.

Legislation

- Control of Asbestos at Work Regulations 2002
- Control of Lead at Work Regulations 2002
- Control of Substances Hazardous to Health Regulations 2002 (COSHH)
- Data Protection Act 1998
- Disability Discrimination Act 1995
- Health and Safety at Work Act 1974
- Health and Safety (Display Screen Equipment) Regulations 1992 (amended 2002)
- Health and Safety First Aid Regulations 1981
- Human Rights Act 1998
- Lifting Operations and Lifting Equipment Regulations (1992) (LOLER)
- Management of Health and Safety at Work Regulations 1999
- Manual Handling Operations Regulations 1992 (amended 2002)
- Mental Health Act 1983
- Noise at Work Regulations 1989
- Personal Protective Equipment at Work Regulations 1992
- Provision and Use of Work Equipment Regulations 1998 (PUWER)
- Regulatory Reform (Fire Safety) Order 2005
- Reporting of Injuries, Diseases and Dangerous Occurrences Regulations 1995 (RIDDOR) (amended 2008)

Further reading and research

Workplace health, safety and security is an important and complex issue. This section has dealt with the key factors and below is details of opportunities to find out more.

- www.dh.gov.uk (Department of Health – health and safety, emergency planning)
- www.hse.gov.uk (Health and Safety Executive (HSE), tel: 0845 345 0055)
- www.healthandsafetytips.co.uk (Health and safety tips, tel: 01506 200109)
- www.neli.org.uk (National Electronic Library of Infection)
- www.nice.org.uk (National Institute for Health and Clinical Excellence)
- www.nric.org.uk (National Resource for Infection Control)
- Bowmen R. C., Emmett R. C. (1998) *A Dictionary of Food Hygiene*, CIEH
- Hartropp, H. (2006) *Hygiene in Health and Social Care*, CIEH
- Horner J. M. (1993) *Workplace Environment, Health and Safety Management; A Practical Guide*, CIEH

Unit HSC 038

Promote good practice in handling information in health and social care settings

Recording information is important and serves many valuable purposes. You need to understand the significance of what you record and how it is recorded, and the requirements relating to record keeping and confidentiality.

In this unit you will learn about:

- **requirements for handling information in health and social care settings**
- **how to implement good practice in handling information**
- **how to support others to handle information.**

1. Understand requirements for handling information in health and social care settings

Once something is written down or entered on a computer, it becomes a permanent record. For this reason, you must be very careful what you do with any files, charts, notes or other written **records**. They must always be stored somewhere locked and safe. People should be very careful with files that leave the workplace. There are many stories about files being stolen from cars or left on buses!

Key terms

Records – information that is written and retained, either electronically as a computer record, or on paper as a hard copy. Records must be accessible, stored securely and be easily retrievable if necessary

Data Protection Act 1998 – a law to ensure the safety of data held

Records kept on computers must also be kept safe and protected. If you work for an organisation, your workplace will have policies relating to records on computers, which will include access being restricted by a password, and the computer system being protected against the possibility of people hacking into it (accessing it illegally).

If you work as a personal assistant, the person you work for may have records on a computer, or kept as written documents. You must check with your employer the steps they want you to take to keep information safe and secure. They may have a password-protected file, a firewall on their computer or use antivirus software. Someone who is directing their own services has the same rights to confidentiality and to have their personal information kept securely.

1.1 Legislation and codes of practice that relate to handling information

The **Data Protection Act 1998** gives people a right to see the information recorded about them. This means that people can see their medical records, or social services files. Since January 2005, the Freedom of Information Act 2000 has provided people with a right

Reflect

1. Do you always think about keeping information safe?
2. If you are working in someone's home, does keeping information secure seem less important than if you were working in a hospital or residential care home?
3. Do you sometimes leave notes and files lying about?
4. Do you always make sure that neighbours or other visitors are not able to access personal information?
5. Think about your own practice in relation to confidentiality – does it really measure up?

Doing it well

Recording information

The purpose of a file is to reflect an accurate and up-to-date picture of somebody's situation, and to provide a record that can be referred to at some point in the future. Some of it may be required to be disclosed to other agencies, and the person it has been written about will have access to it. Always think about what you write. Make sure it is ACES:

- Accurate
- Clear
- Easy to read
- Shareable.

to access general information held by public authorities, including local authorities and the National Health Service. Personal information about other people cannot be accessed and is protected by the Data Protection Act.

The information that you write in files should be clear and useful. Do not include irrelevant information, or opinions that are not backed up by facts, and write only about the person concerned. Sign and date the information. Anything you write should be true and able to be justified. Information you record should be clear and factual.

If you work as a personal assistant, you will keep only the records that your employer asks you to keep. Direct Payments may require certain information to be recorded, and it can be useful to keep some notes for reviews and providing feedback on how well a support plan is working out.

1.2 Main points of legal requirements and codes of practice for handling information

All information, however it is stored, is subject to the Data Protection Act 1998, which covers medical records, social service records, credit information, local authority information and so on. Anything relating to a person, whether fact or opinion, is personal data.

Anyone processing personal data must comply with the eight enforceable principles of good practice laid down in the Data Protection Act 1998. These say that data must be:

- fairly and lawfully processed
- processed for limited purposes
- adequate, relevant and not excessive
- accurate
- not kept for longer than necessary
- processed in accordance with the data subject's rights
- kept secure
- not transferred to countries without adequate protection.

All of the organisations responsible for inspecting quality in the delivery of social care in the UK (see Table 1) also have national minimum standards about how confidentiality must be maintained. The inspectors from each of these organisations will check the systems for recording and storing information, and make sure that they comply with regulations.

In addition to the requirements on organisations, all people who work in social care, regardless of whether it is for a large organisation or an individual employer, should be bound by the professional **Codes of Practice** of the regulatory bodies (see Table 1).

Country	Inspecting organisation	Regulatory body
England	Care Quality Commission	General Social Care Council
Wales	Care and Social Services Inspectorate	Care Council Wales
Scotland	Care Commission	Scottish Social Services Council
Northern Ireland	Regulation and Quality Improvement Authority	Northern Ireland Social Care Council

Table 1: Organisations responsible for inspecting and regulating the quality of social care.

Key term

Code of practice – guidelines for professional behaviour that set out clearly the expectations of those who are working in a professional area

Activity 1

Complying with the Data Protection Act 1998

1. Take the last six actions you have performed with information. These could include:
- writing records/notes
- entering data on to a computer
- sharing information with someone manually or electronically
- receiving information in writing or electronically.

2. Check each of the six actions with the Data Protection principles listed earlier, the national minimum standards for the UK country you work in and the professional code of practice to see if they comply.

3. If they do – excellent! If not, think about what changes need to be made and how you can go about making them.

2. and 3. Be able to implement good practice in handling information and support others

If you think about the purpose for which the information is to be used, this should help you to decide on the best way to record it. There would be little point in going to the trouble of typing out a piece of information that you were simply going to pass over to a colleague on the next shift. Alternatively, if you were writing something which was to go into someone's case notes or case file and be permanently recorded, then you would need to make sure that the information is likely to be of use to colleagues, or others who may need to have access to the file.

Doing it well

Keeping records

- All information needs to be clear.
- It needs to be legible (particularly if you are handwriting it).
- It should be to the point, not ramble or contain far more words than necessary.
- Any record should cover the important points clearly and logically.

Case study

Maintaining records and reports
Look at the following.

> K has been bad this week. On Monday he wouldn't go to college. He said he felt ill but he didn't have a temperature or anything. I think he wanted to stay here and see his new girlfriend in the next lodge.
>
> Tuesday 12 noon. After I had just fed him he vomited all over me. I know he can't help throwing up, but he could give me some warning so I didn't have to change all my clothes. I cleaned him up in the usual way.
>
> Thursday we had archery in the lounge. K wanted to go in his wheelchair but he's supposed to use his sticks, so I told him he had to try with them. He got really stroppy and refused to go in the end. I think we ought to arrange some other activities for him that he can do in his own lodge. Then we won't have these fights about him getting about. What do you think?

A report on K by CS, K's key worker.

1. What is your opinion of this report? Consider the factual detail, the attitude shown towards K by his key worker, and the practical suggestions made.
2. Could you do this better?
3. If so, how?

You may need to record and report:

- signs and symptoms indicating a change in the condition of a person
- signs of a change in a person's support needs
- decisions you have made and actions you have taken relating to a person's needs or condition
- difficulties or conflicts that have arisen, and actions taken to resolve them.

Functional skills

English: Writing; Reading

When writing records for your organisation, you will use the skills of formal writing to communicate information. You will be required to write coherently and clearly, and include an appropriate amount of detail for the purpose of the document. You will need to present information in a logical sequence using language that is relevant for health and social care settings. All work will need to be proofread to ensure accuracy in spelling, punctuation and grammar.

Policies are formal documents that are produced by organisations. By reading through a range of policies, you will develop the skills of skimming and scanning to pick up relevant information that you can use for other purposes, such as note taking to keep records on information you need.

Activity 2

Policies on record-keeping

Find out if your organisation has a policy about record-keeping and about where different types of information should be recorded and kept. Check whether there are clear guidelines on what should be handwritten and information that needs to be word-processed.

Follow the guidelines and provide information in the format that your employer needs. If you are unsure about how you should produce particular kinds of records, ask your manager.

2.1 and 2.2 Security of manual and electronic information storage systems

Imagine going into a record shop which has thousands of CDs stored in racks but in no recognisable order. They are not filed by the name of the artist, nor by the title of the album. Think how much time it would take to trace a particular album. This is exactly what it is like with a filing system – unless there is a system that is easily recognisable and allows people to trace files quickly and accurately, it is impossible to use.

Records are stored in filing systems. These may be manual or computerised. All organisations will have a filing system, and one of the first things you must do is learn how to use it.

Some organisations have people who deal specifically with filing, and they do not allow untrained people to access the files. This is likely to be the case if you work for a large organisation, such as an NHS trust. Smaller agencies are likely to have a general filing system to which everyone in the organisation has access. This is exactly the kind of situation where files and records are likely to go missing and to be misplaced.

If you learn to appreciate the importance of records and the different systems that can be used for their storage, then you can assist rather than hinder the process of keeping records up to date, in the right place and readily accessible when people need them.

Manual systems

In a manual filing system, the types of file used can vary. The most usual type of file is a brown manila folder with a series of documents fastened inside. Other types include ring binders, lever-arch files and bound copies of computer printouts.

All of the files have to be organised (indexed) and stored in a way that makes them easily accessible whenever they are required.

Alphabetical system

If there are not too many files, they can be kept in an alphabetical system in a simple filing cabinet or cupboard. In this sort of system, files are simply placed according to the surname of the person they are about. They are put in the same order as you would see names in a telephone directory, starting with A and working through to the end of the alphabet, with names beginning Mc being filed as Mac and St being filed as Saint. GPs' patient records are usually kept using an alphabetical system.

Numerical systems

Where there are large numbers of files, an alphabetical system would not work. Imagine the numbers of M. Johnsons or P. Williamses who would appear as patients in a large hospital! In that situation an alphabetical filing system would become impossible to manage, so large organisations give their files numbers, and they are stored in number order. A numerical system needs to have an index system so that a person's name can be attached to the appropriate number.

A hospital is likely to give a patient a number that will appear on all relevant documentation so that it is always possible to trace their medical notes. However, there still needs to be an overall record to attach that person's name and address to that particular set of case notes, and these days this is normally kept on a central computer.

Other indexing systems

It could be that, instead of files being organised alphabetically, they may be organised according to the different services an agency offers. For example, they could be kept under 'Mental health services', 'Care in the community services', 'Services for children' and so on. Within these categories, files would be kept in alphabetical order. In a similar way, files may be organised under geographical areas.

Computerised systems

Your organisation is likely to use a computerised system, and there will be very clear procedures that must be followed by everyone who accesses the system. The procedures will vary depending on the system used, but usually involve accessing files through a special programme, which may well have been written either especially for your organisation, or specifically for record-keeping in health and care.

You are unlikely to be able to delete or alter any information which is in someone's file on a computer. It is possible that you will only be able to add information in very specific places, or it could be that files are 'read only' and you cannot add any information to them. This process, because it will not allow people to change or

Why do you think access to a computer system has clear procedures?

alter files, does have the advantage that information is likely to remain in a clear format. It is less likely to become lost or damaged in the way that manual files are. After all, it is really not possible to leave a computer system on a bus!

A computerised system enables organisations to keep a great deal more information in much less space. Although they can be expensive to install, the advantages outweigh the disadvantages in the long run. It also means that everyone in the organisation has to learn how to operate the system and how to use the computer – this is a new skill for many people. It is, however, a skill worth learning if it enables you to record and use information more accurately and effectively.

Other types of records

Most organisations maintain electronic records for accounts, suppliers, personnel and all essential business records. There will be a back-up for any electronically held information; this may be a paper system or an off-site electronic back-up.

Useful information about advice and support services in the area could be maintained in a resource area or filing system, so that helpful leaflets and information packs are not left in a heap on a shelf or a window sill. An electronic index of useful websites, with links, can be very valuable for people and their families if they have computer access and are comfortable accessing information in this way.

Filing systems can work extremely well if they are properly run. They work efficiently and effectively in most organisations as long as a few basic rules are followed by everyone who uses them (see Table 2).

2.3 Maintaining records that are up to date, complete, accurate and legible

There would be little point in finding out about effective means of communication with someone and then not making an accurate record so that other people can also communicate with that person.

Be sure that you record:

- the nature of the communication differences
- how they show themselves
- ways which you have found to be effective in overcoming the differences.

Functional skills

English: Speaking and listening
Using the records you have produced, initiate an informal discussion with a member of staff in your place of work about somebody you suppport. Use the notes you have made to help you get your points of view across clearly. Use listening skills to pick up on points made by your colleague and, where appropriate, use terminology that is appropriate for the work setting.

Do	Do not
Leave a note or card (or something similar) when you borrow a file from a manual filing system	Remove an index card from a system
Return files as soon as possible	Keep files lying around after you have finished with them
Enter information clearly and precisely	Alter or move around the contents of a file, or take out or replace documents which are part of someone's file
Be sure that you access electronic files strictly within your permitted level of access	Make any changes to files unless permitted to do so
Make sure you log in and out correctly	Copy any part of an electronic record system
	Forget to log out

Table 2: Some basic rules about filing.

Activity 3

Sharing records

Think of a person you have worked with where you have experienced communication difficulties. Write notes that would be useful for your colleagues, describing:

- the communication issues involved
- the approaches you use to promote effective communication
- approaches that worked well, and the ones that did not.

If you record the activity, it may contribute to the achievement of learning outcome 4.

Updating and maintaining the accuracy of records and reports is vitally important in any care setting, whether it is a residential home, hospital or a person's own home. The information in records or reports could be:

- about someone who is being supported in your workplace
- about a relative or friend
- about the organisation itself
- about or for someone who works there
- for administrative purposes.

The information could come to you in a range of ways:

- verbally — for example, in a conversation either face to face or on the telephone
- on paper — for example, in a letter, a person's health record or instructions from a health professional
- electronically, by fax or on a computer.

Whatever the purpose of the information, it is important that you record it accurately. It is also important that you pass on any information correctly, in the right form and to the right person. Recording information is essential in health and care services, because the services that are provided are about people rather than objects, so it is vital that information is accurate, accessible and readable. Information about the communication and language needs of people is of daily importance.

Ways of receiving and passing on information

Today within health and care there are many ways in which information is circulated between agencies, colleagues, other team members, people employing their own personal assistants, carers, volunteers and so on. The growth of electronic communication has meant a considerable change in the way that people receive and send information, in comparison to only a few years ago when information sharing was limited to face-to-face meetings, telephone calls or posted letters.

Telephone

One of the commonest means of communication is the telephone. It has advantages because it is instant, straightforward and is a relatively safe and accurate way of communicating and passing on information. However, disadvantages are that it can often be difficult to ensure that you have clearly understood what has been said. There can be problems with telephone lines that cause crackling and technical difficulties. It is also possible to misinterpret someone's meaning when you cannot pick up other signals, such as facial expression and body language. If you regularly take or place messages on the telephone, there are some very simple steps that you can take to cut down the risk of getting a message wrong, as follows.

Make sure that you check the name of the person who is calling. If necessary, ask the person to spell their name and repeat it to make sure you have it right. It is easy to mix up Thomas and Thompson, Williams and Wilkins, and so on. You may also need to take the person's address, and again it is worthwhile asking them to spell the details to ensure that you have written them correctly.

Always ask for a return telephone number, so that the person who receives the message can phone back if necessary. There is nothing more infuriating than receiving a message on which you have some queries and no means of contacting the person who has left it for you. You should read back the message itself to the person who is leaving it, to check that you have the correct information and that you have understood their meaning.

So the message is: you don't know the answer to the query and you're going to Alaska?

No – I said I don't know the answer to the query but I'll ask her.

What other misunderstandings can you think of that could occur over a bad phone line?

Texting

Texts are useful for passing on short communications, such as arranging meetings or letting someone know you will be late. Texts are not appropriate for transmitting detailed or confidential information.

Incoming post

If it is part of your role to open and check any incoming post, you must make sure that you:

- open it as soon as it arrives
- follow your own workplace procedures for dealing with incoming mail – this is likely to involve stamping it with the date it is received
- pass it on to the appropriate person for it to be dealt with or filed. See page 31 for advice on how to deal with confidential information.

Faxed information

The steps for dealing with an incoming fax message are as follows.

- Take the fax from the machine.

- Read the cover sheet – this will tell you who the fax is for, who has sent it (it should include telephone and fax numbers) and how many pages there should be.
- Check that the correct number of pages have been received. If a fax has misprinted or has pages missing, contact the telephone number identified on the cover sheet and ask for the information to be sent again. If there is no telephone number, send a fax immediately to the sending fax number asking for the fax to be resent.
- Follow your organisation's procedure for dealing with incoming faxes. Make sure the fax is handed to the appropriate person as soon as possible.

Email

Email is used very frequently as a means of communication within and between workplaces. It is fast, convenient and easy to use for many people. Large reports and complex information that would be cumbersome to post or fax can be transmitted as an attachment to an email in seconds. However, not everyone in all workplaces has access to email and not all electronic transmission is secure. Be aware of this if you are sending highly sensitive and confidential material. If you do send and receive information by email, you should:

- follow the guidelines in your workplace for using email and the transmission of confidential material
- open all your emails and respond to them promptly
- save any confidential messages or attachments in an appropriate, password-protected file or folder, and delete them from your inbox unless that is also protected
- return any emails you have received in error promptly
- be careful not to give your password to anyone.

Outgoing post

If you have to write information to send to another organisation, whether it is by letter, fax or email, you should be sure that the contents are clear, cannot be misunderstood and are to the point. Do not write a rambling, long letter that obliges recipients to hunt for the information they need.

It is likely that, in many organisations, you will need to show any faxes or letters to your supervisor or manager before they leave the premises. This safeguard is in place in many workplaces for the good reason that information being sent on behalf of your employer

Email can be useful, but can you think of any drawbacks?

must be accurate and appropriate. As your employer is the person ultimately responsible for any information sent out, they will want to have procedures in place to check this.

Reflect

Your employer should have a policy for dealing with the filing and storing of emails and attachments about people. Check this policy to ensure it is up to date with the latest data protection legislation (see page 31). Even if you are directly employed as a personal assistant to one person, stored information should comply with the law.

1. How careful are you with emails?
2. Do you always save them and follow procedures?

Legislation

- Data Protection Act 1998
- Freedom of Information Act 2000

Further reading and research

- www.ico.gov.uk (Guide to Data Protection)
- www.bbc.co.uk/schools/gcsebitesize/ict/legal (BBC Bitesize: The Data Protection Act)

Getting ready for assessment

This learning outcome requires you to demonstrate competence in maintaining records. You will need to demonstrate through actual or simulated records that you are able to record accurate and legible information that is valuable for others who may need to use it. You will also need to show that you are able to deal with information that you are given and that you have to pass on to others. You may be asked to produced anonymised copies of work records, or, if that is not possible, you may have to write simulated records of different types.

Unit HSC 3003

Provide support to maintain and develop skills for everyday life

This unit is an option unit and is aimed at those working in a wide range of settings. It provides you with the knowledge and skills required to work with people to retain, regain and develop skills for everyday life. Not everyone needs, or can benefit from, re-ablement, but it important that you understand the principles and process of re-abling and enabling people.

Everyone needs skills to manage their life each day. Sometimes, due to illness or accident or a change in a long-term condition, people may need support to regain skills. In other circumstances, people may need to learn new skills, for example, in order to achieve greater independence or because they are starting out on an exciting new phase in their life.

In this unit you will learn about:

- the context of supporting skills for everyday life
- how to support individuals to plan for maintaining and developing skills for everyday life
- how to support individuals to retain, regain or develop skills for everyday life
- how to evaluate support for developing or maintaining skills for everyday life.

1. Understand the context of supporting skills for everyday life

1.1 Ways of developing and maintaining skills for everyday life

A skill is simply something that someone can do. The skills that people needs depend on the lives they want to lead. Someone who wants to get their own home and have a job will need one set of skills. Someone who wants to learn how to go mountain climbing, or to learn how to use a computer, will need an entirely different set of skills.

Approaches to skill development or maintenance will depend on the person you are supporting and the choice of the most appropriate approach should be based on factors such as:

- type of skill
- capacity
- ability
- living situation
- outcomes someone wants to achieve.

Types of skills

Skills that everyone needs for day-to-day living fall into different groups:

- independent living skills (sometimes called 'instrumental skills'), such as shopping, cooking, cleaning and budgeting
- personal care skills (sometimes called 'activities for daily living'), such as washing, dressing, grooming, continence, mobility and eating
- relationship skills, such as communication and maintaining social networks.

Each of these types of skill contributes to a person's ability to maintain or increase their level of independence and well-being.

Capacity

You have already learned about the legislation around capacity and the implications of the Mental Capacity Act in Unit SHC 34. However, capacity here is not just about capacity to consent, although that is important, but it is also about a person's capacity to respond and

> **Activity 1**
>
> ### Supporting people to use skills
>
> At the end of a day, sit down and identify the number of skills you have used that day. Work out which of the people you support needs help with each of the skills you have identified. Draw a chart or a graph to see which skills are most frequently needed and which need the most support.

to understand important aspects of skills such as safety and the consequences of actions.

Ability

Ability is different from capacity. You need to be sure that people are able to perform some of the tasks involved in everyday living skills. For example, someone with severe arthritis may have difficulty in lifting heavy saucepans or opening jars. Some people with a learning disability may struggle to manage finances. A person with dementia may have difficulty remembering if they have turned the gas off.

You need to consider ability when considering the type of support that someone may need in order to achieve the necessary skills for the outcomes they want.

Living situation

This may seem obvious, but people's circumstances make a great deal of difference to the skills they need and the best ways of supporting them to achieve the skills. Someone who is living, or wants to live, completely independently will need to be confident that they have all the personal, independent living and communication skills they are going to need.

Someone in supported living, with a support worker on a regular basis, may decide that some skills of day-to-day living can be provided by the support worker.

A person in residential care may not want all of the independent living skills, but will still want to regain or develop as many skills for personal care as possible. It is vitally important that people are not 'de-skilled' by the services that are provided. Just because someone is in residential care does not mean that they should lose all their life skills. Maintaining dignity, self-esteem and the ability to choose is even more essential when people may not be using most of their independent living skills.

Outcomes

You have learned about outcomes in Unit SHC 33; they are about the things that people want to achieve. They can be:

- large and complex outcomes such as 'getting my own flat and being independent'
- outcomes about how people feel, such as 'I want to feel safe in my own home'
- about making relationships, such as 'I want to meet people so I'm less lonely'
- practical outcomes, such as 'I want to be able to make myself a cup of tea again'.

Whatever the outcome or its degree of complexity, you need to think about the skills that will be necessary for the person to develop or regain in order for the outcome to be achieved.

Different approaches

One of the most commonly used approaches to developing or regaining everyday skills is **re-ablement**.

Key term

Re-ablement – short-term, intensive support provided in order to work alongside people who, because of poor physical or mental health, have not been able to maintain day-to-day living skills

The point of re-ablement is that people so easily lose basic skills through hospital admissions, illness at home, an emotional crisis or a traumatic experience. Once the skills are lost people become more dependent on services, lose confidence and self-esteem, well-being suffers and there is a downward spiral, leading to increasing dependence on others.

Re-ablement services usually offer intensive support for around six weeks. The support may include home care support workers, health workers, physiotherapy, occupational therapy assessments for aids and adaptations and mobility, sensory support such as hearing aids, and assistive technology assessments.

If you are working in re-ablement, the key is that you work with people to relearn tasks and skills and not do things them for them. Depending on the reasons why someone is on a re-ablement programme, you may need to support people to use technology or an aid to do something they would previously have done for themselves. For example, putting on a sock or shoe may have been easy before someone had a stroke, but now can only be done using a sock aid. A person who happily did their own vacuuming before having a fall may need the security of an emergency call device to restore their confidence.

Research has shown that the intensive support provided through the re-ablement approach has enabled people to retain their independence for much longer than people who have not received this type of intervention.

Train and fade

'Train and fade' is essentially an approach where support is provided initially and withdrawn gradually as people's skills develop. It is used extensively in supported employment for disabled people, but it can be used effectively as an approach to learning everyday skills as well as those needed for a working situation. This approach has the advantage of allowing people to develop confidence gradually as they improve their skills. This approach is particularly useful for people who need to develop new skills in order to promote their independence and choice.

Assistive technology

Assistive technology is a useful method of supporting or replacing a skill that someone has lost, or is struggling to develop. There are no prizes for struggling — so if there is something else that will do the job, use it!

Technology is developing all the time and it is making major differences to people's lives. People who previously needed to have someone to carry out practical tasks like answering the door, switching on the lights or opening the curtains can now do it all from a computer. Technology and practical aids can make it possible for people to retain independence because tasks that would have been impossible can be made easier by using a simple aid. These are available for everyday skills such as dressing, cooking and eating.

Technology also has an important role in making it possible for people to develop living skills safely and in a situation where they can feel confident that they will

> ## Case study
>
> ### Using the train and fade approach
>
> Gareth is 24, and has a mild learning disability. Up until now he has always lived at home with his parents. They have been very protective and have not encouraged him to be independent. He attends day services and has a work placement. This has given him much greater confidence and, when he was offered the chance to develop a person-centred plan, he was very keen to go ahead. In his plan he identified that he wanted to have his own place, ideally to share with someone and to be able to look after himself. As part of Gareth's plan, he identified that he would need help with shopping, cooking and meal preparation. It was agreed that he would have a support worker each day for the first six weeks and then this would gradually be reduced as he learned how to do things for himself.
>
> The support worker spent time with Gareth explaining the basics of a balanced diet and gave him information he could refer back to if necessary. He also went shopping with Gareth, showing him the route to the supermarket and also visiting local shops and showing Gareth the differences in the style of shopping so he could decide which he preferred. Gareth spent time learning what foods he needed to buy for a good diet and how to read the 'traffic light' symbols on packaging. The support worker helped Gareth to work out his money and how much he had to spend on groceries and how to look for good deals and bargains!
>
> He worked alongside Gareth to cook simple meals and showed him how to follow health and safety rules in the kitchen, how to check the right temperatures for cooking and storing food and how to use seasoning properly.
>
> After the first six weeks, the support worker only came every other day, having planned beforehand what Gareth would do on the day he was on his own, once Gareth was confident, he went to the local shops on his own, and the following week to the supermarket.
>
> Finally after about five months, Gareth said that he thought he could manage fine now, but invited his support worker to call in for tea! Gareth says his best moment was when he cooked Sunday lunch for his mum and dad.
>
> 1. Can you see why this approach worked for Gareth?

not be alone if there is a problem. Sensors and call systems can monitor people's activity levels and raise the alarm if something untoward happens. Systems can be installed in people's homes that can check if they are getting up in the night, or leaving the cooker on, or forgetting to lock the door.

Residential re-ablement/rehabilitation

This is a similar approach to 'community re-ablement', but uses residential accommodation rather than homecare support. People are offered an intensive period of assessment and support within a residential setting. In the setting, facilities such as an assessment kitchen and other rooms are used and staff provide support for people to practise old skills and learn new ones.

This approach is useful for people who would be at too much risk in their own homes until they have developed more skills and confidence. It can be used a 'first step' towards a planned return home. It is essential that staff working in this type of unit focus on the promotion of people's independence and the acquisition of skills for them to return home. The risk with any residential setting is always that people will become more dependent and lose skills and confidence. Units operating this type of service are very clear that their role is short term and is about preparation for home and a return to the local community.

Individual approaches

If you are involved in supporting people to regain or develop skills through any of these approaches, you may use a range of methods to engage people in skills development. Much will depend on the factors we have discussed above, but different methods may work better for particular people depending on their circumstances.

Modelling specific life skills

Modelling involves you demonstrating a life skill for someone. This can be useful for people who may need to gain, or regain, confidence. They are able to watch you doing something and then follow your example. They have the chance to ask questions and to try over and over again. You may need patience to use this method well, as you may need to repeat something many times over. As with any approach, you need to constantly review progress, so that you are not continuing with a method that is clearly not working or simply not right for the person concerned.

Explaining a skill

Sometimes you may need to explain why something needs to be done in a particular way. For example, you may need to explain to someone the importance of washing and drying particular areas of the body in order to avoid skin infections. This may help to reinforce the practical skills around personal hygiene and grooming.

Shared learning

People learning from each other can be a useful method of encouraging the development of skills for everyday life. The opportunities for this are limited, but it can be a helpful approach for people in day services or in residential rehabilitation. Discussing any difficulties in developing or maintaining skills as a group can help one person to learn from another on how they have coped or adapted. Bringing together people who want to achieve similar outcomes can provide encouragement as a result of others' achievements. The situation needs close monitoring in order to avoid matters becoming competitive and people taking undue risks in order to outdo others.

1.2 Why people need support to maintain, regain or develop skills for everyday life

Maintaining, regaining or developing skills for everyday life is important for people's independence and well-being. There are many reasons why people need support around everyday skills, but they are usually the result of one of these causes:

- lack of opportunity to develop skills
- loss of ability to perform skills
- loss of confidence.

How may somebody with visual disabilities need support to maintain their skills?

Lack of opportunity to develop skills

For many people this can be the result of their life circumstances to date. Some people with a disability may have lived in a family situation where there was a great deal of support and not many opportunities to try out skills independently. Many families provide a 'cocoon' for relatives with a disability and, have done everything for them in the belief that this is the right thing to do. Unfortunately this can often mean that people do not reach anywhere near their full potential because they have never had the chance to try doing anything for themselves.

Others may have lived in a residential setting where, again, there was little emphasis on people developing their own skills. This is also generally done with the best of intentions. The concept of providing 'care' means that people can become used to the rhythm and pace of life in an institution, that they never have the chance to do everyday tasks such as shopping, cooking or cleaning. Not only was there no chance to do it, but in many situations, people did not even see others doing it so had no role models at all.

In the past, social care services were generally delivered as a 'gift' model where services were decided by professionals and people had very little say or direction over their own lives. The person-centred approach recognises people's rights to make their own choices and to take control. However, for many people this is very new and alien concept, and it takes some time and support for them to change and develop the confidence and new skills needed for everyday living.

Loss of ability to perform skills

People can lose their abilities for various reasons and at all ages. This is not just something that happens to older people, although the effects can be seen most clearly in this group. People can be unable to do things they have always done because of an accident or an illness or a deteriorating condition such as Alzheimer's disease or Parkinson's disease.

To be unable to do something you have always done can be harder to cope with than never having been able to do it in the first place. Imagine someone recovering from a stroke finding they can no longer cook a meal or even make a cup of tea. Or someone involved in a motorbike accident may now be unable to move around unaided and can no longer go out to the shops, go to the pub, get to work, play football or do many of the day-to-day activities that they used to carry out without thinking about it.

Such a loss of skill can be very difficult for people. In some situations, the loss may be more gradual; for example, a person with arthritis may find that, over time, there is less and less that they can manage. Shopping may be too heavy to carry, it can be too painful to lift something out of the oven, or a flight of stairs may seem impossible.

Loss of confidence

Looking at Betty in the case study above, you can see how loss of confidence can have a significant effect on a person's ability to perform everyday tasks. Sometimes the loss of confidence can be more of a barrier than any physical illness or disability.

Case study

Betty's accident

Betty had always been very independent living in her three-bedroomed house on her own. She said it was the upkeep in the house that kept her active and healthy. Betty enjoyed going out shopping and having coffee with friends. She was also a volunteer at her local charity shop, where she would joke about retiring when she reached her 100th birthday. She would often spend hours knitting dolls and clowns to sell for charity. Betty was 75 and had never felt so good. One morning, just before Christmas, she slipped on some snow outside her house and fractured her hip.

Betty spent many weeks in hospital and received support from the physiotherapists and occupational therapists to regain her strength in walking. When Betty left hospital, she was very nervous about walking outdoors. She was frightened of falling down even when there was no snow or ice on the ground. Walking still caused her pain and so she gave up her voluntary work and stopped going out and having coffee with friends. Because she did not go out, she could not purchase wool for her knitting. She did not knit anything in over six months. Due to the pain Betty was in, her health slowly deteriorated to the point where she needed help in getting washed and dressed in the morning.

1. Can you see how Betty had lost some of the skills she had prior to her fall, and the effect this has had on her?

Doing something like walking downstairs is not just a question of learning how to transfer weight from one foot to the other and to move down the steps, it is also about having the belief that you will not fall and that you can do this without a risk. Similarly, if you have tried to cook a meal only to have it go terribly wrong, you will be less likely to feel confident enough to offer to cook dinner for six people!

Confidence is about trust in yourself and the world around you, and it is based on experience. The more often you do something, the more confident you become that you can do it again. People who have not had to use day-to-day skills for a long time are more likely to lose the belief that they can do it and will take time to regain the confidence and trust in themselves.

If you are supporting someone to regain their confidence and regain the everyday skills they need for independence, you will need to offer plenty of encouragement. It is important to give encouragement even when someone gets something partly right or makes progress. We all thrive on encouragement and praise, and an atmosphere where progress is valued and recognised is important for rebuilding confidence.

1.3 Benefits of maintaining, regaining or developing skills

Developing skills for everyday life can help promote well-being and self-esteem. Life skills can enhance personal development and increase people's quality of life. Becoming and remaining independent is the most beneficial outcome for most people.

Maintaining independence is not the only benefit of learning, or relearning everyday skills. People who are able to undertake their own personal care will feel more positive and have higher self-esteem than being dependent on others.

If someone can learn or relearn shopping and cooking skills, then there is a far greater chance that they will eat healthy, well cooked meals, thus improving their overall health and well-being.

Increased mobility reduces the chance of obesity and improves joint movement and suppleness, thus reducing pain on moving and encouraging further exercise with the health benefits this brings.

If people are suffering with dementia, whatever the cause, maintaining or regaining everyday skills is an important way of focusing brain activity and supporting motor co-ordination. The simple patterns of activity involved in some skills can also be useful as they mean that simple movements can be repeated as skills are maintained. Support to keep people with dementia involved in the retention of everyday skills is important as frequent repetition can delay the time when skills are forgotten and cannot be recalled.

People learning new skills for the first time are likely to experience a great sense of achievement and excitement; for example, older people who are learning how to use computers at 'silver surfer's' classes are usually very enthusiastic about the benefits of technology and their new-found skills. These types of skills can have great benefits in giving people access to large amounts of information, and provides intellectual stimulation through accessing information and finding new experiences. The Internet also provides access to social networking, and gives people the opportunity to keep in touch with family and friends. The use of emails and voiceover Internet communication gives people the chance to share live webcam images and to have face-to-face contact with loved ones. This provides enormous benefits for people by reducing isolation and loneliness, and the mental health problems that can go along with this.

Communication skills are a key part of being able to relate to others. Most people like to get on with others and enjoy being in company. Even for those people who like to live a quieter, less sociable existence, being able to communicate with others is an important part of being able to live from day to day. Simple skills like shopping are impossible without some form of communication.

Communication does not have to mean speech; there are many other forms of communication that people can learn or relearn as a key part of everyday living skills. Unit SHC 31 provides detailed learning about communication, but forms of communication can include:

- speech
- written
- telephone
- texting
- email
- web based
- picture cards
- signing (BSL, deaf/blind, makaton)
- lip reading/speaking
- Braille
- text to audio software
- voice recognition software
- artificial voice/larynx machine.

People may be able to use one or more of these ways of replacing or supporting a means of communication lost through illness or injury. For example, someone who is struggling with mobility, or who has difficulty in shopping because of speech loss, may be able to shop online if they learn some basic computer skills.

How can developing skills help somebody to secure employment?

Activity 2

Everyday skills

Think about someone you support who has lost, or not been able to develop, one or more everyday skills. Make two columns; in the first one, note down how the missing skills are restricting their life and in the second, make notes of the benefits that the person could gain by developing or regaining the skills.

Now think about a different person. Make notes about which skills are important for them and suggest the best ways to ensure that the skills are not lost.

2. Planning for maintaining and developing skills for everyday life

2.1 Working with others to identify skills for everyday life

Skills for life are actions or activities that enable people to live as independently as possible. These skills enable people to do things for themselves rather than having to rely on others to do things for them. Skills for everyday life can be broadly though of as being in two categories: personal care (sometimes called 'basic' skills) and independent living (sometimes called 'instrumental' skills for daily living).

The basic activities for daily living include:

- personal hygiene
- dressing and undressing
- eating
- transferring from a bed to a chair, and back
- continence
- mobility.

Independent living skills include:

- doing light housework
- preparing meals
- taking medications
- shopping for groceries or clothes
- using the telephone
- managing money
- using technology
- feeding.

There are many tools that can 'score' people's levels of independence, but the best way to judge a person's level of dependence is to ask how they feel about themselves and what they can do.

Person-centred planning

As part of working with someone to carry out an assessment of their support needs, the level of independence they have and the amount of support they need is what will shape the support plan. Linking levels of independence and the development of skills to what people want to achieve is the key point of person-centred planning.

Most local authorities will have a supported self-assessment questionnaire that guides people to think about the areas where their skills may need development. There are various types of questionnaire, but they cover similar areas.

Essentially, the questionnaires are designed to be filled in by the person themselves, with help if necessary, and this provides a clear picture of what the person is able to do and any areas where they may need some support. Most importantly, it identifies the outcomes that someone wants to achieve in relation to the development or maintenance of everyday skills. Some people may want to achieve significant outcomes to make major changes to their life. Others may want simple outcomes like being able to have a bath without help, or managing to walk to the shops. Regardless of the impact or level of challenge, all outcomes are important to the person who has identified them, and your role is to support the achievement of the outcomes.

The importance of person-centred planning is that it starts with what someone **can do** and then looks at where there are gaps where the person may need support. This is a much more positive way of people working out what support they need rather than the 'deficit' model seen in many of the tools.

Self assessment questionnaires cover main areas such as:

- personal care
- eating and drinking
- moving around the home
- shopping
- doing laundry
- financial management
- staying safe
- work and volunteering
- community and social life.

You will see that important areas of people's lives such as employment or taking part as a volunteer and participating in social activities are viewed as important areas of people's everyday lives. Staying safe is also a vital part of any assessment about everyday skills often missed by scoring methods. More traditional models may tend to look at specific skills rather than considering a broader, more holistic view.

Some traditional assessment tools use skills to assess people's levels independence. People will score the activities listed in the table. The tool is designed to be used in collaboration with the person concerned, they

are the ones who need to assess their own ability in the key areas identified. Table 1 below is the one used in the Lawton Instrumental Activities of Daily Living (IADL).

To score this assessment, circles one number is circled for each area and added up to give an overall total. The lower the score, the more independent the person is.

Category	Scoring
Telephone	1. Operates telephone on own initiative: looks up and dials number, and so on. 2. Answers telephone and dials a few well-known numbers. 3. Answers telephone but does not dial. 4. Does not use telephone at all.
Shopping	1. Takes care of all shopping needs independently. 2. Shops independently for small purchases. 3. Needs to be accompanied on any shopping trip. 4. Completely unable to shop.
Food preparation	1. Plans, prepares, and serves adequate meals independently. 2. Prepares adequate meals if supplied with ingredients. 3. Heats and serves prepared meals, or prepares meals but does not maintain adequate diet. 4. Needs to have meals prepared and served.
Housekeeping	1. Maintains house alone or with occasional assistance (for example, heavy work done by domestic help). 2. Performs light daily tasks such as dishwashing and bed making. 3. Performs light daily tasks but cannot maintain acceptable level of cleanliness. 4. Needs help with all home maintenance tasks. 5. Does not participate in any housekeeping tasks.
Laundry	1. Does personal laundry completely. 2. Launders small items; rinses socks, stockings and so on. 3. All laundry must be done by others.
Mode of transportation	1. Travels independently on public transportation, or drives own car. 2. Arranges own travel via taxi, but does not otherwise use public transportation. 3. Travels on public transportation when assisted or accompanied by another.
Responsibility for own medication	1. Is responsible for taking medication in correct dosages at correct time. 2. Takes responsibility if medication is prepared in advance, in separated dosages. 3. Is not capable of dispensing own medication.
Handling finances	1. Manages financial matters independently (budgets, writes cheques, pays rent and bills, goes to bank); collects and keeps track of income. 2. Manages day-to-day purchases but needs help with banking, major purchases, controlled spending and so on. 3. Incapable of handling money.

Table 1: Scoring ability in instrumental activities.

2.2 Planning for developing or maintaining the skills identified

After someone has assessed what they need, and what outcomes they want to achieve, they will then need to develop their support plan for how to achieve their outcomes. Some people may be happy to do this on their own or with the support of family and friends, and some may want professional assistance to work out the plan.

The plan may include:

- goals
- the type of support required
- who the person wishes to deliver the support
- how and when the support should be delivered
- ways to address any associated risks
- ways to monitor the plan

Goal setting

Most people find it easier to achieve the outcomes they have identified if they have goals or targets as 'milestones' along the way.

An outcome is something that the person wants to achieve. This could be to live independently or to simply make a sandwich. The outcome 'to live independently' may be complex and potentially take a long time to achieve. There will need to be goals and targets along the way. The outcome 'to make a sandwich' may be achieved in a shorter amount of time, but still may need goals along the way, such as:

- walking to the kitchen
- carrying ingredients from the fridge to the worktop
- opening packaging and making the sandwich.

A more challenging goal on the way to achieving the outcome of living independently could be to plan and prepare a cooked meal. To achieve this goal, the person will need to develop many skills, including:

- planning a menu
- identifying the required ingredients
- shopping
- money management
- cooking
- health and safety
- presentation of food.

Supporting people to develop or maintain everyday skills can involve preventative measures that enable people to maintain skills they already have or developmental measures designed to support people to learn new skills.

Preventative measures

Preventative measures are those designed to prevent or reduce the risks to health and well-being that could threaten or affect the person's skills and abilities. Risks are usually in the form of illness, accident or the degenerative conditions that can accompany older age.

Exercise

Encourage and support people to undertake regular exercise or physical activity. This will help to reduce the risk of heart disease, hypertension and depression.

Healthy eating

Encourage people to maintain a healthy balanced diet appropriate for their dietary needs. A healthy diet can prevent conditions such as diabetes becoming life-threatening or obesity causing mobility problems. Conditions caused by being underweight such as osteoporosis or anaemia can be equally as limiting for people's lives.

Aids, adaptations and assistive technology

People who develop health conditions such as arthritis or multiple sclerosis or dementia may be at risk of losing their skills if they are not given the correct support before the condition takes hold of their way of life. The person's living environment can be designed to include aids and adaptations to help them maintain their skills and fundamentally their independence. Aids could include, for example, adapted cutlery and kitchen utensils, handrails, wider doorways, raised toilet seats, shower seats, dressing aids and memory aids.

Activity 3

Planning aids and adaptions

Think about a person you support and identify the types of aids and adaptations that could help the particular person to maintain and regain skills for everyday life. Use your imagination and be creative as you consider the ways in which practical aids and technology could make the person's life easier. Now carry out some research to see if the type of aid you identified is available and, if it is, where to find it.

Functional skills

Maths: Interpreting and representing

There are many tables and charts available to show weight tables for men and women. Devise a table or chart showing weights and ages of people you support, and compare/contrast these to national averages. Look at whether you can draw any conclusions from your findings.

Reminders of things to do is a good aid to the memory and helps the person to maintain their skills.

Regular health checks

Support and encourage people to undergo regular health checks with their GP and optician. These checks could enable the early detection of heart disease, stroke or eye conditions such as age-related macular degeneration. Each of these conditions could result in someone losing their skills for everyday life. Check-ups with the GP would also include medication reviews to ensure the person remains on the correct medication and at the required level.

Maintain and enhance intellectual skills

A person's mental health is just as important as their physical health. To prevent or slow down the intellectual degeneration of a person, it is important that they remain mentally active. Activities such as

completing crosswords or taking part in quizzes can help stimulate the brain, keeping it active.

Minimise inactivity

Keeping active can help prevent people developing stiff joints and joint pain. Skills for everyday life which involve physical activity such as gardening and housework are valuable means of exercise if they are undertaken on a regular basis.

Support and encourage social activities

Supporting the person to take part in social activities such as visiting friends, dancing, going to the cinema or theatre, going to the pub, visiting a luncheon club or going to a computer class will support people to maintain their communication and social interaction skills. Being involved in group activities helps people to feel a sense of belonging. This promotes positive self-esteem, which aids both mental and physical health.

Developmental measures

Support for carers

Provide information to care givers and others involved in supporting someone. Discuss the concept of active participation and encourage carers to promote independence and support people to try skills for themselves.

Support

Give people opportunities and support to develop their skills. You should avoid doing things for someone if there is a chance that they can develop their own skills. Encouraging people to do as much for themselves as possible will help them to develop skills for everyday life.

2.3 Resolving conflicts during planning

Sometimes, there can be conflicts and disagreements in the process of planning with people. However, as long as you bear in mind that the plan belongs to the person, and they are the one who should have control of the pan and decide what is in it, this should help conflicts to be resolved more easily.

The commonest area of conflict is between families and the person you are supporting. Families who have been caring for someone may be very concerned about people wanting to do something that they think is too risky. Families may feel more comfortable doing things for people rather than enabling and encouraging them to do things for themselves. The combination of a protective family and a young person wanting to begin to develop some independence can be an explosive mix!

Different views can also be evident between professionals who may be involved in the support team. Some may hold particular views about the right way to approach the development or maintenance of skills. However, these are professional differences of opinion and should not become a conflict as they should be resolved in a professional manner through discussion.

Occasionally, if someone wants to do something that is dangerous or that would actually be harmful, then you may be in a situation of conflict with the person by explaining that you are unable to support them. This is a difficult decision to make and you should always consult your supervisor. You can never support someone to harm themselves, but you need to take care when identifying the difference between risk, which people have every right to take and danger from which they may need protection. You have looked at this in Unit HSC 024, but you may need to think about how this could affect what you do when planning work around skills development.

Resolving conflicts requires good communication; discussion and sharing views is always the best way to help everyone feel that their opinions have been listened to and considered.

During the planning process, you need to ensure everyone understands what is being discussed. If someone does not understand, or has the wrong interpretation of what has been said, conflict can occur. Going over what has been decided is a useful way of making sure that everyone is clear. When a decision is reached, saying 'So, are we all clear, we have decided to...' is a useful way of just being sure that everyone has understood.

Remember that if someone is using an advocate or has particular communication needs, you will need to allow enough time and to double-check that agreements are understood.

Personal conflict

Sometimes, the way that someone views themselves or their ability can create internal conflict. They may feel that the planned actions to develop their skills are too difficult to achieve. This is almost always an indication of low self-esteem and a lack of confidence. In this situation, it is important to work to develop someone's self-esteem and give them the confidence to try some new skills.

Some people may not feel that they want to develop; their lack of confidence may make them feel that they are happy relying on others. This can be a difficult conflict to overcome, but a gradual process of encouragement and making sure that targets are achievable will be the best approach to enabling people to resolve any personal conflict.

Some conditions may make it difficult for people to accept or adapt to changes; for example, someone with depression may find it impossible to feel motivated to put in the effort required to work on their skills. In this situation, you will need to work closely with the mental health professionals who are supporting the person to find out the approach that is likely to be most effective for the person. Equally, someone who is on the autistic spectrum will find any changes challenging, it is essential that any work that you undertake with someone on the autistic spectrum is in line with their support plan and with their behaviour management plan.

Doing it well

Resolving conflict

- Identify the issue or problem causing the conflict.
- Look at options and alternatives.
- Ensure effective communication.
- Encourage everyone's involvement, input and opinions.
- Help people to understand the views of others.
- Understand and respect each others priorities.
- Manage conflict when it occurs; do not suppress it.
- Assist people to recognise agreement.
- Ensure that everyone understands the agreement.
- Support the motivation of the person.
- Involve other specialists where required.

2.4 Supporting the individual to understand the plan and anything needed to implement or monitor it

People are in control of any planning for anything that affects any aspect of their lives, but there may be some aspects of a plan for skills development that may need to be explained.

Support understanding

In order to be sure that a person has an understanding of their plan, it needs to be presented in a way that meets their needs. It needs to be in the person's preferred method of communication, and it is your role to support them to develop and record the plan in whatever way they prefer. This could be written, or it may be recorded on a DVD or in an audio format. Some people prefer an easy-read format using graphic images. Some people like to be able to think about the whole plan and are motivated by being able to see the outcome they are working towards. Other people find this daunting and prefer to work towards one target at a time, making gradual progress towards the final outcome.

Equipment

In order to achieve a goal, the plan may require equipment. It is essential that you and the person you support know how to use or operate the equipment safely. As you learned in Unit HSC 037, you must not use equipment that does no meet health and safety requirements, or without the necessary training.

Of course, some of the equipment people may be using to support their skills development may be quite simple aids to daily living, such as aids for opening jars or lifting saucepans, or aids to do up zips or put on a sock.

Regardless of the type of equipment, it is important to know how the equipment works and what the risks are. Most aids and equipment are recommended following an occupational therapy assessment, and you should take this opportunity to check that you are clear how to use the equipment and are confident to provide any assistance to the person you support.

How do you ensure people can use equipment safely when developing skills?

Reflect

Think of a time when you were asked to use a piece of equipment that you had not used before. How did you feel before trying to use it? How did your lack of knowledge affect your use of this equipment? Once you were aware of how to use the equipment safely, how did this make you feel compared to the first time you used it?

Monitoring

Monitoring simply means making sure that the plan is still achieving the original aims and is still suitable for the purpose for which it was intended. In order to monitor a plan to develop or regain everyday skills, it is probably best to agree a checklist with the person you are supporting so that they, or you, can easily keep an eye on the key factors, such as:

- is there progress towards targets?
- is the equipment still right for the job?
- is the target set too high?
- is the target too easy to achieve?
- does the person still want the same outcome?

3. Be able to support individuals to retain, regain or develop skills for everyday life

3.1 Agreed support to develop or maintain skills, in a way that promotes active participation

Supporting someone to develop or maintain skills for everyday life should be done in a way that promotes their **active participation**. This means making sure that they are doing as much as possible to support themselves and that you are only providing additional assistance for things that they really cannot do for themselves.

> ### Key term
>
> **Active participation** – recognising somebody's right to participate in the activities and relationships of everyday life as independently as possible

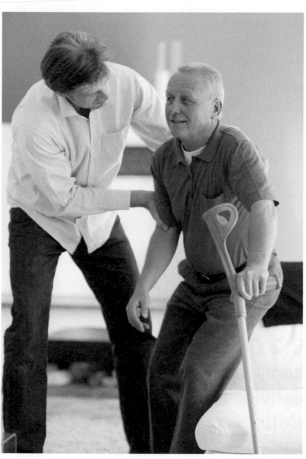
Always agree with the person what support they feel they need.

Providing support

The support that you give someone in the development, retention or maintenance of skills should be appropriate to promote their independence. The person should be at the centre of everything you do. Initially people can require a lot of physical support and encouragement. This may continue until the person's skills begin to develop. The amount of physical support you give

Case study

Agreeing goals to achieve an outcome

Howard is 73 years old and he is recovering from a recent stroke which has left him with speech difficulties and left-side paralysis. Both his speech and his movement are slowly improving, and he is very persistent with the physiotherapy exercises and those that the speech and language therapist has given him. Sadly, just before Howard had his stroke, his wife had died. She had always done the household tasks and the cooking, so not only did Howard have to cope with his reduced movement and co-ordination following the stroke, but he had to learn new skills in order to maintain his independence.

Howard and his support worker agreed on some goals on the way to achieving the main outcome that Howard wanted, which was to be fully independent in his own home again. Both he and his support team knew that there were many challenges ahead as Howard had to relearn speech and mobility, as well as develop new skills in order to be able to be fully independent.

1. How would you begin to tackle the challenges Howard faces?
2. What sort of targets might you agree with Howard?
3. What do you think will be the greatest challenge for Howard, and for his support worker?

should then slowly decrease over an agreed amount of time. This allows their physical skills to increase as they do more and more for themselves. You can continue the support you give using only verbal encouragement until the person's confidence grows. Gradually decrease the amount of encouragement and support you give over a period of time, to the point where the person is able to undertake the skill independent of any support.

Reflect

Think about a challenge you have had to face. It does not matter if it seems quite a small challenge – what is important is whether you found it challenging, not whether others might. Try to recall how you dealt with that challenge. Did you break it down into separate targets? (Even if you did not realise it at the time.) Did you plan how you were going to meet the challenge or just make a start and see what happened? Do you think you dealt successfully with the challenge – or could you have done it better if you had tackled it another way?

3.2 Giving positive and constructive feedback during activities to develop or maintain skills

Feedback on how well someone is doing is an integral part to the development of skills. How you give it and when is also just as important. We all need some form of acknowledgement on what we are doing whether it is at home, work or college. Without feedback the person may carry on doing what they were doing without any changes, or they may simply give up if they feel that no one is interested in their progress.

Feedback

Regardless of the content of any feedback you give, it must be constructive with reasons for any improvements that you may suggest. See Unit SHC 32 about your own personal development for more information on feedback. The same principles apply as for your personal or professional development.

Try to think of helpful and constructive ways you can give feedback. For example:

'Peter, you still haven't got the hang of this bed-making, have you?'

Constructive feedback needs to sound more like this:

'Peter, I can see bed-making is still a bit of a challenge. The pillowcases look great – do you know, if you fit the two bottom corners of the sheet first, the rest goes on so much more easily.'

Can you see the difference? Think about how much more motivated you would feel by having the second style of feedback given to you rater than the first.

Praise and encouragement

Although it is important to give positive and constructive feedback, praise and encouragement are also essential. We all like to have our achievements recognised and valued by others, so make sure that you comment on and praise achievements and progress. Being praised is important motivation for people to keep on working at skills. There is no need to praise excessively and make a huge fuss over every little step and it is important to avoid patronising people and indulging in the sort of comments that you use to a child. There is a world of difference between 'That's great – you've really made some progress this week' and 'Oh wow! Just look at what you've done! Who's clever, then?'

Be aware of how you give praise – do not patronise the person.

Timing

Constructive feedback is useful for helping people to improve their skills. Therefore it should be given either during or soon after the activity that they are working on. Feedback often works well during the activity. If you notice something, comment positively on it there and then. Talk to people about what they are doing so that they can focus immediately on the area that needs further development. Do not wait until a formal review of their development plan; by this time it may be more difficult for someone to remember exactly what they did.

Delivery

How you give feedback is very important, to enable people to accept it. Not everyone is happy to receive feedback, especially if it is suggesting improvements. Ensure that you always begin with the positives and then move on to areas that still need work You may sometimes meet with a negative response to your suggestions, which people are perfectly entitled to make. However, if you can try to turn your feedback around and re-present it in a different way, you may be able to calm matters. For example: 'I'm sorry if it sounded like criticism, I wasn't suggesting that you were wrong, it was just a suggestion that may make things easier for you.'

Activity 4
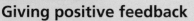

Giving positive feedback

Think about a time when you have provided support to someone during a development activity and have given them detailed positive feedback. Make notes about how you gave the feedback and if there was any impact on the person's performance or self-esteem. You may also want to note down how you think you could have improved how you delivered the feedback.

Functional skills

English: Speaking and listening

This activity will enable you to practise your skills in verbal communication. Your assessor will review and support you by looking at how you adapt contributions to suit the purpose, audience and situation. You will have the opportunity to develop skills in helping to take a discussion forward and to present information clearly.

3.3 Actions to take if an individual becomes distressed or unable to continue

Identifying distress

Distress is a state where people's emotions are aroused and they may behave in ways that are not usual or expected, and they may not interact with others in the ways that they usually would.

People can become distressed for a wide range of reasons and there is more detail in Unit SHC 31. Distress may occur as a result of:

- stress
- loss or bereavement
- illness
- financial problems
- work issues
- relationship problems
- reduced ability.

Being distressed can result in a range of different feelings such as those in the diagram below. Not everyone who is distressed will feel all of things; some people may have just one overwhelming feeling, while others may experience a mix of feelings. You are not expected to resolve all the problems that are making someone distressed, but it is useful for you to understand the possible reasons and to think about how someone may be feeling. This kind of understanding makes it more likely that you will be able to support someone through a period of distress until they are able to take some more positive steps.

Actions to take

Any of us can become distressed at any time if we are unable to deal with external stresses. You may be supporting someone to develop or regain a skill when they suddenly become distressed. There can be several approaches to this depending on what you know of the person and their own circumstances, but it can often be helpful to:

- suggest that the person come with you to a quiet calm environment
- give the person some time and space to compose themselves before encouraging them to talk
- ask them if they can work out what triggered their emotions
- support and encourage the person to express themselves without interruption.

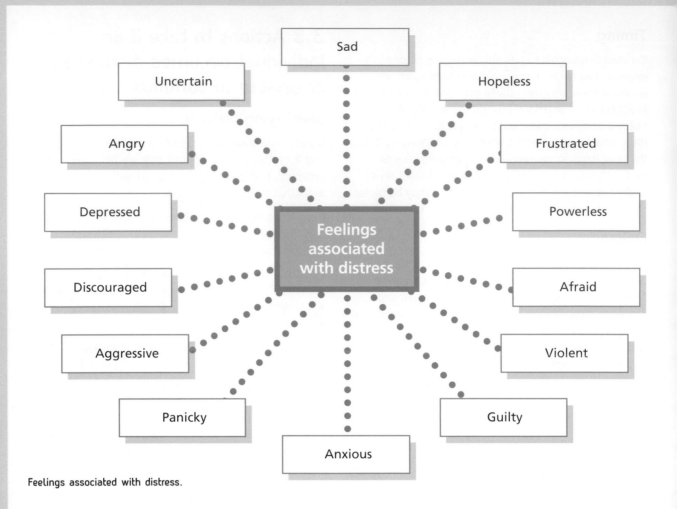

Feelings associated with distress.

They may express that they feel frustrated at not being able to regain or develop their skills as quickly as they would like, or they may say that the activity is too hard and they cannot cope. In response, avoid using phrases such as 'don't be silly'. You may mean to be supportive, but using words such as 'silly' or 'daft' can appear patronising and condescending, and fail to value the reality of the person's distress.

If someone is becoming distressed with the development activity, you could discuss leaving it for a couple of days until the person feels more positive. You could also ask if they would like to change some parts of the plan, perhaps making the goals smaller and more achievable. This approach can sometimes prevent the person from giving up on their progress.

If you have any major concerns someone's physical or mental health, it is important that you speak with them and report your concerns to the appropriate professional. Depending on your role and responsibilities, this could be your manager, line supervisor, the person's GP or consultant, mental health team, psychiatrist or psychologist. Reporting your concerns will enable the person to receive the support they require.

4. Be able to evaluate support for developing or maintaining skills for everyday life

4.1 Criteria and processes for evaluating support

The evaluation of the support given to someone is an important process. You may need to support someone to develop the criteria for evaluation.

Process of evaluation

The most important part of any evaluation is the views of the person to whom the support plan belongs. Any services have to meet the needs and outcomes for the person, or they are not fit for purpose. Only the person is in a position to say if the support is working for them. There may be other key people who could be involved in the evaluation process. These include:

- you, as the support worker
- your line manager

- the person's advocate (if applicable)
- specialists – for example, a physiotherapist, an occupational therapist
- others who are important to the person's well-being.

The process of evaluation could be through a simple questionnaire with specific questions relating to the support the person received. They may not necessarily have to write any comments if the questionnaire was graded for the person to state scores between 1 and 5. Alternatively, tick boxes could be provided to select the answer the person feels most relates to the feedback they wish to give. Below are examples of both of these types of questionnaires.

Questionnaires can sometimes be a cold way to obtain feedback. Not everyone will be happy or able to fill in a questionnaire. To address this, feedback could be obtained through a short interview. The person

Scoring: 1 = Excellent 2 = Very good 3 = Good 4 = Satisfactory 5 = Poor					
	1	2	3	4	5
How good was the support that you received?					
Was the support sufficient for what you needed?					

Rating: A = I agree fully B = I agree mostly C = I neither agree or disagree D = I disagree mostly E = I disagree fully					
	A	B	C	D	E
The support was good					
There was enough support for what I needed					

Examples of questionnaires.

Not everyone will be happy to give verbal feedback.

conducting the interview may need to be impartial to achieve an unbiased result. Face-to-face interviews allow for a more personal, individual response which is not always achievable through written questionnaires. Some people may feel uncomfortable being interviewed, especially if their feedback is not very positive. The pros and cons of both questionnaires and interviews need to be taken into consideration when agreeing on the process of obtaining feedback.

Criteria

Developing the criteria will involve close working with the person to choose criteria that reflect what they want to be the outcome of their plan. Criteria need to cover all aspects of the support given. This will depend on what people want, but the following areas may be a helpful list of suggestions.

- Planning — the support given to the person to:
  - identify skills
  - plan the development or maintenance of the skills identified
  - develop the plan
  - use of any equipment
  - resolving any disagreements.

- Retaining, regaining or developing skills — the support given to the person to:
  - develop skills
  - learn new skills
  - ensure active participation
  - review and change approaches if needed.

Criteria have to be measurable, so you will need to give some thought to what the person wants to measure about the areas they have chosen to evaluate. For example:

- 'I was able to decide what was in my plan'
- 'The plan was easy to understand'
- 'Support staff arrived on time'
- 'Progress was made towards my chosen goals'.

Can you see how someone would be able to use these types of statements to measure if their plan was working well?

Once the criteria and processes for evaluating support have been identified by the person, they must be fully documented and shared with all those involved.

Evaluation form

Devise an evaluation form and plan an evaluation. If you are working with someone appropriate, try it out with them. If not, imagine someone who has a plan to support them to develop or regain skills and complete the form for them. Go over it and see if you think it would give someone the information to decide if the support they had received was effective. If not, amend your form until it is right.

Functional skills

English: Writing

You will have the opportunity to write a formal evaluation and extend the types of documents you use to express yourself in written texts. You will need to ensure that the work is fit for purpose and that all spelling, punctuation and grammar is accurate and that the meaning of the writing is clear throughout the document.

4.2 Evaluating progress towards goals

Earlier in this unit, you looked at planning the development or maintenance of the skills identified for everyday life. You learned about goals — or targets and their importance in making progress towards the outcomes that someone wants to achieve. As part of the process of a person setting goals and targets, they will have decided how often they wanted to review progress.

The progress that people make will be the result of several factors, including:

- motivation
- physical conditions
- mental health/cognitive conditions
- personal circumstances
- quality of support
- frequency of support
- realistic and achievable planning
- appropriateness of approaches/methods.

All of these factors will need to be taken into account when undertaking a review of progress.

4.3 Revising a plan

Identifying issues which require revisions in a development plan does not mean that the plan has been a failure. Some changes that are made may be as a result of the person achieving their goals earlier than expected. The revision may also be as a result of unforeseen difficulties or developments. This is why plans are reviewed. If it was the case that each time a goal was set it would be achieved without question, then no reviews would ever need to take place. Unfortunately, very few things in life have that level of certainty. Sometimes it is very difficult or even impossible to plan for every eventuality.

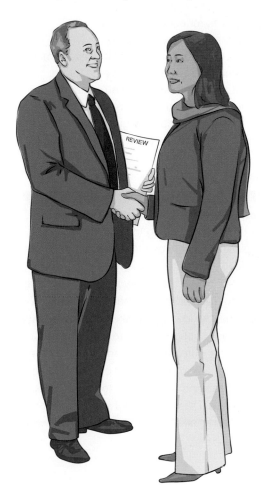

To ensure a plan will work, it must be led by the person concerned.

A plan may need to be revised many, many times before someone achieves their goal. It does not matter how many times the plan is revised providing the person is progress towards their identified outcomes.

4.4 Recording and reporting

The provision of support to maintain and develop skills for everyday life needs to be fully documented in line with legislation such as the Data Protection Act and your organisation's policies and procedures on records and record keeping. These areas are covered in more detail in Unit HSC 038.

It is very important to record the whole process to ensure that everyone is clear about the plan. Areas which will need to be documented include:

- identification of skills to be developed
- methods to be used to develop identified skills
- identification of goals
- timescales for achieving goals
- support required by the person
- names of those involved in the development
- equipment required to achieve goals
- timescales for reviewing/evaluating the plan
- summary of feedback given
- any distress and support given (if applicable)
- new revisions to the plan.

Legislation

- Data Protection Act 1998
- Putting People First (Department of Health 2007)
- Our Health, Our Care, Our Say (Department of Health 2007)

Further reading and research

- http://disabilityuk.com/index.html (Disability UK: information on disabilities including aids to support skills for everyday life)
- http://en.wikibooks.org/wiki/Assistive_Technology_in_Education/Life_Skills (information regarding assistive technology as a tool for supporting people to develop skills)
- www.gcflearnfree.org/everydaylife (interactive Internet programmes designed to give the person everyday life experience without the real-life consequences)
- www.goal-setting-guide.com (informative site on setting and achieving goals)

Getting ready for assessment

Most of this unit is going to be assessed in the workplace. You will need to show your assessor that you are able to work with people to help them develop, maintain or regain their everyday skills. Your assessor will look at how you approach people and how you are able to help them to identify the skills they want to work on and how you support people to look at the best ways of achieving the outcome they want. You will have to show that you are able to review and evaluate progress towards goals and targets, and to support people to change plans if they are not achieving what it needed.

In addition to being able to demonstrate your skills in supporting people, you also have to show that you understand what everyday skills are, why they are important and the situations that can arise where people lose, or never had, the ability to perform day-to-day skills. You may have to prepare an assignment or a presentation for this, or your assessor may ask questions as part of an observation of your practice in the workplace.

Unit HSC 3004

Facilitate learning and development activities to meet individual needs and preferences

This unit is an option unit and is aimed at those working in a wide range of settings who support people in learning or development activities. It provides the care worker with the knowledge and skills required to support people to plan, take part in and evaluate learning or development activities.

All people, regardless of age or ability, have the right to participate in activities of their choice. Learning and development activities can provide enrichment to the person's life and should therefore be supported by the care worker.

In this unit you will learn about:

- the role of learning and development activities in meeting individual needs
- how to identify learning and development activities to meet individual needs and preferences
- how to plan learning and development activities with individuals
- how to prepare for learning and development activities
- how to facilitate learning and development activities with individuals
- how to evaluate and review learning and development activities.

1. Understand the role of learning and development activities in meeting individual needs

1.1 Benefits of engaging in learning or development activities

Before you begin looking into the benefits of learning or development activities, you need to understand the differences between them.

- A learning activity generally involves increasing knowledge.
- A development activity is one that aids the mastering of new skills.

Some people feel that learning and development go hand in hand, that you cannot do one without the other.

Learning and development activities may include:

- intellectual pursuits
- activities to promote fitness or mobility
- activities relating to skills development
- activities to promote participation and interaction.

Benefits

Learning and development does not have to be a chore – it can be fun. Apart from the benefits of being able to do something or knowing about something, learning or development activities can have many benefits for the person including physical, intellectual, emotional and social benefits, otherwise known as PIES.

Physical benefits

Physical inactivity is a major risk factor for developing coronary artery disease. It also contributes to other risk factors including obesity, high blood pressure, high cholesterol and diabetes.

Some physical activities build muscular strength while others increase endurance. Some forms of physical activities involve using the large muscles in your arms or legs. These are called endurance or aerobic exercises.

These activities help the heart by making it work more efficiently during exercise and at rest. People who start regular physical activity after a heart attack have better rates of survival and a better quality of life. Healthy

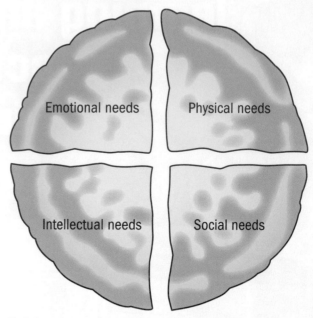

To help you remember, think of a pie.

people – as well as many people with cardiovascular disease – can improve their fitness and exercise ability with physical activities such as brisk walking, skipping, jogging, cycling and dancing. These are all examples of aerobic activities that increase endurance and in turn the heart's performance. You will look at these in more detail on page 264.

Other physical benefits can include:

- an increase in muscle strength
- an increase in joint mobility
- an increase in appetite
- the normalisation of sleep patterns
- the lowering of blood pressure
- an increase in lung capacity (how big a breath can be taken)
- an increased ability to carry out tasks of daily living.

Intellectual benefits

Your brain is an organ that learns and grows by interacting with the world. Mental stimulation can improve the brain's function and can protect against **cognitive** decline. The human brain can continually adapt and repair itself. Even when the brain becomes older, it can grow new neurons. Severe cognitive decline is usually caused by disease, whereas most age-related losses in memory simply result from the brain's inactivity and a lack of mental exercise or stimulation.

Activities which stimulate the brain through learning can often bring about understanding. In turn, understanding can lead to acceptance. These intellectual benefits can bring about harmony within a multiracial society or inner peace to a person who has experienced ill health.

Other intellectual benefits can include:

- the ability to communicate more readily
- becoming more mentally alert
- an increased interest in surroundings and other people
- an increase in memory ability
- an increase in concentration levels.

Emotional benefits

Learning or development can improve a person's self-esteem. This is how the person thinks of themselves. Activities which stimulate the brain or body can help the person to feel better about themselves. The person's self-confidence can be improved and they can become calmer and less stressed about things going on around them. Depression and anxiety have often been lifted with exercise or activity. Think about it – would you be happy sitting around all day every day doing nothing? You would soon become bored or, more seriously, depressed. The process of developing or regaining skills can help the person to become more independent. This in itself is a large emotional benefit, especially for people who may have lost some of their skills or abilities due to ill health.

Other emotional benefits can include:

- the ability to relax more
- the feeling of having more to contribute to life
- the ability to express themselves more readily
- a reduction in confusion.

Social benefits

Learning or development activities for people can be undertaken on a one-to-one basis with their care worker or in groups with other people. The activities can take place within the person's own environment or in the community using public facilities. Activities within the community give the person opportunities to interact and socialise with other like-minded people. Learning or development activities where the person meets other people can lead on to the development of friendships and other social activities one would have with friends.

1.2 The purpose of a range of learning or development activities

There are two types of activities – sedentary and non-sedentary. Sedentary activities are those that are undertaken mostly while sitting down, whereas non-sedentary activities involve much more movement.

Sedentary activities	Non-sedentary activities
Jigsaws	Gardening
Drawing	Walking
Reading	Dancing
Listening to music	Sightseeing
Board games	Aerobics
Surfing the Internet	Bowling
Arts and crafts	Swimming

Table 1: Sedentary and non-sedentary activities.

Most learning or development activities have a specific purpose or reason for the person to take part in them. You will look at these in more detail below.

Intellectual activities

As you saw previously, intellectual activities are those which stimulate the brain. Some people may believe that intellectual activities are not fun, too difficult or you need to have a high IQ to do them. This is not always the case. The following activities can be stimulating to the brain and enjoyable too.

Reading

Reading is a good activity for people of any age. It not only updates knowledge on the latest happenings, but can also increase the depth of knowledge. Reading books, novels, fiction, poems and even the daily newspaper is a good way of keeping the brain stimulated. For those people who are not able to read, many books are now available on audio. Reading can be undertaken personally or as a group (see 'Group participation and interaction' on page 267).

Memory activities

Activities where the person needs to remember items can help keep the brain stimulated. Memory activities can be set up fairly quickly by simply collecting a number of household items and covering them with a towel. The person is encouraged to list all the items they can remember. An alternative way to use this activity is for the person to memorise all the items before one item is removed. The person then needs to try to identify which item is missing.

Board games

Board games such as chess can help keep the brain alert. Not only does the person have to plan their own move, they also have to anticipate the moves made by their opponent.

Sudoku

In this activity the person needs to work out where numbers fit into a grid so that they are not repeated within a section. Sudoku can be purchased in a book or accessed on the Internet.

Quizzes

Played in small groups within the person's environment or by attending a local pub quiz night, this activity can help keep the brain active. The competitive side of this activity can be very stimulating to some. Taking part in a quiz may also offer its rewards in the form of a prize if the person is successful enough to win.

Fitness/mobility activities

When you hear the words 'fitness activities', you may automatically think of strenuous exercise in the gym, exercising to the point where perspiration is dripping from your brow. Fitness activities fall into two categories: low-impact exercise and high-impact exercise. Identifying the difference between these is simple. If you are moving

Board games can help stimulate the brain.

Swimming is a good form of aerobic exercise.

and at least one foot is always in contact with the ground, you are doing low-impact exercise. If both feet are off the ground, you are doing high-impact exercise. Low-impact exercise can include walking, swimming or cycling. High-impact exercise can include running, skipping or jumping.

Improving joint mobility

Various exercises are designed to improve the flexibility and movements of joints. These types of exercise are important to keep the person supple and can aid the reduction of pain caused by stiffness.

Head and neck exercise

All moves should be performed in a controlled and gentle manner and should not be uncomfortable.

- The person should turn their head to the left then return it to the central position, looking forward.
- They should next turn their head to the right then return it to the central position, looking forward.
- Encourage the person to repeat the left and right head turns three times.
- Facing forward, they should tilt their head to one side, taking their ear closer to their shoulder. Remember to encourage the person to do this slowly with no jerking. They should feel a gentle stretch up the opposite side of their neck. Return to the central position.

- This should be repeated by tilting their head to the opposite side.
- Encourage the person to repeat this four times on both the left and right side.

Shoulder mobility

- While sitting or standing, encourage the person to bring their fingertips of both hands towards their shoulders (like imitating a flapping bird). It is not a problem if they cannot reach their shoulders; just make sure they are comfortable.
- The person should rotate their elbows slowly, making circles in the air, moving their arms in a clockwise direction.
- Encourage them to repeat the exercise, making the rotations in an anticlockwise direction.
- Repeat both clockwise and anticlockwise rotations a further two times.

Ankle mobility

- Encourage the person to sit or stand and lift one foot off the ground. Encourage the use of a chair or table to balance against if needed while standing.
- Encourage them to rotate the lifted foot in a clockwise direction five times, slowly and gently.
- Repeat the rotations in an anticlockwise direction.
- Encourage the person to swap over to stand or rest their weight on their other leg and repeat the exercise with the other foot.

Hip mobility

- Encourage the person to stand next to a chair or table (something to help them balance) sideways on, and hold the back of the chair with one hand.
- They should gently swing one leg forwards and backwards in a smooth, slow, pendulum-type movement 10 times.
- Encourage the person to repeat the exercise with their other leg a further 10 times.

Aerobic activities

Walking, swimming and cycling are all types of aerobic activities and are designed to increase the person's heart rate. The heart is a muscle and it needs to keep fit and healthy just like any other muscle in the body, if not more so. The human heart should beat approximately 60–80 times per minute while at rest. With every beat the heart is pumping blood around the body. As the heart muscle becomes stronger through aerobic activities, it is able to pump a larger volume of blood with every heartbeat. As more blood is being pumped, the heart does not need to beat as fast. This means the heart rate of a fit and healthy heart is slower when at rest and does not beat as fast when exercising. The heart is no longer working as hard as it was. Like most things, if it is not used as much, it can last longer.

Functional skills

Maths: Understanding data

Look at figures that identify how calories are burned doing various exercises – for example, aerobics, walking or swimming. Devise a chart to show a minimum of five exercises and the rate at which calories are burned when exercising for one hour. Use this information to plan an exercise routine for a person who wishes to lose a moderate amount of weight over a two-month period (burning 300 calories a week through exercise may be reasonable to aid weight loss). Show your calculations on a weekly and monthly basis.

Development of skills

Skills such as painting, drawing, sculpture, music and singing are some examples of art. If a person once had the skill to be artistic, they would never forget or lose that ability, not even as they grow older. Art remains with the person throughout their life. The person may never have had the opportunity or inclination to express themselves through art and may not therefore know of any hidden talents they may have. Art can allow the person to communicate their thoughts and feelings through their chosen medium. It can help to wash away any feelings of sorrow, anger, anxiety, guilt or depression.

Bird watching

Bird watching is both a sedentary and non-sedentary activity. While watching the birds, the person is mainly sitting down. However, to get to the place where the person may find different birds, they may have to walk. Many avid bird watchers often form or join a group and visit exotic locations for bird watching. The person does not necessarily have to travel any further than their own back garden to start bird watching. The hobby is a lot of fun but is also a skill. It helps the person to discover various facts about nature which were unknown to them previously. Bird watching can provide both entertainment and learning.

Gardening

Planting flowers and growing your own fruit and vegetables is becoming increasingly popular. As an activity it can be undertaken for as long or as short a time as the person prefers. If the person does not have access to a garden, an alternative could be potted plants or window boxes. Both of these can provide the person with many hours of enjoyment. The activity is good for the brain and can be physically demanding.

Whatever the person prefers to grow, they may need to brush up on their plant-growing skills. A trip to the local library or garden centre can help the person collect the information they need. Once the flowers have bloomed or the vegetables have sprouted, the person can feel a sense of achievement. Comments from family and friends on how nice the garden looks or how tasty the fruit and vegetables are can lift the person's self-esteem.

Collecting items of interest

Hobbies or pastimes such as coin or stamp collecting are often seen as uninteresting activities, yet millions of people worldwide do these activities on a daily basis. The collecting of items such as coins can involve a high level of skill. The person would need to develop the ability to identify coins, including their age, country of origin and currency. These are skills which can be developed from researching books, specialist magazines and the Internet.

Whatever the items of interest being collected by the person, many hours hunting around car boot sales, markets, charity shops and collectors' fairs could be spent trying to find the items they are looking for. In their hunt the person would be interacting with many different people, sharing their hobby with others with similar interests. In turn this interaction could help the person to develop their communication and social skills.

Group participation and interaction

Group participation and interaction can promote qualities and skills such as sharing, understanding, acceptance, turn-taking, communication and listening. The groups can be small with only two or three participants, or they can be much larger. The size of the group could encourage or inhibit the person's interaction and participation. If the group is small, the person may have more chance of interacting with others, but may feel quite exposed or embarrassed with such few numbers that they cannot hide away. On the other hand, a large group could allow the person to feel quite relaxed as the spotlight is not constantly on them, but they may not be able to interact or participate as much with everyone else taking their turns. Group activities could include the following.

Book clubs

A group of people, either in their own environment or in the community, could read and discuss books of varying interests. The discussion could be based on the people's feelings towards the characters in the book – promoting expression – or simply how they enjoyed the book, and which parts they enjoyed the most.

Dance clubs

Some organisations such as Age UK run clubs where the person can go along to socialise with other people of a similar age. The club may play music where members can get up and dance or simply sit and enjoy the music in the company of others.

Some clubs are especially designed for people to learn how to dance. Examples of these include country and western, line dancing and ballroom. A person can join the club to interact with others, while developing a skill and keeping fit all at the same time!

Whatever organisation or club the person takes part in, the interaction with others is beneficial to their identity and feeling of belonging. It is also beneficial for their social skills and communication skills.

Dancing can help develop friendships as well as keep you fit.

1.3 How individual needs and preferences may influence how learning and development activities are accessed or delivered

A person's physical or psychological health can have an impact on how they access learning and development activities. Other factors such as religion, belief, social isolation, environmental barriers and finance can also play a major part.

The needs of the person are paramount and must be taken into full consideration when accessing or taking part in learning or development activities.

Physical health

It is advisable before the person takes part in any physical activity that they undergo a physical examination by a doctor. Activities which could potentially threaten the health of a person must be adapted or omitted under the direction of a GP. Those who have a physical disability should be assessed by a physiotherapist or occupational therapist as to the suitability of the planned activity. Those who have not undertaken a form of exercise for a while should be introduced to the activity slowly and their strength and stamina built up gradually. For a number of people with certain health needs, high-impact exercise is not a safe option. These include people with:

- extreme obesity
- chronic issues such as stress fractures, osteoporosis or arthritis
- bone, joint or connective tissue injuries
- pregnancy.

A person's health may prevent them regularly attending learning or development activities. In some activities such as attending college, there may be a requirement for a certain level of attendance to be achieved in order to pass the course successfully. Missing learning or development activity sessions could result in the person missing large amounts of important information and potentially not passing the course. To meet the person's needs, learning and development activities could be tailored around their health requirements. This could mean the person would not necessarily be able to attend a regular activity session such as college courses unless their health permitted this.

Psychological health

Some people may have phobias or mental health conditions which inhibit their interaction with the outdoors, large groups of people, or water, for example. Activities which involve, for example, a person with **agoraphobia** going outdoors will need to be introduced slowly to allow them time to acclimatise themselves. Insisting or encouraging the person too quickly could cause their fears to intensify, making going out increasingly difficult. If the person joins a club or activity programme that requires them to attend weekly, then the support in helping them to overcome their fears must be introduced sooner to enable the person to be ready by the time the activity programme starts. Practice runs can be undertaken so that the person becomes accustomed to the journey they will take.

Key term

Agoraphobia – the fear of open spaces

Religion and belief

A person's religion or belief can have an impact on how they access or participate in learning and development activities. Certain religions forbid females being in the company of males without covering their head and face. This could make it very difficult to participate in some activities. One way of meeting the person's need could be to access specialist organisations which deliver activities while meeting particular religious needs.

Social isolation

Some people may live in areas where community facilities or public transport are not readily available. This can cause the person to be socially isolated. The person may not see or even speak to others from one week to the next. In a recent report by Help the Aged, 22 per cent of older people were effectively isolated as they needed help to get out and about, but did not have it. Only 33 per cent of the older generation has a car. This means 67 per cent rely on public transport to travel away from the home. Over half of these people are reported to have age-related bowel or bladder problems. If the community in which they are travelling does not have public conveniences, many will not want to go out.

Case study

Supporting an autistic person to start a new activity

Jean Claude is a 25-year-old man who has a mild form of autism. He is very interested in photography and has often spoken with his care worker about wanting to improve his photography skills. Jean Claude's autism affects the way he reacts to change. Providing the change is explained fully, Jean Claude will accept the change with little difficulty. Jean Claude's care worker, Dieudonne, telephones the local college and enquires when the next course of photography will start. He is informed the course will start in five weeks' time.

Jean Claude agrees to enrol on the photography course but is concerned about going to college as he has never been there before.

1. How should Dieudonne approach the subject of the photography course with Jean Claude?
2. Should Dieudonne have made the enquiry with the college without consulting Jean Claude?
3. What support should Dieudonne give Jean Claude?

You may need to read the rest of this unit to enable you to answer these questions fully.

Environmental barriers

Under the Disability Discrimination Act 1995, all public facilities must provide suitable access for all people, regardless of their abilities or disabilities. However, some people's needs are still unmet by premises which are not able to undergo adaptation due to their structure. Some colleges and places of education still have limited access for people with physical disabilities. These organisations will often alter the course venue or delivery to meet people's needs.

Finance

A person's financial situation can influence how they access learning or development activities. Some people may be unable to afford learning or development activity fees; it may be possible to obtain support following a financial assessment. Many activities provided by organisations are often free of charge, or have a minimal charge. For some people it could simply be the cost of getting to and from the venues of learning or development activities that they cannot afford.

2. Be able to identify learning and development activities to meet individual needs and preferences

2.1 Supporting the individual to communicate their goals, needs and preferences about activities

To ensure the person accesses the correct learning or development activity to meet all of their needs, it is important that you encourage them to communicate fully what their goals, needs and preferences are. A goal would be what they want to achieve.

Formal and informal discussions

Discussions with the person about what learning or development activities they would like to do could be undertaken informally or formally. An informal discussion could be carried out on a one-to-one with the person while they were relaxing at home or over a meal. This can help them to relax, making the conversation easier. The discussion could be part of a general conversation about the types of things they like to do or it could be instigated from watching something on the television. The person themselves may start up a conversation about the things they like to do or would like to try out.

A formal discussion is one that is purposely set up to identify the person's goals, needs and preferences. Usually these discussions are part of a multidisciplinary review or meeting which includes the person and those who are involved in their care. Formal discussions would have an agenda, and minutes of the meeting would be recorded.

All people being supported, either in their own home or in a care home, should have a multidisciplinary review on a yearly basis. Prior to the review taking place, it would be beneficial to the person to have an informal discussion with their care worker about the pending review and the various topics that will be discussed within it. This would give the person time to think about what they would like to say within the review.

Reflect

Think about an appraisal you have had with your manager. Were you given notice about items to be discussed? How did you benefit from knowing what was on the agenda before the meeting actually took place? Compare your appraisal with a multidisciplinary meeting that you have attended with a person you support.

Functional skills

English: Speaking and listening

By taking part in a multidisciplinary review, you will have the opportunity to take part in a formal discussion about a person you support. You can practise skills of giving relevant and cogent responses to others in the team and to present your ideas clearly.

Case study

Discussing a multidisciplinary review

Gibson is a young man living in sheltered housing for people with substance reliance. Constance is a care worker who supports him to access community facilities for learning, development and recreational activities. Gibson has been notified that his first yearly multidisciplinary review will take place in a couple of weeks. Over lunch, Constance discusses with him what will happen at the review.

1. What should Constance discuss with Gibson about his pending review?
2. What concerns may he have about the pending review?
3. Why would Constance discuss the review over lunch with Gibson?

2.2 Providing information on possible learning or development activities

As a care worker you may already have some ideas for learning or development activities, but do you have all the information relating to them that you could provide to the person and **others** involved in their support?

It is very important that information on possible learning or development activities is shared with the person and others so that all involved can assess its suitability – whether or not the activity will meet the person's needs. The information the person and others would need would include:

- a description of the activity, including the aim or purpose
- benefits of the activity – the intended outcome, including any potential risks
- preparations needed – for example, whether the person needs to register or enrol for the activity
- any resources needed – would these be provided in the activity, can they be purchased or do they need to be specially made?

- any cost involved – if the activity has a cost, and if so, whether it is paid in advance or weekly. Will there be any further costs for resources, specialist clothing or tools? Is the person entitled to any discounts or grants?
- duration of the activity – including when it will start, how long it will last, and if it is a one-off or weekly session (if weekly, how many weeks?)
- the venue of the activity – will the activity be in their own home or would the person need to travel to the activity?
- means of transport, if travel is required – how will the person get to the activity? Does transport need pre-booking? How much will it cost?

Once all of the essential information is made available to the person and others, a decision can be made as to whether or not the activity will fully meet the person's needs. It can also be identified if any of the details of the activity need to be adapted to meet the person's specific needs.

Information on learning or development activities should be provided in a suitable format to meet the person's preferred method of communication. Organisations which offer learning or development activities are usually able to provide information in different languages, larger print or Braille. Some may even provide information in audio format. For those activities which can be planned, prepared and delivered by the care worker or members of their team, the information will need to be gathered and shared in the same way. It is essential the information is provided to the person in a way that they can understand, so that they can make an informed choice.

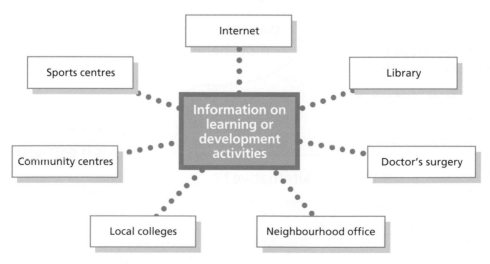

Sources of information on learning or development activities.

2.3 Assessing whether a tailor-made activity may be more beneficial than other learning or development opportunities

A tailor-made activity is designed with the person in mind. These types of activities have their advantages and disadvantages, as do **regular activities**.

> **Key term**
>
> **Regular activities** – activities designed for anyone to access

Tailor-made – advantages and disadvantages

The biggest advantage of a tailor-made activity is that it has been designed with a particular person in mind. The activity content can be planned around their interests, abilities, needs and preferences. The timing and duration of the activity can be set around the person's day including mealtimes, health and treatments. The

activity can be shortened or lengthened to meet how they are feeling at that time. Some tailor-made activities often cost very little, if anything. The resources can usually be sourced from within the person's own environment or can be home-made.

This all sounds so good that you could ask why all learning or development activities are not tailor-made. The answer is that one of the biggest advantages is also the biggest disadvantage. Because the activity is designed for a particular person, it may only be suitable for that one person. It may not therefore be suitable for a group. This could isolate the person and restrict their social interactions. Professionally tailored activities can be very costly compared with home-made tailored activities. The professional's time would need to be paid for. For a group, this cost could be split between all participants, but if there was only one person, they would have to pay for all of it on their own.

When you assess whether a tailor-made activity would be beneficial to the person, you need to ask yourself a number of questions, such as those below, to ensure you come to the correct answer.

2.4 Agreeing learning or development activities that will suit the individual

Identifying the person's goals, needs, wishes and preferences will enable you to begin the identification of suitable learning or development activities. Obtaining the relevant information on these activities will enable the person to begin making appropriate choices. From this, the person and others can begin agreeing and planning those learning or development activities that will suit the person.

The person and others should be supported in being fully aware of the potential activities and their benefits in meeting the person's needs. Without this, there is a risk that agreements could be made on activities which may not be totally suitable.

Under the Human Rights Act 1998 the person has a right to choice, to be aided in agreeing or disagreeing with the support they may require. A suitable learning or development activity may be identified by the care worker which the person does not agree with. They may disagree to the activity for a number of reasons, including:

- cost
- distance required to travel
- potential risks involved.

If the identified activity meets the person's overall needs, then it will be beneficial to look into those areas that they disagree with.

- Could the cost be reduced, shared or paid over instalments to spread out the payments?
- Is there the same activity closer to where the person lives, to reduce the distance required for travelling?
- Can any potential risks be reduced by implementing safety measures?

Obtaining the agreement of the person and others is essential. There is no point in pursuing a learning or development activity if agreement has not been reached with those concerned.

3. Be able to plan learning and development activities with individuals

3.1 Factors that may affect the way a programme of learning or development activities is implemented and supported

A person is an individual. What makes them an individual is their personality, culture, religion and beliefs. These traits can affect the way a learning or development activity is implemented and supported.

As a care worker, you may work with a number of people who each have their likes and dislikes, their individual needs and preferences. It would be wrong to provide the same type of support to all the people you work with. Some may need more support, while others may need very little. When implementing and supporting learning or development activities, it is important you remember the person's physical, intellectual, emotional and social abilities, or PIES (see page 262). To ensure the person is able to take part in the activity fully, some adaptations may be required to the programme or the resources used within the activity. How adaptations can be made is discussed in more detail on page 249.

Physical ability

The physical ability of a person is a factor that could affect the way an activity is implemented and supported. The person may have difficulties using their hands, such as holding small items. This could be caused by arthritis, cerebral palsy, multiple sclerosis, muscular dystrophy, Parkinson's disease or paralysis. They may have physical disabilities caused by a stroke or head injury which impacts on their mobility. This could affect their interaction within the activity. The person may have visual disabilities where they have difficulty seeing small items. The person may have a hearing difficulty which affects how they interact with others; they may also need to use equipment such as hearing aids or loop systems. All these can have an impact on how learning or development activities are implemented or supported by ensuring the delivery of the programme meets the person's needs and accommodates their requirements.

Activity 1

Physical factors affecting the implementation of an activity

Choose somebody you support who has a physical disability, or select one of the physical disabilities identified in this unit. State how the health condition affects their physical ability and the impact this can have on how an activity is implemented or supported.

Intellectual ability

Conditions such as autism, Down's syndrome, dyslexia and learning disabilities can have an effect on the person's level of understanding. Learning or development activities may need to be adjusted to meet the abilities of the person. In order for them to develop and progress, a level of understanding must be established. The programme may need to be delivered at a slower pace to ensure people are able to understand and follow without too much difficulty. The use of essential technical words should be kept to a minimum and those words explained fully.

Activity 2

Intellectual factors affecting the implementation of an activity

Identify a person you support who has a disability which affects their learning, or select one of the learning disabilities already listed. State how the condition affects their learning ability and the impact this can have on how an activity is implemented or supported.

Emotional ability

There are times in everyone's life where emotions play a large part. For most the emotion is short-lived and people carry on with their lives. For some people, their emotional state has a huge impact on their daily living. This could be as a result of mental health conditions such as anxiety disorder, depression, bipolar disorder or obsessive-compulsive disorder. The emotional state of a person can affect how a learning or development activity is implemented or supported. The person may only be able to concentrate for a very short period of time or they may be easily distracted. This would require the programme to be very stimulating with a regular change of activities to keep the person's attention. Those with depression or anxiety can find it very difficult to learn, if not impossible. The programme needs to aid the person to look on things in a more positive light. To support those who are anxious, the programme needs to include relaxation methods first to help them unwind a little.

Activity 3

Emotional factors affecting the implementation of an activity

Identify a person you support who has a condition which affects their mental health, or select one of those already listed. State how the condition affects their emotional ability and the impact this can have on how an activity is implemented or supported.

Functional skills

English: Writing

Write a document that shows you can communicate information, ideas and opinions effectively.
Present your information concisely, clearly and logically. Use a range of sentence structures, including complex sentences, and paragraphs to organise your work. Ensure that you have proofread your work so that the finished text has accurate spelling, punctuation and grammar, and your ideas are clear.

Case study

Planning Julie's collage

Julie is a 47-year-old lady who was recently involved in a car accident which resulted in her losing much of her memory. Julie's husband informed the rehabilitation unit which she attends each week that she used to enjoy arts and crafts. It is agreed that Julie will use this as an activity, in creating a collage, to help regain some of her knowledge. In order to achieve this aim, small goals are set for Julie to work towards over a four-week period. These include planning the design, identifying colours, describing textures and purchasing equipment

Social ability

A person's social ability can affect how they interact with others. In the context of a learning or development activity, the person who struggles with social interaction may need additional support to take part in group activities or discussions. The person may need to be encouraged to take turns or to accept another's point of view. The learning or development programme may need to be extended to include the development of social abilities.

3.2 Establishing a plan for implementing the programme of activities

Planning for the **implementation** of learning or development activities is as important as the delivery itself. A well-planned activity should be one that meets the needs of the person with all involved being clear about their roles and responsibilities.

Key term

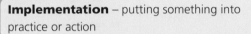

Implementation – putting something into practice or action

A plan for a learning or development activity may include:

- the purpose of the activity
- how the activity will be implemented
- timescales for implementation
- the roles and responsibilities of those involved
- the level and type of support required
- resources or equipment needed
- ways to minimise risks.

from the craft shop. The plan now needs to be documented.

1. What is the overall aim or activity?
2. Over what timescale is the implementation of the activity planned?
3. Describe the four goals that have been planned to help Julie achieve the aim.
4. What benefits do you feel Julie would receive in achieving her aim?

Learning or Development Activity Plan

Name Julie Hunt

Activity Creation of a collage using paints and natural materials to be displayed in foyer on open day

Agreement Julie Hunt, Mrs Hunt (mother), Rassol Marche (key worker)

Purpose

1. To support Julie to express herself through art
2. To aid Julie's identification of colours
3. To aid Julie to describe textures
4. To encourage Julie to exercise by walking to the park to collect natural materials for her collage
5. To encourage Julie to plan ahead
6. To contribute to the open day activities, promoting Julie's self-esteem

Start Date 18th October 2010   **End Date** 15th November 2010

Day Monday   **Weekly**/~~One off~~

Time 10.30 – 12.00noon   **Duration** 1.5 hours

Preparation required	Date required	Action by
Arrange for money to be available for purchase of materials	15th Oct 2010	Rassol Marche

Staff involved	Role/responsibility
Rassol Marche	To lead the activity with Julie
	To support Julie in purchasing items required
	To support Julie in collecting natural materials from the park
	To support Julie in creating the collage design
	To encourage Julie to identify colours during each session
	To discuss textures with Julie during the activity
Mariana Phillips	To accompany Rassol and Julie in purchasing items required
	To accompany Rassol and Julie to the park

Resources required (tick when acquired)

Paper	Leaves	Aprons	Newspaper
Paints	Twigs	Paint pots	
Brushes	Flower petals	Glue	

Implementation of activity	Meeting purpose
Week 1 – Planning – Rassol to work with Julie in designing the collage and identifying natural materials required. Support Julie to purchase resources.	1, 2, 5
Week 2 – Collection of materials – Support and encourage Julie to walk to the park to collect natural materials. Discuss colours and textures on collecting items.	2, 3, 4
Week 3 – Begin collage – Support Julie to use the paints, glue and natural materials to begin her collage. Discuss the colours and textures to reinforce learning.	1, 2, 3, 6
Week 4 – Finalise collage – Support Julie to finish collage and display in the foyer.	1, 6

Potential risks	Actions to reduce risks
Wandering off alone when out of the unit	Double staffing, talk to Julie when out to retain her attention on the activity
Spillage of paint, glue on the floor	Cover floor with newspaper
Spillage of paint, glue on Julie's clothes	Encourage Julie to wear old clothes and an apron
Drinking the paint and glue	Purchase toxic-free paint and glue

A learning or development activity plan.

Holding a planning meeting with the person and others involved is essential before implementing a plan.

To plan the implementation of a learning or development activity, you need to look at the overall aim or activity and decide how it is going to be achieved. You need to look at the steps or goals that need to be met by the person in order for them to achieve the activity. Including a timescale for each goal to be met will help the person focus on the activity.

Activities that require a professional input should be planned by the professional in conjunction with the person and others involved. An example of this may be an exercise programme. It would be important to enlist a professional such as a physiotherapist to aid the planning, to ensure harm does not come to the person.

The activity plan should be fully documented so that the person and others can refer to the record as and when needed. The plan should be detailed sufficiently to allow any care worker to implement or carry out the activity at any point in the programme. This ensures continuity of care in supporting the person as required. A completed learning or development plan is shown on the previous page as an example. You can copy this layout or develop your own if your organisation does not already have a template.

3.3 Assessing risks in line with agreed ways of working

People who wish to take part in learning or development activities may face various levels of risk depending on the activity and the ability of the person. In everyday life, we all face potential risks in everything we do. Some levels of risk may be very low while others are relatively high. Simply crossing the road has its risks. To reduce that risk, we may use a zebra crossing or traffic lights to help us cross safely. Doing this does not take away the risk completely, but it does reduce the risk.

Agreed ways of working

A risk assessment is a document which predicts potential harm to the person and others. Acting upon the risk assessment helps to prevent that potential harm or reduces the risk to a minimum. The General Social Care Council Code of Practice and the Codes of Practice of all the UK countries state that all social care employers should implement and monitor written policies on risk assessment. As a social care employee, you must recognise that people have the right to take risks and that you should help them to identify and manage potential and actual risks to themselves and others. You must also ensure that relevant colleagues and agencies are informed about the outcomes and implications of risk assessments.

The Department of Health's *Best Practice in Managing Risk* is a guide for mental health professionals working with people to assess risk. It underpins risk assessment with principles of good practice for all mental health settings and provides a list of tools offering structure to risk management. The guide states that decisions about managing risks should be based on improving the person's quality of life. It also states that avoiding all possible risks is not good for the person and can create more problems than it solves. Although this document is designed for working with people with mental health problems, it has some useful principles and approaches that are relevant for all people using support services.

Risks associated with activities

Within learning or development activities, there are some risks which may be obvious and some less obvious. Some risks are generic and can arise within many activities — for example, a heart attack is an extreme risk associated with many physical activities; it is far more likely that someone may have a muscle sprain or have a fall. Some risks are more specific to a particular activity; for example, the risks associated with swimming could be drowning in the extreme, but this can be reduced by swimming in a pool with a lifeguard rather than in the open sea. Do you see how this risk has immediately been reduced by putting some restrictions in place? Table 2 gives examples of generic risks within activities.

Many risks associated with activities are increased with underlying health problems. For example, a person who has diabetes could risk developing hypoglycaemia (low blood sugar), if they exercise too much at one time.

Activity	Potential generic risks
Physical activities such as walking, swimming or gardening	<ul><li>Muscle sprains and strains</li><li>Heart attack</li><li>Blisters</li><li>Heat exhaustion</li><li>Weight loss</li><li>Dehydration</li></ul>
Intellectual activities	<ul><li>Eye strain</li><li>Frustration</li><li>Reduction in self-esteem</li><li>Challenging behaviour resulting from frustration</li></ul>
Social activities	<ul><li>Increase in behaviours caused by stress</li><li>Over-competitiveness</li><li>Feeling overwhelmed</li></ul>

Table 2: Potential risks for different activities.

Activity 4

Learning or development plan

Using the information you have learned so far, devise a learning or development plan with a person you support. Show the plan to your assessor and discuss how it was developed.

Functional skills

English: Writing

Devising a plan for somebody you are working with will give you the opportunity to develop your writing skills. The plan will need to be laid out using a selected format. The plan needs to be clearly written using appropriate language. Information needs to be presented concisely and work needs to be proofread to ensure accuracy in grammar, spelling, punctuation and meaning.

4. Be able to prepare for learning and development activities

4.1 Resources or equipment needed for the activity

For an activity to run smoothly, you need to think ahead as to what resources or equipment you will need. This should be included in your planning of the activity. It is important, however, that you collect together all the equipment or resources needed before the activity starts. For some people, a break in the running of the activity while you search for a piece of equipment could result in them becoming frustrated or losing interest. If this occurs it could be very difficult to bring them back on track.

Use a checklist

If you planned to make a cake at home, you would generally compile a list of the ingredients you need. You would then look in your cupboards to see what ingredients you have and tick them off your list. You would know you needed to purchase those items not ticked. The same applies to learning or development activities. You need to write up a checklist of all the items you require, identify those you already have and those you need to obtain. Items could be glues and paints for arts and crafts activities, tickets and train times for social activities or simply petrol in the car for a ride out in the country.

Obtaining items

Some resources or equipment are easily sourced from around the home or learning environment, while others may need to be purchased or made specially. To save on money, items such as coffee or jam jars could be saved, cleaned out and used for paint pots. Items such as sweet wrappers and tin foil could be collected and used in collages. Bits of string, odd shoelaces, buttons or cotton reels can be turned into creative sculptures with a bit of imagination and a spot of glue.

Some activities will require specific resources that cannot be created from items you would normally throw away. The items needed for a relaxation session, for example, would be gentle relaxing music, a CD player, comfortable warm flooring, mats or towels, dimmed lighting and a comfortable room temperature. Some of these you may need to purchase, such as the music or CD player. Others you would need to prepare in advance, such as the room temperature and lighting.

Preparing items

The items you require will depend on the learning or development activity and the abilities of those taking part. You will need to ensure the contents of board games are not missing any vital components. Trying to play cards with one or more of the cards missing would be very disappointing, as would playing Monopoly without any money!

If you are preparing an arts and crafts activity, you may want to prepare the materials in advance. This may include mixing the paint, cutting out shapes or collecting pictures from magazines. The preparation of materials will save time when the activity starts. You do not want people losing interest before they have even started.

Alternatively you can use the preparation of resources or equipment as an activity in itself – for example, supporting the person to measure how much water to mix into the powder paints or encouraging them to cut out pictures from a magazine. The whole activity, including its preparation, implementation and clearing away afterwards, could be turned into a learning or development activity.

4.2 How resources or equipment might be adapted to meet the needs of an individual

Obtaining and preparing equipment or resources for a learning or development activity is vital, but it will not be of any benefit to the person if they are not able to use them.

Some people may have specific needs where they require the use of adapted equipment or resources. People with physical disabilities affecting their hands may require thicker handle grips on pens, paint brushes or garden implements. Grips for pens, pencils and brushes can be made quite simply from a short length of pipe insulator. This then slides over the handle of the utensil and can be removed for use on other items.

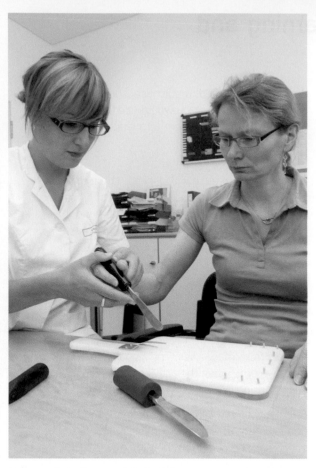

Grips can help the person to hold items more comfortably.

Activities to develop coordination such as playing catch can be adapted by using larger balls, foam balls or beanbags. For people with a visual disability, activities such as playing cards can be adapted through the use of larger playing cards.

Reflect

Think about the abilities or disabilities of the people you support. What adaptations do they currently use for eating, drinking or getting dressed? If they were not provided with the adapted aids, how would they cope? How would they feel if they could not feed or dress themselves?

Intellectual activities such as chess can be adapted using talking chess games. These are of benefit to people who have a visual disability. They enable the person to play a game of chess and know where all the pieces are.

4.3 Support preparation for an activity so as to minimise risks and maximise participation

Preparing for learning or development activities also includes preparing the person. To ensure that the person is fully able to participate in the activity and to do so safely requires support and preparation from the care worker.

Preparing the person

Before you leave home in the morning or the evening to go to work, you prepare yourself suitably. You ensure you are wearing suitable clothes and that you have eaten a good meal. You check that you have everything you need such as a packed lunch, money, car keys or bus pass. You know where you are going, how to get there, how long it will take and then leave the house at a suitable time to arrive at work safely. The way you prepare yourself will be similar to supporting the person in preparing for an activity.

Clothing

You need to support the person in wearing appropriate clothes. If the activity is a physical one, they may feel more comfortable wearing a tracksuit, so that movement is not restricted. Shoes should be flat to give the person better balance and they should be comfortable and well fitting to prevent the person's feet becoming sore. The person's choice of clothes may be different if they were going to the theatre or taking part in an arts and craft session. You would support them to dress appropriately for the occasion or activity while respecting their preferences and ensuring they were comfortable.

The choice of clothes worn during an activity can increase or decrease the risk of injury. Non-restrictive, baggy or loose clothing allows for freedom of movement and therefore can decrease the risk of strains during physical exercise. However, if the clothes were too baggy, the person could trip up or catch their clothing on equipment, which could cause them harm.

Items required

Some activities may require the person to take personal items with them. For example, if the person was going to college to learn maths, they might need to take a pen and paper with them. Activities such as sports or exercise may require the person to take a drink with them in case they become thirsty and a towel in case they get hot. If the activity falls over a mealtime, does the person need a packed lunch or will lunch be provided? This should be identified in the planning stages, as finding out during the activity could result in the person going without food. In terms of risk this can potentially cause the person to feel faint, light-headed or nauseous, which could result in them not being able to participate in the activity fully.

> It is very important to ensure that the person takes with them any medication they may need during the learning or development activity. This includes regular medication and those that are taken as required, such as inhalers.

Information

You should support the person in being fully aware of what the activity entails and what is expected of them. This will enable them to participate fully in the activity while reducing any risks. For example, if the person was taking part in a game of rounders, the rules of the game should be explained to them, including turn-taking, the use of the bat and being run out. If they have all of the information in advance, this will maximise their participation and minimise any risk.

4.4 Preparing the environment

Learning or development activities planned and organised by the care worker will also include the preparation of the environment. In the planning stages you would have identified the type and size of environment required. If the activity involves running around or throwing or kicking a ball, it may be safer to undertake the activity outdoors unless there is a suitable indoor area large enough which is free from obstacles.

Safety first

Regardless of the activity, the safety of the environment is paramount. The environment needs to be free from anything which could cause harm or injury to the person. As a care worker you need to be mindful of health and safety. This is covered in detail in Unit HSC 037.

The environment needs to be prepared to the requirements of the activity. If the learning or development activity is physical, the care worker needs to check the area and remove any obstacles which the person could bump into or fall over.

The temperature of the room, or indeed outdoors, needs to be taken into consideration when preparing the environment. Unfortunately you do not have much control over the temperature outdoors, but you can create shade if the weather is hot and sunny. Indoors the room temperature needs to be suitable for the activity. Sedentary activities may require the room temperature to be warmer as the person will not be moving around much. Activities that require the person to move around more may require the room to be a little cooler, but not cold.

For the activity to be implemented successfully it is advisable to prevent, where possible, any interruptions. A notice can be put on the door requesting not to be disturbed and any telephones, televisions or radios can be switched off. It is also advisable to inform your manager where you are and what you are doing in case of an emergency.

Coverings should be placed on the floor and tables, if required, to prevent spillage and damage to any furnishings. Any trailing wires from electrical equipment should be securely fastened to the floor to prevent trips and falls. Any electrical equipment used should be fitted with a circuit breaker to prevent accidents caused by electric shocks.

Finally, the environment should be risk assessed to identify any potential hazards and actions taken to reduce the risks. You can find more information about how to do this on page 195.

5. Be able to facilitate learning and development activities with individuals

5.1 Your agreed role in facilitating the activity

Supporting people in learning or development activities will include facilitation. Facilitation simply means to 'make easy' or to 'smooth the progress of'. As a care worker you will want the person to participate in the activity with as little difficulty as possible. The person will benefit more from the activity if it runs smoothly and without any problems.

Facilitation

Your role in facilitating learning or development activities is to make the activity possible for the person. As a facilitator you support the person within the activity; you do not do the activity for them. Your role is to encourage learning or development to take place within the person.

As a facilitator you may start the ball rolling with introductions within a group if you introduce yourself first. This would make it easier for people to follow, as they would learn from what you have done. You may wish to lead the group in identifying ground rules and ensure that all people agree to them. For example:

- all ideas are valid and should be respected
- listen to what others have to say
- all participants in the group are equal
- turn off mobile phones
- be punctual to prevent holding up the start
- all information about people in the group is confidential and not discussed outside the group.

Ground rules should be identified by the participants. It is their activity and therefore they should be the ones saying what behaviours they will or will not accept during the activity.

Your facilitating role would also include encouraging everyone to take part. Some people may be naturally quiet and can often be spoken over by other more confident people. Your role would be to try to bring these people into the group by asking them questions directly.

Starting off discussions will facilitate or help the group to continue. If the discussion starts to dry up, your role is to bring it back again by asking questions. The participants can start answering your questions and discussions should arise from there.

5.2 Supporting engagement with the activity in a way that promotes active participation

To encourage and support people to engage with an activity, it needs to remain interesting. The person needs to feel relaxed and safe within their environment. If either of these is missing, then the person will not achieve **active participation**.

> **Key term**
>
> **Active participation** – recognising a person's right to participate in the activities and relationships of everyday life as independently as possible

The relationship between yourself and the person should be built on trust. The person needs to feel accepted, understood and respected if they are to engage fully in activities. Those who do not feel part of the group or the activity will remain on the outside of the activity, taking the role of spectator rather than participant. Your enthusiasm and overall approach will support the person to engage fully in the activity. If you seem uninterested or bored during the activity, this could be picked up by the person and they will find it harder to be motivated.

Avoid the temptation of taking over from the person or doing things for them. If you can see them struggling to cope, adapt or change what they are struggling with to make it easier. Give the person motivation, encouraging them with positive communication such as 'you can do it' or 'you're doing very well'. Avoid using patronising phrases such as 'good boy' or 'aren't you clever'. No matter what tone of voice you use, these phrases are not appropriate within adult services.

Giving encouragement can help people succeed.

People will readily embrace activities which are fun. If a learning or development activity appears to be nothing more than hard work, the person is likely to shy away from it. Research has shown that people learn more when they are engaged in meaningful activities. Simply being fed information does not always give rise to learning.

5.3 Encouraging feedback about how the activity is implemented and the support provided

The reviewing of learning or development activities can aid learning. The person usually develops during the activity, whereas learning usually takes place after the activity has finished. Supporting and encouraging the person to reflect on the activity and feed back their thoughts will help their learning process. If people feel valued, respected, listened to and supported, they will be more likely to give feedback on the activity.

Supporting and encouraging feedback

Not all people will feel comfortable about giving feedback, especially if what they need to say is not positive. You must support all people in giving honest, truthful feedback, and not just feedback that they feel you would want to receive.

Verbal feedback

Some people have no concerns regarding the giving of feedback; however, some may feel awkward. Organise the people into small groups to give feedback. The person may feel more comfortable while being supported by their peers. Within the small group, you should encourage everyone to have their say. It is often the case that one person gives their feedback and others join in to agree or disagree with what has been said. Empower people to give feedback by keeping quiet or referring any questions or comments back to the group.

Written feedback

Following a learning or development activity there may not always be time to obtain people's thoughts and feedback on the activity. In these cases you should use questionnaires. Prepare a simple questionnaire to give to each of the participants at the end of the activity. Encourage the person to complete it there and then, as you may not receive it back if they take it away with them. If the person is unable to complete the questionnaire themselves, they should be provided with support by someone who is impartial to the activity. The person should be given the opportunity to remain anonymous when completing the questionnaire. However, this may not always be of benefit to the review of the activity implementation if the feedback relates to meeting a specific person's need.

The questionnaire shown below is an example of the type of form you could produce to enable written feedback.

Encouraging and supporting feedback following learning or development activities will show the person that you care about:

- how they feel
- how they are developing
- the support they are receiving to develop.

Movement to Music

Feedback Questionnaire

Date of Activity _____ Venue_____

Springfield Recreation Department appreciates your views and feedback on the activity you have recently taken part in. We would be grateful if you could spare a few minutes to complete the following questions and return this form using the box provided in reception. Your comments and views will be taken into consideration when organising future activities.

Please use the following to score your answers
1 – Yes   2 – No   3 – Indifferent   4 – Don't know

	1	2	3	4
1. Has the activity met your needs and expectations?				
2. Was the music suitable to the activity?				
3. Was the facilitator knowledgeable for the activity?				
4. Was the facilitator polite and courteous?				
5. Was the venue suitable for the activity?				
6. Did the venue meet your physical needs?				
7. Would you recommend this activity?				

Thank you for your time and cooperation. Please place your completed questionnaire in the box provided.

An example of a questionnaire about an activity.

5.4 Adjustments in response to feedback

The reason for obtaining feedback following an activity is to highlight any areas of the activity which may require alteration. It would be a complete waste of everyone's time and energy if the feedback was ignored and the activity left unaltered. When the activity is implemented again to either the same or another group, the activity may once again prove to be unsuitable or unbeneficial to the person, which may result in learning or development not taking place.

The feedback received from people should be reviewed in connection with the activity to identify any changes that may need to be made. However, not all feedback would result in the activity being adjusted.

Content of feedback

Feedback can be positive or negative. Positive feedback will mean the person was happy with the activity. Negative feedback does not always mean the person was entirely unhappy. They may be expressing their views on certain areas of the activity which they feel could be improved. The types of feedback people give may relate to:

- **room size** – if the room was too small for the activity, your responsibility would be to identify a bigger room, especially if more than one person gave this feedback
- **lighting** – the lighting may have been too bright for relaxation activities or not bright enough for arts and crafts activities
- **heating** – if a room is too warm it can make people tired and unable to concentrate, while cold rooms can make people feel uncomfortable
- **resources** – if these were unsuitable or insufficient, your responsibility would be to ensure that future activities have sufficient resources which meet the person's needs
- **timing** – the activity may be considered too long or even too short. Your judgement on the timing should be included when reviewing this feedback and adjustments made as appropriate.

Functional skills

Maths: Measurement

Find a suitable room for your activity to take place in. Measure width and length of the room and use these measurements to calculate the area and perimeter of the room. Check your answers carefully and show how you worked them out.

Feedback from the person is important in identifying adjustments to be made, but your feedback on the activity should also be taken into consideration. You need to review the activity objectively for yourself. It may appear to have run smoothly, but you may be aware of certain difficulties you had which need to be adjusted for the next time.

6. Be able to evaluate and review learning and development activities

6.1 The process and criteria for evaluation of the activity and the support provided

You may ask: What is the difference between obtaining feedback and evaluating the activity?

- **Feedback** generally looks at the specific goals to ensure they are being met. It helps to inform the progress that the person is making.
- **Evaluation** looks at the bigger picture; it looks at the overall aim to ensure it has been met in its entirety at the end.

Process of evaluation

To ensure the evaluation of the activity and the support provided is evaluated fairly, key people may be included in the evaluation process. These include the:

- facilitator
- line manager
- training manager (if applicable)
- person
- person's advocate (if applicable).

At the end of the learning or development programme, the person should be encouraged and supported to identify what they have learned, and how they can implement their learning or development into their lives. If they are unable to identify what they have learned or how they can implement it, it would be difficult to show that learning has taken place.

For the evaluation to be fully effective, the whole learning or development activity may be reviewed to include the following criteria:

- the identification of goals, needs and preferences
- information received on possible learning or development activities
- the planning of the programme
- the identification of risks
- the resources used within the programme
- support received by the person
- the learning or development environment
- the facilitation of activities.

The process and criteria need to be agreed with the person and others to ensure the correct information is being collected.

Activity 5

Evaluation

Your organisation may already have a policy or procedure on the evaluation of learning or development activities. Speak with your manager to help you locate and understand the policy. If your organisation does not have a policy or procedure, you may want to devise a checklist to enable you to evaluate activities. Do not forget to obtain agreement from your manager on its use.

6.2 Collating and presenting information for evaluation as agreed

Once you have collected the evaluations of a learning or development activity, you need to collate or bring together the responses. How much time this may take will depend on how many evaluation forms you need to go through and how detailed the forms are in terms of questions the people need to answer.

If you have the responsibility of devising and collating evaluation forms for people, do not allow the thought of time required to govern what questions you set. If you truly want to identify and ensure the people's learning needs are being met, your questionnaire should be sufficiently detailed to extract all the information you require.

In collating the responses to the evaluation forms, you need to look at the same question on each form. Evaluation forms that are devised using a score system are generally easier to collate. You may wish to bear that in mind if you are devising your own. Look at the scores for a particular question and add them up. If the possible scores range from 1 to 5 and you are collating 10 forms, then the minimum score you can obtain would be 10 (10 forms x lowest score of 1). The

Evaluating the activity

On collating the information from some evaluation forms, Cynthia finds that one of the areas is just slightly under its required score. She knows that this should result in that particular area of the activity being reviewed and adjusted as required, but she feels the score is only minimally under the agreed level so she ignores it.

1. Is Cynthia right to ignore the results as she did? Explain your answer.
2. What benefits or problems could this create for future activities?
3. Should Cynthia be evaluating the results on her own? Give reasons for your answer.

highest score you could obtain would be 50 (10 forms x highest score of 5). If you have 3 forms which all score 5 and 7 forms all scoring 4, your total would be 43 out of 50. You need to do this for every question on the evaluation form.

You may wish to present your totals from the completed evaluation forms plotted on a graph. This will enable a visual representation of the areas which are stronger than others and areas where improvements need to be made. You could compare this graph with previous graphs or figures to ensure improvements have been made in those areas that required improvement.

6.3 Agreed criteria to evaluate the activity with the individual and others

Earlier in this unit in section 6.1, you looked at agreeing the criteria for the evaluation of the activity and support provided. You should use these criteria that you identified with the person and others to evaluate the activity. Any agreements should be adhered to. If at any point changes are required, you should meet with the person and others to discuss the possible change and agree new criteria if required. For example, it may have been agreed that for each question answered by the person, a specific score needs to be obtained for that area of the activity to remain unchanged. All alterations to the evaluation criteria should be documented fully.

6.4 Recommendations for any changes in the activity, its implementation or the support provided

Following detailed evaluation of a learning or development activity, you and those involved should be in a position where you can identify any changes that may need to take place with the activity, its implementation or the support provided.

Looking at the evaluation forms will give you a valuable insight as to what each person felt about the programme, the areas that they enjoyed the most, and those they did not enjoy. At this stage you need to be asking yourself the question: 'Why?' Why did the person

Activity 6

What would you recommend?

Following a learning programme, ten people gave their views in their evaluation with the following outcomes.

1. Four people felt very nervous throughout the six-week programme.
2. Two people did not feel the facilitator was very polite.
3. Six people felt the resources used were very poor.
4. One person felt the tea provided at breaktime was too strong.
5. Five people were not happy with the toilet facilities.

Discuss the recommendations you would make for each of these results with your assessor. State why you would make these recommendations and explain anything else you would like to do with these results.

not enjoy it? Why did the person feel they did not benefit?

An evaluation comment such as the room was too hot or too cold is easily rectified. You could recommend that a fan be put in the room, or the thermostat be lowered if the room was too hot. You could recommend that the heating is turned up or additional safe heating is made available if the room was too cold.

Any recommendations you make need to be in the best interest of the person. You also need to remain professional and polite when evaluations of the activities you have facilitated are not what you expect. Remember that people have the right to express their views, and any comments on the activity should not be taken personally. You are only a part of the planning, developing and implementation outcomes, and you are part of a team.

6.5 The importance of recognising progress achieved through a learning or development activity

Most people like their achievements to be recognised and valued. This applies equally to people who are participating in a learning or development activity. It is important to recognise progress and to recognise it in some way. This may just be verbal, or your workplace may have a system of progress charts or individual development records. However it is done, it is the recognition and feeling that others value their progress that motivates people to continue.

Recognition and acknowledgement of the progress achieved by the person can lead to further progress being made. The person may feel a sense of pride in their achievement, which can encourage them to continue with their learning or development activities. Without the acknowledgement of progress, the person may feel that they are not achieving anything. This could potentially lead to them giving up on their learning or development activities.

Progress made by the person could also be evidence that the learning or development plan is working. It can show that the implementation of the activity is set at the correct level and pace.

People who see others achieve may be motivated to work a little harder so they can also share in the satisfaction of success.

Although the recognition of progress is important for the person, the identification of progress is just as important for you. When you can see that someone has made progress, you may wish to discuss altering the development plan by adding a new goal. This adjustment or addition must be made with the person and others to gain agreement in the new learning or development plan. New goal setting promotes continued development. If the person has met their goal, you should encourage further progress.

Doing it well

Supporting learning or development

- Support the person to identify learning or development goals.
- Provide the person with information on activities to meet their goals.
- Assess the type of activity for the person – 'tailor-made' or 'off the peg'.
- Identify appropriate implementation of the activity to meet individual needs.
- Identify and action potential risks relating to the activity.
- Plan a programme of activities for the person.
- Obtain or prepare appropriate resources to meet individual needs.
- Prepare the person for the activity.
- Prepare the environment for the activity.
- Facilitate the activity.
- Support the person's active participation in the activity.
- Encourage feedback from the person after the activity.
- Adjust the activity in response to feedback.

Legislation

- Disability Discrimination Act 1995
- Human Rights Act 1998

Getting ready for assessment

LO1

You need to be able to demonstrate or show that you have the knowledge for each of the assessment criteria listed in the standards. You can demonstrate your knowledge with written or verbal explanations. This can be achieved by answering questions, either in written form or verbally, which have been set by your assessor. Your knowledge can also be demonstrated using case studies or professional discussions. You may demonstrate some of your knowledge when being observed by your assessor. You will only be able to achieve this by explaining to your assessor what you are doing and why. This may not always be appropriate when you are being observed working with people.

LO2–4

You need to be able to show to your assessor that you are competent or that you have the skills in doing these things. The main way your assessor will be able to identify your competency will be through observing you

working with people and others who are important to the person's well-being. Your assessor will need to see you working in a real work environment on at least two separate occasions.

For your first observation, your assessor will need to see you helping people to plan how they are going to maintain or develop skills for everyday life. For your second observation, your assessor will need to see you helping people to gain or keep their everyday life skills, and giving positive, constructive feedback. This can be incorporated with you evaluating the support given and revising people's support plans as appropriate. At the end of your second observation, you will need to discuss with your assessor the actions you would take if the person, or other people, became distressed or unable to continue their everyday life skill activity.

You can also ask work colleagues, as an additional form of evidence, to provide you with a testimonial if they see you working.

Further reading and research

- www.bhfactive.org.uk/downloads/Top_tips_booklet_final.pdf (Tips on how to engage people in physical activity)
- www.bhfactive.org.uk/index.html (British Heart Foundation National Centre (BHFNC) – the BHFNC Information Service offers a wide range of services to help keep professionals up to date on the latest developments in physical activity and health)
- www.braingle.com (Intellectual activities to stimulate the brain)
- www.brainmetrix.com (More brain stimulating activities)
- www.lifelonglearning.co.uk (Lifelong learning, a site which provides information on learning opportunities)

- *Isolation and Loneliness* (POL/00 ID6919 03/08) – Help the Aged Policy Statement 2008.
- **General Social Care Council Code of Practice** (updated April 2010) – Codes relating to the standards of how social care employers and employees should work.
- *Best Practice in Managing Risk* (Department of Health 2007) – Principles and evidence for best practice in the assessment and management of risk to self and others in mental health services.
- *Opening Doors to an Active Life: How to Engage Inactive Communities* (2008) – Information-sharing booklet published by the British Heart Foundation.
- *Working Together to Deliver Physical Activity Programmes* (2009) – Information-sharing booklet published by the British Heart Foundation.

Unit HSC 3013

Support individuals to access services and facilities

In this unit you will have the opportunity to think about how you can best support people to identify and communicate their needs, and how you can pass on information that will enable them to gain access to the most useful services and facilities. Regardless of your role and area of work, you will at some point need to provide information to those you work with or their relatives or friends. It is important that you understand how to access and update that information and how you can assist people, not only to consider services but also to use them where they need support.

Information is knowledge, and knowledge empowers people. Familiarity with the services and facilities that are available and accessible will provide people with the opportunity to increase their level of independence.

In this unit you will learn about:

- **the benefits of and barriers to accessing community services and facilities**
- **how to support individuals to select community services and facilities**
- **how to support individuals to access and use community services and facilities**
- **how to evaluate and review individuals' access to services and facilities.**

1. Understand the benefits of and barriers to accessing community services and facilities

1.1 Benefits to identity, self-esteem and personal development from accessing community services and facilities

The key word in this unit is 'people' and establishing what it is that people want in order to achieve the outcomes that they have identified. This is not about what you think would be best for someone, tempting as it may be to try to persuade people to make use of a facility you think would benefit them. That is not your role. Your role is to support people to identify and communicate what they want in order to improve their own health and social well-being. Family carers should also be encouraged to identify support that would help them fulfil their caring role. You need to give both the people you support and their carers information that will help them to reach their own conclusions.

This learning outcome looks at how people's identity, **self-esteem** and personal development can be affected by using community services and facilities. It may not seem immediately obvious, but the impact can be significant if people are able to participate and to get out and about and meet others. Your role is to support people to access services, so you can help to make it possible for people to take part and do things that they have previously thought were impossible.

Key term

Self-esteem – how you value yourself, and therefore how you believe the rest of the world sees you

Self-esteem

Oscar Wilde once said, 'To love oneself is the beginning of a life-long romance.'

Self-esteem is about how we value ourselves. Feeling good about yourself has a great deal to do with the level of confidence that you developed as you grew up, but behaviour and opportunities as adults also have

a major influence. Everyone needs to feel that they have a valuable place and a valuable contribution to make within society. Participating in activities in a local community can support people to feel good about themselves and give them more confidence. Feeling accepted and part of a group, such as an art class, a discussion group, a choir or a gardening club, can help people to develop or recover confidence and self-esteem.

Also, gaining knowledge by using local services can make a contribution. Being unsure or not knowing makes people feel uneasy and damages confidence. Most of us can remember situations where we were confused or felt that we did not know what was going on. Supporting people to find out about and to use facilities and services can help them to feel more confident and more comfortable.

The importance of identity

If self-esteem is about how we *value* ourselves, identity (or self-image) is about how we *see* ourselves.

Identity is about those things that make people who they are. Everyone has a concept of themselves — it can be a positive image overall or a negative one, but a great many factors contribute to an individual sense of identity.

All of these things are aspects of our lives that contribute towards our idea of who we are. As a social care support worker, it is essential that you consider how each of the people you work with will have developed a self-concept and individual identity.

You will need to consider how you can promote people's own sense of identity. This is not as difficult as it sounds! It is about recognising that the values, beliefs, tastes and preferences which people have — the things that make them who they are — must be supported, nurtured and encouraged, and not ignored and discounted because they are inconvenient or do not fit in with the system. You need to make sure that people know about and can use facilities and services that fit in with who they are and the factors that are important to them; anything from the local swimming pool to an art class at the college or a day centre or an advice centre is an important part of your role in providing support.

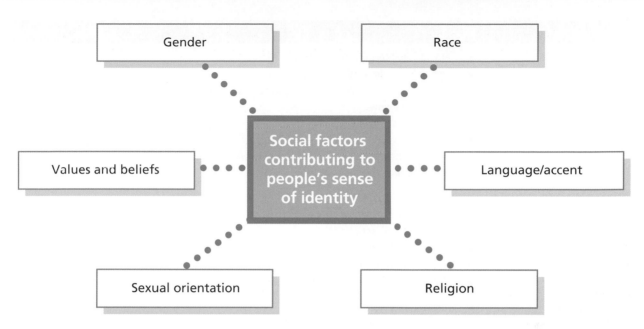

Social factors contributing to people's sense of identity.

Identifying concerns

Joel, who is 87 years old and very deaf, was becoming increasingly angry and unpleasant with the staff who were providing support for him. Several of them had complained about his attitude and one said that she was afraid that he would become violent. Julia, the senior practitioner, decided to try to get to the bottom of the reasons for this. She had always known Joel as a pleasant man who was reserved but always polite. Since her promotion, Julia had not seen Joel for months, but had quite a soft spot for him.

When she visited, she discovered over a cup of tea that Joel was worried about his benefits and the fall in value of his small pension from work. He had no idea where to turn for help, and had become increasingly worried and consequently short-tempered with everyone. Julia told him about the local Citizens Advice Bureau (CAB), gave him information about where to find it and offered to make an appointment.

After visiting the CAB, who helped him to sort out both his benefits and his pension, Joel was very relieved and felt much more confident and happy.

1. How did Julia's support benefit Joel?
2. What might have happened if she had not spoken to him?

1.2 Barriers to accessing services and facilities

There are many barriers that can restrict access or prevent people from using facilities or services. Information is one of the keys to overcoming barriers. A person with plenty of accurate and current information, which is clearly understood and found well in advance, is far more likely to be able to challenge and overcome difficulties than someone who feels uncertain because of a lack of information, and who is unprepared for any difficulties.

Barriers to access tend to fall into four categories:

- environmental
- communication
- psychological
- financial.

Environmental barriers are the most common.

Barrier	Examples
Environmental	• lack of disabled toilet facilities • high-risk or threatening location, for example, near a busy pub or parade of shops which is a known hang-out for gangs of young men • narrow doorways • no ramps • no lifts • lack of transport or lack of access by transport • lack of wheelchair access
Communication	• lack of loop system • poor-quality communication skills in staff at the facility, for example, an unhelpful or obstructive receptionist • lack of translators or interpreters • lack of information or publicity about the service or facility • lack of information in an appropriate language or format
Psychological	• unfamiliarity • lack of confidence • fear or anxiety • concern at loss of independence • unwillingness to accept help
Financial	• cost • anticipated cost

Table 1: The four main types of barriers and examples.

People don't know what they don't know

Do not assume that everyone will be in a position to ask directly for the information they need. To be able to ask for what you need, you must know the right questions to ask and something about the solutions that exist. For example, how could an older person ask about attending a luncheon club unless they knew that such a thing existed? How could a carer looking after a parent with Alzheimer's ask about a local carers' support group unless they were aware of its existence?

Asking the right questions

To establish what is getting in the way of someone getting the services or information that they need, you may have to ask quite a few questions. You cannot always rely on people being able to identify exactly what it is they want. You will sometimes need to use your listening skills in order to pick up what it is that someone is looking for.

It can also help if you ask some prompting questions. This may help to point people in the general direction of a service or facility that they would like to use. You could use questions beginning:

• 'Would you like...?'
• 'Would it help if...?'
• 'Would you enjoy...?'

To give people the maximum possible choice in reaching their decisions, it may be better to phrase your questions generally. 'Would you enjoy some company sometimes?' may be better than 'Would you like to go to the luncheon club at the community centre once or twice a week?'

Asking a question in this way allows someone to consider a new idea and to think about whether or not they would like it. It also allows people to stop at the point where they feel they have made enough commitment for the present. It may be sufficient for a first conversation to establish as an outcome that someone would like to feel less lonely; it may take a little more time to decide how they want to achieve that — for example, by joining a group of other people at a

> **What sort of things would you like to do to keep active, Mr Thorpe?**

> **I don't know. I don't have any idea of what's available for me to do.**

People don't know what they don't know.

luncheon club, or arranging for someone to visit once or twice a week. The general question has supported the person in thinking about the outcome they want to achieve. Later discussion can establish exactly the circumstances in which company would be welcome. If you had begun the discussion with full details of a luncheon club and the community centre, this might have provoked a negative response from someone who may not be keen on meeting a lot of strangers in a strange building.

1.3 Ways of overcoming barriers to accessing services and facilities

Start by checking that all possible information is available about the facilities and services, the challenges and the alternatives. Work alongside people to help plan ways to challenge and overcome any discrimination and barriers.

For example, you may need to support someone to search out alternative facilities if the ones originally found do not have wheelchair access or a **loop system** or ground floor access.

Key term

Loop system – a system enabling partially deaf people to hear dialogue and sound in theatres, cinemas and so on

If the local theatre does not have wheelchair access, encourage the person to make arrangements to travel to one that does. You could also encourage the person to raise the issue with the local theatre and point out to them that they are in breach of the Disability Discrimination Act 1995.

If there are problems finding suitable transport, it will be necessary to find out about transport with the right kind of provision by checking local taxi or public transport facilities that have the necessary adaptations. Most train companies have support services for people with disabilities, such as ramps and a porter service to enable people to get on and off trains.

Overcoming barriers is not always about finding alternatives; sometimes it is about ensuring that people have the right equipment and any aids in order to help to overcome the barrier. This can include everything from hearing aids to mobility scooters. If the barrier is financial, it may involve finding resources to meet the costs.

Psychological barriers will need different kinds of support; you may need to offer to accompany someone or to spend a long time slowly convincing them that what is on offer is not charity or that it will not compromise their independence. Providing reassurance is about much more than just telling people and expecting them to trust you. You may have to spend a long time supporting someone to overcome their anxiety or concerns, or you may be able to support someone by going with them on the first few occasions that they use a new facility or go somewhere they have not been before.

Activity 1

Barriers to access

1. Choose three different types of facility that people in your locality may wish to access.
2. For each, list the potential barriers to access and the ways in which you could support people to begin to tackle the barriers.

You may also need to encourage people to think about any **risks** involved in accessing and using new services and facilities. For example, if a person has to travel to a facility, or will be involved in a new physical activity or in meeting new people, they may need to think about any associated risks and decide how they want to handle them. Everyone has the right to take risks. If people have full information and decide that the benefits outweigh the risks, your role will be to assist them in managing those risks, not to try to discourage them.

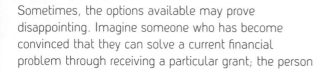

Key term

Risk – the likelihood of a hazard's potential being realised

Sometimes, the options available may prove disappointing. Imagine someone who has become convinced that they can solve a current financial problem through receiving a particular grant; the person has heard about the grant and has built up hopes of it. When you support them in finding out about the grant, you discover that they are not eligible.

In all such cases, it is good practice to prepare the ground in advance by encouraging the person to consider all possibilities and to make contingency plans in case of disappointment. Be ready to suggest alternative approaches to problems, and new areas to explore.

1.4 Support to challenge information about services that may present a barrier

People have a right to challenge information about services that proves to be misleading, inaccurate or discriminatory. For example, if information about a concert was only available in written form, with no option for audio or Braille information, then how is someone with a visual impairment to find out about the concert?

Can you see why this would be unacceptable?

Case study

Challenging services

Tom had recovered well from a hip replacement and wanted to maintain regular exercise. The local swimming pool had advertised an 'over-60s session'; Tom chose this session because it would be quiet and he did not expect to get jostled and splashed by people jumping in and playing noisy games. When he arrived at the pool, it was full of children and young people. He complained to the attendant and was told, 'Well, we don't get many in for the over-60s and it's the school holidays, so we let the kids in too.'

1. Can Tom challenge this?
2. How would you go about supporting him in this?

If you are planning particular arrangements with a facility or service to provide access, you must make sure that this has been agreed with the person concerned. If a person who uses a wheelchair has to make an important visit to a particular location that cannot be changed and there is no wheelchair access through the main entrance, it may be suggested that the person use a back entrance or goods entrance and the goods lift. You should always check with the person before agreeing to this type of arrangement, as not everyone is prepared to access a building through a goods entrance. Many people with disabilities take the perfectly reasonable view that they should have the right to access buildings in the same way as everyone else. In such a case, you may need to support the person challenging the acceptability of this and in arranging for the visit to take place at a different location. It is essential you never compromise the right of someone to choose their own means of access and to set boundaries as to what is acceptable in terms of personal space and dignity.

1.5 How power and influence may be used or abused

Taking a back seat

You may need to encourage many people to use services after they have found enough information to make a properly considered choice. However, you must be careful not to cross the boundary between encouraging and pressurising them into using a particular facility or service. Everyone has a right to choose not to take up the services and facilities that are available.

You are unlikely to pressurise anyone into reading a particular book or seeing a particular film just because you think it is good — you would simply say how enjoyable you found the book or film, and strongly recommend it. However, it is easy to step over the boundary when you believe somebody needs to be encouraged to find out about and use a service that seems to be in their interests.

For example, you may feel that receiving additional support services, attending a physiotherapy session or making a claim for additional benefit would be of great advantage to the person concerned. But your role is limited to supporting the person in finding the information necessary to make an informed choice. You should avoid putting pressure on anyone to take a particular course of action.

Similarly, you should not attempt to prevent someone from following a course of action because you believe it is risky or unsuitable. Professional support workers can be faced with difficult situations when people have obtained information about facilities or activities that may expose them to risk of injury or other dangers. There is a fine line between neglecting your duty of care and imposing unfair restrictions. Most people working in social care are likely to be cautious, rather than careless. Although this concern for the safety of people is well intentioned, it can result in restricting people's rights to enjoy some of what life has to offer.

Case study

The right to take risks

Jemma spent all her childhood in a residential facility for young people with learning disabilities. She is now 21 and has moved into supported group accommodation in the community. She is able to care for herself and has also started a job at the local supermarket, where she collects and returns the trolleys. Jemma has been very happy in the supported accommodation, and she enjoys her job and the independence it brings her.

At work, Jemma has met a boyfriend, who is now suggesting that she move out of the supported accommodation and into a bedsit with him on the other side of the town. She is very keen to do this, but she still requires a considerable degree of protection as she has an extremely naïve view of the world and has very little understanding of any risk to her personal safety. Her boyfriend is very attached to Jemma, but he has had recurring problems with drugs in the past and finds keeping a job difficult. At the moment, however, he is free from drugs and has a steady job.

Staff at the supported accommodation are concerned that Jemma would be at risk if she moved in with her boyfriend, because she has very little understanding of the issues to which she could be exposed. They are therefore considering whether they are able or ought to prevent Jemma from moving out of the supported environment.

1. Do the staff have any legal right to stop Jemma moving in with her boyfriend?
2. Do the staff have any moral right to stop Jemma moving in with him?
3. To what extent should she be allowed to make her own choices?
4. What might be the effect on Jemma of losing the opportunity to make this change?
5. Would the situation be different if she wanted to move in with another resident in the supported accommodation?

2. Be able to support individuals to select community services and facilities

2.1 Identifying and agreeing preferred options for accessing services and facilities to meet assessed needs and wishes

Once you have found out what someone's needs are and referred to your own store of information or made further enquiries, you need to provide the information in a way that is useful to the person concerned. When you are providing information, you will need to give careful thought to:

- the needs of the person receiving the information
- the nature of the information.

The needs of the person

First, you must be sure that you give the information in a way that can be understood by the person concerned. You must ensure that any specific communication needs are met. For example, people may require information to be in a particular format, such as large print or in Braille, or to be communicated using signing. You will need to find out how to change the format of the information or how to access it in a suitable format.

You will also need to consider the circumstances when you offer information about a particular service or facility. You should take into account a person's overall situation at that particular time. For example, you would not pass on information about social clubs and outings to someone whose partner had just died. That sort of information may be appropriate after a few weeks or months, but it is unlikely to be of any value at that moment. This principle also applies in situations where you are aware that someone is particularly upset by problems or difficulties. You also need to take into account a person's state of health and any medical treatment that may affect the relevance or usefulness of the information.

Make sure that information is accessible by:

- presenting it in the most useful format
- making it available at the right time
- taking all the circumstances into account.

There is also a right way and a right time for supporting people to access information. It is important you do not rush what you say. People are more receptive to information if they are comfortable and at ease. Do not attempt to pass on information when you are rushing out of the door – it is unlikely that someone will remember the details of a hurried remark.

Oh Betty, I did check and there is a painting class on Tuesday afternoons at 2.30, or Thursday mornings at half past 10, and you can go along to either of them if you just phone the library first...

Would you be able to remember information given to you like this?

Directly accessed information

When people are accessing information themselves, they may come across problems. Information may not be available in a useable format. For example, information about a local theatre production may not be available in large print, or a poster advertising an exhibition may be at the top of a flight of stairs, making it inaccessible for some people. A local information office may not have a loop system, making it difficult for people with impaired hearing to access verbal information. Encourage people to identify specific problems and discuss supporting them to make a complaint to the relevant organisation, so that the information can be improved.

You may come across situations where services clearly discriminate against people on the grounds of race, gender or disability. For example, someone finding out information about a job may be told they need not apply because they have a disability. If you find any instances of discrimination, you should offer to support the person concerned in informing the relevant body — see Unit SHC 33.

The nature of the information

For many people who would have real difficulty accessing information for themselves, it can be helpful if you write down basic information or give them a relevant leaflet. This may be enough for some people, who may undertake the next stages of research on their own. Others may want you to do some further research with them. Do not forget that throughout this process, the point is for you to support people in finding out information for themselves, not to do it for them.

Plenty of people know exactly what information and services they want.

Taking decisions

With careful thought and full information given at the right time, decisions can be taken at a pace that suits the person. This careful pace will also enable you to be sure that the person has access to all the information necessary to prepare a support plan.

You may not always be in the position of supporting someone to explore new options. There may be circumstances where you are faced with the opposite — some people are full of ideas and have a very clear picture of exactly what they need in order to achieve the outcomes they want. Your role in these cases may simply be to support the accessing of information.

The person you are supporting sets the pace, whatever that may be. Your role is to provide the access to information they require about the services they consider important. Be careful not to limit the information you provide, or the ways in which you provide it, because you believe that a particular facility or service is unsuitable for someone. The choice is theirs, and the job of supporting them to access the information is yours.

Doing it well

Finding out what is needed to achieve outcomes

- Get to know the person's interests and needs.
- Proceed at the person's pace.
- Do not impose your views about suitability or appropriateness on them.
- Be honest and realistic about what is available.
- Keep your information about access accurate and up to date.

Identifying strengths and areas for support

Your job is to support people to identify their own strengths and capabilities, and those of their current support network. Any gaps in the current arrangements and any opportunities to improve health and well-being should be areas for them to consider.

If you have worked with someone for a period of time and have got to know them, and possibly their carers too, it will be much easier for you to know about their needs and interests, and the types of services and facilities that are likely to be useful to support the achievement of their outcomes. It is then easier to raise questions about any new facilities or services that they may wish to try.

However, you will also need to take care that you do not encourage unrealistic expectations about services and facilities available in the local area. When you are asking questions about services and facilities that someone may like to use, take care only to provide definite information about those of which you are certain. If you have any doubt whether a particular service or facility is provided in your local area or is restricted because of lack of resources, you should make that clear so that people can check it out.

It may be useful to have a list or database of the potential services and facilities for the people you support that you keep up to date. Facilities vary greatly from area to area and from setting to setting. Table 2 shows a general picture of the services and facilities that people may find useful, and you should consider these for inclusion in an information database.

How to obtain accurate information

No one expects you to have your head full of information to pass on to people! However, you do need to know where to find information and the best and most efficient ways of doing so. This will mean you can explain to people how to go about finding out information for themselves. You also need to know how to keep information so that you have access to it whenever you need to use or update it.

What	Who	Where
Meals	Social services or voluntary organisation, commercial organisation	Social services department, Internet
Home care	Social services or independent provider, private care agencies	Social services department
Family support	Social services or independent sector	Social services department
Shopping	Local voluntary organisations, local shops	Library, Citizens Advice Bureau (CAB), social services department, local place of worship, Internet, local supermarkets
Lunch or social clubs	Social services or local voluntary organisations	Social services department, library, CAB, local place of worship
Holidays and outings	Specialist travel companies, social services, specialist voluntary organisations	Social services department, library, CAB, Internet, travel agent
Pensions and benefits	DWP, social services, Welfare Rights, voluntary organisations	Welfare Rights Centre, Claimants' Union, DWP, CAB
Education	Local education office, college of further education, library	Town or county hall, telephone directory, Internet
Sports	Leisure services department, specialist voluntary organisations	Town hall, CAB, library, Internet, *Yellow Pages*
Mobile library	Libraries, leisure services department	Town hall
Cinema, theatre, clubs and pubs	Leisure services department, theatres and cinemas, local tourist office	Town hall, library, Internet, *What's On* guide, tourist office, local newspapers

Table 2: Services and facilities: what they are and where to find them.

We now live in an information society — a great deal of information is available on any subject. It is easy to become confused and end up with information that will not serve a useful purpose for the people you support.

How many sources of information can you think of that are available in your local area?

Local sources of information

One of the most useful sources of information is the 'one-stop shop' approach of organisations such as the Citizens Advice Bureau (CAB). You may also find that your local Council for Voluntary Service or your local authority have an information point; these are often located in libraries, town halls, civic centres or other easily accessible places. At these points you can usually obtain leaflets and information, and staff are available to find out more for you and to offer advice on specific areas of need. Most advice centres will find information for you if they do not have it to hand.

You may be looking for specific information in response to someone's request, or you may be generally updating your own information database so that you are ready to deal promptly with any information requests. In either case, any of these facilities provide you with a very good starting point.

Special interest groups

Another excellent source of information is the range of specific interest groups such as Age UK, the Alzheimer's Society, Mencap, Mind and Scope.

These groups offer plenty of information about facilities and services specifically related to those with a particular condition. You can find the websites,

Case study

Finding out about needs

Vijay is a young man in his mid-twenties who uses a wheelchair following a spinal injury. He is provided with 24-hour care and has a team of support workers. Recently Vijay appeared somewhat unhappy. He said he was bored and wanted something more exciting to do. His support worker suggested a range of options including visiting the cinema and the theatre, going to a social club or visiting an art gallery — all of which were interests of Vijay's. However, every suggestion was rejected without Vijay giving any clear reason why.

A few days later, another support worker decided to approach matters in a different way. Through questioning, she established that Vijay would very much like to take up any of the suggestions made earlier, but had assumed that to do any of them he needed to take a taxi, and this was something he felt unable to afford.

Vijay had not liked to say that he could not afford the taxi and so had simply refused any of the suggestions.

The second support worker was able to explain to Vijay that the local authority operated a dial-a-ride service with a small bus specially adapted for wheelchairs, and that he could book this service and use it for a nominal charge. There was also a taxicard scheme entitling eligible users to a certain number of taxi journeys per month at dial-a-ride prices. Vijay was delighted and began to make plans for a range of visits and activities.

1. What mistake did the first support worker make when giving information to Vijay?
2. What might have happened if the second support worker had not spoken to Vijay?
3. What can you learn from this?

How easy do you find it to support people to access the Internet?

contact addresses and telephone numbers for these organisations on the Internet or at an advice centre, your local library or voluntary services.

The Internet

One of the best sources of information is the Internet. To use this you will need access to a computer connected to the Internet and some skill or experience in using the various search engines in order to locate relevant websites.

The information that you can obtain from the Internet is almost unlimited and covers every possible subject. However, you must be aware that this information is often not subject to any form of verification or control, and therefore it is not always possible to confirm its accuracy. If you are finding information from the Internet to pass on to people, you should obtain it primarily from official websites of relevant organisations for the particular area of interest.

Other useful websites are official government sites and those of universities and research establishments. You may find that there are government reports and results of inquiries, or research findings, that are relevant to

people you support. Using the Internet can be a very quick and easy way of gaining accurate and up-to-date information, often before it has appeared in print or become readily accessible in other ways.

Encouraging people to use the Internet

For many people, accessing information for themselves over the Internet can be useful and motivating. It can provide people with a new outlet and interest, as can be seen from the massive interest in 'Silver Surfers' groups being run around the country by Age UK. The take-up of these classes for older people has been huge, and many older people now have the skills to access information for themselves. Beware of assuming that anyone over the age of 60 knows nothing about surfing the net – you may find that they are much more able than you are!

The Internet can also allow people to network with others who have similar interests and issues. This form of social networking can help to broaden the social contacts of those who may otherwise have limited opportunities for meeting people. However, you should make sure people are well aware of the basic precautions that should be taken when using the Internet in this way.

- Remember that because of free and unrestricted access to the Internet, not every message is genuine and truthful.
- Never give out your address, telephone number or any financial information.
- If you arrange to meet someone you have come into contact with via the Internet, meet in a public place and do not go alone, or tell someone where you will be and when you expect to return.

There are also many useful opportunities for education and training via online learning materials. These can make learning more accessible and may offer the chance for new knowledge and understanding which may not be available through traditional teaching approaches.

There are increasing opportunities for people to access the Internet even if they do not have their own computers. Cyber cafés, libraries, local town halls, colleges and universities have facilities for public access to the Internet, usually for a small fee. You might encourage people to take advantage of these if appropriate. As always, the best approach is to support people to find out information for themselves.

Legislation about information

Access to information is broadly governed by two Acts of Parliament. The first is the Data Protection Act 1998, which restricts the way in which personal information can be used and limits those who can access information about people. There are basic principles that govern the way information must be handled.

All information, however it is stored, is subject to the rules laid down in the Act. This covers medical records, social service records, credit information, local authority information — anything which is personal data (facts and opinions about a person).

Anyone processing personal data must comply with the eight enforceable principles of good practice. These say that data must be:

- fairly and lawfully processed
- processed for limited purposes
- adequate, relevant and not excessive
- accurate
- not kept for longer than necessary
- processed in accordance with the subject's rights
- kept secure
- not transferred to countries without adequate protection.

You will need to be aware of these restrictions in case someone asks you for help in finding out information about another person.

The other piece of relevant legislation is the Freedom of Information Act 2000. This Act is about accessing information held by public bodies such as local councils, the National Health Service (NHS) and the government. It is concerned with records about the activities and plans of public bodies, not about people.

Each public body must set out the details of information it will routinely make available, how the information can be obtained and whether there is any charge for it. Each public authority must comply with requests for the information it holds unless an exemption from disclosure applies. Public authorities normally have a maximum of 20 working days to respond to a request.

This will be useful if you are helping someone find out about the activities, policies or decision making of a public body.

How information is stored

Once you have obtained information for someone, or to keep your own knowledge up to date and current, you need to be sure that you can store it in an accessible way. You need to record individual addresses, telephone numbers, website addresses and detailed information about the services provided.

It is a good idea to create an information store where you can keep leaflets, notes, telephone numbers and cuttings from newspapers or magazines which may be of interest to people you currently support, or to others in the future. A simple filing system, either alphabetical or grouped by subject, in a concertina file or a filing drawer, is probably the easiest way to deal with this.

A small library of information is very useful, provided that you keep it up to date. It is important that on a regular basis — for example, every three months — you go through it, discarding outdated information and replacing it with the most current information. If you prefer to store information electronically, create a folder on a computer in which you record the website and email addresses of relevant services. The easiest way is to create a simple database in a spreadsheet. Remember to back up your electronic records regularly, in case of accidental loss.

Activity 2

Information store

Create an information store, either in hard copy or on computer, for yourself and your colleagues. Decide on the categories of information you want, and create a set of headings. Then collect the information and enter it under the appropriate headings. Show the results to your colleagues and ask for feedback.

After three months, review the usefulness of this information store.

1. How many times has it been used?
2. Does it need to be updated?
3. Is it suitable for everyone to access?

Write a short evaluation of what you have learned from this task.

Functional skills

English: Writing; Speaking and listening

A number of staff in your place of work have decided to devise an information store so that information can be accessed more easily. In a group, discuss and take notes of what information your place of work needs to store and the headings for doing this and then delegate responsibilities so that each heading is covered. Ensure that all the group are actively involved in the discussion.

Using your headings and the information you have gathered, document your findings in an organised way so that the information is clear for staff in your place of work. Use an appropriate layout for the information and check that spelling, punctuation and grammar are accurate.

2.2 The relevance to the individual of the services and facilities available

It is important to spend time with people to make sure that the available services and facilities are what they want and will help to support the achievement of their desired outcomes.

The changes in the way that care services are provided mean that people no longer have to fit into whatever services are available. Person-centred social care means that services have to meet the needs of the person, not be a 'nearest fit' into services that are planned to meet the needs of the majority.

This very different approach means that people are better able to access services that are suited to their own needs.

Everyone should be encouraged to evaluate how useful or relevant the services are for them and to identify if there are gaps in provision that mean they are unable to find the service they need.

Working alongside people, you could suggest that they consider firstly which of their outcomes the service is contributing to meeting. Secondly they could consider criteria; for example, is the service:

*   in the right place
*   available at the right time
*   delivered by the right people
*   accessible
*   affordable?

Encouraging people to look at service availability in this way means that they are more likely to be able to identify if a particular service or facility is really what they need, or if they need to look for an alternative that will be more effective at meeting their needs.

3. Be able to support individuals to access and use community services and facilities

3.1 Identifying the resources, support and assistance required to access and use selected services and facilities

The range of services and facilities that people may want to use is large and varied. Not all are provided by the health and social care services. Many other services and facilities provided by commerce, industry, entertainment and retail organisations will also be useful for day-to-day living and enjoyment. Once people have the information on what is available, the next stage is to support them to make use of it.

Do you see how she is providing support – not doing it for him?

This may involve completing application forms or other paperwork, and you may need to support people to fill in any forms that are needed. As always, your role will be to assist in gathering the information and, if necessary, to help with the writing involved. But you should not simply take over the task; people should do as much as they want to for themselves and be able to call on your support if they wish.

Home services

Depending on circumstances, some people may wish to take advantage of services that can be supplied to them in their own home rather than having to travel. If you support someone who is unable or unwilling to travel, you may need to support them in finding out if services can be provided at home. Many organisations provide an off-site service. Examples are:

- mobile shops
- mail-order shopping catalogues
- mobile libraries
- solicitors
- homecare services
- meals services
- doctors and other health services
- pharmacists
- mobile hairdressers.

Most banks and building societies provide services online and by telephone, as do many large and small retail shopping facilities. Home delivery take-away food and films via rented videos/DVDs or through satellite or cable television are readily available in most areas. Most local councils allow payments online, and many social services departments carry out self-assessments for services online. The benefits are enormous for those people who have access to a computer and the skills to use the Internet.

Travelling to services

People have to travel if they want to participate in many forms of entertainment and culture, such as the theatre, concerts, art galleries or sporting events. They will also have to travel to essential appointments, such as an appearance in court or a visit to the hospital. When you are supporting people to make maximum use of services, you may need to discuss travel arrangements with them. You may need to assist someone to identify any problems with accessing the services they want to use and work with them to find ways to overcome the problems and issues.

Imagine how much easier people's lives are because of online services.

3.2 Supporting the individual to apply for and arrange any required resources and assistance

As you saw in Unit SHC 31, one of the most significant influences on communication and the way people deal with decisions or stressful issues is the life stage they have reached. You will need to take this into consideration when deciding on the appropriate degree of support to offer a person in accessing and using services.

Some people may lack confidence in their own skills and abilities, and therefore find the prospect of accessing and using new services and facilities very daunting. In this sort of situation, you will need to be prepared to offer considerable encouragement and support, while ensuring that you do not cross over the line into a situation where you misuse the power and influence you have.

Encouraging people to select and use services

- Make sure that you support people to access a full range of information.
- Try to identify difficulties and answer as many questions as possible.
- If you do not have information or cannot answer questions, tell the person you will find out – and make sure you do.
- Give any information you have about the consequences of using the service or facility, including information about others who may have benefited.
- Encourage people to find out all they need to know about how to access the service or facility, such as whether they can use the service at home or if travel is necessary, and if so, what the travel arrangements need to be.
- Offer to assist and support people in any way you can, such as offering to introduce them (by previous agreement) to others who may be using the service or facility.
- Make sure you do not use undue influence over someone to persuade them to act in a particular way simply because you think it is best.

3.3 Agreed responsibilities to enable the individual to access services and facilities

The level of support that you need to provide to a person will vary depending on the circumstances. Some people may simply need you to make the initial contact for them. Others may need you to accompany them on a first visit to a new facility or to meet a new group of people, and then to withdraw gradually as they grow in confidence in using the service. On other occasions your role may be to enlist the support of other people who are better qualified or more experienced, or who have the resources or time to provide a better service for the person.

It is important you encourage people to dispense with your support as soon as they feel able to manage independently. You should do this when they tell you that they are becoming more confident in using the facility or service. Do it by gradually and appropriately reducing the level of support.

For example, you may have accompanied someone on a first visit to a Welfare Rights Advice Centre. The person may have needed you because they were unfamiliar with the service and did not understand the benefits system enough to be able to explain the information required. However, as the visits continue and the work of the Welfare Rights Advice Centre is under way, you may be able to withdraw from accompanying the person as they become more familiar with the workers in the centre. Your involvement may then be limited to providing transport, or holding a feedback session on their return.

It may take people a while to adjust with confidence to new social situations. For example, if you have supported someone to find out about and then visit a new day centre or social club, it may take a few visits before they are confident enough to go alone. As always, your role is to do only as much as they require, to allow people the maximum opportunity to make their own lives and to be as independent as possible.

4. Be able to evaluate and review individuals' access to services and facilities

4.1 Information needed to evaluate the effectiveness of community services and facilities for the individual

Evaluation is often thought to be a difficult and complex process, but in fact it is straightforward. The process of evaluating an event or experience is extremely useful because it allows you to find out what:

- worked well, badly or not at all
- was wrong and can or cannot be fixed
- you would or would not do/use again
- was better or worse than you expected
- needs to be changed or should stay the same
- you need to do next time.

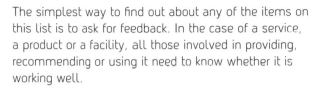

Key term

Evaluation – the process of gathering and reviewing evidence, then reaching a judgement

The simplest way to find out about any of the items on this list is to ask for feedback. In the case of a service, a product or a facility, all those involved in providing, recommending or using it need to know whether it is working well.

The basic requirement for any sort of information is that it should be:

- accurate
- relevant
- up to date
- easy to understand
- accessible to everyone
- within the law.

You need to encourage people to check that information is accurate and relevant for their purposes. It also helps if information is interesting!

People who provide information need to know whether it is all of those things listed above, so feedback is essential. You should encourage and support people in providing feedback about information they have accessed or tried to access.

Case study

Compiling a directory

Learners at a local college were studying for a health and social care qualification. For one of their assignments, they were asked to produce a directory of information about entertainment and leisure facilities in the local area. When they had completed the project, the learners decided to present the finished directory to a supported living unit which provided supported living for eight people with a disability, some of whom have complex needs.

The directory was printed out and stapled to form a booklet. The work had been done very neatly and each facility was identified in bold lettering, followed by a short description of the facilities, like this.

> **Royal Theatre**
> Plays, concerts and shows. Weekly programme of events. Seats 500. Tickets through box office 10.00hrs–20.00hrs, 01234 567890.
> Café available 11.00hrs–18.00hrs.
> Facilities DT, WA, L, B, H (see key on p. 5).

A few weeks later, staff noticed that the directory was lying in the lounge and no one seemed to have used it.

1. Why do you think the directory was not used?
2. How could it be improved?
3. What sort of information should be in it?
4. How should it be presented?

If you have tried to obtain information about welfare rights and it was not available in large print, this fact can be fed back to the co-ordinator of the Welfare Rights Centre. However, it will be important that you encourage the person concerned to check that the information has improved, otherwise the feedback will have been wasted.

In the case of commercial businesses, shops, supermarkets, cinemas, entertainment centres or theatres, feedback should be given to the manager on site. Some businesses may be part of a national or international chain, and information may be handled centrally. Where this is the case, you should encourage and support people to seek out those who have responsibility for the information policy of the company, and make sure they receive the feedback.

Information is no use if it does not serve the purpose for which it was needed.

How many different ways of getting information can you think of?

4.2 Working with others to evaluate the experience of accessing services and facilities

You will need to spend time discussing with people how the use of services or facilities has contributed to their well-being. People's needs do not remain the same, so services and facilities that met someone's needs at one time may no longer be appropriate after quite a short period of time. Regular review and feedback will therefore be needed. Feedback should identify:

- the services and facilities the person has selected and used
- any discrimination or exclusion that they have experienced
- what has been beneficial and why
- what has been less helpful and why.

As a professional support worker, you should know that receiving feedback is not always easy and that criticism can sometimes make you feel resentful. So you should encourage people offering feedback to ensure they make positive suggestions alongside any complaints they may have. No one likes receiving a long list of complaints and criticism, even if it is well deserved. People are much more receptive to feedback if it is accompanied by useful suggestions about how matters could be improved. This will help them to improve the quality of the services they provide, and should mean that others will not experience the same problems in the future.

Reflect

Think about the process of evaluating services and facilities used in your workplace, including documentation used.

1. How useful is it?
2. How much notice is taken of the feedback?
3. Can you identify any specific changes that have come about as the result of feedback?
4. If not, what does that tell you about attitudes to feedback?

4.3 and 4.4 Changes to improve access

Constructive feedback involves identifying the changes necessary to improve the outcomes for people using services and facilities. Your role in supporting this process may include collecting together information, records and reports connected with the evaluation. You must follow organisational procedures and remember the rules of confidentiality when you are working with such information.

Evaluation is of no use unless it results in the appropriate changes being made. You will need to work with the people involved to achieve the necessary changes. You will also need to support people in challenging any discrimination or exclusion they have experienced.

However, as with the selection of services, it will be important that you do not misuse your position of trust in order to influence the feedback a person gives so that it reflects *your* opinion of services and facilities. There will be channels through which you can communicate your own experiences and opinions, and these will have their own value, but you must ensure they are kept clearly separate from the feedback given by the person themselves.

Legislation

- Data Protection Act 1998
- Disability Discrimination Act 1995
- Freedom of Information Act 2000

Further reading and research

You may find it most useful to research services and facilities in your area, as these will be easiest to access. Here are some ideas to help you start this process and build upon what you have already learned in this section.

- www.citizensadvice.org.uk (Citizens Advice Bureau)
- www.goodaccessguide.co.uk (Good Access Guide – tel: 01502 566005)
- www.drc-gb.org (Disability Rights Commission – Disability Equality Duty)
- Leader, A. (1995) *Direct Power; A Resource Pack for People Who Want to Develop Their Own Care Plans and Support Networks*, Pavilion Publishers
- Sobczak, J. (2001) *Alive and Kicking*, Age Concern
- Stalker, K., Duckett, P., Downs, M. (1999) *Going with the Flow; Choice, Dementia and People with Learning Difficulties*, Pavilion Publishers

Functional skills

English: Reading

Collect information from a minimum of three sources about services and facilities in your area. Select the services and facilities you think would be most useful for people you support and produce a fact sheet summarising this information for your place of work.

Getting ready for assessment

Most of this unit is about demonstrating good practice, but you do need to be able to show that you understand the issues that some people experience in accessing services. You may have to do this through an assignment or it could be a presentation. It will be important for you to show that you understand the main aspects of identify and self-esteem, and how having access to services can help to support this is a positive way. You will also need or show that you can identify the barriers and the best ways to overcome

them. Of course, this will be different for people, but you will need to understand all the basic principles.

The rest of the unit will be assessed through observing your work in supporting people to overcome barriers and difficulties, and to access the services that they need. Your assessor will want to see that you support people to overcome their own barriers and meet challenges rather than doing it for them. This will mean giving encouragement and possible advice, but be careful not to take over.

Unit HSC 3020

Facilitate person-centred assessment, planning, implementation and review

Person-centred means activities based upon what is important to a person from their own perspective and which allow them to be fully included in society. One of the most important roles a care worker has is to find out what type of service a person wants and to work alongside them and others to provide the best and most effective level of service to meet their needs.

In this unit you will learn how to have a holistic approach to planning care services through supporting people to lead the assessment and planning process. You will look at how to facilitate person-centred assessment, how to implement and monitor the support plans, and how to manage and record support plan reviews.

In this unit you will learn about:

- the principles of person-centred assessment and care planning
- how to facilitate person-centred assessment
- how to contribute to the planning of care or support
- how to support the implementation of care plans
- how to monitor care plans
- how to facilitate a review of care plans and their implementation.

1. Understand the principles of person-centred assessment and care planning

1.1 The importance of a holistic approach to assessment and planning

One of the essential aspects of planning care services is to have a **holistic** approach to planning and provision.

> **Key term**
>
> **Holistic** – looking at the whole situation

This means recognising that all parts of a person's life will have an impact on their care needs and that you need to look beyond what you see when you meet them for the first time.

The idea of person-centred planning comes from the *Valuing People* (2001) White Paper. It contains some broad principles that are of relevance to work with all people. Key principles of person-centred planning assessment are that:

- the person is at the centre
- family and friends are full partners
- others involved in the person's wider life may be included
- person-centred planning reflects the person's capacities, what is important to the person (now and for their future) and specifies the support they require to make a valued contribution to their community.

> **Reflect**
>
>
>
> Draw a spider diagram showing the people that have an effect on your life on a daily basis. Put yourself at the centre with those with the most influence nearest you and those with the least further away.
> 1. Has that surprised you in any way?
> 2. If you were one of the people you support, whom would you want to include in your support planning?

1.2 Ways to support the person to lead the process

Throughout the process of obtaining information, you should make sure you constantly check that people are fully aware of what is happening and feel they are in control of the process. One of the problems with the way services are provided, regardless of whether they are services for health, for social care or for children and young people, is that many people feel they play only a passive role.

It is easy to see how this can happen. Agencies and service providers have well-organised systems which can often involve filling in a great many forms, attending meetings and working through the bureaucracy. If you work for such an organisation, these things are a regular part of your life. They do not represent a threat to you. But you need to remind yourself that many of the people you deal with will not be familiar with the workings of your agency and may not feel confident enough to question or challenge what is happening.

Personal budgets mean that people are now in control of their own services and they can determine how they want to spend the budget that is allocated to them. For many people who have been using services, this is a new experience. They will have been used to being asked to be involved in planning for their services, but have always had to fit in with whatever services were available. Person-centred planning now means that services must fit around their needs. This will take some getting used to for many people — and for staff!

Often those who influence the person's life the most are not those traditionally at the centre of the support planning process. On a day-to-day basis, the social services may have little influence on a person's life, but the postman who stops for a chat every day may be very important.

There are several steps you can take at each stage of the process to ensure that people understand they are in charge of their service.

Step 1

People should make clear who needs to be involved in the process of thinking about and planning their service provision. You may need to prompt them to think about the people they would like to be involved. Sometimes it is helpful to make some suggestions. For example, you could ask, 'What about your neighbour, Mrs Smith, the one who pops in with your dinner? Might it be a good idea to ask her?' Or, 'Your niece Susan might have some ideas about the sort of services you could use.'

Step 2

At each stage of the process, you should check with the person that the plan is following the ideas they have for how they want their service to be delivered. You should do this using the means of communication which the person prefers. For example, if your normal means of communication is to talk, then you could have a regular chat to ensure that the service proposed is what the person wants and to ask whether there are any specific ways in which they want tasks to be carried out. Alternatively, if the person has a hearing impairment, your means of communication to establish the same information may be by writing or using signs. If any extra support is needed to enable somebody to communicate their views, such as interpreters, translators or signers, make sure that this is provided.

Step 3

The use of any additional sources of information — for example, previous records from other agencies that may be involved with a person — must be agreed in advance before you approach the sources for the information.

It is important you do not take this agreement for granted and that you explain exactly what you intend to do, so it is clear to what the person is agreeing.

Step 4

Make sure they know the range of options that are open to them. Explain that they do not have to think only in terms of traditional service options. There are many flexible ways services can be delivered and the best plans are usually a mix of informal and professional support, with effective use of assistive technology and plenty of innovation and creative thinking.

Step 5

Support the person and their family, friends or carers to feed back their views about the assessments made. If the process goes smoothly the feedback will be positive, but you may also need to support people in challenging some points or in complaining about an assessment that does not meet their expectations. Make sure that you understand the appropriate channels to use for passing on any concerns, and that you communicate them not as your own views, but as the views of the person in question.

Help people to decide what they want to say and to work out the best way to present it. This could be in a written form or they could prepare some notes in advance to ensure that they cover all the points they want to make.

There may be special communication issues that you need to take account of in order to enable people to express their opinions effectively. You might be able to use advances in technology to make the support planning process more personal, accessible, meaningful and fun for the person. Interactive technology can help to produce plans that are developed, designed and produced by people themselves with assistance from support staff as required.

Make sure they know the different results which could come from the meeting so that they will not be surprised by any of the decisions that could be made. Explain to them that there could be a range of options for the meeting to consider.

You may need to work with an advocate who is acting on behalf of the person, or you may need to consider engaging an independent advocate in order that the person's needs and wishes can be effectively understood and explained at the meeting. Your agency may have a procedure for engaging advocates.

Where necessary, make practical arrangements for a person to attend. This could include ensuring accessibility of the meeting room, providing transport where necessary, or providing translation or other communication assistance.

1.3 Ways the assessment and planning process can maximise an individual's ownership

One-page profiles and action plans

An effective way to identify somebody's needs and wishes leading to a full and person-centred action plan is to complete a one-page profile with them. One-page profiles can be developed generally or around a specific area, such as their health. They provide the person and others with an at-a-glance snapshot of the most important aspects of the person's life.

You can support a person to put together a one-page profile in two ways:

- by gathering and recording the information with the person bit by bit, in stages
- by collecting the information when the person and those who know them well are gathered together, perhaps for a planning meeting or a review.

The profile should include:

- the person's strengths and particular skills and abilities
- what is important to them
- what is important for them, what they need and what support they need to meet their choices.

Identifying people's strengths and abilities is important because this means that you are starting from a positive perspective, introducing others to the sort of person somebody is and what great attributes they have.

After one-page profiles have been completed on various aspects of a person's life, the facilitator can help them (and those who know them well and care about them, if the person wishes them to be involved) look at what is working and what is not working right now. This helps the person and their assistants identify what areas need attention and where extra support might be required. From the information on the one-page profile, an action plan can be created. This would note what needs to be done, who the person is who will help do it, and when it will be done by.

Activity 1

Create a one-page profile

Choose one of the people you support and design a one-page profile around an aspect of their life – for example, their social needs or health needs. What do they enjoy? What questions would you ask them to find out what they want? How could you support them to achieve this? Who else might need to be involved to meet their wishes?

2. Be able to facilitate person-centred assessment

2.1 Assessment partnership

Most local authorities have a supported self-assessment process. This will vary depending on where in the UK you work. The processes may be different, but the underlying principles of the person being at the centre are the same wherever you work.

Self-assessment is usually a questionnaire that identifies people's needs through a series of questions about what they can do and what they need help with. The questions will cover areas such as mobility, eating and drinking, being safe, work, education and personal care. Following completion of the assessment by the person, this will then be shared with a social worker or care manager who has to agree that the assessment seems appropriate. They will usually record their view on the assessment alongside that of the person concerned.

2.2 Agreeing the process

The supported self-assessment process is quite straightforward, but people who have not experienced it before may need some support and encouragement to participate fully. For many people who may already have support from family and friends, it is important that they have the opportunity to be involved in both the assessment and in the planning process. Following the completion and agreement of the assessment, the results are used to identify the resources that will be available to fund the person's support/care plan.

Most social services departments use a Resource Allocation System (RAS) that matches the results of the supported self-assessment to an allocation of money.

Following the agreement of the self-assessment, the person will be told how much money is available for them to plan their support package.

Doing it well

Preparing people for meetings
Go through the procedure of the meeting with them so that they know exactly:
- who will be there
- what will happen
- in what order matters will be discussed
- the type of contributions that all of those present at the meeting will make.

2.3 Outcomes

Person-centred plans are based on the outcomes that someone wants to achieve. Outcomes are about the end result of the support plan. They answer the 'so what?' question.

Think about it like this: every support package has inputs, outputs and outcomes. At a simple level, they look like this:

INPUT: Mary has four hours of support each day.

So what?

OUTPUT: Mary can make a meal and go shopping.

So what?

OUTCOME: Mary is more independent.

Outcomes are what planning and support are all about. It may take some time for people to think about the outcomes they want to achieve, but with some discussion and some prompting to remind people about things they have previously said they wanted to do, most people will get there in the end. Some people may need the support of an advocate to ensure that they are able to complete their assessment and make their plans.

2.4 Focus on strengths

Person-centred plans are about building on what someone can do, not the things that they find difficult. Previously in social care, we have operated using a 'deficit model'; in other words, we have started from a position of providing services based on what most people in a particular client group are unable to do.

The person-centred approach is about identifying people's strengths and building on those, so that services are only provided to 'fill in the gaps' between what people are able to do for themselves and what informal support they have from family and friends.

Concentrating on what people are able to do promotes independence and encourages people to do as much as possible for themselves.

2.5 Identifying support requirements

Plans are about achieving outcomes. Once the outcomes are decided it is then easier to see:

- what the person can do for themselves
- what can be done through informal family and friend support
- what additional paid support is needed.

A person-centred plan should be developed by the person for whom it is intended. Some people may want to do this with the support of family or friends, and some people may want the involvement of their support worker. If you are asked to support someone to develop their plan, remember that it is their plan and not yours, and it is up to them to decide the outcomes that they want to achieve through their plan. People need to maintain contact with social services through their social worker so that social services are aware of what someone wants to achieve through their plan, and how they want to achieve it.

It is essential that people are comfortable and confident about deciding on their plan. Some people may need some help to start work on it as this will be a new experience for most. Many people like to work on their plan with their family and share it with professionals after it is completed.

There does have to be a 'sign off' of the plan by social services. The professionals involved may make suggestions as to how the plan may be most effectively put into practice. Social workers also have a role in looking at whether the plan will meet the outcomes that people have identified. The plan will only be agreed when it is clear that it will meet the outcomes that the person wants to achieve. If changes are needed, they will be discussed and agreed.

The planning process looks like this:

Assessment $\longrightarrow$ Allocation (£) = Paid / natural support = Support plan

---

Activity 2

Assessing needs and preferences

Check out the processes used at your place of work for assessing the needs and preferences of people.

1. Are there clear guidelines as to how information is obtained?
2. Are all those with influence in a person's life involved in the process?
3. Are the roles and responsibilities of managers and care workers clearly defined?
4. Is the person at the centre of all consultations?

If appropriate, you could propose improvements to the system.

3. Be able to contribute to the planning of care or support

3.1 Factors that influence support

There are many factors that will affect the outcomes people want to achieve and the support that they will need. All of the following are likely to have an influence on people's hopes and dreams and what they are able to do for themselves:

- health
- employment
- education
- social factors
- religious and cultural factors
- risks
- availability of services.

Health

The state of people's health has a massive effect on how they develop and the kind of experiences they have during their lives. Someone who has always been very fit, well and active may find it very difficult and frustrating to find their movement suddenly restricted as the result of an illness, such as a stroke. This may lead to difficult behaviour and the expression of anger against those who are delivering services. Alternatively, the person may become depressed. Someone who has not enjoyed good health over a long period of time, however, may be able to adjust well to a more limited physical level of ability, perhaps having compensated for poor health by developing intellectual interests.

Employment

Health is also likely to have had an impact on an adult's employment opportunities, either making employment impossible at times or restricting the types of jobs they could do. Whether or not adults are able to work can have a huge effect on their level of confidence and self-esteem. Employment may also have an effect on the extent to which people have mixed with others and formed social contacts. This may be an important factor when considering the possible benefits of residential care as opposed to care provided in a home environment.

Income levels are obviously related to employment, and these will have an effect on standards of living — the quality of housing, the quality of diet and the lifestyle people are able to have. Someone who has had a well-paid job is likely to have lived in a more pleasant environment with lower levels of pollution, more opportunities for leisure, exercise and relaxation, and a better standard of housing. It is easy to see how all of this can affect a person's health and well-being.

Education

People's level of education is likely to have affected their employment history and their level of income. It can also have an effect on the extent to which they are able to gain access to information about health and lifestyle. It is important that the educational level of a person is always considered so that explanations and information are given in a way which is readily understandable. For example, an explanation about an illness taken straight from a textbook used by doctors would not mean much to most of us! However, if the

---

Case study

Supporting somebody with autism to find employment

Tom is a 24-year-old with autism. One of the effects of this is that his sleep patterns are very disrupted and he is often wide awake in the early hours of the morning. Tom wants to gain employment, but his sleep patterns make it hard for him to work a regular 9–5 job.

As he is often up early in the morning, he has developed a good relationship with the milkman, who often stops for a chat during his rounds.

1. What job opportunities could there be for Tom?
2. How would you help him to realise his ambitions?
3. Are there any other people who could get involved?

information is explained in everyday terms, we are more likely to understand what is being said.

Some people may have a different level of literacy from you, so do not assume that everyone will be able to make use of written notes. Some people may prefer information to be given verbally, or recorded on tape. Also, remember that some illnesses such as a stroke or dementia can affect a person's ability to understand, assimilate and communicate information, regardless of their educational level.

Social factors

The social circumstances in which people have lived will have an immense effect on their way of life and the type of care provision they are likely to need. Traditionally, the social classification of society is based on employment groups, but the social groups in which people live include their family and friends, and people differ in the extent to which they remain close to others. The social circumstances of each person who is assessed for the provision of care services must be taken into consideration, to ensure that the service provided will be appropriate.

Religious and cultural factors

Religious and cultural beliefs and values are an essential part of everyone's lives. The values and beliefs of the community people belong to and the religious practices which are part of their daily lives are an essential aspect for consideration in the planning of services. Some people may also have a specific ethnic identity and a sense of belonging to a specific ethnic community. Any service provision which has failed to take account of the religious, ethnic and cultural values of the person may provide a poor quality of service.

Risks

All plans have to consider risks. Sometimes a person's choice of plan may involve them in risks. A risk assessment will provide information on the level of risk and proposals for how it can be reduced, but if a person has capacity (see Unit SHC 34 for information about the Mental Capacity Act) and they are fully informed about the risks and potential consequences, then the choice is theirs to make.

Being creative about services

Not all outcomes will be met by using services. In fact, one of the important aspects of person-centred planning is that it encourages everyone to think about how to achieve outcomes rather than just about what services to use. Thinking creatively and being innovative is an important way to support people to think about what they want their support package to look like.

Some people may prefer to use some money to help friends and family to provide support, not necessarily by paying them, but perhaps by meeting transport costs or some other form of practical help. Sometimes, making good use of universal services that are already in the community may be part of a plan, for example, leisure services, transport, libraries, galleries or lifelong learning.

Universal services	Targeted services
• Public transport	• Social services for adults
• Swimming pools	• Children's social services
• Leisure centres	• Medical treatment
• Libraries, museums, galleries	• Sensory support services
• Roads	• Dental treatment
• Street lighting	• Occupational therapy
• Parks and open spaces	• Physiotherapy
• Waste collection	• Counselling
• Schools and colleges	
• Public health information	

Table 1: Examples of universal and targeted services – can you see the difference?

It takes a while to get used to the idea that not all problems are solved or all needs met by providing professional services. There will always be some areas where professional support is needed, but actually looking creatively at where support may come from and ways in which people can be creative can yield some interesting and exciting results.

Case study

Putting together Amir's support plan

Amir has cerebral palsy; he is 25 years old and wants to live as independently as possible. He decided to hold the meeting to organise his support in the back room of the local pub and invite all his friends and family. As he was explaining the plan and identifying the different tasks for which he would need support, friends and relatives volunteered to offer help for activities such as going to the football match, going to the pub, driving him to his girlfriend's house and supporting him at the local chess club.

When his plan was complete, Amir only needed paid support for personal care, because he was not happy

for family and friends to do that, and for support on the days he was working, as the hours needed were too many for people to volunteer. Amir was really pleased because there was enough money left in his budget for him to give music vouchers to his friends from time to time as a thank you for helping him. Amir's social worker agreed to 'sign off' the plan as she agreed that it would meet his outcomes of wanting to progress in his career and maintain his social life.

1. How is this way of arranging support person-centred?

Keeping all parties informed

One of your key roles in this process is to provide information to the person and all those who are involved in the process about the precise services proposed and what options are available. For example, if you are giving information to somebody about a proposal for providing day care, this will include details about:

- the exact nature of the day care proposed
- the location of the day care
- the type of care offered
- the general aims and atmosphere of the facility
- the number of people who attend
- what the transport arrangements will be.

Informed choice can only be made with this kind of detail. If necessary, you should offer to make arrangements for the person and their relatives or carers to visit any establishments that are part of the proposal for care services.

3.2 Options and resources for delivery of the plan

A person may feel confident and well able to put across their own point of view. If so, your role is simply to support and encourage. However, if somebody does not feel able to put their views across adequately, or if there is a difference of opinion as to how their needs are best met, it may be your role, or the role of an advocate, to ensure that their views are clearly represented and understood.

Reflect

Try to remember a situation where you have felt you were not in control and that other people held the power. This may have been a medical situation – for example, where you were a patient and felt that you were unable to ask all the questions that you wanted to because the doctor simply did not seem to have time to answer them. It may have been a situation that involved lawyers or other professionals, or your child's teacher or head teacher. Think how much easier it might have been if someone had been acting as a support for you.

Remember how you felt in those situations, and choose one of them to act as your 'trigger' to recall those feelings whenever you are in a support planning meeting, or a similar situation, with a person. This should remind you to encourage and help the person to put across their views.

There is a fine balance between representing people's points of view and putting across your own views about what you think may be best for them. You will need to be careful to represent a person's views even if you think they are not the most appropriate. When you are making contributions at a meeting, you should always introduce remarks with, 'Mr X has told me that...', or 'Mrs Y has explained to me that she would prefer...', rather than, 'I think that...' or 'In my opinion the best course of action would be...'. It is important not only for accuracy, but also to make sure the person knows that their views are being represented, not your own, and that they are the person in control.

Difficult situations

You can find yourself in a difficult position when somebody's views and expectations of the service needed are different from the views of the other professionals, or of the person's own relatives or carers, and particularly if they differ from the views of your own agency. Your role is to represent the views of your person, but you should not get drawn into the role of attempting to manipulate the procedure to ensure that the person achieves their desired outcome.

Neither should you become involved in disputes with other professionals; you should simply ensure that the person's views are clearly expressed. You may also wish to add your own views as a professional, and these will be based on the person's needs and wishes.

People are able to decide which services they want, and how and by whom they want them delivered. People will know how much money they have to spend and so will be able to see where support from family and friends or the local community can be used. Sometimes, the funding contribution to their budget may need to be used creatively in order to do everything someone wants, and it can be difficult if people feel that their budget is not adequate for their needs.

Your role in this situation is to encourage people to think about alternative ways of using resources and making the most of any informal support opportunities. Very often, people will have grown so used to having professional support that they cannot think of other ways to achieve outcomes. In some situations, it can be relatives who are unhappy with the size of a budget and you may have to explain how the Resource Allocation System works and suggest ideas about how outcomes can be achieved. Frequently you may find that people and their families may only be able to think about using traditional services and may need encouragement to think about how to put together informal support, universal services and paid support to achieve what they want.

In the past few years, a number of different ways of including the person in the planning process in a meaningful way have been developed. Some of these have already been mentioned above. They include:

- advocacy
- **self-advocacy**
- facilitated decision making
- providing mentors and/or other support for family members
- providing training for staff and family members.

The system of having a person to speak on behalf of another person is called advocacy. An advocate will go with a person to a meeting, for example, and make sure that the person's views are fully expressed. The advocate must be someone who has known the person well over a long period and who therefore knows their views, likes and dislikes. Self-advocacy involves empowering people to speak for themselves by building their confidence, self-esteem and communication skills.

A key element in achieving person-centred planning is to have a **facilitator** to help people not only say what they want, but also know what's available.

> ## Key terms
>
> **Self-advocacy** – speaking up for oneself
>
> **Facilitator** – a person who helps make something happen. This is often associated with decision making or planning

In your present work role, it may be possible to assist someone in the support planning process by acting as an advocate, or even as a facilitator or mentor.

3.3 Agreeing delivery

People will have developed their person-centred plan using a range of methods to look at what is important to them in their lives. There are various different approaches to support plans, but they should all include the following, which is used by at least one large council.

People are able to say what support they want and how and by whom they want it delivered. Of course, what they want has to be able to be delivered within the budget that is available to them. Person-centred planning does not deliver an unlimited budget!

Delivery of paid support is an important aspect of someone's plan. They may want some support delivered by someone they know, or they may have a preference for a particular agency or individual worker.

Question	The plan should include:	Your plan will not be agreed if:
What is important to you?	All about you: Important people and places Interests and hobbies	It is not individual It is not specific
What do you want to change or achieve?	Changes you want to make: Your lifestyle Things to achieve Things that need to stay the same Where you live Long term	It is not clear Changes are imposed by others Changes would make life worse
How will you be supported?	The help you need: When and where Staying safe and well	There is no detailed plan for support The plan puts you or others at risk
How will you use your individual budget?	Detailed cost for one year: How much money for the next two years? Direct Payment, trust, individual service fund or arranged through social worker	You do not say how the money will be spent
How will your support be managed?	How your support will be organised: Contingency plans How will the money be managed? Details of how you will directly employ people if needed	You do not say how your day-to-day support will be managed
How will you stay in control of your life?	How you make decisions: How are you involved in decisions if other people help you to make them	Others make decisions that you can make
What are you going to do to make this plan happen?	A clear action plan of who is going to do what	It isn't clear how the support will be delivered

Table 2: Example approach to support plans.

Some people like to employ their own support workers, while others do not want that level of responsibility.

People may not be able to choose all parts of their support, particularly within health services where there is not yet the ability to make those choices. The delivery of social care support can usually be delivered according to the choices made by the person in their plan.

3.4 Recording the plan in a suitable format

Once someone has produced a plan that they are happy with, and changes have been discussed with any relevant people, you should ensure that those decisions are recorded in such a way that all of those involved with the process can access them readily. You may want to consider using a form for recording the outcomes of the planning meeting and simply add to it any subsequent changes made and agreed.

Doing it well

Maintaining good communication

- Communicate all information clearly and in a way that can be understood.
- Make sure people are able to be in control of the planning process, using an advocate if necessary.
- Support people to communicate their decisions if necessary.
- Make sure that the person and any others they wish to be involved have recorded the plan and included all the necessary elements.
- Ensure that people are able to discuss their plan in an environment where they feel comfortable.
- Ensure that the plan is agreed by the relevant social worker/care manager.
- Ensure that all final proposals for care provision have the agreement of the person and those who are involved in their care.
- Ensure that all of those involved with the process are kept informed of any changes and updates made to the proposals.
- Ensure that records are stored securely and that confidentiality is maintained.

Reflect

Think about a person you are currently working with. Consider all your actions in respect of that person and whether they were given a choice in the services provided.

If you believe the person was given every possible choice, then list the ways in which you ensured that was the case. If you believe the person's choice was restricted unnecessarily, identify the reasons why this happened and the steps you could take to ensure that it does not happen again.

You may be involved in a support planning meeting organised to develop or review a person's support plan.

The person you are working with will have identified the outcomes they want and will have chosen the support to help achieve them. You need to be clear about what you need to do to ensure that the outcomes are achieved, but the way you relate to the person you are working for is also important, as many people will have had experiences that have damaged their confidence and self-esteem.

The format for recording a plan is important. It must be in a format that is useable by the person. Many of the templates for drawing up plans use graphics rather than text, as this is easier for many people to access. One commonly used design uses a 'map' of a road, showing where people want to go and the people who are important along the way.

Another design is based on a graphic that has a graph in the shape of a star identifying what is important in someone's life, the bits they are happy with and the bits they want to change. The most important thing is that the plan is accessible to the person it belongs to and that it can be easily understood by them. It also needs to be able to show:

- information about the person and how the plan relates to their life
- how changes will improve someone's life and evidence that this is their plan and not developed by someone else
- what support the person will need and how this will keep them safe and well and reduce any risk of harm. There needs to be a detailed breakdown of how the support will be used
- detailed information about how the budget will be spent

- information about how support will be managed and organised — will it be done by the person themselves? Or a relative or friend? Or by an agency?
- clear information about how decisions are made and how the person is in control of the decisions. This may involve the use of an advocate
- an action plan for how this will all work on a practical level.

Each of these aspects will need to be recorded or the plan may not be agreed by the social worker/care manager.

4. Be able to support the implementation of care plans

4.1 Your role in implementation

Your role could be one of several depending on the nature of the plan. You may need to:

- provide practical support or personal care
- support independent living skills
- support someone to engage with social networks
- support someone to become active in their local community
- support someone to access education and training
- support someone to access transport or work
- assist in managing the budget
- coordinate the delivery of the plan
- liaise with other professionals.

Whatever role you have in the implementation of the plan, you must carry it out in the best interests of the person you are supporting and always remember that it is their plan and, more importantly, their life! They can choose how they want to live their life and your role is to support, not to direct, what they do.

You may need to be flexible in the way you work in order to fit in with people's plans and the way they want to do things. Everyone is able to change their minds about activities and plans, so an ability to respond to changed plans is important. Sometimes this can create tensions with other commitments, but flexibility should be built in as far as possible.

4.2 Support others

If you are involved in working with other people in the implementation of a plan, or in coordinating some parts of it, you may have to offer support to others, especially if you are the one who knows the person best.

Sometimes if people are coming in to provide a specialist part of the plan, such as a physiotherapist or a speech and language therapist, they may not know the person well. It will be helpful if you are able to provide some additional support.

Carers may also need your support from time to time. Caring for a family member, no matter how much they are loved, is never easy. It can be very stressful and people are often glad of support, even if it is just a chat and a sympathetic ear.

Reflect

Think about how your life has changed in the past six months. The changes could be major or very small in impact. For example, you could have discovered a new TV programme that you want to watch regularly, or you may have gone on a diet or stopped smoking. Write a list of these small changes and how they impact on your quality of life.

Now think about a time when you had a big change in your circumstances. Maybe you left school and got a job, moved home, got married. How did you deal with these changes emotionally and physically? What support did you have?

Doing it well

Developing and implementing support plans

- Support the person to be central to the process of planning their own care programme, and in expressing preferences.
- Check that proposals made by professional agencies meet with the agreement of the person before starting any programme of care.
- Ensure that you are able to carry out the support plan activities for which you are responsible.
- Support colleagues to carry out the support plan activities for which they are responsible.
- Make arrangements to feed back regularly on the provision of the service.
- Contribute to arrangements for regularly reviewing the service and make sure that the person is involved throughout the process.

4.3 Making changes

Throughout the life of any plan, you are looking for and responding to change. It is important you are clear about the difference between types of changes that require action, and those which are simply a part of everyday life and do not involve a major rethink of a support package. For example, somebody who inherits

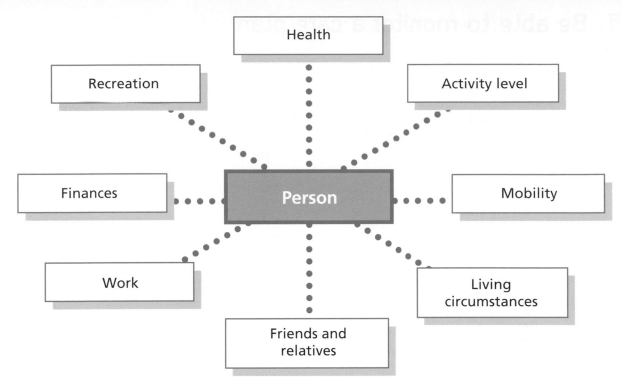

You may be asked to report any significant changes in somebody's performance.

£50,000 will experience significant change, whereas someone who receives a £1.20 per week increase in income support will not! Both, however, have experienced a change in their financial circumstances.

Similarly, someone who changes from working two days each week to a full-time job experiences a significant change that will involve alterations in the support package they receive. But someone who changes from working two days each week as a telephonist to working the same two days as a receptionist is unlikely to need significant changes in their support plan.

There are many different types of changes that people experience; some are shown above.

Case study

Acknowledging change

Miss Pugh is aged 73. She lives alone and is a retired floor manager from a large local department store. She has had support from the home care and mobile meals service since her mobility deteriorated with the increasing severity of her arthritis over the last five years. She was a fiercely independent lady who had always refused to accept any benefits or support in addition to her state pension. After finally getting her agreement to review her finances, her key worker had identified that she had some additional benefits due to her from her company pension scheme. This had increased Miss Pugh's monthly income considerably and had eased her financial situation. However, this change in circumstances had also put her income above the payment threshold for home care service and she now has to pay for the service that she had previously received at no charge. Miss Pugh is angry at this and is considering cancelling the home care service, although she would find it extremely difficult to manage without it.

1. How would you explain the situation to Miss Pugh?
2. What are the skills you would need in order to encourage Miss Pugh successfully to continue using support services?
3. Should such a possibility have been discussed with Miss Pugh in advance of obtaining her agreement to review her finances?

5. Be able to monitor a care plan

Whatever approach your agency takes to monitoring, it will be decided at the outset how a particular plan of support will be monitored and the methods will be agreed with the person and their carers. Your feedback will be an essential part of the process. A monitoring process will involve:

- the person receiving the service
- their carers or family
- other health care professionals
- the service provider – whose performance will be monitored.

5.1 Monitoring the way a care plan is delivered

Monitoring is essential to ensure that any plan of support is continuing to meet the needs it was designed to meet. A plan of support will have originally been assessed, planned and put in place to meet a particular set of circumstances. The original individual plan should include plans for monitoring and review that have been agreed by all concerned, because plans put in place with even the most thorough assessment and careful planning will not necessarily be appropriate in six months or a year, or continue to provide services of the quality or at the level originally expected.

Monitoring may seem a complex process but its principles are very simple. Most of us monitor many things in our lives on a regular basis without realising it.

Monitoring of a support plan needs to pick up changes in the circumstances of the person who developed the plan, their informal carers and any service providers. The original support plan will include forms of care and support that reflect the person's needs at the time. For example, someone recently discharged from hospital following treatment for mental health problems may receive quite extensive support under the care programme approach, consisting of day care, community psychiatric nurse visits, and access to a support group of carers. However, feedback on that person's progress may show their mental health has improved to the point that day care is no longer needed on the previous level and that an alternative service, such as support in finding employment, is now far more appropriate. A plan that is frequently monitored is likely to be one which is responsive to the needs of the person, and is also an effective use of the resources of the organisation responsible for funding.

Checking resources

Checking on resources can also be important if changes in the availability of those resources means that a care package will have to be altered in some way. A reduction in available funding or an increase in demand for a particular resource may mean that adjustments in the level of service provision will have to be made. Regular monitoring makes it easier to be aware of where resources are being used and where changes need to be made.

Case study

Monitoring behaviour changes

Claire is 75 years old and lives alone with daily support for cooking and personal care. She attends a day centre on a regular basis. Until recently, she has been enthusiastic about gardening and enjoyed working on the centre's allotment. Recently, you have noticed that she chooses to spend more and more time indoors, and has refused to participate in physical activities.

1. What questions would you ask Claire to find out why her behaviour has changed?
2. How else would you encourage her to monitor her own changes?
3. Who else could you talk to about this?
4. What parts of Claire's support plan might need to be revisited?

What resources are used for activities in your workplace?

5.2 Collating monitoring information from agreed sources

Obviously the most important person in any monitoring process is the person at the centre of the plan, so they must be clear about how to record and feed back information on the way the care package is working. This can be through:

- completing a checklist on a regular basis (weekly or monthly)
- maintaining regular contact with the care manager/coordinator, either by telephone or through a visit
- using an electronic checking and monitoring form which would be emailed on a regular basis to the care manager/coordinator
- recording and reporting any changes in their own circumstances or changes in the provision of the care package.

Monitoring by carers and families

Carers and families are likely to participate in the monitoring of a care package in similar ways. You will need to make sure that carers are willing to participate in monitoring and they do not feel you are adding yet another burden to their lives.

Regular monitoring and feedback should cover the needs of carers, to make sure the provisions are still meeting their needs. Carers should also be included in providing feedback about the service. Regular feedback from carers, and the knowledge that they will contact you if circumstances change, can be taken into account when monitoring.

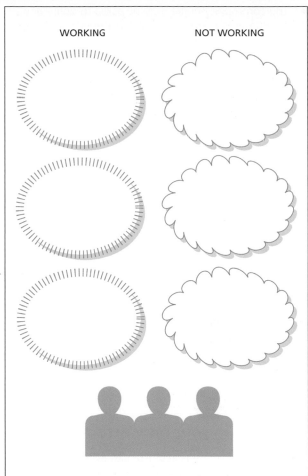

A feedback form from a person in care.

However, it is not appropriate or reasonable to put all the responsibility on a carer to notify you when changes take place. Carers cope with tremendous demands on their time and energy, both physical and emotional. Whatever systems you agree in order to keep up to date with feedback from carers, you must make sure you are not placing even more demands on their time.

Monitoring by other health care professionals

Maintaining contact between reviews with other professionals who may be involved with the person is an essential part of the monitoring process. The most effective method of doing this is to agree the types of changes that will trigger contact. For example:

- the GP may be asked to notify the care manager of any significant health changes or hospital admissions

- the community nurse may be asked to notify any problems in compliance with treatment, or changes in the person's ability to administer their own medication, or changes in home conditions
- the physiotherapist may be asked to notify any significant changes in performance.

There may be other professionals involved, such as occupational or speech therapists, depending on the circumstances of the person. The principles of monitoring remain the same. Professionals will need to be particularly vigilant in reporting any changes which could mean that the person is at risk of receiving inadequate care under the current plans.

Feedback from care professionals

Your role in administering the plan of support means that you are in an ideal position to identify changes in somebody's circumstances that may mean a service is no longer appropriate. It may need to be increased, decreased or changed in order to meet a new situation. The changes do not have to be major, but they can have a significant impact on a person's life.

5.3 Recording changes

Support plans may need to be altered as the result of changes. You will need to make sure that any changes that are agreed are recorded on the plan and that all the relevant people, including carers and other professionals involved, have a copy of the changes. You may also need to record changes in line with the procedures of your organisation, so that official records, statistics and finances are all kept in order and information sent to the relevant people.

Possible changes in people's circumstances

There are many aspects of people's lives that could change. Some examples are shown on the following page.

Activity 3

Changes in your own circumstances

1. Look at your own circumstances over the past 10 years and make a list of the ways in which they have changed. For example:
   - you may have more children than you had 10 years ago
   - some children may have left home and moved away
   - members of your family may have died or been born
   - you could be living in a larger or a smaller house
   - you could have more money or less money
   - you could be doing a different job.

   All these are major changes which have taken place in your life in just the relatively short period of 10 years. Listing them will help you see the types of situations that change and affect people's lives.

2. Then take a much shorter period – for example, the past year – and look at much smaller changes which may have happened to you during that time. They could be changes in your finances and your job role. For example:
   - you could now be undertaking a qualification
   - you may be driving a different car
   - you may have acquired digital television.

   Any number of small changes such as these have affected the way you are living your life. Again, make a list of these changes and consider the impact each of them has had.

   Although the second list may have had a smaller impact than some of the big changes you listed in your first reflection, they will nonetheless have combined to bring about some quite significant changes in your lifestyle.

Have any of these aspects changed in your life in recent years?

Case study

Changing levels of support

Katherine is a woman in her early 50s. She has Parkinson's disease, her level of mobility has been decreasing gradually over the past three years, and she has recently begun to fall frequently. She lives with her two sons who are aged 19 and 25, and her only contact with health and care provision so far has been through her hospital consultant and the primary care team. Her service requirements have been mainly medical with regular support from a physiotherapist.

Her increase in falling has coincided with a major change in her circumstances. Her younger son has been offered a place at an excellent university and her older son has been headhunted for his dream job in the United States on a two-year contract. Katherine does

not want either of her sons to miss the opportunities they have been offered – so she now wants to discuss the ways in which she can arrange support that will allow her to remain as independent as possible.

1. Who should be the first professionals Katherine holds discussions with?
2. Who else should be involved in planning?
3. How would you help to ensure that Katherine retained control of the process?
4. What feelings would you anticipate Katherine would have about her change in circumstances?
5. What steps do you think should be taken to make sure that Katherine remains independent?

6. Be able to facilitate a review of care plans and their implementation

The purpose of reviews

Reviews are essential because care situations very rarely remain the same for long periods of time. As circumstances change, the package of care may need to be reviewed in the light of those changes. At agreed intervals, all of the parties involved should come together to reflect on whether or not the package of care is continuing to do the job it was initially set up to do. If there were no reviews, the arrangements could continue for years, regardless of whether they were still meeting care needs.

A review will gather together all the information about the circumstances of the person, the service provided and the service provider. It will give all those concerned with the care of the person the opportunity to express their opinions and to be involved in a discussion about how effective care provision has been and the changes, if any, that need to be made.

6.1 Who should be involved in the review process and criteria to judge effectiveness of the care plan

As in the initial planning, the person is central to the review process. They need to agree who will be involved and how to judge whether the plan is still effective However, any review should attempt to obtain feedback from as many people as possible who are involved in

Reflect

Nothing stays the same – everything is subject to change. This includes all aspects of people's circumstances. You must make sure that the support people receive changes in line with any changes in their lives.

People who might be involved in a review.

the care of the person. So, the most important people at the review are the person and their carers or family. You, as the person (or one of the people) providing services from the plan of support, are a very important contributor. The key worker or care manager/coordinator is also important in the review process, as is any organisation providing the care.

It is also key that others with an interest in the care of the person have the opportunity to participate in a review. For example, a GP, health visitor, community psychiatric nurse, community occupational therapist, physiotherapist, speech therapist, welfare rights support worker, representative of a support group, or anyone else who has been a significant contributor to the life and care of the person concerned, should be involved if at all possible. Everyone should have the opportunity to give a view and to contribute to the discussion. However, the person who must agree to any review decision is the person concerned.

How the review process is managed

The care manager/coordinator or key worker is likely to be the person responsible for organising the review itself and making sure that it takes place at the appropriate time. If the person receiving support is receiving direct payment, they are likely to take responsibility for initiating a review if it is felt to be necessary. Where direct payments are involved your role is very different; it is simply one of being there to provide support and assistance if it is required by the person. You would only become involved in a review if they requested this.

The person managing the review is likely to go through a checklist similar to the one on the right to make sure that the review meets the needs of the person concerned.

During the review, everyone should be given a chance to contribute. If the person receiving support has chosen to use an advocate to present their point of view, this person should have every opportunity to contribute on the person's behalf. If some choose to communicate in writing or by other means, such as email, then those comments must be taken into account. If there have been any changes in organisational policies or access to resources, or changes in the circumstances of the service provider, these are also key matters and should be fed into the review for consideration.

Review checklist

1. Does the person understand what a review is?
2. Do the person's carers also understand what a review is and its purpose?
3. Is the review arranged at an appropriate time to check progress?
4. Is this an annual review or has it been triggered by a change in the person's circumstances?
5. Does the review cover whether the person continues to need the same level of support and services, whether there have been any changes, what the original support plan intended, and the results of monitoring?
6. Has the person been asked when and where would be convenient for the review?
7. Has it been explained to the person which decisions the review is able to take in respect of their continuing care provision and the development of a new support plan?
8. Has the person been offered an advocate in order to help them prepare for the review, to support or to speak for them at the review?
9. Does the person know who is responsible for making sure that the review meeting is managed?
10. Has the person agreed to all of the people who will be at the review?
11. Can all of the participants contribute either in writing or verbally to the review?
12. Do all the participants in the support plan know that they can request a review?
13. Have carers been consulted about the appropriate time and location for the review?
14. Have crèche facilities been offered for anyone who needs them so that they can attend the review?

If any conflict or difficulty arises in relation to the support plan because of feedback or observations, you must ensure that organisational procedures are followed to address the issues raised.

Supporting people to contribute

You may need to support the person to recognise the impact of significant change and to identify the differences between important and unimportant changes. You may wish to use a prompt.

You may also need to support people to complete any paperwork that is necessary for the review or for the implementation of any revised support plan.

Care workers and other members of your team may also need support in order to contribute to the review meeting. They may feel intimidated, particularly if they are unfamiliar with speaking in front of a roomful of people.

You can encourage them to prepare for the meeting by:

- putting together a list of all the records they have kept on the person
- informing them of their role in the meeting and preparing them for questions they may be asked
- checking they are familiar with your organisational procedures and that they understand the process.

6.2 Feedback about how the plan is working

Once all the information has been gathered and all contributions have been made, those taking part in the review will need to make a decision about any necessary changes to the support plan and the care package for the next period of time. Decisions should clearly be based on the monitoring of evidence and should particularly take account of contributions from the person and their carers.

You should plan regular contact with the person to get feedback on how the plan is working. Ideally, this should be through visits so that you can observe first hand any conditions that might be changing. At the very least, there should be the opportunity on a regular basis for the person to contact you by phone or letter to inform you of how the plan works in practice.

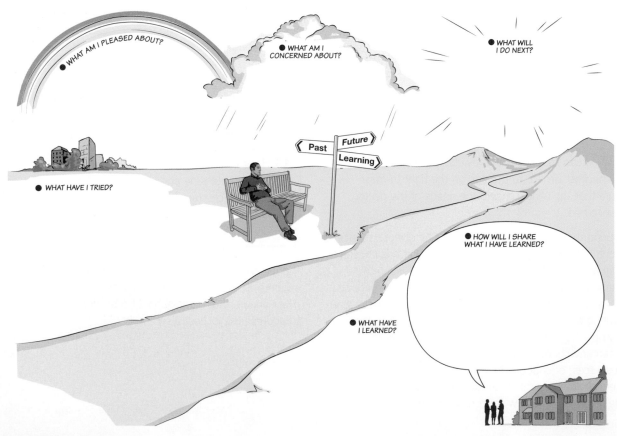

An example of a review map.

6.3 Feedback and monitoring/ other information to evaluate the plan

Two aspects of the support plan must be monitored:

- any changes to the person's situation
- how well the service provision works and any adjustments needed in the way it is delivered.

One way to do this is through the use of checklists. You can devise a checklist which you can go through with the person on a regular basis, and provide another checklist to others involved in the person's care. Both checklists should show the objectives agreed in the planning meeting and how far they have been achieved.

Activity 4

Devising a checklist

Use the support plan for somebody and devise a checklist to show how far the outcomes agreed have been met.

Include:
- the aspect of the person's life, for example, health, diet, cultural needs
- the outcomes agreed on the plan
- support needed
- scale of effectiveness
- any changes.

6.4 Agreeing any revisions to the plan

A review should not take a decision about changing provision with which the person fundamentally disagrees. If the proposed changes are because of a change in the level of available resources and result in a reduction in service to the person, it may be that such a decision is inevitable. However, it is important that the alternative which will be in place is acceptable to the person.

If the person is dissatisfied at the end of the review, it is important they are informed about the complaints procedure and the process for asking for a further review of the resources available. Full access should be ensured by offering advocacy or any other support services that may be required for people to take full advantage of any complaints system or further routes to changing decisions, such as approaching decision makers or accessing pressure groups.

Setting the next review date

At the end of each review, it is essential that the date is set for the next review and that all the participants, particularly the person and their carers, find the date acceptable, both in terms of their own availability and the length of time before the review is due to take place.

Reviews must be undertaken at least once a year and if somebody is receiving a care package under the care programme approach system through the mental health services, any admission to hospital must generate a review within a month of discharge.

Activity 5

Analysing a support plan review

Carry out an analysis of the last support plan review in which you were involved. Consider:
- the roles and responsibilities of the people involved in the review
- the quality and detail of the feedback
- whether changes were identified
- whether the review was person-centred
- how any conflict was handled
- how the review was recorded.

Keep your notes for your portfolio.

6.5 Documenting the review process and revisions as required

Many organisations still have their own documentation (although under the single assessment process, joint records are increasingly being produced). They are likely to cover most or all of the following points.

Doing it well

Recording a care package review

All reviews must be recorded in the person's records. Confidentiality must be respected and the records must include:

- written reports from each care service included in the care package
- a record that all relevant staff have been invited to attend the review or to contribute in writing
- a record showing how the person has been prepared for the review and the access they have to an advocate if required
- evidence that relevant carers and others who offer support have been invited to contribute
- a record of all those who attended or who contributed
- a careful record of any changes
- the revised support plan as a separate document.

It is important that all those who have contributed, even if they have not been present at the review, are informed of the outcome and that they know of any changes to the support plan for the person.

Recorded reviews contribute to the overall quality of the service any organisation offers and they are likely to be included in any file audit undertaken during inspection processes. The review process, if it is well conducted, provides a vital opportunity for people to contribute and to make choices about the care package they receive.

Reviews that are badly prepared and carelessly undertaken rob people of the opportunity to take decisions which affect their lives significantly, and they also result in an ineffective use of scarce and valuable resources.

Further reading and research

- www.alzheimers.org.uk (Alzheimer's Society)
- www.cqc.org.uk (Care Quality Commission)
- www.dh.gov.uk (Department of Health)
- www.gscc.org.uk (General Social Care Council)
- www.nationalcareforum.org.uk (National Care Forum)

Getting ready for assessment

Most of this unit will be assessed in the workplace. You will need to show your assessor that you understand the principles of person-centred assessment and support planning. You may be able to do some of this through a professional discussion, but much of it will need to be demonstrated through the way that you work with people. Your assessor will look at how you work with people to establish a partnership approach both to the assessment process and to how the process should be carried out and who else should be involved. They will want to see that you ask people about what they want to happen and how they want their support plan delivered.

You will have to show that you are able to contribute to the planning of care or support, and to the implementation of support plans, by encouraging people to think about the kind of support they may want and to explore the skills and abilities that they already have.

In addition, you also have to show that you are able to monitor support plans, recording changes that affect their delivery. Your assessor will want to see how you keep records for monitoring the plan and how you support people to monitor their own plans so that they can be sure that they are delivering services and support in the way they want.

When reviewing support plans and their implementation, you will need to demonstrate how you seek agreement with the person and others about who should be involved in the review, and how you support the person to judge effectiveness of the support plan.

If people are not willing or able to review their own plan, you will also need to show how you seek and use feedback from the person and others about how the support plan is working, and demonstrate cooperative working to revise the plan as required.

Unit HSC 3029

Support individuals with specific communication needs

Fundamentally you will have learned the basis of communication from the mandatory Unit SHC 31. This unit will expand on your knowledge and will look at supporting the communication of people who have specific communication needs. This will include people with learning disabilities, physical disabilities, mental and physical health problems, or sensory disabilities.

All people have the need and right to express themselves through their preferred format. It is our responsibility to support people to do this by assessing their needs, providing the appropriate support, aids or equipment and by monitoring the effectiveness of that support.

In this unit you will learn about:

- **specific communication needs and factors affecting them**
- **how to contribute to establishing the nature of specific communication needs of individuals and ways to address them**
- **how to interact with individuals using their preferred communication**
- **how to promote communication between individuals and others**
- **how to support the use of communication technology and aids**
- **how to review an individual's communication needs and the support provided to address them.**

1. Understand specific communication needs and factors affecting them

1.1 The importance of meeting communication needs

All people have a right to **communication** and we are governed by standards, codes of practice, guidelines, morals and law to ensure those communication needs are met. Unit SHC 33 looks at these areas in greater detail; we will only examine them here in relation to specific communication needs.

Rights to communication

Imagine if you were unable to communicate. How would you make an appointment to see the doctor of your choice? How would you tell the hairdresser or barber what style of hair cut you wanted? How would you stop people from calling you names or taking advantage of you?

Communication is a basic human right. Without communication the person is unable to realise or exercise their rights. Under the Human Rights Act 1998 all people have the right to 'freedom of expression'. This is just one right under the Act which relates to communication. If we did not meet people's communication needs, many may be denied their rights. Table 1 covers some of the people's rights based on the General Social Care Council (GSCC) Code of Practice and shows how their rights can be affected. These may vary for the Scottish Social Services Commission, the Care Council for Wales and the Northern Ireland Social Services Council.

1.2 How your role and practice can impact on communication with an individual who has specific communication needs

How you interact with people is very important. Your role and practices can have a big impact on the communication with somebody who has specific communication needs. Your role as a support worker is to support and encourage the person in everyday activities. Your practices may be affected if you do not

> **Key term**
>
> **Communication** – the passing on and receiving of information through a variety of methods including verbal and non-verbal communication

Person's right to...	Effect when communication needs are not met
diversity, or to be different	The person will not be able to express their own identity or culture.
equality	The person will not be treated equally if they are unable to communicate their views or opinions.
control their own life	The person will not be able to make choices regarding their life.
dignity	The person is not being treated with respect by denying them their right to communication.
effective communication	The person will not be able to communicate effectively.
safety and security	The person will not be able to express their safety concerns or report acts of abuse.
take risks	The person will not be able to choose the risks that they take.

Table 1: Communication rights of people.

have a good understanding of the person's specific communication needs. You may not be able to communicate fully with the person, which could result in their needs being unmet. Some people may even concentrate on the person's communication needs so much that they forget the basic skills of effective communication.

You can find more on basic communication skills in Unit SHC 31.

Basic communication skills

- Use closed questions to obtain yes or no answers.
- Use open questions to encourage more in-depth answers.
- Avoid asking too many things at once to prevent confusion.
- Allow the person time to respond.
- Do not interrupt the person while they are communicating or anticipate their response.
- Show the person that you are interested in them. Use appropriate body language such as nodding, smiling and leaning towards the person when communicating to show interest.

1.3 Features of the environment that may help or hinder communication

The environment

How many times have you tried to communicate with someone and found it very difficult or frustrating because of the environment you are in? The environment can both help and hinder communication. The following features of the environment are described to show you how they can do this.

Lighting

Is there sufficient lighting to enable people with hearing loss or poor sight to be able to see you clearly? Poor lighting can hinder communication especially if the person has a hearing or visual disability, as they may rely on looking at your facial expressions and lips to understand what you are saying.

Distractions

Are there any background noises or activities which could distract the person or make hearing difficult, such as noise from the television or radio? Some people may find it difficult to concentrate with background noise. People with a hearing difficulty may find it difficult to hear you clearly if the television or radio is on.

Positioning

Is your seating position and that of the person such that you can see each other's face and body language? It is important for effective communication that each of you can see each other's body language and facial expressions, as these support verbal speech.

Barriers

Are there any obstacles between you and the person that could create a barrier, such as a table or desk? Barriers can block the view of each other's body language. They can also create a sense of unease or hierarchy, such as when you go and see your bank manager or attend an interview.

Space

Is there sufficient distance between you and the person? We all have a need for personal space. If someone sits or stands too close to you, it could make you feel uncomfortable. For communication to be effective, people need to feel comfortable and unthreatened.

1.4 Reasons why an individual may use a form of communication not based on a formal language system

Some people, because of a health condition, may communicate using a method that is not formally recognised. This could include the use of hand gestures, alternative use of words or sounds and behaviour.

Some people may develop their own way of communicating because they do not have the ability to communicate in a more formal manner. This could be because they have a learning disability, a physical disability, a mental health condition, a sensory disability, or as a result of their upbringing or social development.

Learning disabilities

Up to 90 per cent of people with a learning disability have some form of specific communication need. Many people with a learning disability have no identified cause of their communication difficulty.

How can physical disabilities affect communication?

Some theorists believe it is the learning disability that affects the person's communication. Others believe it is the lack of communication skills which affects the person's ability to learn. Despite much research, no certain conclusion can be found.

There are many different types of learning disability that can affect the person's communication — for example, Down's syndrome. The level of learning disability for people with Down's syndrome can vary. Often their social ability tends to be higher than their intellectual ability. Approximately 75 per cent of people with Down's syndrome have difficulties with their hearing. Combine this with a learning disability and people have an increased difficulty in communication. People with Down's syndrome can have difficulty in forming words and speech sounds, resulting in their speech being difficult to understand. People with this condition may develop their own way of communicating.

Physical disabilities

Some people may, quite wrongly, think that those who have a physical disability also have an impairment of their intellect. People with physical disabilities do not necessarily have any form of learning disability. Having a physical disability can be difficult to come to terms with, especially when the person's communication is affected.

When the physical disability affects the person's facial muscles or vocal cords, their verbal communication can be affected. If it affects their bodily movement or head control, it can also affect their non-verbal communication.

Physical disabilities can be congenital or acquired; the most common form of physical disability affecting communication is cerebral palsy.

Cerebral palsy

The causes of this condition are vast, all leading to damage of the person's brain. Cerebral palsy can cause differing disabilities depending on the part of the brain affected. Someone with any form of cerebral palsy may have difficulty communicating or developing recognisable speech.

Mental health conditions

A mental health condition is one that affects how somebody relates to their environment due to changes within the brain caused by injury, infection, age or substance abuse. It is not only the changes to the person's brain that can create a specific communication need — the lack of understanding and acceptance from society can create communication difficulties also. It is for this reason we need to develop a better knowledge of mental health conditions so we can support the person and their communication needs more effectively.

Dementia

The most common mental health condition within older people is dementia.

Dementia is a progressive disorder that can affect the person's short-term and sometimes long-term memory. It also affects their recognition of people or things, speech, understanding, concentration, orientation and motivation. Their personality may change dramatically. Hallucinations may occur when they believe they can see something or someone who is not really there. Inevitably communication will be affected from the initial stages of dementia. With the person developing forgetfulness, you may need to repeat yourself, or constantly remind them of certain things. A change in the person's personality or behaviour will require a change in the way communication takes place. (See Unit DEM 301 for more on dementia.)

Sensory disabilities

Disabilities which affect somebody's senses, and in turn affect communication, include hearing loss and sight loss. These are the two main senses on which humans rely to interact with their environment. Without sight or hearing (or indeed both), communication will be affected and alternative ways of communicating will need to be used.

Hearing loss

The world in which we communicate relies heavily on sound; people talking or singing, or radio and train platform announcements are just a few examples. Sound is all around us every day from the birds singing to the wind rustling through the trees. Some sounds are more important for communication, such as the sound of a car horn to let you know of an oncoming car or the sound of a fire alarm to let you know to evacuate a building. Imagine you could not hear any of these sounds. What effect would this have on your communication?

The term 'hearing loss' can apply to someone who is profoundly deaf (someone who has no hearing at all), as well as to people who are hard of hearing (someone

Activity 1

Sensory disabilities

Undertake this exercise with a friend or colleague.

1. Sit in a quiet room with your colleague or friend and put on a blindfold.
2. Hold a normal conversation between the two of you as you would at any other time. Continue the conversation for at least 20 minutes so that you become acclimatised with being blindfolded.
3. After the conversation, remove the blindfold and identify how you felt communicating without sight. Discuss this with your colleague or friend and ask them how they thought your communication differed while you were blindfolded.
4. Repeat this exercise but instead of wearing a blindfold, wear headphones to block out the sound. You may need to play music through your headphones to block out your colleague's or friend's voice altogether.

who can hear but has difficulty). Some people are born deaf, known in professional terms as pre-lingual deafness, while others can lose their hearing later in life. This is known as post-lingual deafness.

People with pre-lingual deafness will have usually learned to communicate using a specific method from an early age. However, those with post-lingual deafness may have difficulty communicating as they can no longer use their only method of communication, speech. Such people will need to develop a way of communicating which may not be a form of communication that is based on a formal language system.

Functional skills

English: Speaking and listening

Using information gained from the discussion with a friend about how it feels to have a conversation blindfolded, sit down with others to share your thoughts and ideas. You need to take an active part in the discussion and use points brought up by others to take the discussion forward. Present your ideas clearly and adapt your body position to show you are attentive.

Sight difficulties

Sight plays an important role in communication. More than 90 per cent of what we communicate is through non-verbal communication. This is communicated through our body language – how we stand, our facial expressions, movements we make with our hands. If what we communicate is less than 10 per cent verbal, then somebody without sight will miss out on a huge amount of information needed to make the communication effective.

When we talk about people with sight difficulties, we are referring to people whose sight cannot be corrected through the use of glasses or contact lenses. A person's sight can be affected to varying degrees, ranging from partial sight loss to complete blindness.

Much like hearing loss, sight loss can occur before birth (congenital) or after birth. People who lose their sight after birth may experience different difficulties in communication to those who were born without sight. Losing your sight at a later stage in life can create acceptance difficulties and the need to learn a new method of communication which may not be part of a formal language system.

The main cause of sight loss in the UK is, like hearing, age-related. Eighty per cent of people with sight loss are over the age of 65 and have conditions such as macular degeneration or cataracts.

Deaf-blindness

Having no sight or no hearing can cause major problems with communication. Imagine having neither sight nor hearing at the same time – the problems created for communication could be enormous.

Deaf-blindness, as defined by the organisation SENSE (the leading national charity that supports and campaigns for children and adults who are deaf-blind), is a 'unique disability'. Many may have heard of this condition as 'Dual Sensory Impairment' (DSI). People who have deaf-blindness have a complete loss, or nearly a complete loss, of both sight and hearing.

Some people can be born with deaf-blindness, known as congenital deaf-blindness, while others may develop the condition, which is known as acquired deaf-blindness. Both groups of people may develop a form of communication which is not part of a formal language system.

The main cause of deaf-blindness is rubella. This happens when the rubella virus (German measles) is transferred from a pregnant woman to her unborn child. The rubella virus affects the foetus in the womb, causing damage to its developing sensory organs (eyes and ears) as well as to the heart and brain.

Social development

It is gauged that people begin developing language between the ages of 12 and 24 months. Some people may develop earlier, others later. It is during this stage of development, and as the child gets older, that it is important to encourage social interaction, which in turn helps develop communication further. People who have been socially deprived may not have the ability to communicate fully or may use alternative forms of communication, such as behaviour, to express

---

Case study

Garfield's expressions

Garfield is an 18-year-old man who has a learning disability and no formal verbal speech. He enjoys sitting by the window looking out over the back garden. Whenever a bird lands on the bird bath, Garfield screams and claps his hands. If a squirrel comes into the garden, he becomes very excited. He draws his legs up to his chest and rocks back and forth, biting his hand. At mealtimes Garfield will occasionally throw his food on the floor and cover his head with his arms. If his mother sees this and approaches Garfield, he will say

'Na na na na' and quickly pick up his food off the floor and put it in the bin.

1. What do you think Garfield is communicating when he sees a bird or a squirrel in his garden?
2. What could he be communicating by throwing his food on the floor?
3. Why do you think Garfield covers his head after he has thrown his food on the floor?
4. What do you think Garfield means when he says 'Na na na na'?

themselves and their needs. If the person's inappropriate expressions have not been corrected, they may go on to develop this behaviour further into their adolescent and adult lives.

1.5 Communication methods and aids to support individuals to communicate

Regardless of a person's disability, if it affects their communication, they will require support to be able to express themselves effectively. Communication support can be given through human **aids**, symbolic aids and technical aids. You will look at technical aids later on in this unit.

Any form of communication which is supported or replaced by materials or equipment is classed as aided communication. The materials or equipment used can be simple everyday items such as a pen and paper to write messages, pictures or photographs and symbols.

Well, I never know what I'm going to need... I suppose photographs would be much easier.

Objects can be used as a point of reference to aid communication.

Augmentative and Alternative Communication (AAC)

AAC is the description given to the different ways communication can be supported or replaced. This can include the use of the following.

- **Objects** can be used as a point of reference. For example, holding up a cup when you ask somebody if they would like a drink. The object can help the person to understand what you are talking about.
- **Photographs** of people or items are a good aid in supporting communication. They can be used as objects are used, but photographs are more portable.
- **Symbols** can benefit those with or without disabilities. They are used around us all the time in everyday life, from instructions in how to use a new appliance, to signs and symbols on the roads.

Many of us use some form of AAC to supplement our communication every day without really thinking about it. We will wave our hand to mean goodbye, nod our head for 'yes' or shake it for 'no'. This non-verbal communication is known as unaided communication because equipment or people do not aid it.

Other communication methods and aids

British Sign Language (BSL)

BSL is the main communication method used by people who have a hearing loss. BSL uses the hands, body and face to make signs which represent words or phrases. It also has its own alphabet which is expressed using the fingers on each hand. This is also known as finger spelling. BSL is a language in its own right, developed over many hundreds of years, and was formally recognised by the UK government on 18 March 2003 as an official language. BSL can be learned in stages by attending college or training days offered by selected organisations.

Makaton

Makaton is a form of signing which is intended to support speech, not replace it. It is a simple form of signing which can be used with any people who have difficulty forming words. People and their network of carers use it in over 40 countries worldwide and it is available in English, Urdu, Gujarati, Hindi and Punjabi text to ensure equal access to communication support.

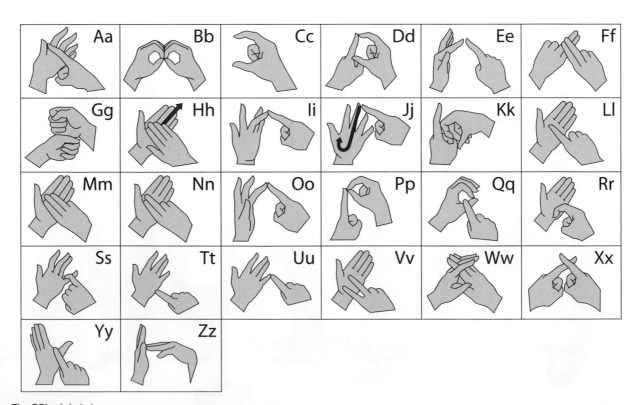

The BSL alphabet.

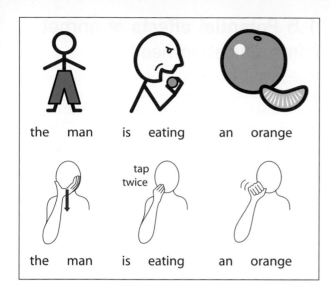

the man   is   eating   an   orange

tap twice

the man   is   eating   an   orange

Makaton can be signed to support speech or used as symbols to support the written word.

Following recent government legislation on public and commercial services providing information for everyone, Makaton signs and symbols are being used more and more around the community.

Picture Exchange Communication Systems (PECS)

PECS is a communication system where the person exchanges a picture they select, from a carefully compiled album of pictures, for the item they want. This method of communication gives the person independence and allows them to express their needs or feelings easily and quickly. This system also has the advantage of being portable and easy to use and understand. It is also very encouraging for the person, as their communication is instantly rewarded. The album of pictures can be compiled to include simple symbolic pictures related to the person's needs, interests and preferences. The types of pictures you could include may be basic such as a drink or biscuit. As the person becomes more confident with the communication system, more pictures can be added to the album.

Touch

The use of touch in communication may play an important role with those people who have a sight or hearing loss, or both. However, some touch may be seen as inappropriate. This includes touching the intimate parts of the person and patronising touch such as patting them on the head. People who have no verbal speech may tap you on the arm, place their hand on your shoulder or may hold your hand if they require your attention. They may also take your hand and place it on their head or neck if they require comfort. Some people who have dual sensory disabilities may touch others' faces to identify who they are. In this case it is the face that is communicating to the person.

Activity 2

Touch

Communication through touch may not be seen as an appropriate form of contact with certain groups of people. Speak with your manager to ascertain what is deemed appropriate contact with the people you work with and write up your findings to present to your assessor.

Deaf-blind manual alphabet

For people who are deaf-blind, a slightly modified version of the BSL finger-spelling alphabet is used. The person signs letters on to the hand of the recipient to spell out what they wish to communicate. The recipient then responds by signing on to the hand of the person. Both parties in this form of communication need to be well skilled at signing as well as being able to spell accurately.

Braille

Braille is a method of communication used by people who are blind. It is a series of raised dots on paper formed into set patterns which represent letters of the alphabet. The person reads Braille by running their fingers over the dots to feel the pattern and identify the letter it represents. Braille is becoming more widely used on everyday objects such as medication packs and buttons on a lift as well as for information leaflets provided by organisations such as social services.

Human aids

There are three main types of human aids to communication — an interpreter, a translator and an advocate.

An interpreter is a person who supports the communication between two people who do not share the same language. This would include the sign languages, such as BSL. In this case, the interpreter would act as the link between the person using BSL and people they wished to communicate with who did not know sign language.

A translator changes the written word into an easier-to-read format for the person with communication needs. This could be written text translated into Braille or symbols.

An advocate is someone who speaks on behalf of another when they are not able to do so. An advocate can help a person to make choices, ensure their rights are met and make sure they are listened to. As a support worker, you may act as an advocate for people you support on a daily basis. There may be times, however, when an impartial advocate is required to support the person's views — for example, if the person needs to make a serious complaint or allegation. These advocates, known as 'citizen advocates', are independent and are paid to act on behalf of the person. A citizen advocate is totally independent of the person, their family and the organisation providing the care.

Methods and aids to communication include:

- pen and paper
- writing
- interpreters
- translators
- advocates
- touch
- pictures
- symbols
- photographs
- objects of reference
- British Sign Language (BSL)
- Makaton
- Picture Exchange Communication Systems (PECS)
- deaf-blind manual alphabet
- Braille.

1.6 Potential effects of unmet communication needs

Having difficulties expressing oneself can lead to both physical and emotional problems. You may have experienced some of these emotions yourself during Activity 1 earlier on in this unit.

People who experience a gradual loss of effective communication may become increasingly withdrawn, depressed or isolated. These emotions reduce the person's self-esteem as they start to develop feelings of frustration and uselessness. Their behaviour may change as they vent their frustrations with acts of anger or even violence.

People who have grown up with specific communication needs do not necessarily have it any easier. Just because they have been born with a condition affecting their communication does not entirely mean that they have learned to cope with the difficulties. The effects will still be the same.

Some people who have not received the required support to communicate effectively may become indifferent to others. They may begin to feel that there is no point in trying to express themselves, their needs or their views, when no one appears to be listening or attempting to understand them. Unsupported communication needs can result in the person being denied their rights. As a society, if we deny somebody their rights in life we are, in effect, abusing that person.

Hearing loss is not a new condition, nor is it one that people are not aware of. Despite this, people do not fully realise the true implications of not having the ability to hear. *A Simple Cure* (RNID 2004) reported that 77 per cent of people who use British Sign Language as their first language were not provided with a BSL interpreter when they were admitted to an accident and emergency unit (A&E). It is hard to imagine how these people were able to express themselves effectively and receive the care that they required when they were not able to communicate in their first language! In addition to the fear, pain or anxiety caused by the medical problem leading them to go to the A&E department in the first place, these people must have faced extreme frustration when trying to communicate their needs.

For information relating to how the person's rights could be affected, see Table 1 on page 338.

2. Be able to contribute to establishing the nature of specific communication needs of individuals and ways to address them

2.1 The individual's specific communication needs

Before we can effectively support somebody with their communication, we need to identify what specific communication needs they have. To ensure this support is effective, we must work in partnership with the person and **others**.

>
> **Key term**
>
> **Others** – this may include family, advocates, specialist communication professionals and others who are important to the person's well-being

The law

The Care Quality Commission (CQC) is responsible for ensuring care service providers meet the National Minimum Standards in England (see page 32 for other countries). In relation to communication this includes:

- the assessment of sight, hearing and communication needs
- identifying a person's preferred communication method
- meeting communication needs
- enabling access to appropriate aids to communication.

The CQC undertakes inspection of care services looking at policies, procedures, records and reports, observing daily life in the environment in which the care is provided and interviewing people and their families to ensure set standards are being met. The CQC also investigates complaints made against care services.

Working with the person

There are various ways in which you can work with the person to identify their specific communication need. These can include talking to them, asking them questions and observing them in a variety of situations.

When you observe somebody, you may find that they communicate in a completely different way with their family compared with their doctor, for example. For this reason it is important that you observe the person's interaction with as many different groups of people as possible to ensure you obtain the correct information. You should also observe the person in different environments, such as:

- in the care home/ward
- in the family home
- at the day centre/school/college
- in the community.

A person's communication need may change depending on how confident or comfortable they feel at that time. This is why it is good practice to identify their needs in different places and with different people. You could also observe somebody's communication while they undertake different activities, such as those that they really enjoy and more everyday tasks.

It would be good practice to undertake the same observations again but on a different day of the week, as the person may not have been feeling very well, or could just have been having a bad day!

Having the person know that they are being observed can also affect the outcome. They may become nervous about being watched, which may affect their communication needs. For this reason it may be of benefit to observe the person discreetly without them knowing.

Talking to the person about things they enjoy such as a favourite hobby, pastime or special interest could enable you to identify a specific communication need. Asking questions, both open and closed, could help you identify things in more detail. This may include what the person feels they need support with in terms of their communication and how they view their communication needs.

Working with others

If you are required to identify the specific communication needs of somebody you are working with, you may well benefit from speaking with:

- professionals
- advocates
- the person's family
- the person's close friends.

However, the care working environment can be a very busy place. You need to ensure that those people you wish to speak to have the time and are prepared to speak with you. For example, you cannot expect to approach a consultant in the middle of their ward round and ask them to provide you with information on a particular person or their potential communication needs. This action could present many problems; it may not be appropriate to interrupt the consultant at this particular time, the open ward would not be an appropriate place to discuss confidential matters or the consultant may not have all the information you need, as they were not given time to prepare for the questioning!

In order to obtain all the information you require, arrange a suitable time and place to meet with the person. Let them know in advance what information you need, so that they can prepare themselves for the meeting and have the answers to your questions.

It is important to remember that family and friends may not always be able to give you the information you need. This could be because they know the person well, which can 'blinker' their perception of that person. If you know someone very well, you do not always fully identify with any difficulties they may have. You can become accustomed to the way things are and the way people behave to the point that you do not see any difficulties.

2.2 Identifying communication methods or aids that will best suit the individual

Have you ever tried on an outfit in a clothes shop and thought to yourself, 'This doesn't suit me'? You try on clothes before buying them so that you can be sure they fit and are suitable. This is similar when you are identifying communication methods or aids that will best suit the person. You may not always identify the best method or aid first time around and you may have to try different methods until you find one that suits the person.

Matching communication needs with methods or aids

Having looked at the various methods and aids to communication earlier, you may be able to start identifying what communication needs they could meet. For example, British Sign Language may be suitable for someone who is deaf. However, not all methods or aids are that easily matched to the communication need or indeed to the person. Table 2 examines different types of method or aid and abilities they may suit.

When a communication method or aid has been identified as being potentially suitable for the person, it is good practice to allow the person sufficient time to become accustomed to it. After an agreed amount of time, the method or aid should be assessed as to how well it meets the person's needs. This is discussed in more detail in section 6.2 of this unit.

2.3 How and when to access information and support about identifying and addressing specific communication needs

As a support worker you will be continually up-skilling and updating your knowledge and practices as required by the General Social Care Council's (GSCC) Code of Practice in England (see page 32 for other countries). This is covered in detail in Unit SHC 32.

In relation to communication, it is important that you access information about identifying and addressing specific communication needs so that you support the person in the best possible way that you can. It may be that you are a new support worker or the person is new to your area of care. Whatever the reason may be, accessing information and support will help you to work with the person, giving them the best support that you can.

Method or aid	Abilities needed	Need suitable for
Pen and paper	Reading or writing	Unable to speak or hear, short- and long-term memory loss
Photographs	Seeing	Unable to speak or hear, short- and long-term memory loss
Objects of reference	Seeing	Unable to speak or hear, short- and long-term memory loss
Symbols	Seeing	Unable to speak or hear
BSL	Using both hands	Unable to speak or hear
Makaton	Using hands	Difficulty speaking
PECS	Seeing	Unable to speak or hear
Finger spelling	Using hands and spelling words	Unable to speak, hear or see
Interpreter	Using a recognised language including BSL	Unable to speak the language of others
Advocate	None required	All needs, especially learning disabilities
Braille	Using hands and fingers	Unable to see

Table 2: Communication methods/aids and the abilities they suit.

Accessing information

The organisation for which you work will have its own policies and procedures detailing how to work with people with specific communication needs. Some of these policies will have been written to include parts of the country's regulatory body's Code of Practice as well as the National Minimum Standards. As a support worker it is your responsibility to ensure you are aware of your organisation's policies and adhere to them accordingly.

People's records

All organisations, whether they are a local authority, the National Health Service (NHS), private or voluntary sector, are required to keep individual records on the care given to all of their patients. Speech and language professionals as well as psychologists and psychiatrists would generally compile records relating to specific communication needs.

As you will be aware from other units, all information and records kept relating to a person are protected by the Data Protection Act 1998. This Act governs who is able to gain access to personal information and how that information can be used. Under this Act it is illegal

What useful information can records contain?

349

to disclose certain information about one person to another. This is also true in the case of medical records under the Medical Records Act 1990. Accessing computer records will usually require a password. This is to prevent the records being accessed by others who do not have the right to see them. In larger organisations, such as the NHS, you may need to access records, both paper and computer, through the medical records officer or another similar person who is responsible for the storage and maintenance of patients' records. In smaller organisations, accessing records may be easier as they are available to most members of the care team.

There may be times when you are unable to access records or information relating to the specific communication needs of people. Some may not have used specialist services for many years, therefore records might not have ever been created. Where information is not available, you will need to use alternative strategies in accessing it. This could be from the Internet, books, journals or reports and reviews.

Using the Internet

The Internet is a very good way of obtaining information, providing you know what you need. When accessing information on specific communication needs through the Internet, it is helpful to know what disability or health condition you are looking at in relation to the communication need – for example, communication needs for people with hearing and visual disabilities.

It is important to remember that the Internet contains a vast array of information from many sources. To ensure the accuracy, currency and validity of the information, you may want to access sites of organisations that are relevant to the disability you are researching.

Reading books, journals, reports or reviews

Your local library or college library should have a section on communication. Within this section you should be able to find some books on specific communication needs. The information can be very detailed and extensive with so many books to choose from. Again, as with the Internet, you need to be clear on what information you are looking for.

Ensure the information you find is up to date.

Doing it well

Accessing records and information

- When accessing information relating to people, you must always be mindful of confidentiality.
- Ensure that no one else can see the information when you are looking at paper records or computer records.
- When speaking with others, make sure no one can overhear your conversation.

Accessing support

To ensure you are able to support somebody's communication needs fully, you may need to work in conjunction with other professionals and specialists. There are a number of specialists who can work with people to support their communication either directly or indirectly. Each specialist's role is very detailed, but a brief overview of their involvement with people with specific communication needs is given here.

Do you know how occupational therapists can help the person develop communication skills?

- **Behavioural support service workers** are professionals who work with people and their care givers in developing appropriate methods for the person to express themselves in non-challenging ways. Any form of behaviour can be seen as communication. However, for it to be effective, the behaviour displayed needs to be acceptable.
- **Occupational therapists** support the person to develop fine motor skills (hand and finger skills) to maximise their potential for independence. Some methods of communication require the use of fine motor skills, including the use of keyboards (see section 5.1).
- **Psychiatrists** are medical doctors who look into why people behave in certain ways. They assess and treat people who have conditions such as learning disabilities, mental health problems, dementia, behaviour disorders and epilepsy. As behaviour is a form of communication, the input from a psychiatrist can be very informative in supporting the person's communication needs.

- **Psychologists** are involved in assessing patterns of behaviour associated with certain conditions. These could include depression or anxiety. In addition to this, psychologists offer assistance to support workers in ways of working with people, following a psychological model such as the cognitive behavioural approach (how the person sees or understands things).
- **Speech and language therapists** assess and support the person's speech development. They may also work with people who have difficulty swallowing. The therapist works closely with other professionals and the family of the person to ensure the communication methods are used correctly to maximise effectiveness.

Accessing support from others is not an admittance of failure – rather the opposite. As a support worker, you are not expected to know everything and be able to support everyone. Admitting that you do not know something or that you need support is a strength. By seeking and accessing support for yourself and the person, you are ensuring that they receive the most appropriate help to enable their communication needs to be met.

3. Be able to interact with individuals using their preferred communication

3.1 Preparing the environment to facilitate communication

The environment in which you support somebody to communicate effectively is just as important as the support you give that person. They must feel comfortable and secure in their surroundings if communication is to be effective. The acronym LISTENS describes how the environment should be prepared when you are communicating with people (see Table 3).

The environment on the whole needs to feel welcoming. People who feel uncomfortable either physically or emotionally will find communicating very difficult.

3.2 Using agreed methods of communication to interact with the individual

Identifying a suitable method of communication for those who have a specific communication need can take much time and effort. Therefore it would be a complete waste of time if you did not use the methods identified and agreed. More importantly the person you are interacting with may not understand what you are communicating if you did not use the agreed communication method. By using this agreed method you are recognising the need of the person and respecting their individuality. The method would have been agreed by professionals, colleagues and family members as well as by the person. For you to ignore

Lighting	The lighting needs to be bright enough for people to see each other's faces clearly, especially if they have a visual disability. However, it should not be so bright that it makes people squint.
Interruptions	The environment should be free from interruptions. You could put a 'Do Not Disturb' sign on the door, or take the telephone off the hook.
Seating	The seats should be comfortable to sit in and arranged so that those involved in the communication are facing each other without any obstacles, such as desks, blocking the view of each other.
Temperature	The room should be warm but cool enough to be comfortable without sweating. If the room is too warm or not warm enough, those involved in the communication will not be able to concentrate fully.
Empowering	The needs of the person should be put first. They should be supported to feel that they are in control and for this to be the case, the environment should be suitable for their communication needs, containing all of the tools needed to support their communication fully.
Noise	Any background noise such as radios or televisions should be reduced to a minimum. Background noise can be very off-putting and may cause the person to lose concentration or be distracted by what is going on around them.
Secure	The person needs to feel safe to aid effective communication. They need to feel the safety of their personal well-being as well as the safety of the information they disclose.

Table 3: LISTENS.

Supporting Ian's communication

Ian has no speech and no hearing. He makes his needs known by pointing. He also has some limited use of Makaton, but has difficulty in grasping new concepts. You would like to assist Ian in devising an activity programme for each day of the week.

1. How are you going to establish what Ian's interests are, taking into account he has no speech or hearing?

2. Once you have established his interests, how are you going to enable him to plan what he would like to do each day? Describe the format you would use.

3. Identify the advantages and disadvantages of your chosen format. Provide evidence of the format that you would use.

the agreed method and use a different way to communicate with the person would be the same as you saying to the professionals, colleagues and family that you know better than they do. You would be disrespecting everyone. Your actions would be unprofessional and potentially damaging to the person and the support they require.

Reading the support plan

The person's support plan should detail the communication method to be used when you interact with them. It should detail the specific communication need and any aids you may require. It is important that you read the support plan on a regular basis to keep yourself up to date in supporting the person's communication needs.

Request training

If you are unsure about using the agreed communication method, ask someone to explain it to you. You may benefit from attending a formal training session to improve your skills to enable you to use the agreed method. Alternatively, you could watch another member of staff who is experienced in using the agreed method.

3.3 Monitoring the individual's responses to check the effectiveness of communication

Is the communication method being used suitable for the person? Does it meet all of their needs or only some of them? Is the person left satisfied after the interaction or are they confused or frustrated? These are the types of questions you need to be asking yourself during and after any interaction with somebody who has a specific communication need.

Suitability

Using the example in section 2.2 on page 348, if you purchased an item of clothing and on getting it home decided it really did not suit you, you would take it back to the shop and exchange it for another item of clothing. It can often be the case that what we once thought suited us is no longer suitable. This change can come about for a number of reasons. Within communication, the person's ability may have changed, making the agreed method of communication unsuitable. The change could be a positive or a negative one. The person's ability could have improved or decreased. If the person's method of communication is no longer suitable, it will most likely be ineffective.

Monitoring responses

When you are interacting with the person, you need to be aware of the responses they make. These responses can be verbal or non-verbal. If you ask them a question, using their agreed method of communication, and the answer you receive back is known to be incorrect, it could be that the method of communication you used was not suitable. The answer the person gave may be incorrect because they did not understand the question. As well as the verbal response, you also need to monitor non-verbal responses such as facial expressions and body language. Does the person look confused when you interact with them, or do they look frustrated? Either of these responses could be an indicator that they are finding it difficult to understand you; the communication method you are using is ineffective.

Remember to monitor the person's responses after your interaction. If they repeat what they initially communicated with you, then the interaction you have just had was not successful. If the person approaches another member of staff communicating to them what they had to you, then it could mean again that your interaction had not been successful.

Observe the person's body language. Clues to frustration or confusion can include:

- interwoven clenched fingers — usually hands would be on a table or held across stomach or on lap
- thumb(s) clenched inside fist(s) — this can be a signal of repression
- hand clasping wrist — clasping a wrist, which may be behind the back or in open view, can be a signal of frustration, as if holding oneself back.

Know what information you are looking for.

The above examples of body language are given as a guide only. It should also be remembered that reading a person's body language is not an exact science.

3.4 Adapting your practice to improve communication

When communicating with people who have a specific communication need, you must be aware of your use of formal and informal language, as both could cause confusion in certain situations. Confusion often occurs when one person interprets a word or gesture to mean something different to how it was intended. An example of this can be seen when informal words are used such as 'kid'. Informally this is a child, but some people may interpret the word kid as a young goat. Table 4 shows some other examples.

Activity 3

Formal and informal words

Look at the informal words in the left-hand column of Table 4 and see if you can identify another meaning for the word other than the formal word given in the right-hand column.

Informal	Formal
Lit up	Illuminated
Job	Occupation
Take on	Employ
Give	Donate, contribute
Times	Multiply
Dad	Father
Spud	Potato
Guts	Courage
Need	Require
Jam	Preserve
Won't	Will not
Gutted	Devastated
OK	Satisfactory
Ask	Enquire
Phone	Telephone
Plane	Aeroplane

Table 4: Examples of informal versus formal terms.

When you are using non-verbal communication to support somebody, you must be aware of potential cultural differences. What is acceptable in one culture can cause great offence in another. Some examples are as follows.

- In Makaton, pointing one finger on each hand from the top of your head is the sign for a cow. In Japan, this same gesture means angry.
- The French use pulling down their cheek from below the eye to mean, 'I don't believe you.'
- In Iran the thumbs-up sign is extremely obscene.
- In Japan, the raising of your eyebrows is indecent.
- Some Asian cultures smile to cover emotional pain or embarrassment.
- In the Philippines and Korea, showing your palm up is rude.
- In Turkey, nodding of the head with a hand gesture to the heart is a polite refusal.

As you can see, many gestures you might consider as day-to-day could land you in a great deal of trouble in other parts of the world!

Think about how you communicate — do you speak quickly? If so, you may need to slow down to enable people to follow what you are saying. Do you tend to speak quietly? If so, you may need to raise the volume of your voice to enable people who have a hearing difficulty to hear you clearly.

Be mindful of how you interact with people. It may not always be the case that the person is the cause of the communication difficulty. If you do not adapt the way you communicate to meet their needs, then it is you that is causing the communication difficulty.

Limit your own words

To encourage the person's communication, reduce your own words to those that the person will be able to understand and take in. If they become agitated or upset, reduce your communication to visual aids only. Hearing sounds or seeing mouth movements that you cannot follow can cause confusion if they are made too quickly or become excessive — just think how you might react to hearing a long stream of jargon!

Reflect

Think back to a time when you have needed to adapt your own communication to support others to communicate effectively. What was it about your communication that you had to change? Was the change effective?

4. Be able to promote communication between individuals and others

4.1 Supporting the individual to develop communication methods

Communication is important in everyday life. Not just verbal speech but everything that is needed for effective communication. As a support worker you have a duty of care to ensure the needs of a person are met; this includes communication.

Developing communication methods

If you are a parent or are close to a young child, you will appreciate the feeling you get when that child says its first word. Because you are so pleased, the child wants to continue pleasing you by saying more and more. The child receives praise and attention, which motivates them to continue. This could be worked in the same way for the people you support. The praise that you give will need to be age-appropriate, but the motivation may come from other means.

Activities in everyday life

To develop communication methods, the person could take part in various development activities. As with any activity, they need to be motivated.

Whenever somebody with a specific communication needs attempts to interact with you, you must acknowledge that interaction straight away. Ignoring the person is a sure way for them to regress or remove themselves from interacting with others, in the fear that they will be rejected again.

You need to acknowledge that you have understood what the person has communicated to you. You can do this by repeating back part of what the person has communicated to you, or you can fulfil their request if one has been made.

The television is often a distraction within communication but it can also be used effectively to develop communication. You could ask the person what they are watching, what they think is going to happen next, who their favourite character is and why.

Turn a shopping trip into an activity by encouraging the naming of grocery items in the shopping trolley. Use certain items as a reward if the person is able to name the item or describe its colour or shape.

Whatever activity you encourage and support the person to take part in, it is important that you acknowledge and praise any attempts they make to communicate.

4.2 Providing opportunities for the individual to communicate with others

Communicating with the same person can sometimes become boring or stale as you run out of things to communicate about. To support somebody's communication development, it is important that they interact with others so that they can experience differing levels and types of communication. These opportunities can be set up purposely or they can be spontaneous whenever the chance arises.

Discussion groups

Regardless of whether the person lives alone or in a large care home, there are various discussion groups they could join in the community. If you cannot find one, why not set up your own discussion group?

If you work in a care environment where there is more than one person that you support, you could set up reminiscing groups. You can arrange different areas to look back on and discuss weekly, fortnightly or however often the group would like to meet. As a group you could talk about activities that have been undertaken together or holidays. You could discuss local news articles, films or special events such as the World Cup.

Reminiscing can often occur naturally, such as when an older person is watching an old film.

There are various materials that can be used to aid reminiscence:

- photographs, personal mementos, postcards or comics
- records, films, videos or slides, including holiday slides or videos

- television programmes, radio programmes
- ration books, local history books
- famous events (for example, D-day or the Queen's coronation).

Activity 4

Discussion groups

Set up a discussion group with some people. Ask your assessor to observe you encouraging and supporting the people's specific communication needs.

Functional skills

English: Speaking and listening

Set up a discussion group with a minimum of three other people. In the group, discuss how you can encourage and support people you support to communicate. Use this opportunity to encourage others to express themselves by asking relevant questions. Give clear and relevant responses to others, and adapt what you say to suit the range of people within the group. Present all your information and ideas clearly.

Support independence

While you are supporting somebody, natural opportunities may occur where you could encourage them to communicate for themselves. This may be going to the doctor's, catching the bus, ordering food in a café or restaurant, or purchasing items from a shop. It would not be a good idea to insist the person communicates if they do not feel ready. This could possibly leave them distressed, which might cause their communication to regress.

Doing it well

Providing opportunities to communicate

- Give the person a reason to communicate, and encourage them to make choices.
- Limit your own words to prevent confusing the person.
- Arrange the environment to maximise interaction.
- Do not forget your basic communication skills.
- Use reminiscing as a communication tool.

4.3 Supporting others to understand and interpret the individual's communication

It is not always people who have a specific communication need that people find difficult to understand. Some people speak so fast, or have such a broad accent, that it can take some time to get used to that person before you can start understanding what they are saying. Sometimes, however, you do not always have the opportunity to get used to a person's way of communicating and someone has to interpret what they are saying to you.

As a support worker, you will have plenty of time and opportunities to understand what the person is communicating to you, but not everyone will be so lucky. It can be very frustrating to communicate with someone who does not understand what you are saying. It may also be embarrassing for the person to have someone else translate what they say to help others understand.

Within a support environment the solution can be quite simple — send staff on specialist training to develop a better understanding. Unfortunately you cannot send every member of the public on a training course but you could help family and friends of the person to gain a better understanding of the communication method that the person uses. This can be done through training or one-to-one explanations.

To save the person embarrassment while they are in the community, you need to be discreet when translating what they communicate. You can do this by repeating what the person communicates and end with, 'Is that right?' This way you are still involving the person and are not presuming what they have said. Try not to start with 'he said' or 'she said', as this tends only to bring more attention to the person's communication difficulty.

With time and patience from community members, the person's communication method will be better understood, making it easier for them to take a fuller part in community activities.

4.4 Supporting others to be understood by the individual by use of agreed communication methods

Much like supporting others to understand the person, it is equally important for them to understand others. Some may have a specific communication method when they are communicating but are able to understand clearly when others communicate with them. The following case study explains this a little further.

Case study

Memory's bell

Memory lost her ability to speak when she had a stroke four years ago. Despite her obvious physical disability, Memory enjoys a full life. She lives on her own, does her own shopping and enjoys going to bingo on a Wednesday evening. The local bingo club know Memory very well and often greet her, saying, 'Are you feeling lucky tonight? Don't forget to ring that bell loudly.' Memory has attended the Wednesday evening bingo session for months and she is well known by others who attend the session.

One week, however, Memory was not able to go to the club on the Wednesday so she went on the Thursday instead. When she purchased her bingo tickets she wrote down how many tickets she wanted so the bingo staff could understand her. Behind her was a group of young men and young ladies. The ladies started laughing, saying, 'How is she gonna play bingo when she can't speak? What if she gets a full house?' At that Memory turned round to face the group, smiled and rang her bell as loud as she could. The faces of the ladies in the group went very red with embarrassment and one of them said, 'Well, we didn't know that she could hear, we thought 'cos she doesn't speak she couldn't hear either.' How wrong they were!

1. Does Memory need any support in understanding what others are communicating? Explain the reason for your answer.
2. How do you think Memory enabled the staff in the bingo hall to understand that when she rang her bell she was calling a full house?

5. Know how to support the use of communication technology and aids

5.1 Specialist services relating to communication technology and aids

Technical aids

Although technical aids to support communication have become increasingly more complex over the last few years, they have also become more accessible. As our understanding and development of electronics increases, so do the ever ingenious aids to support communication and promote independence. For example, people with sight loss can have access to a talking microwave; a hand-held CCTV scanner which magnifies print on an ordinary television, and computers which read out the text on the screen.

Each year an organisation called 'Communication Matters' holds a conference on the latest communication aids available. An association closely related to this organisation is the UK Trade Association of Communication Aid Suppliers (CASC). The CASC organises roadshows around the country demonstrating all the aids available to support communication.

> **Activity 5**
>
> ### Obtaining information
>
> Identify and attend an organised event which demonstrates the availability and uses of communication technology and aids. Obtain any literature on aids you feel could benefit those you support. The following link is for CASC roadshows: www.communicationmatters.org.uk/page/road-shows

Some examples of the types of technology aids available include the following.

- Talking photo album – a 24-page photo album that allows you to record a 10-second message. This is a useful communication aid for people with learning disabilities, dementia and sight loss.
- 'Listen to me' – this device has 12 message buttons on which you can record up to 10 seconds of speech, sound or music. Each large button has a clear sleeve in which to put a picture or symbol relating to the sound. It is very portable and lightweight, making it easy for the person to take anywhere. This is a good aid for all people with a specific communication need.
- 'Go Talk 9+' – an easy-to-use speech output device, which has nine message keys, each having five levels. The message keys are large and can be changed using the overlays stored in the back of this portable, slim communication device.
- Lightwriter – a portable device into which the person types what they want to say. The screen is large enough for the recipient to read, enabling private conversation when required. This device comes with a synthesiser option, which allows the typed text to be played back through speech.

There are many more sophisticated communication aids available, which are designed to translate text into speech. Many computers are now able to take the software required to provide this facility; however, the person still needs to have the ability to input the text into the computer.

The cost of technical aids varies considerably but this is often outweighed by the benefits to the person in providing a means of communication and all that comes with this ability.

5.2 Types of support to use communication technology and aids

In today's society the use of technology is becoming second nature. This does not mean, however, that all people will be efficient in using communication technology or aids. Many may have never used a form of technology before.

As a support worker, you have the responsibility to ensure that the person uses any communication technology or aid for its intended purpose. You should make them aware of any potential dangers such as using electrics near to water. Risk assessments should be carried out to determine any possible harm coming to the person while using the aid, and measures put in place to reduce any possible risks.

A Lightwriter has many benefits.

Support

The level of support required by people using communication technology or aids may vary from person to person. It is important that support is arranged from the beginning. In many cases the communication technology or aid fails simply because the person received little or no support in using the aid. Support can be provided in various ways at various times. Some people may require regular support in using the communication technology or aid while others may require very little support after the initial set-up.

Training

In order to ensure that the person uses the communication technology or aid correctly, training must be given. This may need to be given not only to the person but also to significant people who may be involved in using the aid, such as staff, family and friends.

The first thing the person and significant others may need training on is the basic functions of the technology – how to turn it on, how to charge it up.

The training may need to continue over a period of time, especially as the person's needs may change or the equipment is upgraded.

When training is given to the person, it may be good practice to introduce the technology or aid gradually. Just receiving the aid for some people may be an emotional upset. The aid could signify to them that their own verbal communication is never going to return. For some this could be a significant change in their lives. Other people may not be able to cope with a large amount of information being given in one go. For these the training will need to be given in small steps to ensure they do not experience information overload.

5.3 Ensuring communication equipment is correctly set up and working properly

On first receiving a communication aid or technological piece of equipment, it is vital that it is set up by a professional. This is to ensure the piece of equipment is working correctly and is free from faults. If the equipment is set up by an inexperienced person, it may not be set up correctly, which could affect how it is used by the person.

Most communication aids are designed to be portable and are usually built to withstand knocks. However, the equipment should be checked daily, before use, to ensure any mains cable is free from damage and that there are no loose or exposed wires. This is to prevent the person being exposed to potential electrical shocks.

Consideration also needs to be given to the health and safety of the person when using electronic aids. Following health and safety guidelines a qualified, approved electrician must first check all pieces of electronic equipment to declare fitness for use. This is known as Portable Appliance Testing (PAT). This topic is covered in more detail in Unit HSC 037. It may be important to identify a key person who will be responsible for the day-to-day maintenance of the equipment, ensuring that it remains fully charged and ready to use at all times. This task will be very important to the person who uses the communication aid. They would not want their only means of communicating failing during an interaction with others. This would be like you losing your voice halfway through a conversation. This could leave the person without any means of communicating effectively. Look back at section 1.6 to remind yourself of how this may affect the person.

6. Be able to review an individual's communication needs and the support provided to address them

6.1 Collating information about an individual's communication and the support provided

Collating or collecting information about somebody's communication and the support that is provided is essential in monitoring the effectiveness of the person's communication. You can collect the information you require through a number of methods.

Observing the person

Observation of somebody is a useful tool in identifying a specific communication need, as we saw in section 2.1. It is also an important tool in collecting information on the effectiveness of the support that is given.

You may have used this method with your own family or friends, watching them and noticing changes. For example, you may have observed a younger sibling riding their bicycle for the first time without stabilisers. You can recognise that the support you gave your younger sibling has worked.

Feedback from others

Talking to family and friends about how they feel the support the person receives is helping their communication is another way of collecting the information you require. The feedback you receive from the person's family may be invaluable in filling in those gaps when you do not work with the person.

Talk to other members of staff, professionals and the person themselves. How the person views their communication and the support they receive is very important. Colleagues, professionals and family and friends may feel the person's communication is developing well and may be happy with the support they receive. If this view is not shared by the person themselves, then this needs to be addressed. If they are not happy, they may not be motivated to continue using the form of communication which has been identified as being suitable. They may even opt not to use any method at all, which could leave them without any means of communicating.

Recording information

The information that you collate needs to be documented or recorded. This is so everyone involved in the person's support can be kept up to date with their specific communication needs. You may have gathered a lot of information about the person's communication and the support that they receive, but you should not keep your findings to yourself. To benefit the person, your findings must be shared and discussed further with everyone involved in the person's support. This is discussed in more detail in section 6.2.

Your organisation may have recording sheets of its own or methods by which you need to record your findings. It is important that you record factual information, meaning things that you see, hear and touch rather than feel emotionally. All records that you produce must be placed in the personal file of the person you support to maintain confidentiality and to ensure that other members of the care team are able to access your findings.

You may want to devise your own recording format, providing it meets with your organisation's approval and the requirements of the Data Protection Act 1998, which states entries should be accurate, legible and complete.

An example of a recording format which you may wish to use or adapt to your own area of work is shown opposite. This example shows findings following initial observations of a person.

Once you have more factual reports from subsequent observations, you may need to discuss them with other members of your team to obtain their views on what they feel the person is communicating. You will need to record your team's discussion and agree on what the person is communicating before giving your baseline assessment outcome.

Your findings may look something like the example on page 364.

Name: Amy Maxwell	**Date of Birth:** 17.06.48

Details of disability

Amy has moderate learning disabilities, no verbal speech and right-sided weakness following a stroke six months ago

Observation 1	**Observation 2**
Details	**Details**
Amy is working with her key worker Martine preparing breakfast	Working with a new member of staff, Mark, in cleaning her bedroom
Date: 18.2.11	Date: 19.2.11
Obs start time: 08.15	Obs start time: 16.25
Obs finish time: 08.40	Obs finish time: 17.15
Obs undertaken by: Daljit Kaur	Obs undertaken by: Daljit Kaur
Communication observed:	**Communication observed:**
Touch	Touch
Amy touched Martine's arm and smiled	None
Object of reference	Object of reference
Amy picked up coffee jar while nodding her head	Amy held up can of polish
Smell	Smell
Amy sniffed at a jar of jam and put it back in fridge	Sniffed Mark's jumper
Visual	Visual
None	Amy looked at her photograph of her family
Movement	Movement
Amy was standing on tiptoes, moving quickly	Amy kept her back to Mark, moved very slowly, head down
Sound	Sound
None	Amy made clicking sound with her tongue

An example of a recording format.

6.2 Evaluating the effectiveness of agreed methods of communication and support provided

In order to evaluate the effectiveness of agreed methods of communication, you need to establish a baseline of the person's ability and communication method. This should be done when they first arrive into your care and is often called an initial assessment. The baseline details where the person is at with regards to their specific communication need, before any support is initiated. Everyone involved with the care and support of the person should be made aware of this baseline so that they can evaluate the effectiveness of any agreed methods of communication.

FINDINGS ON COMMUNICATION OBSERVATIONS

Name: Amy Maxwell   **Date of birth:** 17.06.48

Date of meeting: 23.2.11

Present: Martine Davies (key worker), Mark Forth, Daljit Kaur, Diane Rathband, Dionne Solomon (manager).

Action	What is being communicated
1. Touching your arm and smiling	1. Greeting you hello
2. Picking up coffee jar and nodding	2. I would like a cup of coffee
3. Sniffing at staff clothing	3. I'm checking you out, who are you?
4. Sniffing at food	4. Do I like this food?
5. Putting food away after sniffing	5. I don't like this food
6. Standing on tiptoes	6. I'm happy or excited
7. Moving quickly	7. I like what I'm doing (activity)
8. Moving slowly	8. I do not like what I'm doing (activity)
9. Turning back to staff	9. I do not know you, I'm shy
10. Making clicking noise with tongue	10. I'm nervous or worried
11. Looking at her family photograph	11. I miss my family and want to talk about them

An evaluation of what a person is communicating.

Using your baseline assessment you will now be able to evaluate the effectiveness of the way the person communicates. To do this you will need to compare your baseline assessment with your current findings. These findings could be from your own observations or from feedback of others.

Comparing the baseline with your current findings will help you to identify the effectiveness of the agreed methods of communication.

If changes have occurred, it is important to identify why these have come about. Positive changes may indicate that the agreed communication method is effective; it is helping the person to communicate and interact with others. This would mean the current support they are receiving should be encouraged to continue or possibly adapted to make even more improvement.

Findings which show a decrease in the person's communication ability need to be investigated further to identify the cause. The person may have an underlying health condition or may have developed emotional difficulties which have affected their communication. It could simply be that the agreed method of communication is not having the effect it should. Whatever the cause, the person should be supported to manage their communication ability, to prevent further decrease, and identify alternative methods of communication where possible.

The effectiveness of the person's agreed communication method can be recognised formally, through the reassessment process, or informally by support workers, while working with the person on a day-to-day basis. The formal evaluation of effectiveness should be undertaken yearly and should involve the person and key people in their lives, including their family, friends, partner, speech therapist, GP, psychologist, psychiatrist, occupational therapist, care staff and any other

Many people can be involved in a multidisciplinary review.

significant people involved in the person's life. This is known as a multidisciplinary review.

The most obvious recognition of effectiveness is when the person is no longer able to do what they used to do. Not all changes are for the worse, though! Recognising somebody's ability to do something which they could not do before is an important change which needs to be recorded.

Reasons for recording information on communication changes

Regardless of how changes are recognised, recording and reporting must be undertaken. If you identify the change while working with the person, you should make an entry in their records, stating the date with a factual entry of what was observed or how you identified the change. You should then formally report the changes to the manager or person in charge so that any required actions can be taken immediately. Significant changes in a person's ability to communicate should be referred to the speech therapist or GP involved in their care for professional investigation and monitoring.

For more information on records and record keeping, see Unit HSC 038.

Doing it well

Evaluating effectiveness
- Compare your findings with a baseline assessment to identify effectiveness.
- Encourage support workers, family and friends to note the effectiveness of communication.
- Record and report observations immediately following your organisation's policies.
- Be factual when recording – report what you see or hear, not what you think.

6.3 Ways to support the continued development of communication

Once you have helped to identify and supported the person to use an agreed method of communication, your support should not end there. You will need to work with others to identify ways of supporting the person to develop their communication continually. Once a young child has said their first word, you do not leave it at that. You encourage that young child to say more and develop their communication further.

Progressive development of communication

When somebody masters their agreed method of communication to support their specific communication need, it may be time to introduce alternative methods to aid them to develop their communication further.

The person may be using objects of reference to communicate their needs and be able to make their needs known clearly using this method. To support them to develop further, you may agree that the person should be encouraged and supported to say verbally the word of the item they want. Some may argue, 'Why change something if it is already working?' or 'Why fix something if it is not broken?' The answer is development. If you did not develop yourself either personally or professionally, your practices would become stale. Your self-esteem would reduce and you would lack motivation. This is the same for a person's communication.

You would not be expected to work on your own at this. You would work with others to identify ways to support the continued development of communication. Others may include:

- speech and language therapists
- psychologists
- psychiatrists
- occupational therapists
- behavioural support service specialists.

For more information on each of these job roles, see section 2.3.

Legislation

- Data Protection Act 1998
- Human Rights Act 1998
- Medical Records Act 1990

Further reading and research

- www.ace-north.org.uk (Ace Centre North: 'Giving people a voice'. Tel: 0161 358 0151)
- www.patient.co.uk/showdoc/12 (Patient UK: comprehensive health information as provided by GPs and nurses to patients during consultations)
- www.inclusive.co.uk/infosite/aac.shtml (Inclusive Technology. Tel: 01457 819790)
- www.gscc.org.uk (General Social Care Council)
- *A Simple Cure* (RNID 2004).

Getting ready for assessment

LO1 and LO5

You need to be able to demonstrate or show that you have the knowledge for each of the assessment criteria listed in the standards. You can demonstrate your knowledge with written or verbal explanations. Your knowledge can also be demonstrated using case studies or professional discussions. You may demonstrate some of your knowledge when being observed by your assessor, by explaining what you are doing and why. This may not always be appropriate when you are being observed working with people.

LO2–4 and 6

You need to be able to show to your assessor that you are competent or that you have the skills in doing these things. The main way your assessor will be able to identify your competency will be through observing you working with people and others who are important to the person's well-being.

Your assessor will need to see you working in a real work environment on at least two separate occasions, working with a person in identifying their specific communication need and ways this can be addressed, and helping the person communicate with others. Your assessor will also need to see you reviewing the person's communication needs to ensure the support given meets their requirements.

You can also ask work colleagues to provide you with a testimonial if they see you working.

Unit HSC 3047

Support use of medication in social care settings

This unit is about the way you can understand the principles of support for use of medication in social care settings, for yourself and those who work alongside you. Your workplace may be a home environment or any other facility that provides a health or care service. It provides you with the basic knowledge and skills to support the use of medication to ensure that you understand how to handle medicines safely and to ensure that others are aware of the importance of the safe handling of medicines, regardless of where support is being provided.

In this unit you will learn about:

- **the legislative framework for the use of medication in social care settings**
- **common types of medication and their use**
- **roles and responsibilities in the use of medication in social care settings**
- **techniques for administering medication**
- **how to receive, store and dispose of medication supplies safely**
- **how to promote the rights of the individual when managing medication**
- **how to support use of medication**
- **how to record and report on use of medication.**

1. Understand the legislative framework for the use of medication in social care settings

This section will enable you to identify the legislation that governs the use of medicines in the care and support setting. It will outline the legal classification for **medicines** and also explain the importance of policies and procedures, and how they must incorporate legislative requirements.

1.1 Legislation that governs the use of medication in social care settings

This section covers:

- legislation relating to medicines
- Acts relating to your practice at work
- the Health and Social Care Act 2008 (Regulated Activities) Regulations 2009
- the Mental Capacity Act 2005 (Deprivation of Liberty Safeguards)
- patient records and confidentiality.

Legislation relating to medicines

There are a number of pieces of legislation in place to manage the administering of medicine to people.

- The Medicines Act (1968) requires that the local pharmacist or dispensing doctor is responsible for supplying medication. They can only do this on the receipt of a prescription from an authorised person — for example, a doctor.
- The Misuse of Drugs Act (1971) controls dangerous or otherwise harmful **drugs**, designated as Controlled Drugs (CDs). The main purpose of this Act is to prevent the misuse of Controlled Drugs.
- The Misuse of Drugs and the Misuse of Drugs (Safe Custody) (Amendment) Regulations 2007 specifies about handling, record keeping and storage of Controlled Drugs correctly.
- The Safer Management of Controlled Drugs Regulations (2006) specifies how Controlled Drugs are stored, administered and disposed of. Controlled Drugs must be kept in a Controlled Drug cabinet that complies with these regulations. Records must be made for all Controlled Drug transactions.

Key terms

Medicine – a type of drug, used in the treatment or prevention of a disease

Drug – any substance which, when taken into the body, may modify one of its functions

Guidance documents

The Handling of Medicines in Social Care, published by the Royal Pharmaceutical Society of Great Britain in 2007, is designed to give the reader guidelines for the safe handling of medicines. A copy should be at your place of work. Alternatively you can download it from www.rpharms.com

Acts relating to your work practice

- The Health and Safety at Work Act (1974) underpins regulations intended to reduce the risk posed by hazardous substances.
- The Control of Substances Hazardous to Health (COSHH) Regulations (1999) requires employers to take all reasonable measures to protect their employees from the potentially dangerous substances or materials that they may come into contact with while at work.
- The Hazardous Waste Regulations (2005) defines household and industrial waste and includes medicines that are no longer required. Basically, care homes with nursing must use a clinical waste company to dispose of their unwanted medicines. Other care homes can return medicines to the supplying pharmacy for destruction.

These regulations all direct you towards maintaining high standards of safety when dealing with medicine. Accidents, such as spillages of medicines, needle stick injuries, handling of cytotoxic medicines and safe disposal of excess medication are examples where these acts and regulations relate to medicines. To avoid these, equipment must be provided to deal with any known risk you may have to deal with, in order to reduce the risk of harm to you. This may include gloves, aprons, washing facilities, and spillage kits and sharps disposal containers.

Medicines should not be touched and extra precautions (for example, wearing gloves) must be taken for certain medicines that may cause harm if inadvertently handled – for example, **cytotoxic medicines**. It is also important that all creams and ointments should be applied using gloves to reduce the risk of cross-contamination and also potential harm to you.

Key term

Cytotoxic medicine – any medicine that has a toxic effect on cells

---

Activity 1

Hazardous substances

List hazardous substances in your workplace and how they are stored. Include medicines. Do any medicines or appliances require you to take extra precautions? Does this happen in your workplace?

Reflect

Think about your practice of handling medicines. What health and safety issues do you think occur handling medicines? How do you overcome these? Does your workplace support you in handling medicines safely?

The Health and Social Care Act 2008 (Regulated Activities) Regulations 2009

In England, all providers of health and adult social care must comply with the new Health and Social Care Act 2008 (Regulated Activities) Regulations 2009 and the Care Quality Commission (Registration) Regulations 2009. These regulations describe the essential standards of quality and safety that people who use health and adult social care services have a right to expect.

The new system of regulation is focused on outcomes for people rather than systems and processes. This will make sure that all people can expect services to meet essential standards of quality and safety that respect their dignity and protect their rights.

You can download this information from the **Care Quality Commission's** website at www.cqc.org.uk

---

Key term

Care Quality Commission (CQC) – the independent regulatory body responsible for the regulation of health and adult social care services in England. It also protects the interests of people whose rights are restricted under the Mental Health Act (1983)

In England, the regulation that relates to medicines is Regulation 13 of the Health and Social Care Act 2008 (Regulated Activities) Regulations 2009:

- **13(1)** The registered person must protect service users against the risks associated with the unsafe use and management of medicines, by means of making appropriate arrangements for the obtaining, recording, handling, using, safekeeping, dispensing, safe administration and disposal of medicines for the purposes of the regulated activity.
- **13(2)** In making the arrangements referred to in paragraph (1), the registered person must have regard to any guidance issued by the Secretary of State or an appropriate expert body in relation to the safe handling and use of medicines.

Different standards apply in Wales and Scotland. The regulations are supported by outcome groups that state what the people who use health and adult care services should experience.

Outcome 9: Management of medication

People who use services:

- will have their medicines at the times they need them and in a safe way
- wherever possible will have information about the medicine being prescribed made available to them or others acting on their behalf.

This is because providers who comply with the regulations will:

- handle medicines safely, securely and appropriately
- ensure that medicines are prescribed and given by people safely
- follow published guidance about how to use medicines safely.

Activity 2

Prompts

Look at the prompts for outcome 9. In summary they detail how and what you care for regarding medicines you should provide.

- 9A – providing personalised care through the effective use of medicines
- 9B – managing risk through effective procedures about medicines handling.

Part 2 relates to guidance that you should consider.

- 9C – taking into account relevant guidance
- 9D – promoting people's rights and choices
- 9G – support for their medicines
- 9H – administration of emergency medicines.

Consider these prompts and how you would think about your service, and how you would put these into practice to improve the outcome of the service you provide.

The Mental Capacity Act 2005 (Deprivation of Liberty Safeguards)

The Mental Capacity Act 2005 details that:

- a person is assumed to have capacity to make a decision regarding their care
- a lack of capacity must be clearly demonstrated
- you must take all reasonable steps to help the person make a decision. For example, using counselling or changing the formulation to help a person take their medicines
- an unwise decision by a person does not mean they lack the capacity to make a decision
- if it has been decided that a person lacks the capacity to make a decision about their medication, any further decision made on their behalf must be made in their best interest (not the interests of the care staff, for example)
- the person's rights and freedom of action must be taken into account. The decision taken should show that the least restrictive option or intervention is achieved. For example, it would not be acceptable to sedate somebody in order to stop them wandering around the home.

Overview of Deprivation of Liberty (DoL) safeguards

The DoL safeguards give clear directions that providers must take to protect people not covered by the Mental Capacity Act 2005 to deprive someone of their liberty if it is necessary to protect them. This includes the administration of sedating medicines, so it is important that you are aware of these safeguards.

Patient records and confidentiality

There are two Acts that relate to patient records that are important to you as a care worker.

Access to Health Records Act 1990

This Act defines who can see medical records. The person can see their own medical records, but nobody else can without permission from that person. This includes next of kin and friends.

Data Protection Act 1998

This Act requires any organisation that keeps personal records on computer to register as a data user and they must comply with specific regulations. They must:

- keep information secure
- allow the person to have access to their records
- record only relevant information
- only use and disclose the information for its stated purpose.

Maintaining confidentiality

It is important that you maintain the person's confidentiality at all times. Apart from the person, you should never discuss their clinical condition and the medicines they take with anyone else except the healthcare professionals involved in their care, unless you have the person's written permission. Even then you will only be able to discuss their case with those other specific named people. For example, you may be given permission to discuss the case with the person's next of kin – you could not then talk to your neighbour about it!

Ultimately you are responsible for maintaining the confidentiality of the people you support and you are accountable for your actions if you do discuss their condition and treatment with anyone else without consent.

Case study

Maintaining confidentiality

Rose wishes to know what medicines she is now taking, as she does not feel very well since starting her new tablets.

Rose's daughter Kerry has recently visited her mother and asks you about the medication she is currently taking, as she has noticed that her mother is very drowsy and difficult to wake.

1. Is it acceptable to discuss Rose's medication with her?
2. Can you show Kerry her mother's medical records?
3. What should you say to her?
4. To whom would you address Kerry's concerns?

1.2 The legal classification system for medication

Classification of medicines

Medicines are all classified by the Medicines Act 1968. It is important when working with medicines that you have a good working understanding of the common types of medication. Table 1 shows the main classifications of medicine. You can use it to work out under which category the various medicines you work with should go.

Individual knowledge

Not everything you need to know will be taken from written sources. The person is also an important source of information about the medicines they take. They are the one taking the medicines and have unique and important information about what they want to take and why. Imagine if you were given no say in any medicine you were taking – would you feel comfortable? Similarly if a certain medicine made you feel unwell, you would want to tell the person giving it to you – they will want to do the same.

Activity 3

Using medicine information

Look at three medicines in the home you commonly administer and read the PIL (Patient Information Leaflet), MIMS (*Monthly Index of Medical Specialities*), BNF (*British National Formulary*) and the NHS website on medicines.
- How do the sources of information differ?
- Which was easier to understand?
- Did you learn anything new about these medicines that could benefit the person who takes them?

Functional skills

Maths: Carry out calculations

Liquid medicines are often more expensive that tablets or capsule formulations. Using the BNF for the general costs of medicines, calculate the difference in price for a 28-day cycle of five medicines in liquid or solid formulations, for example, Risperidone, Digoxin, Furosemide, Senna or Metformin. Calculate the cost of the individual dose, then multiply it by the number of doses per day, then the number of days in the cycle (28). (Note that the dose can also be found in the BNF.)

Classification	Abbreviation	Definition	Example
General Sale List medicines	GSL	These must be licensed and are sold in shops, supermarkets and so on, and do not require a pharmacist to be present unless they are purchased from a pharmacy.	Paracetamol (maximum 32 tablets) Gaviscon liquid
Pharmacy medicines	P	These can only be sold in registered pharmacies under the supervision of a pharmacist.	Paracetamol (maximum 100 tablets) Chloramphenicol eye drops
Prescription Only Medicines	POM	These must be prescribed before a pharmacist or dispensing doctor can supply them.	Eumovate cream Oramorph oral solution 10mg/5ml
Controlled Drugs	CD	These must be prescribed by a doctor or other designated clinician. Different rules apply in writing the prescription. Storage and recording are also different.	Oramorph concentrated solution 100mg/5ml Ritalin 20mg/1ml

Table 1: Classifications of medicine.

Names of medicines

There are two names for medicines — the generic (non-proprietary) name and the trade or brand name. The generic name is based on the medicine's main ingredient and the brand name is the manufacturer's name. Normally medicines are prescribed by their generic name, so the pharmacist can then dispense the most cost-effective medicine.

Examples of generic and brand names include:

- Ventolin — this is the brand name for the generic medicine Salbutamol
- Istin — this is the brand name for the generic medicine Amlodipine.

Activity 4

Classification of medicines

Can you name three medicines that are classified as GSL, P, POM and CD that can be found in your workplace?

List five other examples of medicines which are commonly prescribed in your workplace. Write the generic name and an example of a brand name for each.

Controlled Drugs

The Misuse of Drugs Act 1971 legislates the use of Controlled Drugs. These are classified according to the harm that they may cause, if misused. There are three classes: A, B and C. The regulations define the classes of person authorised to supply and possess Controlled Drugs while undertaking their professional duties. There are also five schedules of Controlled Drugs. These specify the requirements governing activities such as manufacturing, supply, possession, prescribing and record keeping.

You may see Schedules 2, 3, 4 and 5 in the course of your duties.

The common Controlled Drugs are listed in Table 2, including examples of branded preparations.

Schedule	Generic name	Brand name (common examples)
3*	Buprenorphine	Temgesic®
2	Diamorphine	
2	Fentanyl	Durogesic®; Durogesic DTrans®; Actiq lozenge®
2	Hydromorphone	Palladone® capsules and SR capsules
2	Methadone	Physeptone®
	Methylphenidate	Ritalin®; Concerta XL®; Equasym®
5**	Morphine (strengths below 13mg/5ml)	Oramorph oral solution®; Oramorph® unit dose vials; Sevredol® oral solution
2	2 Morphine (strengths above 13mg/5ml)	Oramorph® unit dose vials 30mg, 100mg and concentrated solution; Sevredol® tablets and concentrated oral solution; Morcap SR®; MST®; MXL®; Zomorph®
2	Oxycodone	OxyNorm®; OxyContin®
3***	Phenobarbitone	
2	Pethidine	
3*	Temazepam	

Table 2: Common Controlled Drugs (CDs) and brand names.

* CD storage but no register.

** No CD storage or register.

*** No CD storage but register required.

Some exemptions do apply, but often for good practice they should all be stored in a CD cabinet and all transactions recorded regardless of schedule.

1.3 How and why policies and procedures must reflect and incorporate legislative requirements

Outcome 9, regarding the management of medicines, lists the prompts that relate to this outcome group. It states that to provide personalised care to people who use services, the care and treatment they receive must be supported by clear procedures, which must be followed in practice. The procedures should be monitored and reviewed, and explain how up-to-date medicines information and clinical reference sources are made available.

Policies and procedures should not only promote the safety and well-being of the person in the home, but also the safe practices of all care home staff. A good policy should be specific to the service provided. You should be able to read a copy of it easily and undertake any duties to a high standard as expected by the new regulations regarding the safe handling of medicines.

Functional skills

English: Writing
Read through the home's policies for medicines in the care home. In your own words, describe how you could improve the policy to ensure the safety of people you support. Document what you would include or change in the policy on ordering medicines. This needs to be laid out clearly using a suitable format and accurate spelling, punctuation and grammar.

Reflect
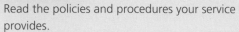

Read the policies and procedures your service provides.
- Do you think they are clear enough to enable you to comply with the standards?
- Could you pick up the policy and follow it to do the required job?
- Could it be better written?
- Does it relate to the specific service you provide or is it a generic (more general) policy?

Activity 5

Policies and procedures
1. Imagine you have just administered the wrong medicine to somebody in your care home. Does the policy in your care home guide you through the process to ensure the safety of the person? Is there any way you could improve the policy?
2. You have recently started as a care assistant in a care home and have been asked to order a medicine for somebody. Does the policy in your home give you enough information for you to do this? What could you include or change to make the policy easier to understand?

Doing it well
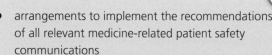

Following policies and procedures
The policies and procedures should include obtaining, safe storage, prescribing, dispensing, administration, monitoring and disposal of medicine.

For the social care setting these should include:

- how medicines which are prescribed 'as required' (PRN) are handled and used
- ensuring that staff handling medicines have the competency and skills needed
- correct arrangements for giving medicines covertly in accordance with the Mental Capacity Act 2005
- recording arrangements when administering medicines
- arrangements for reporting adverse events, drug reactions, incidents, errors and near misses and to reflect on them to prevent further occurrence

- arrangements to implement the recommendations of all relevant medicine-related patient safety communications
- an up-to-date list of medicines for all people who use the service
- arrangements for the management of discharge medicines to allow for continuity of care
- arrangements for medicines management following the death of a person receiving care
- the use of homely remedies
- supporting people to self-administer their own medicines
- procedures that are followed in practice, monitored and reviewed for Controlled Drugs and other medicines that comply with current legislation (Medicines Act 1968, Misuse of Drugs Act 1971 and the Safer Management of Controlled Drugs Regulations 2006).

2. Know about common types of medication and their use

2.1 Common types of medication

As discussed earlier, medicines are classified according to how potent they are. Four classes of medicine were listed: GSL, P, POM and CD. In addition to these there may be other medicines that you come across.

Complementary or alternative medicines

These can be purchased from chemists and supermarkets but a few may be prescribed by medical practitioners. They include vitamins, minerals, nutritional supplements, herbal remedies, aromatherapy, Chinese medicines and homeopathic medicines.

Homeopathic medicines

Homeopathy works by treating the whole person. Homeopathic remedies are believed to work by a principle of 'like curing like'. This means that a substance, which in high doses can cause harm, can cure the same symptoms when given in tiny doses. It is believed that the small dose stimulates the body to heal itself.

Herbal remedies

These can be prescribed by a herbal medical practitioner and are also available from health food shops and pharmacies. They should be used with caution in the elderly, pregnant women and breastfeeding women. Some are known to interact with traditional medicines, and advice should always be taken from a medical practitioner (doctor or pharmacist) before any herbal remedy is administered. A common example of a drug interaction with herbal and traditional medicine is St John's Wort when taken with some medicines used to treat epilepsy.

Chinese medicines

These are used to restore the imbalances in the body that have caused the disease. They are usually prescribed by a traditional Chinese medical practitioner, but some can be purchased over the counter.

2.2 Conditions for which each type of medication may be prescribed

You will need to be familiar with all the types of medicines you administer and what they are for. Access to information about the medicines is important and recognising side effects and common doses is essential for good care of people.

- You should know what all the medicines you administer are for.
- You should know or have a reference source to identify common side effects.
- You should understand why you administer all the medicines you handle.

Activity 6

What are medicines you administer for?

Look at three Medicine Administration Record (MAR) charts. Do you know what each medicine has been prescribed for and what it does?

Look at a person's support plan. Does this include information on the clinical conditions the person has? Can you identify the medicine they have been prescribed to treat it?

Functional skills

English: Reading

Select a minimum of three medicine administration records for people you support. Research information about illnesses and medicines you are unfamiliar with using a range of texts. Summarise succinctly your information on three types of illness and the medications given for them. Use this information for the task above.

Level 3 Health & Social Care Diploma

Activity 7

Commonly used medicines

Complete the following table. Fill in the name of a medicine that you may have administered with the dose and record the common side effects. The first one has been filled in as an example.

You will need good reference sources, for example, BNF, MIMS, PILs or NHS websites. Try to give examples of medicines you have actually administered.

Medicine for the treatment of	Example	Common adult dose	Common side effects
Chest infection	Amoxicillin	250mg three times a day	Sickness, nausea, rash, diarrhoea
Allergies			
Heartburn			
Anticoagulation (to prevent blood clots)			
Depression			
Insomnia			
Anxiety			
High blood pressure			
Asthma			
Nausea			
Pain			
Epilepsy			
Diabetes			
Parkinson's disease			
Dementia			
Cancer			
Anaemia			
Inflammation of the joints			
Eye infection			
Fungal infection			
Ear infection			
Eczema			

Table 3: Medicines, doses and common side effects.

Useful reference sources

The *British National Formulary* (BNF) is a useful book that includes information about medicines including their indications, dose ranges, side effects and possible drug interactions. This is updated and republished every six months, and is a good reference source that every care service should consider buying. It can be viewed online at www.bnf.org or purchased from all good bookshops. However, it is important that you only use the most recent edition – otherwise you could be making important care decisions based on out-of-date information!

Another good reference source is the *Monthly Index of Medical Specialities* (MIMS). This contains the latest information about drugs that are available on prescription or sold over the counter (GSL and P medicines). It can be accessed online at www.mims.co.uk or purchased from MIMS, Haymarket Subscriptions, 174 Hammersmith Road, London W6 7JP.

Information can also be taken from the Product Information Leaflet (PIL), which must be supplied by the pharmacist for each medicine dispensed. This is written by the drug manufacturer and explains all about the medicine, giving essential information about its use – for example, how to take it, any side effects, cautions and correct doses. In all these cases it is crucial that you follow the information and guidance given from these sources of information. Again this can be found electronically at www.medicines.org.uk. You can download the PIL or the SPC (Summary of Product Characteristics) which gives more detailed information about the medicines.

The NHS site is another good reliable website for medicine information (www.nhsdirect.nhs.uk or www.nhs.uk). It documents what medicines are prescribed for and also gives detailed information about most clinical conditions. It may be useful when writing support plans and finding information about symptoms of medical conditions, for example.

If any information is unclear, speak to your pharmacist, who will be able to offer you advice.

2.3 Changes that may indicate an adverse reaction to a medication

Any person may experience side effects or adverse reactions to any medicine they may take. You will learn how to recognise the difference between the two, when to seek help and how and where to document them.

Common side effects

Examples include:

- rashes
- breathing difficulties
- swelling
- nausea
- vomiting
- diarrhoea
- stiffness
- shaking
- headaches
- drowsiness
- constipation
- weight gain.

All medicines cause side effects or adverse reactions. These can vary from person to person. All details should be recorded in the person's daily records. Side effects

Case study

Why are medicines prescribed?
- Senna tablets. Dose: two at night when required.
- Lactulose syrup. Dose: 15ml twice a day when required.
- Movicol sachets. Dose: one daily when required.

The care assistants have been administering all three medicines every day. After a week or so Kathleen began having mild diarrhoea, which became progressively worse. The care assistants took advice and stopped giving all three medicines and gave Loperamide 2mg capsules, as prescribed. When Kathleen's health improved they resumed giving the three medicines again and continued to give Loperamide 2mg capsules.

1. Why did Kathleen keep having diarrhoea on a regular basis?
2. Why were Loperamide 2mg capsules prescribed?
3. What further action should the care assistants take to prevent this happening again?

may be minor and self-limiting, and stop over time, or they may become so unpleasant that the clinician may have to discontinue prescribing the medicine. This should be documented to prevent the medication from being prescribed again and so that care assistants are aware of problems with a particular medicine.

Adverse effects are unwanted or unexpected reactions after taking a medicine. They may be serious enough to seek immediate medical help – for example, in the case of **anaphylactic shock**. Again these must be recorded on the Medicine Administration Record (MAR) chart, facing page and care notes to alert staff if the medicine is accidentally prescribed and dispensed.

Key term

Anaphylactic shock – extreme immediate reaction by the body to a medicine

Reflect

Your duty of care does not stop at just administering medicines. You must monitor and record any adverse reactions or side effects to the medicines you administer. The best place is the daily records and the MAR chart, and a support plan may need to be written for some clinical conditions. The pharmacist should be informed of all adverse drug reactions and allergies to enable them to make a clinical judgement for all medicines prescribed to be dispensed.

Doing it well

In the event of an adverse reaction to a medicine

- Inform the manager and seek professional help immediately (this may include calling an ambulance).
- Observe the person.
- Document all adverse reactions and what you have done.
- Treat the symptoms following clinical advice or take the person to the hospital if you cannot treat the symptoms as directed by the clinician.
- Record the medicine and the reaction in the person's care notes and MAR chart to prevent it from happening again.
- Inform the person's own doctor and pharmacist as soon as possible if you have not already done so.

Case study

Adverse drug reaction

Anna has recently been prescribed Flucloxacillin for an infection in her toe. You have administered two capsules only and she has developed a red rash all over her body and her hands are beginning to swell up. She is also taking Aspirin 75mg daily, Ramipril 5mg daily and Bendroflumethiazide 2.5mg daily.

1. What is the most likely reason for the red rash and swollen hands?
2. What action would you take if this happened to somebody you support?
3. What records would you keep?
4. How would you prevent this from happening again?

Functional skills

Maths: Carry out calculations with numbers of any size in a practical context

Anna is prescribed digoxin elixir 50 micrograms/ml. Her newly prescribed dose is 62.5mg od. Calculate the volume of digoxin in millilitres (ml) that she must be administered and the volume needed for a 28-day cycle.

You must:

- be aware of the common side effects of the medicines you administer
- have current, up-to-date medicine information and be familiar with how to use these reference sources
- know what action to take if the person's condition deteriorates rapidly
- make sure you fully document all your actions and observations so other staff are also aware of a potential problem.

Case study

Taking professional advice

Mrs Ghuman had been prescribed Tramadol 100mg, to be taken four times a day for severe pain. She has recently been crying and complaining that there is a crocodile at the end of her bed waiting to eat her and that it is following her around the home. Care staff thought this might be due to her underlying dementia and decided to inform the old-age psychiatrist at Mrs Ghuman's next appointment. A pharmacist visited the home during his routine visit and staff told him about Mrs Ghuman's recent behaviour. Tramadol was prescribed at the maximum daily dose of 400mg and she had been taking it regularly for three weeks.

The pharmacist advised that the Tramadol might be causing Mrs Ghuman to hallucinate and advised the staff to contact the doctor to discuss a change in medication to treat the pain.

1. Look up the medicine Tramadol in a good reference source. List the side effects.
2. What action should the care staff have taken to enable them to identify this adverse drug reaction earlier?
3. Who could have been contacted earlier to give advice?

Activity 8

MAR charts

Look through some MAR charts and see if any person in your care home is allergic to any medicine.
Complete Table 4.

Question	Your response
Was the allergy recorded in the pre-assessment form?	
Is it recorded in the support plans and/or MAR chart?	
Has the allergy been recorded on every MAR chart? Check the last 12 months to see if it is always recorded and by whom.	
Have you informed the pharmacist so they can add the allergy to the pharmacist records?	
Does your medication policy support you through the process of what to do in the event of a person's adverse reaction to a medicine?	

Table 4: Questions on allergies to medication.

3. Understand roles and responsibilities in the use of medication in social care settings

This section will enable you to describe the roles involved in the process of prescribing and dispensing medicines. Homely remedies will be discussed.

3.1 Roles and responsibilities of those involved in prescribing, dispensing and supporting use of medication

You will need to be familiar with what a legal prescription looks like and also the number of people who are able to write them. You will learn prescription jargon to enable you to read and check prescriptions you will see.

The prescription

Most prescriptions you will come across will be NHS prescriptions but you may also occasionally see private prescriptions or hospital prescriptions. People normally receive medicines prescribed by a clinician, such as a doctor, dentist and in some instances a nurse or pharmacist. NHS prescriptions (FP10) are written by a doctor before being dispensed by a community pharmacist or dispensing doctor. The majority of medicines administered by carers will have been dispensed against a prescription written by a clinician. As a care assistant, your most important job will be to check the prescription before it is dispensed and to check the dispensed medicine and MAR chart received into the service for accuracy before you administer the medicines. Any discrepancy must be addressed with the prescriber or pharmacist immediately. You cannot alter any prescription even if you believe it to be incorrect.

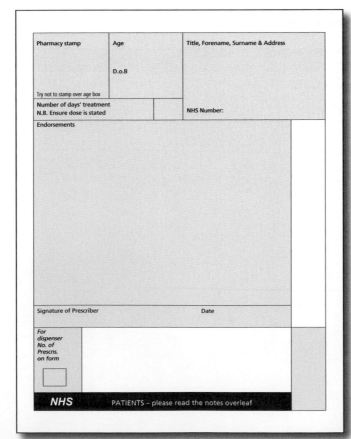

- A prescription is valid for 13 weeks from the date it was written.
- The only exception is a prescription for Controlled Drugs, which is valid for only 28 days from the date of issue.
- The name and address of the doctor must be stamped on the prescription.
- Prescriptions can be computer written or hand written, but must be signed by the doctor or other registered clinician to be valid.

An example of a prescription.

Prescription jargon

Doctors once used to write prescriptions in Latin and many directions on prescriptions today are still written in Latin, albeit an abbreviated version. Table 5 lists some common abbreviations you may see on a prescription.

Latin abbreviation	Direction
Od	Each day, daily, once a day
Bd	Twice a day
tds, tid	Three times a day
Qds, qid	Four times a day
Ac	Before food
Pc	After food
Cc	With food
Prn	When required
om, mane	In the morning, each morning
on, nocte	At night, every night
mdu	As directed
stat	Given at once
I.U	International units
mg	Milligram
mcg	Microgram (this should normally be written in full)
ml	Millilitre
im	Intramuscular
iv	Intravenous
neb	Nebule
Guttae, G	Eye drops
elix	Elixir
susp	Suspension

Table 5: Latin abbreviations for direction.

You are responsible for signing the back of the prescription and ticking the reason for exemption from prescription charges, if applicable, if you are responsible for the person's medication within the service you provide. Evidence for exemption may be asked for by the pharmacist.

The Medicines Act 1968 permits the administration of a prescribed medicine by a third party in accordance with the prescription for that person (with the exception of injections). This enables you to administer to people you support.

3.2 Explaining where responsibilities lie in relation to use of 'over the counter' remedies and supplements

Over the counter or homely remedies

Some medicines that have not been prescribed can still be administered to people. These are usually described as homely remedies. These are medicines which can be purchased over the counter, so are either a GSL or P medicine. They can be administered for certain clinical conditions for a maximum number of doses per day for a set period of time (usually 48 hours). Their purchase and administration must be supported by a homely remedy policy and their use must be fully documented. It is normally up to the registered manager or designated person to decide what homely remedies they purchase and whether their staff have the competence to administer them. Table 6 shows an example of how one homely remedy, paracetamol, can be used.

It is important that all homely remedy policies are checked by either the doctor or the pharmacist to ensure that they are clinically correct.

Indication	For general pain, headaches, period pain
Dose	One or two tablets every four to six hours
Maximum number of doses	Eight tablets in 24 hours
Maximum number of days to be administered before referral to a doctor	Two days (48 hours)
Cautions and warnings	Do not administer if already taking any product containing Paracetamol

Table 6: An example of a homely remedy policy for Paracetamol 500mg tablets.

Reflect

- Do you have a homely remedy policy in your care home?
- Have medicines been purchased to support this policy?
- Could you draft a homely remedy policy for medicines requested to be purchased by the person?
- List common medicines that could be purchased to be administered under a homely remedy policy for your service.

Activity 9

Homely remedy policy

Draft a homely remedy policy for a simple linctus for chesty coughs and a magnesium trisilicate mixture for indigestion, using the format shown in Table 6.

4. Understand techniques for administering medication

This section will enable you to understand the different routes by which medication can be administered and also the different forms in which medicines may be presented for administration. Materials and equipment that can be used to assist the administration of medicines will also be discussed.

4.1 Routes by which medication can be administered

There are various routes in which a medicine can be administered to somebody. This section will discuss the various routes most commonly used to administer medicines.

Routes of administration

There are various ways that people can take medicine — for example, by swallowing, by injection, application on the skin. There are many more ways to take medicine than are commonly thought.

Orally

The majority of medicines are administered via this route. Tablets, capsules, liquids, suspensions and mixtures are all examples of medicines administered orally.

Sublingually

This is where tablets or liquids are administered under the tongue for speed of absorption. Common examples of medicines administered sublingually are GTN spray and tablets for angina or Buprenorphine tablets (Temgesic®) for pain.

Inhalation administration

This method is used mostly for patients who have chronic respiratory problems such as asthma. This enables the medicine to be delivered to the site where it is most needed — the lungs. Inhalers and nebules (for use in a nebuliser) are common examples of this route of delivery.

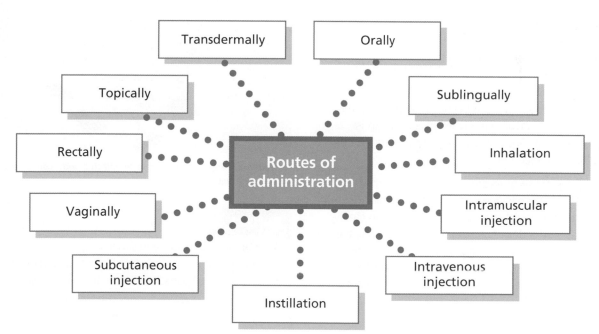

Routes of administration.

Do you use one of these or know anyone who does?

Intramuscular (IM) injection administration

The medicine is injected directly into large muscles in the body, usually in the legs or bottom. This can only be performed by a doctor or trained nurse.

Intravenous (IV) injection administration

The medicine is administered directly into the veins. Medicines are rapidly absorbed into the body via this route, which is advantageous when a situation is life-threatening. Again this can only be performed by a doctor or trained nurse.

It is good practice to record on the MAR chart when the next IM or IV dose is due and who is to administer it (for example, the district nurse). This way you can clearly see whether the dose has actually been administered or not on the due date and appropriate action can be taken if it has not been. It is also advisable to record in the diary when the medicine should be ordered, to ensure a continuous supply.

Subcutaneous injection administration

With this injection, the medicine is administered directly under the skin. A common example of a medicine administered via this route is insulin. Medicines are injected in the fat layer beneath the skin. Care staff may, after suitable training, administer medicines via this route. You should be supported by policies regarding this practice. Again, written consent from the person is required, and their doctor or community nurse must give you permission and training to carry out this procedure.

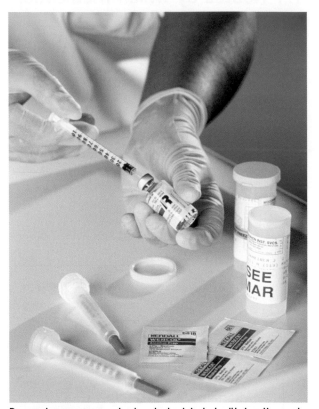

Do you know anyone who has to be injected with insulin, such as someone with diabetes?

Reflect

Think about the people you support.
Do you have any diabetic people who require regular insulin injections? What insulin do they use and what type of injection system do they use? What training is available in your area to enable you to administer insulin?
Look in the BNF to see what different products are available to administer insulin.

Instillation administration

With this method, the medicine is in the form of a suspension or liquid that can be instilled in a number of ways: via the eyes, nose or ears. Again, care staff may administer via this route after suitable training. Ear drops for wax removal and eye drops for the treatment of glaucoma, dry eyes or an eye infection are good examples. Nose drops or sprays are available for allergic conditions such as hayfever or inflammatory conditions of the nose.

Do you find it difficult to put in eye drops?

Rectal administration

Medicines administered into the body by this route are absorbed very quickly. Suppositories are available for this route of administration and are inserted high into the rectum. Again, only members of staff who have received suitable training and been given authorisation should administer medication via this route, as this is an invasive route of delivery.

Rectal diazepam is used for the treatment of epilepsy. In order to treat this condition, diazepam needs to be rapidly absorbed into the bloodstream. Any people prescribed this medicine should have a written protocol recording the correct use of the drug, ideally prepared in conjunction with a clinician. Training is essential for all care workers to ensure they understand the exact clinical symptoms for when it should be administered, the technique of application and any measures to be taken following administration.

Activity 10

Diazepam rectal tubes

This medicine is effective at treating epileptic fits. It is administered rectally for ease of administration as oral medication cannot be taken during a fit. It is rapidly absorbed, so will work faster.
- Are any people you work with prescribed this medicine?
- Is there a protocol detailing its use?
- Look at the PIL and other reference sources to confirm the dose and how to administer it.

Vaginal administration

For medicines administered by this route, pessaries are formulated or creams applied using a special applicator. These are normally used to treat conditions of the vagina – for example, vaginal thrush. Again, only trained staff who have been given authorisation should administer medicines via this route, as this is another invasive route of delivery.

Topical application administration

This is where creams, ointments and gels are applied directly to the skin. They can be used to treat skin conditions or can be used as a delivery route for an analgesic (a painkiller). Care workers are often required to apply external preparations to people. Gloves should always be worn (normally either latex or latex-free) to protect against absorption of the medication through your skin and to prevent cross-contamination.

How often have you been required to apply external preparations to people?

Transdermal patch administration

The transdermal patch is a more common route of administration than a few years ago. Examples include fentanyl patches, Hormone Replacement Therapy (HRT) patches and nicotine patches. The drug is released slowly from the patch over a set period of time and is absorbed through the skin into the bloodstream. The Product Information Leaflet will state the preferred sites of application. Normal sites are the chest, upper arm

and the backs of hands. The skin should be clean, dry and hair-free. The site of application must be varied, in order to reduce the risk of the skin becoming sensitive to the patch. This is important as sensitive skin could lead to inflammation and irritation, and ultimately the discontinuation of the patch. The site of application should be recorded. The person should still be able to have a bath or shower. Once the patch is removed, it should be folded in half to prevent re-application and to deactivate the patch.

Activity 11

Routes of administration and formulations of medicines

Table 7 is a list of medicines. Write down the formulations that are available for each medicine and the route through which they can be administered. The first example is done for you. You will find the information in the BNF, MIMS and SPC.

It is always best to talk to the person and try to understand why they do not want to take a medicine. For example, it may be that the tablets are too big or leave a funny taste in the mouth, make the person feel unwell or they simply cannot swallow them. An alternative preparation or medicine is often available and this can be discussed with the doctor to improve compliance. Your knowledge of alternative formulations will help the person make an informed choice to aid compliance.

Medicine	Formulations available	Route of administration
Salbutamol	Injection	Subcutaneous injection or intramuscular injection
	Solution for intravenous infusion	Slow intravenous injection
	Aerosol inhaler	By mouth by inhalation
	Dry powder inhaler	By mouth by inhalation
	Nebules	Via a nebuliser by mouth
	Tablets or capsules or syrup	Orally by mouth
Buprenorphine		
Clotrimazole		
Fusidic acid		
Sodium valproate		
Bisacodyl		

Table 7: Medicines, formulations and routes of administration.

4.2 Different forms in which medication may be presented

The majority of medicines are formulated for oral administration. This means they are to be taken via the mouth, in the form of a tablet, capsule, liquid or suspension. These medicines come in a variety of shapes and sizes, colours and tastes. Solid dose oral formulations are made either as tablets or capsules, and are formulated to aid compliance and reduce adverse effects. Table 8 shows some of the tablets and capsules that are taken by this route.

As well as tablets and capsules, oral medicine can also be delivered by liquids, suspensions and syrups. Again, these are formulated to aid compliance. Liquid preparations are measured when administered, using a 2.5ml or 5ml spoon, oral syringe or a medicine tot. All liquid preparations must be shaken before measuring out the dose. This is particularly important for suspensions.

It is your responsibility to ensure that the right person receives the right drug at the right dose at the right time via the right route, and to involve a clinician if the person constantly refuses.

Activity 12

Measuring medicines
Compare a 5ml measurement of liquid using a 5ml syringe, a 5ml spoon and a measuring tot. Does the quantity vary? Consider this when you next administer liquid medicines.

Formulation	Reason	Example
Enteric coated (ec)	Used to avoid absorption in the stomach, which helps to protect the stomach from adverse effects caused by the medicine	Prednisolone EC Aspirin EC
Modified Release (MR) Controlled Release (CR) Slow Release (SR)	Used to release the medicine over a period of time. This enables a medicine to be given once or twice a day, which may be advantageous to the patient. These should never be crushed	Sinemet CR Adalat retard Securon SR Maxolon SR
Soluble, effervescent	Used to dissolve the medicine in water to make the medicine easier to take	Soluble aspirin
Sugar-coated	Used to improve the taste of a medicine	Ferrous sulphate
Chewable	Used as the tablet is too big to swallow and is chalky	Calcichew D3
Sublingual	Used to dissolve rapidly into the bloodstream and taken to the site of action quicker. The tablet is placed in the side of the mouth or under the tongue	Temgesic Buccastem

Table 8: Some tablets and capsules taken via the mouth.

Case study

Refusal to take medicine
Jennifer consistently refuses to take her medication.
She is prescribed:

- Aspirin 75mg EC tablets 1m
- Ramipril 5mg capsules 1od
- Simvastatin 20mg tablets 1n
- Nifedipine capsules 20mg od
- Ferrous sulphate 200mg tds
- Senna tablets 2–4n.

1. What could you do to enable Jennifer to take her medicines?
2. Should you hide them in her food?
3. Who should be involved in decisions regarding medication?
4. Are alternative formulations available?

4.3 Materials and equipment that can assist in administering medication

There is a variety of medical devices to enable people to take their medicines. As a care worker, you should be aware of the different products on the market to aid compliance with prescribed medicines.

Compliance aids

These are used to encourage and support people to take their medicines. They may promote both concordance and compliance.

Monitored Dosage System (MDS)

The pharmacist may dispense medicine in bottles and boxes or in a Monitored Dosage System (MDS). There are various systems available on the market, for example, Manrex®, Venalink®, Nomad® and BioDose®. The choice of system supplied may depend on what the pharmacist can offer, but the ultimate choice of what system suits the care home is up to the staff or the person receiving domiciliary care. Those supported by domiciliary care may be assessed by the pharmacist under the Disability Discrimination Act 1995 to enable people to self-administer their own medicines via a Monitored Dosage System (compliance aid).

An MDS is usually used for solid oral dose medicines such as tablets or capsules. More recently a system has been marketed that dispenses unit doses of liquids. Other formulations such as inhalers, eye drops, creams, ointments and effervescent tablets cannot be dispensed by an MDS. This results in two different systems of medicine administration being used in the home (MDS and containers), which may cause problems.

It is vital that good practice prevails and the MAR chart is always referred to before the administration to ensure that all the medicines prescribed are given to the correct person, regardless of how they are dispensed. When medicines are dispensed using the MDS, the expiry date is compromised, resulting in an increase in medicine waste (more so for 'when required' (PRN) medication). Usually it is eight weeks from dispensing.

Tablets or capsules which cannot be identified and are similar to each other should not be placed together in an MDS. All medicines must be identifiable and the description labelled by the pharmacist. Medicines which

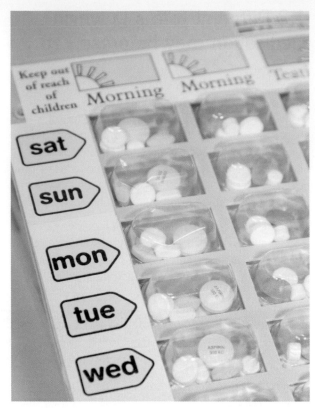

Have you used Monitored Dosage Systems with people?

cannot be dispensed in an MDS as their stability is compromised include Lansoprazole fastabs, omeprazole, sodium valproate, rabeprazole (as they may absorb water and disintegrate) and nifedipine capsules (as they are light-sensitive). However, there are many more medicines that cannot be dispensed in an MDS — you should ask your pharmacist, who will be able to tell you if a medicine cannot be dispensed in this way.

A number of significant drug interactions can occur when medicines are taken at the same time. This may have a profound effect on the person. Good reference sources such as the *British National Formulary* (BNF) identify drug interactions and side effects of medicines.

Activity 13

MDS

1. List three medicines in solid dose form that cannot be dispensed in an MDS.
2. Can you think of difficulties that the staff may have because of this?
3. How could these be overcome?

Other compliance aids

As well as the MDS, there are a number of other compliance aids to help people take their prescription. Examples of these include Medidose® and Dosette®. These devices are particularly useful in adult placement settings, such as domiciliary care, and they can be used for 'leave medication' in care homes when people leave the home for any length of time and medication is required to be administered. It is advised that the pharmacist fills these wherever possible but in exceptional circumstances, secondary dispensing by specifically trained care staff may occur against a written policy.

Inhalers

A variety of different inhalers are available on the market. Aerosols, dry powder inhalers, nebules and powder inhalers are marketed in a variety of preparations from turbohalers, autohalers, accuhalers and evohalers, to name but a few.

Compliance aids such as 'spacers' can be prescribed to help with the delivery of the medicine from an inhaler. Again there are many marketed, such as Aerochambers® and Volumatic®.

For eye drops

There are appliances that aid the instillation of drops into the eye, which may be useful if the person does not like eye drops being applied.

Reflect

Do any of the people you support use an inhaler? How do you assess that they use the inhaler correctly for maximum benefit?

Does the person have regular check-ups with the asthma nurse or doctor? What appliance can be prescribed if the person's technique is poor?

Look up in the BNF the variety of spacer devices available.

Percutaneous Endoscopic Gastrostomy (PEG) and Naso Gastric (NG) tube administration

Some people may not be able to swallow medicines in the conventional way but they could be administered via NG (Naso Gastric) or PEG (Percutaneous Endoscopic Gastrostomy) tubes.

All medicines should be checked with the drug company for current information on administration. The suitability of medicines to be administered by this route, in addition to drug–drug interactions and drug–food interactions, should be considered and supported by documentation. Side effects from drugs reacting with either other drugs or certain foods should always be considered carefully. The community or hospital pharmacist will be able to help you compile information on the best formulations to use. Again, all care workers should be suitably trained to administer medicines with a PEG tube – you should only administer medication through this route if you have been trained to do so.

Training involving these techniques is important. You should always be completely clear what it is within your competence to do.

Reflect

- Do you have any people you support who require medication to be administered via a PEG or NG tube?
- Compile a list of the various medicines and formulations. You may need to obtain information from the manufacturers.
- Record the advice on the most suitable formulation and any precautions that must be taken when administering via this route.

Note: Liaison with the doctor may be essential if a formulation prescribed is not recommended by the manufacturer.

5. Be able to receive, store and dispose of medication supplies safely

This section will enable you to receive supplies of medication in line with agreed ways of working. It will also cover the safe storage of medicines and where to dispose of medicines.

5.1 How to receive supplies of medication in line with agreed ways of working

Firstly you need to identify the medicines that need to be ordered. Ensure that you order them in time to enable you to check the prescriptions, the medicines and MAR charts received before any administration takes place.

Request the prescription from the surgery. Check that you have asked for and received sufficient quantities to last the 28-day (or 7-day) cycle. You can then check the prescription received against the old MAR chart. This is important to ensure that no errors have been made and you have a prescription for what you ordered.

You will need to rectify any problems with the surgery before any medicines are dispensed. Check repeat prescriptions previously issued have not changed. It is easier to correct any discrepancies with the prescription before it is dispensed.

You should photocopy the prescription to check the dispensed medicines and MAR chart received against. Your service may have a different system, but it must be robust enough to identify any dispensing issues.

Once you have done this, send the prescription to the supplying pharmacy or dispensing doctor.

Check the dispensed medicines received and the new MAR charts against the copy of the prescription and address any errors before any administration takes place. Allow yourself enough time to check in the medicines accurately. Keep the photocopy of the prescription with the MAR chart for reference. The photocopied prescription then becomes a working document.

Record the quantity of medicines received on the MAR chart. The pharmacist may print these but you should record the actual quantity received as well and any balances of medicines carried over from previous cycles. This will then show the quantity of medicines available to administer at the start of the MAR chart. This is essential information for quality-assuring administration and record keeping.

Always ensure a second member of staff confirms the accuracy of the MAR chart and receipt of medicines. Both members of staff should sign the MAR chart to record they have accurately checked all the information and receipt of medicines.

Case study

Once or twice a day?

A care home had received a delivery of medicines, but the senior carer did not check them in correctly and instead put them in the trolley ready for use. The doctor had changed the dose of one medicine from one tablet twice a day to one tablet daily. The MAR chart recorded to give the medicine twice a day, but the label on the bottle recorded to administer it once a day. The surgery and the pharmacy are closed so the correct dose cannot be confirmed.

1. What processes should have prevented this from happening?
2. Which dose should the care assistants now give?
3. Who can they go to for advice as the surgery and pharmacy are closed?
4. What are the consequences of the potential error?

Reflect

Think about the processes involved to receive medicines into the home. Does your medicine policy enable you to be able to receive medicines in the care service, regardless of where they have come from, such as:

- hospital
- the person's home
- the supplying pharmacy
- a different pharmacy?

What is the difference in process between the four examples for receipt of medicines? How does this differ if the person is cared for at home?

Activity 14

Ordering and receiving prescriptions

Some common problems occur with ordering prescriptions and receiving medicines. Think of possible reasons and solutions to overcome the following problems.

- Not obtaining prescriptions in time to check the medicines received.
- Running out of medicines mid-cycle.
- Unclear directions or 'mdu' recorded (as directed).
- Pharmacist unable to supply a medicine in time.
- Not obtaining a copy of a prescription written mid-cycle and sent straight to the pharmacy for dispensing.
- The doctor changing the dose of a medicine after the repeat prescription has been ordered.

Case study

Domiciliary care

Joe is looked after in his own home. The domiciliary care staff are responsible for collecting his prescription from the surgery and getting the medicines dispensed at the local pharmacy. A care assistant picked up the prescription and took it to her local pharmacy ready to collect the next day, to take along to Joe. However, the pharmacist was unable to dispense the prescription because the doctor had failed to write the prescription for one of the medicines correctly. The care assistant had to take it back to the surgery to be corrected.

1. How could the care assistant have avoided the situation?
2. What could the care service have done to avoid this happening?

Case study

Which dose?

Janita was recently prescribed an antibiotic for a chest infection. The doctor told the care assistant on duty to give it four times a day before food and handed her the prescription. He recorded the dose as 'as directed', since he had just told her the dose. The care assistant was on leave for two weeks after the evening shift, so put the prescription in the diary ready for dispensing. The next care assistant on duty arranged for the prescription to be dispensed and it was delivered to the home. The following problems then occurred.

- The new care assistant was unaware of what the doctor had told her colleague regarding the dose.
- Staff were unaware of the dose of antibiotic to be administered and many did not administer it to Janita at all.

- Janita's chest infection got progressively worse and the doctor was contacted after 10 days.
- The doctor prescribed a different antibiotic to treat the infection.

1. What procedures should the first care assistant have followed to avoid this situation?
2. When should the second care assistant have contacted the doctor to check the dose?
3. What should have been written on the MAR chart and when?
4. How could this whole scenario have been avoided?

5.2 How to store medication safely

One of the key issues connected with all medicines is the arrangements made for storing them. The ideal storage area for medicines within a care home is in a room specially dedicated to medicines. The temperature of the room must be below 25°C at all times to ensure the medicines are stored within their product licences and their stability is maintained. An air conditioning system may have to be installed to guarantee this.

They should not be stored in damp environments, so keeping medicines in a kitchen or bathroom is not advisable. You may not notice medicines that are no longer stable as they may look the same, but you cannot guarantee their stability if you do not store them correctly at the right temperature and humidity. Other areas not deemed suitable as they may affect the stability of the medicines or are unhygienic are window sills and/or next to radiators, toilets and sluices.

The medication room may contain a number of storage facilities connected to the administration of medicines. A locked medicine trolley must be able to be secured to the wall when not in use. Cabinets for storing excess and new supplies of medicines will need to be locked at all times. Medicines that are no longer used should be held separately or in DOOP bins that are themselves locked in a cupboard. There should be a Controlled Drugs cabinet that complies with current regulations. All dressings and syringes should be held in a locked facility. **External medicines** should be stored separately from **internal medicines**.

Medicine refrigerator

A dedicated lockable medicine refrigerator's temperature must be maintained within a set range between 2°C and 8°C. The maximum, minimum and current refrigerator temperatures should be recorded on a daily basis to demonstrate that the temperatures have been maintained at all times. The refrigerator should be defrosted regularly. Clear instructions should be available if the temperatures fall outside these limits, as the medicine stability may be compromised (in which case a new supply may have to be obtained).

If the medicine refrigerator temperature falls outside these limits of 2°C and 8°C, your pharmacist will be able to advise you what medicines may need replacing.

Controlled Drugs

Controlled Drugs (CDs) must be stored in cabinets which comply with the Misuse of Drugs and the Misuse of Drugs (Safe Custody) (Amendment) Regulations 2007 and the Misuse of Drugs Regulations 2001.

Case study

Missing medicines in domiciliary care

David lives at home and receives domiciliary care three times a day for personal care and help administering his medicines. He has grown-up children who visit on a regular basis. David has always left his medicines on his bedside cabinet. One day staff notice that some of his tablets are missing from a blister pack in his bedroom. David said he had not taken any tablets but mentioned that his young grandchildren had visited the night before and played in his bedroom.

1. How can the care assistant identify how many tablets have been removed from the blister pack?
2. Who should be contacted regarding the missing tablets?
3. What should be done to avoid this happening again?

These regulations specify the details of the construction of the cabinet. A Controlled Drugs cabinet does not have to be a locked cabinet within a locked cabinet. They are specially designed metal cabinets which have a double-skinned casing and a double lock. They must be able to be ragged bolted to a permanent wall (not a partition wall) so they cannot be easily levered off. They are designed to prevent or delay entry into the cabinet, in order to help prevent the theft and, ultimately, the possible misuse of the medicines stored inside.

Controlled Drugs cabinets should be reserved for Controlled Drugs only. Items such as jewellery, money or cigarettes should not be stored in them. Access should be limited only to a key holder on duty, who is responsible for the administration of medicines.

People who wish to self-administer their own medicines must have a personal lockable cupboard in which to store them. They do not have to have a dedicated Controlled Drugs cabinet for their own personal use.

All medicines should be stored securely. This includes medicines that have been refused by people and medicines that are no longer prescribed or needed by the person and are awaiting destruction. It is important that all waste medicines are stored in a locked cupboard awaiting return to the pharmacist or a clinical waste company for destruction.

Key security

The person in charge of each shift should hold the keys to the medication room and units within. Access should be limited in order to maintain security. Hanging keys on hooks outside the room and cupboards is not secure and should never occur in the care environment.

Activity 16

Security

Think about your care service.

1. Does medicine security meet the required standards within your place of work?
2. What would you do to improve the security?
3. How could this be achieved?

Reflect

People in domiciliary care will not have a medication room or even a lockable facility to store their medicines in. If you work in domiciliary care, think of the people requiring help with their medication.

- Is the storage of medicines suitable?
- Would you change any person's medicine storage?
- How could this be achieved?
- Do people visit the home who may compromise medicine security?
- What would you do if somebody's young grandchildren often visited?

5.3 How to dispose of unused or unwanted medication safely

All medicines that are no longer required must be disposed of at the earliest opportunity and not kept on the premises for use at a later time. The disposal of medicines is regulated by law. It could be harmful if they were put out with the ordinary rubbish and ended up on a landfill site, or flushed down the toilet or sink, for example. The following points must be followed for safe disposal.

- Medicines from a care home without nursing care provided can be left in their dispensed containers and placed separately from current medicines, ready for collection by the pharmacist for disposal. These unwanted medicines are classed as household waste so the pharmacist does not need a licence to collect them.

- The pharmacist cannot collect waste medicines from a care home that provides nursing care or a combination of nursing and personal care unless they hold a clinical waste licence, as these medicines are classed as industrial waste. In these instances all medicines must be taken out of their boxes but not removed from blister packs. If the pharmacist does not hold a licence, the care service is responsible for ensuring the waste is collected by a licensed waste management company.
- Needles and syringes (sharps) must be put in a 'sharps box' once used, to reduce the risk of needle stick injuries and cross-contamination.
- Transdermal patches should be folded in half to render them ineffective.
- Liquid waste should be put in a special bin and not tipped down the sink or toilet.
- All clinical waste bins and boxes containing medicines for the pharmacist or clinical waste company to collect must be kept in a locked cabinet at all times, even in the locked medication room.
- All medicines that are no longer needed must be recorded either in a 'returns book' or on the MAR chart.
- Disposal of Controlled Drugs must be under strict control. In a nursing home or a home that provides both nursing and personal care, these must be destroyed using a Controlled Drugs destruction kit. The Controlled Drugs register must record exactly what has occurred and the balance must be updated and checked. Two people must always undertake this task to ensure no mishandling.
- There should be a written policy for the safe disposal of surplus, unwanted or expired medicines.

You may have to destroy medicines because:

- somebody's treatment has been changed or discontinued
- a person transfers to another care service. It is advised that they take all of their medicines with them, except those that are no longer needed
- the medicine reaches its expiry date. Some medicine expiry dates are shortened when the product has been opened and is in use – for example, eye drops. This information is usually on the label or the PIL
- a person dies. Their medicines should be kept for seven days, in case there is a coroner's inquest.

The medicines are the property of each person, so consent must be obtained to destroy medicines. If a person leaves the home, their medicines should be returned to them unless consent has been obtained to dispose of them.

Activity 17

Disposal of medicines

Think about your practice and read your service's medicine policy regarding the disposal of medicines.

1. What would you do if somebody refused to take the medication and you had already prepared it in a tot ready for administration?
2. How and where would you destroy these medicines?
3. Do the records support what you have done – are accurate records made on the MAR chart and returns book?
4. Where do you store these medicines until collection to prevent mishandling?

Case study

Medicine disposal

A care home has a room where medicines that are no longer needed are stored. Staff take the medicines out of the pharmacist-labelled boxes and put the blister packs in the waste medicines collection bin. The bin is not locked away and is accessible to all members of staff. One day a member of the kitchen staff was seen going into the room, helping herself to some blister packs of medicines from the bin.

The kitchen staff member was immediately challenged and searched, and two blister packs of diazepam and zopiclone were found in her pocket and a blister pack of lorazepam in her locker. The kitchen staff said that she had intended to give them to her boyfriend, who had asked her to get him some drugs for his addiction.

1. How could this have been prevented?
2. Who should be informed of the theft?

6. Know how to promote the rights of the individual when managing medication

This section will enable you to explain the importance of principles to adhere to while handling medication. This will include consent, self-administration, rights to dignity and privacy, and also patient confidentiality. It will also explain the importance of risk assessments to manage and promote the person's independence to look after their own medicines.

6.1 The importance of consent, self-medication or active participation, dignity and privacy, and confidentiality in the use of medication

Consent

Before administering any medicine to somebody, you must obtain their consent for treatment. All medication prescribed must be offered to the person, but they have a right to refuse to take any medicines prescribed. You should never force somebody to take any medicines, and they must not be hidden or disguised in food (covert administration). A consistent refusal to take prescribed medication should be recorded and discussed with the person's doctor.

Somebody may not be capable of making an informed choice about whether to take the medication. This could be for a number of reasons – for example, the person could suffer from Alzheimer's disease or another form of mental illness. In certain circumstances it may be essential to treat the person, in which case the medicine may have to be administered covertly.

It would be necessary to undertake a Deprivation of Liberty safeguarding assessment, in these circumstances, to assess whether the person has the capacity to make an informed decision about whether to refuse their medication or not and whether to administer them covertly in the interests of their health and well-being.

If the person can make an informed choice about taking medicines, their right to refuse must always be respected and the doctor informed. It is important to talk to them to try to find out why they refuse to take their medication. Covert administration is not acceptable in these circumstances.

Case study

Refusal to take medication

Ada has dementia and consistently refuses to take her medication, one of which is Donepezil; this is prescribed by the hospital to treat her dementia. Another care assistant said that you could hide it in her food.

1. Should you administer the medicines covertly in this way?
2. What other action could you take?
3. What legislation is appropriate here?

Self-administration of medicines or active participation

This is where the person wishes to take their own medicines and not be administered them. All people should be given the opportunity to self-administer their medicines and they should be risk assessed as able before you allow them to take full responsibility. Compliance checks are equally important to ensure that people do take their medicines safely.

Dignity and privacy

It is important that you maintain the person's dignity and privacy at all times. For example, you must take into consideration their preferred location for where they wish to have their medicines administered. This may be in their own room, or in the communal lounge. You might need to consider when to administer medicines during Ramadan, respecting the person's fasting, or how to administer medicines on a four-times-a-day regime when they leave the service for a trip each lunchtime.

You must also take into consideration the person's preferred way of taking medicines. They may like the medicines placed in their hands for them to put in their own mouths to swallow and not have them placed in their mouth by you. You should apply creams and ointments to people when they are in their own room and not in a communal lounge, as their privacy and dignity need to be considered and respected. The person may be able to apply their own creams with support from you by opening the tube or tub of cream.

Reflect

Think about the people you support.

- Where do you administer medicines?
- Does your practice promote privacy and dignity at all times?
- Do you respect people's cultural and religious beliefs?
- How could you improve your practice to ensure people's dignity and privacy are respected at all times?

Confidentiality

All information about the person's medication is confidential and it is important to adhere to the legislation regarding this as outlined earlier.

Reflect

A simple example of maintaining confidentiality is where you keep the MAR charts. Are they just left on top of the medicine trolley in the dining room, or are they placed inside the locked trolley so no visitors or people being supported have access to this confidential information?

Think about your practice.

- Where are the MAR charts held?
- Where do you keep repeat prescriptions? Are they pinned to a noticeboard for all to see when entering an office?
- Where do you keep archived MAR charts?

6.2 How risk assessment can be used to promote independence in managing medication

Self-administration is where the person wishes to have full responsibility for taking their own medicine. All people should be encouraged to self-administer their own medication and must be fully supported by you to ensure they do so safely. Initially you should assess whether the person can self-administer their own medicines. This may identify where extra support is needed to enable them to take their medicines safely.

All people must be risk assessed as able before they can self-administer their own medication. Again, your care service should have a written self-administration risk assessment policy, which you can check against (see following page).

Reflect

Think about the medicines you administer and their different routes of administration.

- Could somebody be able to self-administer some of their medicines but need support for others?
- How could you assess this?
- Does your policy enable you to identify the medicines separately?
- What steps would need to be taken to ensure that all the person's medicines are taken correctly?

Case study

Ramadan

Raspal will not take any medicines during the fast of Ramadan. He is on the following medicines:

- Metformin 500mg bd
- Aspirin 75mg m
- Simvastatin 40mg n
- Multivitamins 2od
- Flucloxacillin 250mg qds.

1. What approach would you take to ensure his health and well-being?
2. Should you encourage Raspal to break his fast to take his tablets?
3. Could the doctor or pharmacist offer any help or advice?
4. Can these tablets be given at different times outside the medicine round?

Assessment for self-administration

Person's name: ....

DOB: ....

Question	Yes/No	Comment
1. Has self-administration been explained?		
2. Has supply of medication been explained? This should include advice on when to reorder supplies to ensure that medication does not run out.		
3. Does the person understand the requirement for storage of their medicines? e.g. all medicines should be kept locked securely in the drug locker/drawer; the person should keep the key with them.		
4. Has the person been shown their medication with an explanation of the purpose and how it should be taken?		
5. Can the person demonstrate an understanding of: • the name of the preparation • the purpose of the medicine • dose and frequency • when and how often to take PRN medication, and what the maximum dose is?		
6. Has the person been advised to inform staff if they suspect a side effect?		
7. Has the person been advised that they must inform staff if they make a dosage error?		
8. Has the person been advised that they should inform staff of any change in their condition?		
9. Can the person open child-resistant containers, blister packs? If 'no', would the provision of plain caps enable self-administration?		
10. Does the person have good eyesight? If 'no', can this be rectified by the use of spectacles and/or large-print labels?		
11. Does the person have access to a watch or clock?		
12. Is the person able to read and understand written words?		

Special dispensing requirements	✓ if needed	Comment
Tablets out of blisters		
Plain bottle tops		
Large-print labels		
Inhaler aids Is an assessment of inhaler techniques by the asthma nurse/ pharmacist needed? NB. Advise people using corticosteroid inhalers to rinse their mouth out with water after use.		Which?
Individual patient dispensing/MDS		
Reminder cards		

Self-medication approved   Yes/No

Reassessment date: ....

Care staff member's signature	
Name	
Date	
Person's signature	
Date	

A self-administration risk assessment.

For somebody moving into care, it is not enough just to risk assess the person as able to self-administer their own medicines on entry to the home. People's needs are dynamic and can rapidly change. Following the initial risk assessment, compliance checks should be undertaken on a regular basis. These involve auditing the person to demonstrate that they can take their medication as prescribed. It should be part of the agreement between the person and the home that compliance checks are undertaken to confirm the person does take the medicine as prescribed. These compliance checks will also help to reveal if the person is indeed taking their medication as prescribed.

Doing it well

Safe self-administering

- Complete a risk assessment to confirm whether the person can safely self-administer their own medication.
- Give the person the medication and record the quantity given on the MAR chart.
- After a couple of days, calculate the number of tablets that should have been taken and how many should be left in the box.
- Check the actual number of tablets with the person.
- Record on the MAR chart what you have done.
- Re-assess if the audits demonstrate that the person has not taken the medicine correctly and offer more support if needed to continue safe self-administration (for example, medicines dispensed in compliance aids or prompting the person to take the medication).

All people should have their own MAR chart recording all the prescribed medicines. This could be used to record any compliance check you do to assess whether the person takes their medicines safely. When you complete the MAR chart, do not record that you have administered the medicine by signing the MAR chart, as you have not. Record that you have given the person their medicines and the quantity, and use the chart to record the compliance check under the appropriate date.

Case study

Self-administration

Mr Patel refuses to allow the care assistants to count and assess his medicines, and insists he will self-administer his medicines.

1. What should you do?
2. How can you support Mr Patel to enable him to maintain his independence?

6.3 How ethical issues over the use of medication can be addressed

You may encounter different scenarios where ethical issues that may occur which may compromise your views and the people you support.

Case study

Ethical issues

Lesley is a vegan and will not eat any meat or any product from animals. He has recently been prescribed flucloxacillin capsules to treat a skin infection. He refuses to take the capsules, as they are made up of gelatine.

1. What should you do?
2. Which medicine information source would be useful in finding whether animal products are used in the medicine formulation?
3. What alternative products are available?

Case study

Ramadan

Amrit wishes to observe the religious festival of Ramadan. He is a diabetic and must have regular meals throughout the day, and also take some of his medication with food. He refuses to eat during daylight hours, which equates to 14 hours, and will not take his medication.

1. What should you do?
2. Whom should you inform regarding his decision?
3. Do you think that Amrit's wishes should be ignored to maintain his health?

7. Be able to support use of medication

This section will guide you through ways of supporting the person to use their medication, ensure that they do so safely and also how to address any practical issues that may arise when handling medicines.

7.1 How to access information about an individual's medication

In this section you will learn how to support somebody to take their medicines. You need to know where to access this information and whom to ask if you need further advice.

Activity 18

Alternative formulations

One of the people you support has swallowing difficulties and is prescribed tablets and capsules which she finds very difficult to swallow. Think about the references sources discussed in section 2.2, and decide which is best to use to enable you to discuss alternative formulations with the prescriber.

Some liquid preparations are very expensive, especially if they are made specifically for a person. They often take a while to prepare and have a short expiry date. Other formulations may be just as good and a lot less expensive. Look to see if there are patches, soluble tablets or chewable tablets available instead of automatically thinking a liquid is the best alternative.

Reflect

Think of the medicines in your workplace. Are they all administered orally? List those that are not. What supporting healthcare professionals administer medicines that you cannot?

You must only administer medicines by a route that you are both competent and confident to do so, and also know whom to ask if the administration route is outside your competencies. For example, you may not be able to administer a pessary for vaginal use as it is an invasive procedure and the district nurse may have to come in to administer this medicine. However, you may receive specialist training to administer insulin subcutaneously to a diabetic person. It is important that you do not administer medicines that are outside your competencies.

Case study

Swallowing difficulties

Sheila is very poorly with a chest infection and her health has deteriorated over sometime and finds it difficult to swallow her medicines. She is prescribed the following medicines (see table below) and had recently been prescribed an antibiotic for her chest infection.

Medicine	Dose	Alternative formulation and dose
Paracetamol 500mg tablets	1–2 qds prn	
Ranitidine 150mg tablets	1 bd	
Adalat retard 20mg tablets	1 bd	
Ferrous sulphate 200mg tablets	1 tds	
Risedronate sodium tablets 35mg	1 weekly	
Salbutamol tablets 4mg	1 qds	
Senna tablets	2 n	
Amoxicillin 500mg capsules	1 tds	

Table 9: Sheila's current medication.

1. Suggest alternative formulations which may help Sheila take her medicines, bearing in mind cost.

Case study

Administering insulin

John has recently been diagnosed as Type 1 diabetic. He has been prescribed insulin and this must be administered twice a day. The diabetic nurse has prescribed insulin for John and has asked you to administer it to him. You have never done this before.

1. What should you do?
2. Can John inject the insulin himself?
3. Do your medicine policies and procedures support you to administer insulin?
4. Who takes ultimate responsibility for you to administer insulin?

7.2 Support to use medication in ways that promote hygiene, safety, dignity and active participation

Hygiene

All medicines must be stored and administered in a hygienic way. It is not acceptable to touch medicines while you are preparing to administer them or while you are counting them during a quality assurance audit, for example. You should always wash your hands before you handle medicines. You should wear gloves if you run the risk of handling them inadvertently if they are cytotoxic. Any medicine dropped on the floor should be discarded and a new supply sought.

It is important to store medicines in a clean and tidy environment. People have the right to expect the highest standard of hygiene at all times to reduce any risk of cross-infection.

Safety

If you do not have and follow robust systems for handling medicines safely, you may accidentally give the wrong dose or give the medicine to the wrong person, or not give it at all. They could all cause harm to the person you support. This may result in minor discomfort but could result in the death of a person.

While it is important to allow each person choice in their handling of medicines, they must not put others in a position of danger if they fail to follow basic rules.

1. Wet hands with running water

2. Rub hands together with soap and lather well

3. Weave fingers and thumbs together and slide them back and forth

4. Rinse hands under a stream of clean, running water until all soap is gone

5. Blot hands dry with clean towel

Do you know the correct procedure for hand-washing?

It is important that you assess each person to balance the risk.

Medicines should never be used to restrain or sedate people. This has been referred to as 'Chemical COSHH'. It is important that you recognise medicines that do cause sedation and be aware of why they were prescribed in the first place. They should never be used to control behaviour or used as a punishment.

All aspects of good care are centred on the needs of the person. You must be confident that medicines are administered for the benefit of the person and not the staff. You must be sure that the medicines you administer maximise benefit and avoid causing harm to the person.

Warfarin

Darren is prescribed warfarin. He regularly goes to the anticoagulation clinic and his dose changes after each visit. One day the care assistant forgets to order his medicines so she does not give him any warfarin.

1. What could be the consequences of not administering Darren his prescribed warfarin?

2. How could a supply be obtained while waiting for a prescription to be written?
3. List the side effects of too much warfarin.
4. List the adverse effects of administering a sub-therapeutic dose of warfarin.
5. What systems should have been followed to ensure a continuous supply?

Parkinson's disease

Doreen has Parkinson's disease. She has been prescribed a medicine to be administered six times a day. It must be administered every three hours during the day. These times do not fit in with the medicine rounds.

1. What extra systems need to be put in place to ensure that she is administered the medicines as prescribed?
2. Would a compliance aid help or hinder administration?
3. How would you ensure that a dose is not missed and actually administered every three hours?

Simple rules of administration apply when handling medicines. You must be able to identify the medicine from a pharmacist-labelled container, be able to identify the person and know what the medicine is for to be able to support the person's clinical needs fully. Special precautions for administration should be known, for example, before food, and you must be trained to be able to undertake this task. Further training may be required for more specialist administration techniques.

All medicines must be administered from a pharmacist-labelled container. They should be prepared directly before administration and not prepared in advance by yourself or someone else. Each person's medicine should be prepared in isolation and you should never prepare more than one person's medicine at a time. This could result in administering the medicine to the wrong person.

In domiciliary care, somebody's medicine may be prepared in advance for them to take at a later time, if the support plan supports this practice and it has been agreed by the care service and the person. This may be essential if, for example, the person cannot open the blister pack to get the tablet out due to arthritis, and they may only have one visit a day but need to take the tablets three times a day.

Reflect

Look at the medicines the people you support are prescribed.
- Is there an excessive level of sedating medicines prescribed?
- Can the prescribing be justified?
- Do the support plans support the prescribing or is it just to control behaviour or stop the person wandering around?
- Are 'when required' (PRN) medicines administered routinely that are used to control behaviour?
- Are there systems in place to prevent the overuse of medicines?
- Are outcomes always recorded after each administration of a PRN medicine?

Dignity

It is important that you promote the person's dignity at all times. This may be simply securing the MAR charts in a locked office and not leaving them out for all to read. You should never discuss the person's clinical condition in front of other people in the home, as this may cause distress to the person. You should reflect on where you

Case study

Compliance

Barbara wishes to self-administer her own medicines. A risk assessment indicates that she can do this safely. You give her the following medicines:

- 28 × aspirin 75mg tablets: dose 1m
- 28 × Furosemide 20mg tablets: dose 1m
- 56 × Adcal D3 tablets: dose 1bd
- 28 × warfarin 3mg tablets: dose 1 daily at 6pm
- 28 × warfarin 1mg tablets: dose 1 alternate days at 6pm.

1. Write a MAR chart for Barbara. Use today's date.
2. Record what you have given to Barbara.

After five days, you undertake a compliance check in the evening at 8pm. You count:

- 23 × Furosemide 20mg tablets: dose 1m
- 52 × Adcal D3 tablets: dose 1bd
- 25 × warfarin 3mg tablets: dose 1 daily at 6pm
- 21 × warfarin 1mg tablets: dose 1 alternate days at 6pm.

3. Which medicines has Barbara not taken correctly?
4. Could there be any other explanation?
5. What additional support could you offer Barbara to maintain active participation?
6. If you establish that Barbara has taken the incorrect dose of some medicines, whom should you contact?

Functional skills

Maths: Calculations using whole numbers

Using the information on Barbara's tablets, calculate the number of tablets that she should have taken and compare this to how many tablets were left. The difference is what medicines had actually been taken outside the prescribed dose.

administer medicines. It may cause distress if the person is administered their medicine in front of everyone else. Their rights and dignity should always be discussed before any administration of medicines takes place.

Consideration should be given to people of the opposite sex. Some people would be embarrassed if a member of the opposite sex administered their medicines, due to cultural or religious beliefs. This should be discussed and a support plan written if this is an issue.

Active participation

Active participation is a way of working that recognises somebody's right to participate in activities such as self-administering their own medicines. All people should be regarded as an active partner in their own care or support rather than a passive recipient.

It is essential that you support the person to take their own medicine but equally essential to assess whether they can do so safely. It is important to remember that somebody may not be able to take a complex medicine regime of tablets but may be fully competent to apply a cream or use their inhaler. Your assessment must be able to identify the person's needs and not just make a blanket statement that they are not capable of any active participation in looking after some of their medicines.

It may be as simple as the person finding it difficult to open containers to be able to take their own medicines. Alternative dispensed containers could be discussed with the pharmacist to try to maintain the person's autonomy.

Compliance aids could be explored to enable somebody to continue to take their medicines safely.

Even if the person wants to self-administer their own medicines, a MAR chart should still be written with the full medicine regime. This could be used to record the number of tablets given to the person and to record compliance checks.

7.3 Strategies to ensure that medication is used or administered correctly

It is important that you give the correct medication at the correct dose by the correct route at the correct time with agreed support, respecting dignity and privacy, and that records accurately reflect practice.

It is important that you keep records of all the medicines you handle. You should at any time know exactly what medicines have been prescribed for each person and why and what has been administered. You should also be able to identify if these have been administered correctly. This sometimes is known as an audit trail — what has been received, what has been administered and what is left. If people do not receive their medicines as the doctor prescribes, it may compromise their health and well-being.

Reflect

Many errors can occur if correct procedures are not followed, such as:

- administering too many or not enough tablets
- administering the wrong medicine to the wrong person
- not administering the medicine at all
- not recording the actual administration
- administering the medicine at the wrong time.

Think about your practice. Identify areas where possible errors may occur. What would you do to prevent them?

Activity 19

Emotions

1. Write down a list of emotions you would feel if you had made a medicine administration error.
2. How would you feel if a care assistant gave the wrong medicine to your mother?
3. Think of the possible consequences of any error.

You should always refer to the MAR chart before any administration of medicines and then prepare the medicines ready for administration. Following the transaction, you should immediately record the transaction on the MAR chart either by signing it, to demonstrate that the medicines have been taken by the person, or recording the reason for non-administration. This is usually by a code, described on the MAR chart.

Reflect

Many errors occur when a dual system of dispensing is used, where some medicines are dispensed in MDS and some are dispensed in traditional boxes and bottles. If staff do not follow the correct procedures and fail to check the MAR chart before and after signing, serious errors can occur. How could you identify medicines that are not dispensed in MDS on the MAR chart to ensure that they are administered as the doctor prescribed?

Case study

The interruption

A senior care assistant was expected to answer all telephone calls, even if she was in the middle of the medicine round. The phone rang and the senior care assistant answered it. Distracted by the problematic phone call, she then returned to the medicine round. She inadvertently gave Peter Jones's medicine to Peter Smith. She quickly realised what she had done but decided not to say anything, and ignored the policy of reporting all medicine errors. Three hours later Peter Smith became very ill and the doctor was informed. The senior care assistant admitted her mistake and Peter Smith was admitted to hospital for observation. His family were informed the following day.

1. What should the senior care assistant have done when she realised her mistake?
2. When should Peter Smith's family have been informed?
3. What should the care service do to prevent this kind of mistake happening again?
4. Should the home inform Peter Jones's doctor and relatives also?
5. Should the regulatory body be informed of this mistake?

Staff drug audit sheet

Name of staff: ....

Date	Time	Name of person	Medicine	Dose	Quantity received	Quantity recorded as administered	Calculated quantity	Actual quantity	✓ or ✗
	before								
	after								
	before								
	after								
	before								
	after								
	before								
	after								
	before								
	after								

Staff drug audit sheet

Name of staff: *Care assistant June Brown*

Date	Time	Name of person	Medicine	Dose	Quantity received	Quantity recorded as administered	Calculated quantity	Actual quantity	✓ or ✗
20 June 2010	10am before	Joe Bloggs	Aspirin	75mg 1m	28	12	16	16	✓
	10.30am after				28	12 + 1	16 − 1 = 15	15	✓
20 June 2010	10am before	Joe Bloggs	Sodium Valproate	200mg 2 tds	84	44	40	42	✗
	10.30am after				84	44 + 2	42 − 2 = 40	40	✓
20 June 2010	10am before	Edna Green	Amoxicillin	250mg 1 tds	21	14	7	7	✓
	10.30am after				21	14 + 1	7 − 1 = 6	7	✗
20 June 2010	10am before	Ivy Brown	Diazepam	5mg 1m	50	28	22	12	✗
	10.30am after				50	28 + 1	12 − 1 = 11	9	✗
20 June 2010	10am before	John Smith	Paracet-amol	500mg 1−2 prn	100	45	55	60	✗
	10.30am after				100	45 + 1	60 − 1 = 59	59	✓

Drug audit sheets.

Activity 20

Medicine errors

Think about the records in your service.

- Could you demonstrate to a judge in a law court that you had administered all the medicines as prescribed and that records reflected practice?
- Would you be able to identify in a timely fashion if a medicine was due to run out before it actually did, to enable you to obtain more to ensure a continuous supply?
- Could you identify if medicines went missing?
- Is the quality assurance in your practice robust enough to assess individual staff competence?

It is important that you have a quality assurance system in your service to assess staff competence in the safe handling of medicines.

You could use the staff drug audit template on the previous page to assess individual staff.

It is important that you have a baseline assessment of the medicines you choose to audit. You can then assess whether the staff member has given the medicines as prescribed and whether records reflect practice.

- You need to count the quantity of at least five medicines, preferably in bottles or boxes if you use MDS for the majority of the medicines dispensed, as this is the area of greatest risk.
- The count should be done before the medicine round without the knowledge of the care assistant who is due to undertake the round. You are assessing the care assistant as well as the accuracy of the records.
- The care assistant is allowed to undertake the medicine round in the usual fashion.
- You then calculate how many tablets/capsules are left and recount the quantities of these medicines.
- Any discrepancies indicate that the medicines have not been administered as prescribed and/or the records do not reflect practice.
- Further support and training should be undertaken to ensure that these errors are not repeated.

7.4 How to address any practical difficulties that may arise when medication is used

This section will deal with examples of support a person may need that is outside your competency. This may include the monitoring and assessment of clinical parameters.

Monitoring and assessment of clinical parameters

Some medication may require clinical parameters to be monitored before their administration. For example, blood sugar levels should be checked before the administration of insulin, or the pulse should be recorded before the administration of digoxin. With the exception of insulin, there is not an expectation for you to have full knowledge to assess the clinical parameters, or to undertake these clinical activities, but there should be an awareness of the reasons for clinical monitoring and to ensure that these take place as directed by a clinician.

If you do undertake clinical monitoring, it is important that you have regular training to do so and you are confident it is within your competence to do so.

Reflect

Think about your current practice.

- Are you expected to undertake a task that you feel is outside your area of expertise or competence?
- Is there adequate training available that is updated regularly?
- Do you know whom to go to, to access further training?

7.5 How and when to access further information or support about the use of medication

Practical difficulties that may occur include lost, missed and spilt medication. In this section you will understand how to address these issues. Also you will learn what to do if somebody decides not to take their prescribed medicines. Medicine errors will be discussed and what action you must take if you administer the incorrect medicine. You will also learn what to do if the person is unwell and is sick after taking their prescribed medicine in addition to any other adverse reactions the person may have to a medicine.

Lost medication

All medicines must be accounted for at all times and a good-quality assurance system will enable you to recognise if any medicines are missing. It is essential that further audits are undertaken to identify any poor staff practice and systems are put into place to prevent any further loss. If the loss involves a Controlled Drug, the police must be informed.

Reflect

Audits indicate that two temazepam 10mg are missing.
- What would you do?
- To whom should you report this?
- How do you obtain an additional supply to ensure that the person does not go without prescribed medication?
- What records should be made?
- How could this be prevented in the future?

Missed medication

Medicines may be missed for a variety of reasons. The person may be asleep. If this is the case, you should go back when the person is awake. You should respect their privacy and dignity, and not wake them up to administer medicines just because it fits in with your medicine round.

Sometimes people go out of the home on social leave. In this instance you could consider giving them their medication before they go or when they come back. If they leave the home on a regular basis, the pharmacist may be able to dispense a separate supply for them to

take out of the home. You could speak to the doctor to discuss a change in medicine regime or a change in formulation — a slow release preparation may be prescribed to be administered daily instead of ordinary tablets to be administered three times a day — for example, avoiding the need for a midday dose when the person is out of the home.

In exceptional circumstances, secondary dispensing the medicines into a container for the person to take out when they leave the home may be a possibility to ensure they take their prescribed medication.

Medicines are placed in a separate bottle or a compliance aid and given to the person or their carer while outside the home. This must be labelled to the same standard as that dispensed by the pharmacist. The person has the right to expect the same level of skill and care from trained staff as they would from a pharmacist. It is important that secondary dispensing is undertaken by two trained members of care staff following a specific policy to ensure no mistakes are made. Records on the MAR chart must be complete so the audit trail is maintained and it is possible to track how much medicine has been taken out of the home.

Reflect

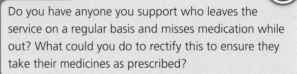

Do you have anyone you support who leaves the service on a regular basis and misses medication while out? What could you do to rectify this to ensure they take their medicines as prescribed?

Spilt medication

This may happen occasionally. You may accidently drop the medicine. In these instances, it is important that the person is still administered the prescribed dose. It is not acceptable just to record that they have not taken it because you have dropped it. You should give the last dose if it is dispensed in an MDS or another dose from traditional bottles and boxes.

Case study

Secondary dispensing

The son of Mr Brown has decided to take him away for a short holiday. He has not told you in advance so you have not been able to ask the pharmacist to dispense a supply separately for Mr Brown to take. You talk to the pharmacist and he cannot help you, as he has already dispensed the medicines.

1. Does your service have a policy to secondary dispense against?
2. How many staff members should undertake the secondary dispensing?
3. How can you suitably label the medicines?
4. What necessary records need to be kept?

You must never take a supply from another person. Remember medicines are the property of the person to whom they are prescribed. You also increase the risk of making an error. In addition, they will be short of the medicine too!

A person's decision not to take medication

Everyone has the right to choose whether to take medicines or not. If the person has the capacity to make decisions and decides not to take their medicines, this must be respected. You should talk to the person to find out why they do not want to take their medicines and also contact the doctor to inform them of the person's decision.

It may be simply a lack of understanding about what the medicines are for, or they may cause unwanted side effects. It is important that you explore all possibilities and inform the doctor of these.

If the person lacks capacity to make an informed decision regarding the medicines they take, procedures must be followed to establish whether the medicines are administered covertly.

Wrong medication used

Unfortunately, mistakes are all too common in social care. This is usually the result of poor systems and staff failing to follow good practice.

It is essential that you identify if a medicine error has occurred and rectify this immediately.

Vomiting after taking medication

This may occur. This may be due to an underlying medical condition or an adverse reaction to a medicine. Professional advice should always be sought and the records must record that the person was sick after taking their medicines. This could be recorded on the back of the MAR chart as well as in the daily records.

You must adhere to the expert advice given. Recording exactly when the person was sick and other information – for example, that it resembled coffee grounds – is important to enable the doctor to make an informed decision about what is wrong with the person.

Adverse reaction

As discussed earlier, adverse reactions may occur when somebody takes any medicines. They may have taken them for a long or short time but it is important that you document the reaction when it occurs, to enable the doctor to make an informed decision later. If the person is allergic to a medicine, you should consider the following.

- Is emergency medicine required?
- Is the pharmacist aware of the allergy?
- Is the allergy recorded on the MAR chart?
- Is there a support plan recording the error? This may include other medicines the person may be allergic to; if, for example, they are allergic to penicillin, what antibiotics are they also allergic to?

Case study

The wrong medicine

A busy care home relies on many agency staff. Existing staff turnover is high and the home has many unfilled vacancies. Medicine management is poor and there is no formal way of identifying the people who live there. Agency staff have trouble knowing who is who.

The agency staff on duty asked each person to confirm their name. One agency nurse said to somebody, 'Are you Andrew Wilson?' He replied 'Yes', and she gave him the medicine.

Unfortunately he was not Andrew Wilson and she had given him someone else's medicine.

1. How could this have been avoided?
2. What should the agency nurse have asked?
3. What improved practice should be put into place to prevent this happening again?
4. What are the consequences for Andrew Wilson and the other person?
5. Who should be informed of the error?

8. Be able to record and report on use of medication

8.1 How to record use of medication and any changes in an individual associated with it

and

8.2 How to report on use of medication and problems associated with medication, in line with agreed ways of working

It is essential that you record all the relevant information regarding the person's care. This may range from simply recording that you have administered a medicine to recording a complex medicine reaction and what you did to prevent it happening again. It is essential that you work as part of a team. If something untoward has happened, you should be able to report this and record exactly what you have to do to prevent further problems. The outcome prompts in the new regulations clearly state that you have to have an understanding of the risks in administering medicines and also have to keep the person informed of any changes.

Reflect

Think about your service. Do your policies and procedures reflect what to do if somebody experiences an adverse reaction to medicines? Does it record what to do to prevent it happening again? Is the person informed of any decisions that are made following the adverse reaction?

Getting ready for assessment

For this unit you will need to demonstrate that you can safely handle medicines. You will be expected to understand the legislation surrounding medication and how this is put into practice. Your assessor will need to be sure that you can order, receive, administer and dispose of medicines safely and accurately record this. You will be required to know what the medicines you handle are for and their common side effects in addition to the various routes of administration. You may be asked to develop a medication policy and also to recognise where mistakes could be made and how to prevent them in existing practice. People's rights regarding medicines and how to support people to take medicines will be assessed. Assessors may decide to shadow a medicine round to assess your competence in the safe handling of medicines.

Legislation

- Access to Health Records Act 1990
- Care Quality Commission (Registration) Regulations 2009
- Control of Substances Hazardous to Health Regulations 2002 (COSHH)
- Data Protection Act 1998
- Disability Discrimination Act 1995
- Hazardous Waste Regulations 2005
- Health and Safety at Work Act 1974
- Health and Social Care Act 2008 (Regulated Activities) Regulations 2009
- Medicines Act 1968
- Mental Capacity Act 2005 (Deprivation of Liberty Safeguards)
- Mental Health Act 1983
- Misuse of Drugs Act 1971
- Misuse of Drugs and the Misuse of Drugs (Safe Custody) (Amendment) Regulations 2007
- Misuse of Drugs Regulations 2001
- Safer Management of Controlled Drugs Regulations 2006

Further reading and research

- *Essential Standards of Quality and Safety* – guidance about compliance, published by the Care Quality Commission (www.cqc.org.uk/_db/_documents/Essential_standards_of_quality_and_safety_March_2010_FINAL.pdf).
- *The Handling of Medicines in Social Care* – published by the Royal Pharmaceutical Society of Great Britain in 2007, this is designed to give the reader guidelines for the safe handling of medicines. A copy should be at your place of work (alternatively you can download it from www.rpharms.com).
- www.dh.gov.uk/en/Publicationsandstatistics/Lettersandcirculars/Dearcolleagueletters/DH_080714 – Deprivation of Liberty Safeguards and Mental Capacity Act 2005 local implementation networks.
- www.drugs.gov.uk/publication-search/drug-licences/controlled-list?view=Binary – the Home Office website has a link to a list of Controlled Drugs and their Schedules.

Glossary

Accommodation — the process by which the eye changes optical power to focus on an object as its distance changes

Accredited — given official recognition or approval

Acquired — anything that is not present at birth but develops some time later

Action Learning Set — a group of between about four and seven people, who meet regularly to support one another in their learning in order to take purposeful action on work issues

Active participation — when a person participates in the activities and relationships of everyday life as independently as possible; they are an active partner in their own care or support, rather than a passive recipient

Advocacy — acting and speaking on behalf of a person who is unable to do so

Advocate — a person responsible for acting and speaking on behalf of a person who is unable to do so

Agoraphobia — the fear of open spaces

Aids — something that helps. This may include technological aids and human aids

Anaphylactic shock — extreme immediate reaction by the body to a medicine

Anatomy — the physical structure of the body

Anthropods — bugs, flies, ticks, fleas, mosquitoes and similar creatures. They transmit infections by biting, sucking or burrowing under the skin

Articulatory — relating to articulation (vocal expression)

Bariatric — a term used for a person whose weight exceeds 25 stone

Bias — influence in an unfair way, whether positively or negatively

Body language — the ways in which people communicate without speaking, such as through posture and how they arrange their bodies

Capacity — the necessary requirements to do, or achieve, something

Care Quality Commission (CQC) — the independent regulatory body responsible for the regulation of health and adult social care services in England. They also protect the interests of people whose rights are restricted under the Mental Health Act

Closed question — a question that requires only 'yes' or 'no' as an answer

Code of practice — a set of guidelines and regulations to be followed by members of an occupation or organisation

Cognitive — mental processes including thinking, knowing and remembering

Communication — the passing on and receiving of information through a variety of methods including verbal and non-verbal communication

Competence — demonstrating the skills and knowledge required by the National Occupational Standards

Congenital — present at birth

Contract — get shorter

Cross-infection — infection that spreads from one person to another

Data Protection Act (1998) — a law to ensure the safety of data held

Dementia — a condition involving a loss of mental powers, in particular, of memory

Demographic — the characteristics of a human population or part of it, especially its size, growth, density, distribution, and statistics regarding birth, marriage, disease, and death

Deprivation — a lack of something important, for example, a physical lack of money, shelter or clothing, or an emotional lack of loving, nurturing and caring

Discrimination — unfair treatment of a person or group on the basis of prejudice

Diverse — being different; people are unique according to their own background, culture, personality, race, any disability, gender, religion/belief, sexual orientation and age

Drug — any substance which, when taken into the body, may modify one of its functions

Dysphasia — a problem with finding the right words or interpreting the meanings of words spoken

Empower — to enable people who had previously depended on others to make decisions and take control of their own lives. People can be empowered through finding access to information and knowledge, or through growing and developing confidence in their own abilities

Evaluation — the process of gathering and reviewing evidence, then reaching a judgement

External medicine — a medicine that is applied to the body and not taken by mouth

Facilitator — a person who helps make something happen. This is often associated with decision making or planning

Hazard — something that could possibly cause harm

Holistic — looking at the whole person or situation

Implementation — putting something into practice or action

Induction — a formal briefing and familiarisation for someone starting at an organisation

Infringing rights — a situation where a person's entitlements have been disregarded and access to entitlements has been blocked through deliberate or accidental actions

Internal medicine — a medicine that is swallowed

Legislation — laws

Loop system — a system enabling partially deaf people to hear dialogue and sound in theatres, cinemas and so on

Macular degeneration — an eye disease that results in blurred vision and can cause blindness

Medicine — a type of drug, used in the treatment or prevention of a disease

Milestone — a scheduled event to show the completion of a part of an overall task or goal

Motor control — the ability to control body movements. Gross motor control is the ability to make large movements, such as waving, and fine motor control is the ability to make more complex movements, such as holding a pencil

National Minimum Standards — these are used by the Commission for Social Care Inspection (CSCI) to inspect the quality of care in services

National Occupational Standards — UK standards of performance that people are expected to achieve in their work, and the knowledge and skills they need to perform effectively

Non-verbal communication — a way of communicating without words, through body language, gestures, facial expression and eye contact

Open question — a question that cannot be answered by just 'yes' or 'no'; it often begins with a 'how' or a 'why', for example. This sort of question encourages people to talk more

Others — these may include family, advocates, team members, a line manager, specialists or others who are important to the person's well-being

Personal development — developing the personal qualities and skills needed to live and work with others

Personalisation agenda — the process of putting people in control of the services they receive by giving them control over how the budget for their support is spent

Physiology — the normal functions of the body

Plan — the plan may include goals (short, medium and long term), the type and level of support needed to achieve goals, roles and responsibilities, ways to address any associated risks and ways to monitor the plan

Positive action — ensuring that people are able to enter into fair competition with others

Positive discrimination — acting more favourably towards someone because of their perceived disadvantage — this is not legal in the UK

Primary research — the collection of data that does not already exist

Professional development — developing the qualities and skills necessary for the workforce

Qualitative research — research that is based on attitudes, opinions and perceptions

Quantitative research — research that is measurable and in numeric form

Records — information that is written and retained, either electronically as a computer record, or on paper as a hard copy. Records must be accessible, stored securely and be easily retrievable if necessary

Regular activities — activities designed for anyone to access

Regulator — someone who ensures compliance with laws, regulations and established rules

Risk — the likelihood of a hazard causing harm

Risk control measures — actions taken in order to reduce an identified risk

Sacrum — the bony part of the back located at the base of the spine

Secondary research — the summary or gathering of existing research and data

Self-advocacy — speaking up for oneself

Self-esteem — how you value yourself, and therefore how you believe the rest of the world sees you

Self-image/self-concept — about how people see themselves

Socially clean — hands that are washed and clean enough to sit down to eat a meal or to shake hands with someone, but not clean enough to carry out a clinical procedure

Stereotyping — making negative or positive judgements about whole groups of people based on prejudice and assumptions, rather than facts or knowledge about people

Trigger — an event that causes other events

Vena cava — a large vein that returns blood to the right atrium of the heart

Whistle-blowing — reporting concerns about practice in your workplace

Legislation

This page lists all the legislation referenced in this book. For more information on any item, please refer to the index.

Access to Health Records Act 1990
Access to Personal Files Act 1987
Adult Support and Protection (Scotland) Act (ASPA) 2007

Care Quality Commission (Registration) Regulations 2009
Care Standards Act 2000
Carers (Equal Opportunities) Act 2004
Carers and Disabled Children Act 2000
Control of Asbestos at Work Regulations 2002
Control of Lead at Work Regulations 2002
Control of Noise at Work Regulations 2005
Control of Substances Hazardous to Health Regulations 2002 (COSHH)
Criminal Justice Act 1998

Data Protection Act 1998
Disability Discrimination Act 1995

Family Law Act 1996
Fraud Act 2006
Freedom of Information Act 2000

Hazardous Waste Regulations 2005
Health and Safety (Display Screen Equipment) Regulations 1992 (amended 2002)
Health and Safety at Work Act 1974
Health and Safety First Aid Regulations 1981
Health and Social Care Act 2008 (Regulated Activities) Regulations 2009
Human Rights Act 1998

Lifting Operations and Lifting Equipment Regulations (1992) (LOLER)
Local Authority Social Services Act 1970

Management of Health and Safety at Work Regulations 1999
Manual Handling Operations Regulations 1992 (amended 2002)

Medical Records Act 1990
Medicines Act 1968
Mental Capacity Act 2005
Mental Health Act 1983
Misuse of Drugs Act 1971
Misuse of Drugs and the Misuse of Drugs (Safe Custody) (Amendment) Regulations 2007
Misuse of Drugs Regulations 2001

National Assistance Act 1984 S47
No Secrets (England) and In Safe Hands (Wales)
Noise at Work Regulations 1989

Offences Against the Person Act 1861
Our Health, Our Care, Our Say (Department of Health 2007)

Personal Protective Equipment at Work Regulations 1992
Police and Criminal Evidence Act 1984 S17
Protection from Harassment Act 1997
Protections of Vulnerable Groups Act 2007
Provision and Use of Work Equipment Regulations 1998 (PUWER)
Public Interest Disclosure Act 1998
Putting People First (Department of Health 2007)

Regulatory Reform (Fire Safety) Order 2005
Reporting of Injuries, Diseases and Dangerous Occurrences Regulations 1995 (RIDDOR) (amended 2008)

Safeguarding Vulnerable Groups Act 2006
Safer Management of Controlled Drugs Regulations 2006
Sexual Offences Act 2003

Theft Act 1968

Work and Families Act 2006

A142475

Level 3 Health & Social Care Diploma

Unit numbers by awarding organisation

Unit no. in Heinemann book	Unit title	Unit accreditation no.	Edexcel/NCFE unit no.	CACHE/ OCR unit no.	C&G unit no.
SHC 31	Promote communication in health, social care or children and young people's settings	J/601/1434	1	SHC 31	4222–301
SHC 32	Engage in personal development in health, social care or children and young people's settings	A/601/1429	2	SHC 32	4222–302
SHC 33	Promote equality and inclusion in health, social care or children and young people's settings	Y/601/1437	3	SHC 33	4222–303
SHC 34	Principles for implementing duty of care in health, social care or children and young people's settings	R/601/1436	4	SHC 34	4222–304
HSC 024	Principles of safeguarding and protection in health and social care	A/601/8574	5	HSC 024	4222–205
HSC 025	The role of the health and social care worker	J/601/8576	6	HSC 025	4222–206
HSC 036	Promote person-centred approaches in health and social care	Y/601/8145	7	HSC 036	4222–305
HSC 037	Promote and implement health and safety in health and social care	F/601/8138	8	HSC 037	4222–306
HSC 038	Promote good practice in handling information in health and social care settings	J/601/9470	9	HSC 038	4222–307
HSC 3003	Provide support to maintain and develop skills for everyday life	L/601/8028	59	HSC 3003	4222–311
HSC 3004	Facilitate learning and development activities to meet individual needs and preferences	L/601/8644	60	HSC 3004	4222–312
HSC 3013	Support individuals to access and use services and facilities	F/601/7927	65	HSC 3013	4222–316
HSC 3020	Facilitate person-centred assessment, planning, implementation and review	H/601/8049	68	HSC 3020	4222–319
HSC 3029	Support individuals with specific communication needs	T/601/8282	74	HSC 3029	4222–324
HSC 3047	Support use of medication in social care settings	F/601/4056	80	HSC 3047	4222–331
DEM 301	Understand the process and experience of dementia	J/601/3538	13	DEM 301	4222–365
SS MU 3.1	Understand sensory loss	M/601/3467	31	SS MU 3.1	4222–393
HSC 2028	Move and position individuals in accordance with their plan of care	J/601/8027	56	HSC 2028	4222–232

■ = Group M ■ = Group C ☐ = Group B

Index

Key words are indicated by **bold** page numbers.

CD chapters are indicated by:
(D) for unit HSC DEM 301
(S) for unit SS MU 3.1 or
(M) for unit HSC 2028
after the page number.